George Moore

George Moore

Influence and Collaboration

Edited by
Ann Heilmann and Mark Llewellyn

UNIVERSITY OF DELAWARE PRESS
Newark

Published by University of Delaware Press
Copublished by The Rowman & Littlefield Publishing Group, Inc.
4501 Forbes Boulevard, Suite 200, Lanham, Maryland 20706
www.rowman.com

16 Carlisle Street, London W1D 3BT, United Kingdom

British Library Cataloguing in Publication Information Available

Library of Congress Cataloging-in-Publication Data

George Moore : influence and collaboration / edited by Ann Heilmann and Mark Llewellyn.
pages cm
Includes bibliographical references and index.
ISBN 978-1-61149-432-7 (cloth : alk. paper)—ISBN 978-1-61149-433-4 (electronic)
1. Moore, George, 1852–1933—Criticism and interpretation. I. Heilmann, Ann, editor. II. Llewellyn,
Mark, 1979– editor.
PR5044.G54 2014
823'.8—dc23
2014020614
ISBN 978-1-6114-9533-1 (pbk : alk. paper)

Contents

Acknowledgments

This book has benefited immeasurably from the support of many individuals and institutions. Our greatest thanks go to Mark Samuels Lasner for his always ready generosity in offering liberal access to the Pearl Craigie/George Moore Papers held in the Mark Samuels Lasner Collection on loan to the University of Delaware Library, and for giving us permission to reproduce the manuscript versions of Moore and Craigie's collaborative plays *The Fool's Hour* and *Journeys End in Lovers Meeting*. We are grateful to both Mark Samuels Lasner and Margaret Stetz for sharing with us their awe-inspiring expertise in *fin-de-siècle* culture and literature. We are also indebted to Michel Brunet's exhaustive knowledge of French literature, which proved invaluable in identifying the source of *Journeys End in Lovers Meeting*. It was a pleasure to work with the scholars in this collection and a privilege to draw on their rich and wide-ranging experience. We further wish to express our appreciation of the delegates of the "George Moore and his Contemporaries" conference at the University of Hull, where the conception for this book first originated, to the British Academy for supporting the event, and to Hull's Department of English and Faculty of Arts and Social Sciences for funding a research trip to the Mark Samuels Lasner Collection. The organizers and participants of Moore conferences at the Universities of Almería (Spain), Galway (Ireland), and Paris helped us develop important ideas. Thanks are also due to the anonymous readers of our proposal for their constructive suggestions. Finally, without the support and patience of Julia Oestreich and Donald C. Mell at Delaware University Press and Brooke Bures, Amie Brown, Joe Miller, Jackie Barnes, and Suzanne Wheatley at Rowman and Littlefield, this project would not have been possible.

Introduction

George Moore: Influence and Collaboration

Ann Heilmann and Mark Llewellyn

George Moore (1852–1933) was a prominent figure in the late-Victorian and turn-of-the-century cultural landscape. Innovative and provocative, his work and personality left a significant imprint on European art criticism, English realism and naturalism, the Irish Literary Revival, and life writing. He was infamous for falling out with almost all his literary and artistic contemporaries because of the way he immortalized them in his memoirs. His indiscreet and satirical portraits reveal as much about the period's movements and its luminaries as do Max Beerbohm's mordant caricatures, but Moore was the kinder of the two. Yet for all his contribution to the literature and culture of the *fin de siècle* and beyond, much of Moore's oeuvre is out of print. Despite the recent burgeoning of Moore studies, he remains marginal to literary histories of the era. As a character on the *fin-de-siècle* stage reconstructed by academic criticism, he is often the walk-on character in volumes about James Joyce, G. B. Shaw, W. B. Yeats, and others. This book seeks to make an important intervention in Moore studies in focusing attention on the diversity of Moore's cultural influence and interaction with his contemporaries in conjunction with providing unique insight into hitherto unidentified archival material relating to two of his collaborative plays. What we seek to achieve in this study is to throw into relief the multiple ways in which Moore's work can serve as a counterbalance to established understandings of late nineteenth and early twentieth-century literary aesthetics through both presenting innovative readings of Moore's work and demonstrating, via textual techniques, his actual collaborative practice. It is this collaborative practice in conjunction with his cosmopolitan outlook, we argue, that turned Moore into a key player in the *fin-de-siècle* formation of an international community that, as as

1

Matthew Potolsky argues, "posited a transnational and transhistorical 'decadent subject' as an alternative to the . . . ideals of national community."[1] For Moore, replace "decadent" with the more generic "aesthetic" in his idiosyncratic engagement with what Potolsky, drawing on Michael Warner, calls a "counterpublic"[2] distinguished by its cross-cultural politics of shared taste.

One of the reasons Moore tends to be overlooked in Victorian studies (a term perhaps too generalist to encapsulate the eccentricity of Moore) is that he espoused so many different and, at times, ostensibly incompatible identities. As an experimentalist who reinvented himself with every new book, Moore—in contradistinction to Joseph Conrad, Thomas Hardy, Henry James, and many other writers he was at war with—is not easy to categorize. An Anglo-Irish absentee landlord from his early twenties, the apprenticeship decadent, newly resident in Paris, moved on to journalism and art criticism in London when his County Mayo rents dried up; a cosmopolitan artist steeped in French aesthetics, the maturing writer exerted considerable influence on British and Irish literary culture; an atheist possessed of an inveterate hatred of religion, the older Moore on his return to Revivalist Ireland converted to the Anglican Church to strike a fatal blow against his Roman Catholic upbringing. Moore's lifelong project of self-transformation and his spirit of innovation steered him towards new aesthetic departures even and especially when some avenues appeared barred to him. Equipped with an exquisite understanding of visual art, he abandoned the painting career he had envisaged for himself when he recognized that his aspirations would always outstrip his ability; his practical and intellectual insights turned him into a sophisticated critic of the art instead. Yet, in subsequently posturing as a diabolist[3] poet, he temporarily sacrificed ambition and originality to the Flaubertian impetus of "épater le bourgeois."[4] A middling playwright, he was keen to launch co-authorship projects, many of which culminated in dramatic bust-ups.

An agent provocateur as an art critic, novelist, short fiction writer, and memoirist, always probing and daring, often deliberately combative, the personality who is pivotal to this book is a prime example of the self-identified *artiste terrible* of the *fin de siècle*. Initially, Moore conceived of himself as "the youngest of the naturalists, the eldest of the symbolists."[5] His key role— as observer-participant and as satirist—within many literary and aesthetic movements at the end of the Victorian period and into the twentieth century owed considerably to the structures and manners of collaboration and exchange that he embraced. Many of his novels were banned by the circulating libraries (including *A Modern Lover* [1883], *A Mummer's Wife* [1885] and *Esther Waters* [1894]; see chapters 4 and 5). His response was to channel such repudiation of his writing into a renewed sense of his artistic reputation. Years before his fellow Irishman Oscar Wilde (one of the many compatriots with whom he jarred) coined the phrase, Moore had decided that infamy was a form of fame, and that an intuitive alertness to personal encounters and relationships could make the materials of great art. His life was his aesthetic product, his fiction no less true or more real than his fabricated memoirs. At the heart of all his output, however, resided a sense of immediacy, honesty, and contemporaneity. Moore's stories live in the moment of the telling, which may explain the drive, even compulsion, to rewrite them at later stages of his career. This revisionary impetus also extended to revisiting earlier cooperative projects. That collaborations, even when long since ended, continued to change shape in his writerly recollection is significant. It suggests that Moore's sense of what individuals could contribute to his development kept on maturing after contact and working relationships were a thing of the past. Moore's authorial self, like those of his characters, was both imagined and observed in the world in which he lived. Similarly, his contemporaries could not fail to recognize themselves in his work because they were left so undisguised by his pen. Even minor figures, picked up from a passing note in an autobiographical distraction, served a purpose: "Dan," his uncle playing the piano to his mistress, "shall become a piece of literature in my hands."[6]

From his earliest *Confessions of a Young Man* (1888) onward, Moore never ceased to challenge established literary conventions, styles, and subject matter in the process of moulding his aesthetics in response to but also against the cultural modes around him. Although too much of an individualist to align himself absolutely with specific cultural groupings, he was associated with most of the key movements of his time, even if such involvement typically shifted into conspicuous rebellion. A pioneer of the French naturalist style in English, he quarreled with Emile Zola and, at the turn of the century, his pivotal role in the Irish Renaissance was partly invigorated by his very ambivalence toward the cause. With the stories of *The Untilled Field* (1903) he made a significant contribution to the development of a distinctive Irish literature in English, only to satirize the leading figures of the Revival in *Hail and Farewell* (1911–1914). In the early decades of the twentieth century, he continued to experiment with form and genre, conceptualizing the Wagnerian "melodic line"[7] and gaining recognition for his use of stream of consciousness in *The Lake* (1905). He revised many of his earlier writings and developed new interests in classical adaptation. In all cases, it was Moore's combination of an original tale or a novel retelling, coupled with a model, style, or method from contemporary or past aesthetic movements reshaped to his own style, which brought new artistic vision to the page. That those influences were as diverse as his imagination could accommodate is important. Whether or not Moore read all the writers with whom his works have an association, or read them particularly deeply—from Balzac, Huysmans, and Zola to Nietzsche, Schopenhauer, and Turgenev—the influence of thinkers and artists on his self-perception and his concept of the aesthetic within the period is vital.

Moore's relationship with other writers and artists is the subject of this collection in both its critical-scholarly (part I) and archival-editorial (part II) dimensions. The literary and cultural engagements the individual chapters in part I present as cross-influence, imitation, or shared purpose can be seen as indicative of Moore's wider networks of contact with friends, family, and, of course, enemies. While his life and career extended to the modernist period, his writing was, and remained, profoundly invested in the prevailing issues and contestations of the Victorian and turn-of-the-century eras. As an author in tune with the range of cultural and aesthetic modes of the *fin de siècle* and, indeed, as a key figure in bringing so many of the definitive markers of late-Victorian literary transformation from his continental friendships to English translation, his knowledge of his contemporaries in all their aspirations and also absurdities was critical to his interpretation of the cultural landscape of the time.

"Nearly every major figure of his era," writes his biographer Adrian Frazier, "worked with Moore, tangled with Moore, took his impression from, or left it on, George Moore."[8] Moore's reputation as a collaborator and an interlocutor with the most significant cultural and artistic individuals in Britain, Ireland, and France in particular, but also in Europe more widely, provides a rich case study of modes of exchange and influence in the period, and a unique and distinctive perspective on Moore himself. To read Moore—by which we mean not only to read his writings but also his character and personality more broadly—is to view the turn of the century through the eyes of Moore the protagonist and Baudelairean *flâneur*.[9] Moore frequently failed to dissociate the two roles: the creation of "George Moore" as self-portrait, and George Moore the author of an auto-biofictional identity, has always been difficult to disentangle. But how did Moore's contemporaries engage with him, exchange ideas, interact with his literary experimentation and modes of writing? And how did Moore project his impressions, opinions, and desires through other artistic figures, either through direct claims of influence or through collaboration?

The chapters in this volume seek to explore new and different perspectives on Moore's perception of his creative responses to other writers and artists. Reading Moore's own performative reminiscences, as well as taking note of studies or memoirs by his contemporaries, one must always consider the retrospective nature of (auto)biographical judgments and the unstable boundaries of memory and interpretation. Moore was a serial rewriter: his works underwent multiple versions, and this passion for revision cannot be divorced from the manner in which his views of particular personalities, and their impressions of him, changed over time.

The creation of the individual through self-portrayal and revision was the principle with which Moore depicted others and by which he wanted to be understood himself. One of the best-known anecdotes about his approach sees Moore as a young man chastized for irritating Edouard Manet by constantly asking for changes to his portrait, prompting the latter to declare that it was not "[his] fault" if Moore's profile was "lopsided" and his face had the appearance of a "squashed egg-yolk."[10] Manet's exasperation illuminates one aspect of the contemporary response to Moore, just as Moore's impulse toward readjustment is indicative of his self-positioning in relation to others. For Moore, the projection of an external image was as much part of the process of (re)imagining the self as was social and cultural interaction with his fellow writers and artists. If one considers that Moore originally trained as a painter, which was the central impetus in his relocation to Paris in the 1870s, one begins to understand how he sought always to change perspective, to see afresh his own image. The act of seeing and reading character was itself a form of collaboration, the blank canvas through which the shape of the other was formed via the lens of the writer.

The roots of Moore's sense that all art is in some respect collaborative in that it relies on the creativity of those who constitute the human environment of the writer or artist derive from impressions he gathered at the outset of his literary career. In *Confessions*, drawing on his experiences as an art student in Paris, Moore defined the relationship with his contemporaries as contingent on the position they were assigned in his writing. Like literary texts in the process of creation, Moore's social environments and the people within them were all aspects of a world that could be enhanced through literary reimagining. The narrator's close male friend Marshall is tellingly depicted as both "a study, a subject for dissection,"[11] and as someone whose life experience can be read by the authorial persona and transubstantiated into a more aesthetic formulation. The narrator constitutes himself as a subject through his omnivorous consumption of his surroundings and its inhabitants. The creation of "George Moore" as a figure generated from the collaborative potential provided by the influence and influencing of others is presented to us in the text with great verve and a spirit of impish enthusiasm that would continue for Moore's entire writing career. There is a sense of overwhelming satisfaction in the "confession" that could serve as an epigraph to Moore's engagement with his contemporaries: "I have had many friends, and of all sorts and kinds—men and women; and, I repeat, none took part in my life who did not contribute something towards my well-being."[12] In one sense, all of Moore's contemporaries were constructed as influences, collaborators, or both. Moore's "well-being" here can be read in terms of his individual development and creative success. As Frazier comments, "Moore was so single-mindedly a literary person that life itself was for him essentially authorship, and he turned all relationships into literary collaborations."[13] That he persuaded Yeats to author a letter in the voice of his not-so-pseudo-Yeatsian character Ulick Deane in *Evelyn Innes* (1898) is a case in point.[14] The act not only suggests Moore's supreme confidence in blurring fiction and fact, and imagination and reality; it also points to the aesthetic belief that these binaries could enrich one another in the service of the artistic good.

Moore's friends, and the cultural and artistic modes they represent, are thus the raw material of his work, but they are also, by the time they appear in his own aesthetic format, his creations, having been "assimilated." Assimilation is a form of collaboration, and yet it carries no exchange value: the individual, his or her experiences and absurdities are subjected to a process that is not mutually beneficial but productive only for Moore. "As I picked up books," he writes, "so I picked up my friends. I read friends and books with the same passion, with the same avidity; and as I discarded my books when I had assimilated as much of them as my system required, so I discarded my friends when they ceased to be of use to me."[15] In this attitude, Moore anticipated Marcel Proust,[16] but he also did more than this in establishing a literary style that acknowledged its indebtedness to and affection for the lives of others even while taking pleasure in exposing the oddities of those same lives.

Moore's eclectic range of influences extends to the key artists of his time: Manet, as already noted, but also the Impressionist movement more generally (see chapter 2); Balzac (as discussed in chapter 1); Zola (aspects of whose works Moore adapted; see chapters 3–5 and 6); Baudelaire, source of "various thefts"[17] especially in Moore's abortive but formative poet phase that produced *Flowers of Passion* (1878) and *Pagan Poems* (1881); Gautier (Moore's "measure of pure aestheticism"[18]); and Flaubert, to name a few. This may raise the question of Moore's relatively broad taste or inability to discriminate, which would miss the point. Moore did discriminate but only when an influence had been utilized to the point that it could be assimilated or naturalized to his own talent.

The quasi-theatrical performance of collaboration (and also its collapse) was not accidental. When Moore worked with others on joint projects, such exchanges were publicly celebrated through proclamation but also always served the purpose of injecting new impulses to Moore's own work. The routes of Moore's approaches to collaboration and competitiveness with his fellow writers and artists owe a great deal to his early Parisian experiences of an aesthetic culture that explored the nature of movements by conceptualizing individual talent through collective endeavor. The sociologist Michael P. Farrell draws attention to seven key stages of collaborative engagement: formation of a partnership; united rebellion against authority; joint pursuit of a quest or shared outcome; negotiation of a collaborative new vision (such as the Irish Literary Renaissance); creatively working together; "collective action" (such as co-authorship or a declaration of a movement's underpinning principles); separation; and finally "nostalgic reunion," when the group comes together again to reminiscence about its achievements, ignoring the bitterness and divisiveness of the earlier events. It is noteworthy that Farrell's opening case study is of the Impressionists in the 1860s and 1870s, given that the latter decade was precisely the formative period in Moore's aesthetic trajectory.[19] In fact, Farrell quotes from *Confessions* to illustrate the competition between Manet and Degas and to provide an account of their collaborative environments. While it would be reductive to apply Farrell's model too indiscriminately to the diverse modes of collaboration and influence in which Moore was involved, it is the fluidity with which Moore moved between the stages that disconcerted his contemporaries. For him, the nostalgic reunion was rarely in prospect but—as his countless semi-autobiographical and frequently reworked memoirs demonstrate—the retrospective reflection offered an alternative, both in objective and outcome, to the collaborative drive. Moore's ability to anticipate his future thoughts on a failed collaboration, to analyze a partnership in order to inspire singular and individual creative aspects of his own writing appears to have been the driving force of much of his work. In blurring the quest and separation stages, Moore often undermined the potential of articulating a joint vision.

If Moore's influence on others and his absorption of others' influence always had a definitive outcome for him in writerly terms, be it in the form of plot, character, or style, the more formal collaborations of his writing life always came to a bad end.[20] The best example of how Moore's literary collaborations reverberate with the relationship models that Farrell places at the center of his approach is that of the Irish Literary Revival and the abortive literary partnership with Yeats. Moore's propulsion to join events in Ireland is described in *Hail and Farewell* as bordering on the prophetic, with a voice enjoining him to return to his homeland. But even in such contexts, his collaborative impetus was usually for the good of Moore rather than for any other purpose. While visiting his Irish cousin, Edward Martyn, a lead player in the Revival and much-invoked character in Moore's fiction, he recalls how he "looked forward to a long *séance de collaboration* after breakfast."[21] Having joined forces with Yeats on the composition of a new Irish theatrical genre, Moore redirects the object of their work to himself: "Literary adventures," he notes as Yeats tells him that he must write dialogue in French in order for it to be translated into English, then into Irish, then back into English again to make it more authentic, "have always been my quest, and here was one."[22] The "quest" here is as much one for Moore as for anything to do with Ireland itself. The centrality of Moore's collaborators to this vision of a new version of "George Moore," refreshed and reinvigorated for the literary world, was pivotal. By self-consciously drawing connections in his own mind and in his writing between the individuals featured in *Hail and Farewell*, Moore rationalizes his experience of them into a replenished sense of self: "analogies can be discovered in all my boon companions. Could it be otherwise, since they were all collected for my instruction and distraction?"[23]

The competing goals between Yeats's vision for a new literary Ireland and Moore's vision for a new literature for George Moore were actually more complex, not least in the similarity of the two men. Yeats's own personality, particularly in writing partnerships, should not be overlooked as part of the psycho-literary dynamic between these two sons of Ireland. As Roy Foster comments, the problems of Yeatsian aesthetic values contributed to the difficulties in their relationship, so that given "the expectations which he cherished about art . . . [Yeats's] later aesthetic quarrels with contemporaries like George Moore were inevitable."[24] In fact, in their literary perfectionism the two men were remarkably alike. Yeats was, like Moore, "a compulsive rewriter,"[25] and their conception of literary production as an unfinished text in constant need of refinement would become magnified in collaboration.

Although the Yeatsian example illustrates the most extreme breakdown in collaborative relations Moore had with another male author, his influence over others was characteristically multiplex. "Devious, uncontrollable, unable to resist the temptations of a demonic sense of humour, Moore was deeply mistrusted by all his acquaintance," remarks Yeats's biographer, "but he was a close and influential observer of literary talent."[26] There were some, like Arnold Bennett, who acknowledged their debt to Moore (proclaiming him "the father of all [Bennett's] Five Town Books"[27]), and others, like Edmund Gosse, to whom Moore offered literary mentorship. It is important to recognize that Moore could be generous and assume an anonymous position in his support for other writers, especially friends. Thus, while encouraging Gosse to write *Father and Son* (1907) and issuing constructive critical advice on the redrafting of the initial materials, he "never went out of his way to claim credit for it," even though, as Frazier notes, "*Father and Son* is more famous and better-selling to this day than any book Moore ever wrote."[28]

Moore's relationship with James Joyce, and indeed Joyce's feelings about Moore, were more complicated. Moore supported the petition for Joyce to receive a Civil List pension in 1916,[29] and that year's publication of *The Portrait of the Artist as a Young Man* owed not a little to Moore's own *Confessions*.[30] The pair's meetings in 1929, at which a rapprochement was reached, presented a stark contrast to those at the turn of the century when Joyce's brother Stanislaus called at Moore's Dublin home in Ely Place to leave a copy of the pamphlet "The Day of the Rabblement."[31] Joyce's 1901 publication was a salvo in the battle for a new form of literature, and most particularly for a distinctive Irish literary voice. Although in the "Scylla and Charybdis" episode of *Ulysses* (1922) Joyce would make the point—tongue-in-cheek—that Moore was the man to write the great Irish epic, in "The Day of the Rabblement" it had been Moore's association with literary contemporaries in Europe that alienated Joyce's confidence in Moore's ability to undertake that work. Joyce wrote that

> Mr. Moore . . . has wonderful mimetic ability, and some years ago his books might have entitled him to the place of honour among English novelists. But though *Vain Fortune* (perhaps one should add some of *Esther Waters*) is fine, original work, Mr. Moore is really struggling in the backwash of that tide which has advanced from Flaubert through Jakobsen to D'Annunzio: for two entire eras lie between *Madame Bovary* and *Il Fuoco*. It is plain from *Celebates [sic]* and the latter novels that Mr. Moore is beginning to draw upon his literary account, and the quest of a new impulse may explain his recent startling conversion. Converts are in the movement now, and Mr. Moore and his island have been fitly admired. But however frankly Mr. Moore may misquote Pater and Turgeuieff *[sic]* to defend himself, his new impulse has no kind of relation to the future of art.[32]

In exploring Moore's indebtedness to other writers, Joyce grants him knowledge and exposure to great cultural figures, only to castigate him for mere mimicry of them. One cannot help but detect a certain anxiety in Joyce's need to acknowledge his understanding of Moore's diversity as both an admission and a denial of the potential of Moore's influence on his own work. Yet, by 1907, Joyce's lecture "Ireland: Island of Saints and Sages" contained the praise that Moore was "an oasis of intelligence in a Sahara of spiritualist, mystic and detective works whose names are legion in England."[33] The intervening period had seen the publication of *The Untilled Field* and, more importantly, *The Lake*. As Frazier has pointed out, it may indeed have been Joyce's "devastatingly well-informed analysis of GM's literary position in Europe [that] . . . pushed Moore away from stories for Irish translators and toward the experiment with stream-of-consciousness in *The Lake*."[34] But the influence worked both ways. Joyce's adoption of "a new style with each new book" as part of a "Flaubertian, modernist principle" may have been inspired by Moore's model, especially given the evidence of Joyce's extensive reading of the older man's work.[35]

Moore's relationships with other Irish writers were often the most volatile and antipathetic. The Yeats example is not an isolated one. George Bernard Shaw and Moore may have shared an interest in Wagner,[36] but when they were both young men in London, Shaw knew Moore only as a braggart who told "silly stories about himself and women," to the point that he was stunned to discover him to be the author of *A Mummer's Wife*. It was only now that Shaw realized "the incredible industry of the man."[37] Later he added that, when telling anecdotes or stories to friends, Moore always

> insisted on an audience, but neither valued nor respected its credulity. He was the most good-humored artist I ever met. We laughed at him until our ribs ached. We pointed out inconsistencies, contradictions, impossibilities, unexplained changes of scene in the romance. He only said, "Ah, wait now, I'm coming to a bit that you'll like." Nothing ruffled him.[38]

Shaw's emphasis on Moore's inclusion of his listeners in his performance is significant. Moore needed a responsive audience, whether writers, artists, or readers. Partly, this audience was meant to derive pleasure from his style and persona, but, as Shaw indicates, it also served the function of a mirror in which Moore could see reflected back signs of the approval, affection, and admiration that he sought to inspire.

Ultimately, Shaw did not think much of Moore: "All the stuff about his being a great prose writer is nonsense." That he might be ranked alongside nineteenth-century prose stylists such as "Scott and Dickens, Ruskin and Carlyle and De Quincey" was out of the question: "he was nothing: he had no heights and no depths except in certain descriptions of Ireland and certain scandalous passages."[39] Yet, even in his dismissal, Shaw expressed respect for Moore's drive, acknowledging that his work was appreciated by a select audience: "his enormous industry, his honesty and fearlessness, and his good-humor, pulled his imagination through. I cannot read him much, because his first sentence is exactly like every other sentence in the book; and I soon feel there is nothing to prevent George going on like that forever; but other people wish he would."[40]

Shaw's recognition that Moore's impact on readers, friends, and fellow artists was divisive is significant. Part of this no doubt relates to Moore's inclination to fictionalize his friends in the service of literary advancement. Thriving on companions, he then consecrates them to sacrifice for the benefit of the ultimate object of art: the individualized achievement of the independence of the artist himself. For Moore, as for "George Moore," it is the dual possibility of engagement with others at the level of the lived moment and the re-imagined nature of that moment recorded as a work of artistic assimilation that provides the key to his understanding of what aesthetic culture means. In this sense, Moore's aestheticism is both like and unlike that of his most prominent fellow Irish contemporary, Oscar Wilde. Moore's aesthetic project resembles Wilde's in that the greatest creation of the artist is himself; yet unlike Wilde's, Moore's artist figure, even in self-portrait, is not idealized or immortalized, nor does he place style above everything. It gives the lie to Wilde's comment that Moore had a "vague, formless, obscene face."[41] Rather, the figure is of human folly, the imperfectible individual, and is consequently embraced as such, with all the foibles and frailties that this entails. Self-creation goes pen-in-hand with self-deprecation if it makes an entertaining tale.

Although Moore did have that very public and (on both sides) long-lasting falling-out with Yeats,[42] this should not be the enduring memory of his engagement with the Irish Literary Revival and the innovations, ideas, and intellectual challenges and changes it brought about. In fact, one might argue that it is precisely Moore's contrariness that adds richness to the account of the Revival and provides an important narrative of diversity and difference to movement-centric analyses. One of his other collaborators, Pearl Craigie—who published under the male pseudonym "John Oliver Hobbes"— was rudely kicked by him in Hyde Park,[43] in a literary memorial that has left an imprint on both their legacies. This end point in a relationship that influenced both writers, and whose abortive collaboration is key to Part II of this volume, would be refashioned in Moore's writing throughout the rest of his life as he sought to get his sense of "the truth" of Craigie (and of the "other" George Moore he became in her company) into literary format with the intensity used in confronting her in the park.

Moore's relationships with women marked a different kind of collaboration, engaging the libidinal alongside the textual in ways that his male-to-male partnerships could never do. As he once remarked to a friend, "when a man has collaborated with a woman it is the same as if he had slept with her. She has no secrets left to reveal."[44] To Moore, writing was an erotic act. His comment reflects on the intimacy with which he associated processes of collaboration, joining together as it did the intellects, personalities, and bodies of the participants. For a writer so fascinated by the possibilities of non-reproductive sexuality, there is something peculiarly fitting about his construction of collaborative authorship as a naked, vulnerable, and possessive act that produces as its offspring a work of art. This idea found most prominent expression in his *Memoirs* fantasia "Euphorion in Texas" (chapter XIII), in which an American admirer selects the author as the most suitably qualified candidate to "give Texas a literature."[45] *Memoirs* contains a number of sexually spiced narratives of collaboration. While "The Lovers of Orelay" (chapter IX) is self-deprecating on the question of sexual performance and textual fulfilment,[46] "Lui et Elle" (chapter II) plays out the story of two different types of female partners, casting Craigie as the sexually, as well as textually, manipulative "Agate" and Maud Cunard as the savior figure "Elizabeth." In the narrator's reflections on the restorative effect of Elizabeth's hospitable approach we can identify aspects of a core Moorean set of values: "Only such impulsiveness as hers" could have effected his recovery; Elizabeth "must have divined it . . . or it may have been that some book of mine stirred her imagination. . . . [A] man loves in the first instance through the eye . . . whereas a woman loves through her imagination."[47] It is through imagination that the love affair takes route, and collaboration is as much eroticized through illusion as through reality. Moore's previous depiction of a romantic quest to Bayreuth for Wagnerian edification becomes a version (improved) of "George Sand's celebrated journey to Venice with Alfred de Musset"[48] in a reverie that invokes Balzac, Turgenev, and Rousseau as authors worthy of bringing the character of Agate to life.[49] By implication, Moore places his own account into the circle of influence containing these same names: here literary allegiance, homage, and self-authorization are aggrandized into one.

If Moore's collaborations were dramatic in nature, then his collaborative impulse also had a theatrical rationale. In the case of Agate/Craigie the romance had begun through a book that might become a play, and as he confessed to others, he was no good at playwriting, seeing his "speciality" and "gift" as "the power to link up a story."[50] In fact, all of Moore's plays were collaborative,[51] which reveals a striking dependency for an author so keen to assert individualism and self-identity in his work. In the late 1880s, we find Moore approaching Clara Lanza, the author of *A Righteous Apostate* (1883), asking if she would "care to write a play with one three thousand miles away?"[52] After a few suggestions, he proposed that "[i]f you like my arrangement of your story, write the play, send it to me and I will alter it and rewrite where I think necessary and send it back to you for final revision."[53]

Significantly, as Frazier emphasizes, Moore's "main, if not sole approach to women was through co-authorship."[54] Whether through writing with female co-authors like Craigie or making them collaborators and subjects of his fictionalization (Honor Woulfe in "Euphorion in Texas" or Cunard in "Lovers of Orelay"),[55] Moore engaged women textually if not sexually. Another collaborator, Julia Davis Frankau (writing as Frank Danby), satirized him in *A Babe in Bohemia* (1889) as Sinclair Furley, a man "only interested" in women "as ways to incite his own sensations, so that he could study these and use them in his books."[56] A more positive writing partnership developed in 1920 with Ethel Maud Harter, whom he advised on *A Love Conference*, a novel published in 1922 to considerable popular success.[57]

Moore's ineffectual endeavor in later life to conjure forth a dalliance with a female writer is invoked in Lorine Pruette's short story "Leda and the Lion" (1934), published a year after his death. A tale of the old Moore, it captures the slippage between textual and sexual connection that he portrayed in *Memoirs* and elsewhere. "Tell me about your book, perhaps I can help you" is the elderly writer's pick-up line.[58] Literary and libidinal collaborations are here figured as authorial desire par excellence. Yet as Moore had affirmed in *Avowals* (1919), intelligence was the principal catalyst for his attraction: "[t]he only women worth while are learned women."[59] Moore's trysts with female writers who visited him were partly exercises in how the erotics of text and sex intersected. Playful games placed literary trade-offs against bodily expression: "Let me see you undressed," says the Moore character in Pruette's narrative, "and I'll *fix your book for you*."[60] To the woman herself, the corruption of her literary corpus is more threatening than bodily penetration: "She would, she thought ironically, prefer that he outrage her body than that he tamper with her book, but she did not try to explain this to him. She saw that he would bargain for bodies or for books, and . . . that he was a great and famous man."[61] The false note here is the comment "for bodies or for books" in that it separates the two in ways Moore would not have recognized. In his conjunction of both reading and writing out desire, there could be no bodies *or* books; they were fundamentally and inextricably intertwined.

With the exception of the Craigie incident in the park, Moore's passionate and violent reactions were, thankfully, undertaken on the page, and remain with us as undercurrents to the reputations of those around him, particularly other writers. Henry James—whom he dubbed "the eunuch"[62]—was a constant source of aesthetic antagonism for Moore but provided a context for his views on the function of fiction. In *Confessions* he mocks the Jamesian text for its depleted plotline:

> Suicide or adultery has happened before the story begins, suicide or adultery happens some years after the characters have left the stage, but in front of the reader nothing happens. . . . The lady, it is true, may have a lover, but the pen finds scanty pasturage in the fact; and in James's novels the lady only considers the question on the last page, and the gentleman looks at her questioningly.[63]

It is James's lack of action and thereby lack of recognizable material text to assimilate that is at the heart of Moore's criticism that his work is not literature from the outside world, the world of shared corporeality, but from within a closed psychological, purely cerebral, in Moore's phrase "drawing-room,"[64] environment. This Jamesian vision contrasts with the enacted powers of enchantment in Moore's descriptions of the erotic value of his infamous "woman of thirty" over "the young girl"[65] in a vision that allows the young man and his older woman not only to look at one another, and to ponder adultery, but also to be together in his rooms "by night and day" or else mentally "she shall consume . . . his life."[66]

In a sense, this also highlights how Moore's *Confessions* serves as a foundation text for his engagement with the influences and collaborative potential of other artists throughout his career. The *Confessions* section on contemporary authors begins with an anonymous actress pointing out that Moore's worst enemy is himself because he has become so French, a reminder that he has lived off French literature, art, and music for so many years that they have become an inseparable part of himself. By the end of the same section, Moore has decided to abstain from reading the work of his English contemporaries (apart from Pater) because of their inferiority. Instead he turns to an older English literature in the proto-modernist belief that there was something more authentic, more "real" in literature before Victorian morality set in; with the Victorians "English fiction became pure, and the garlic and asafoetida with which Byron, Fielding and Ben Jonson so liberally seasoned their works . . . have disappeared from our literature."[67] It is perhaps in this translation of French experimentation into English literature that Moore proved himself to be most innovative, but it was an innovation that only worked because of the supreme confidence of the voice behind it. This

may also be a factor in Moore's increasing shift in focus in the latter stages of
his career, a turn away from work in contemporary fiction to autobiographical or retrospective pieces on the one hand, and to medievalism (*A Story-
Teller's Holiday*, 1918) and classicism on the other (*Daphnis and Chloe*,
1924; *Aphrodite in Aulis*, 1930).

Moore's comments on the failings of other writers, their lack of innovation or experimentation, were also turned on himself. His assessment of his
own position in relation to his contemporaries in a variety of literary forms,
movements, styles, and cultures was just as damning, frequently as harsh,
and always as tongue-in-cheek. In a 1916 interview the year after James's
death, for example, he volunteered an anecdote about having asked James for
help during revisions to the proofs of his autobiographical volume *Ave* a few
years earlier. Moore wanted James to assist with the revision and clarifica-
tion of a particular phrase, and he recounted that

> James rolled his eyes like a man in convulsions. Then he snatched the proof
> from me and started from the room with it. Finally, he came down, having
> composed a line and a half. It looked profound, but what it meant I had no
> idea. However, I put it in. When my secretary came to type it, she asked me if
> it was written correctly, as she could make no sense of it! Later, when the book
> was being set up, Heinemann came to me with the proof containing that
> sentence. "Will you please tell me what you mean by this?" said he. "Neither I
> nor my reader could make it out." I told him I couldn't and then explained to
> him who had written it.
>
> I can never think of that without recalling my first meeting with that great
> French master, Jules Lemaître. At that time he had read nothing of mine, and
> he said, "Tell me, are you clear or are you obscure?"
>
> "I am clear, Monsieur Lemaître," said I. "I have not talent enough to be
> obscure." That remark seemed to please him.[68]

It is a complicated anecdote, moving from Jamesian stylistic reputation (and
repudiation) to Moore's mockery of his own talent and abilities. Self-deprecating is not quite the term for this mockery, but in its conjunction of a series
of aesthetic differences, its humor, and its acknowledgement of human frailty, it is representative of Moore's engagement even with writers that were
unlike him, had different values, and practiced a divergent form of artistic
life. It also serves as a kind of riff on the way he could openly admit to taking
things from other artists with the liberality of a good friend imposing on
another's hospitality for just that little bit longer than even friendship truly
allows.

Hospitality might, in many respects, be the term through which we need
to reassess Moore's interaction with other artists. Open to the cause of the
aesthetic in its myriad forms, he was often at the forefront of finding a place
for new movements and experimental treatments within the public con-

sciousness. And yet, it is always his personalized sense of self-renewal through the aesthetic pleasures to be found in the world around him that is most vivid and tangible in the work itself. His frequent forays into the realm of the memoir, indeed his reinvention of the form into something more hybrid—from *Confessions of a Young Man* (1888) and *Impressions and Opinions* (1891) through *Memoirs of My Dead Life* (1906) and *Hail and Farewell* (1911–1914), to *Avowals* (1919), *Conversations in Ebury Street* (1924) and *A Communication to My Friends* (1933)—exhibit an ever-replenished rewriting of his life's narrative. The restructuring and, one might argue, re-marketing of the "real" provide important evidence of his desire to play with concepts of fact and fiction, memory and truth, and reality and the unconscious, in search of new, innovative literary expression. In reshaping the reality of his associations, friendships, and collaborations with other writers and artists throughout his life, Moore signposted the centrality of the lived aesthetic to his work as a whole. The last of these autobiographical works, *A Communication to My Friends*, was the text Moore was working on right up until his death as he sought to renegotiate his past, and refigure his relationship with writers he had known and reinvented, into yet more revised narrative. In many respects, all his works had been forms of communication with his friends, even when they had ceased—or soon would cease, on seeing what he had written—to use that epithet to describe the collaborative relationships in which they had (sometimes unwittingly) played a part.

Over the last twenty years, Moore has received revived attention. An increasingly vibrant field, Moore studies has established new approaches to the author's impact on the genres, forms, and styles as well as the reputations and portrayals of other artists at the *fin de siècle*. At the forefront of this development were Elizabeth Grubgeld's *George Moore and the Autogenous Self* (1994), which offers a reappraisal of Moore's autobiographical strategies and designs, and Adrian Frazier's magisterial biography, *George Moore, 1852–1933* (2000), a book deeply embedded in the cross-connections and contemporary cultures in which Moore found himself, often helped to shape and nurture, and subsequently turned against. Mary Pierse's collection *George Moore: Artistic Visions and Literary Worlds* (2006), drawn from the first of a series of international conferences on Moore, provides a range of perspectives on the international and European contexts for revisionist approaches to his work. In our five-volume scholarly edition of *The Collected Short Stories of George Moore* (2007), we sought to focus attention on the precision with which Moore revised, and in the process reconfigured, his short fiction. Three further collections of essays—*George Moore: Dublin, Paris, Hollywood* (2012), edited by Conor Montague and Adrian Frazier; *George Moore: Across Borders* (2013), edited by Christine Huguet and Fabienne Dabrigeon-Garcier; and *George Moore and the Quirks of Human*

Nature (2014), edited by María Elena Jaime de Pablos and Mary Pierse—have taken forward novel perspectives on Moore's relevance for readers of the *fin-de-siècle* period and beyond.[69]

Where previous essay collections have embraced the range of Moore's interests and undertaken valuable work in critically re-establishing the openness of Moore's writing to multiple readings and standpoints, the present volume has a more precise focus. It takes these recent reconsiderations of the importance of Moore's diverse body of work as a starting point to reconceptualize through a sustained interrogation his interactions with and impact on his literary and artistic contemporaries. Part I, "Influence," offers new scholarly readings that explore Moore's narrative performances, his use of the autobiographical blurred with fictional, real, and fictionalized encounters with other writers and artists, and his theories of fiction and national identity in conversation—or disputation—with them. The chapters in this section deliver significant and original insights into Moore's position in relation to both popular and mainstream authors and artists of the time. The individual chapters are united in locating Moore's oeuvre at the epicenter of cultural encounters and debates. Importantly, the chapters collectively mount an argument that Moore studies needs to think through the interlinked intellectual cross-currents between his work and that of his contemporaries both as part of a process of canonical reappraisal and as recognition of the impossibilities of placing the truly individual artist into neat categories or movements. Part II, "Collaboration," provides two illustrative case studies of Moore's collaborative practice by making available, for the first time, two manuscript plays he co-authored with Pearl Craigie in 1894.

The book begins by reflecting on different aspects of Moore's self-construction. In an opening chapter inflected with the metafictionally playful and ironic performance of Moore himself, Adrian Frazier examines the concept of writerly "peculiarity," which Moore adopted from his literary model Balzac, tracing correspondences between the two writers in terms of style and self-(re)presentation. Moore's endeavor of claiming cultural-spiritual kinship with Balzac proffered protection from parallels that might be drawn with more contemporary writers. Such self-fashioning continued throughout Moore's career and indicates his awareness of the need to be vigilant with his relationships with other artists and creative figures even as he sought to make use of them for his personal advancement.

While Frazier deals with Moore's literary self-constitution through reference to a "great" (and conveniently dead) writer, Anna Gruetzner Robins places his relationships with the contemporary artists of his Parisian period into the context of art history and the formation of collective (and, one might argue, collaborative) relationships in chapter 2. Positioning Moore as a self-proclaimed curator of the aesthetic experience not least as a result of his proximity to the innovators of Impressionist art, Gruetzner Robins scrutinizes the nature of his visual topography. Significantly, she identifies, in many cases for the first time, the location of the artworks Moore references in his real/imagined visual exhibitions. Moore's art criticism, in *Confessions* as well as in *Impressions and Opinions* and *Modern Painting* (1893), remains important both in its immediacy within the period, and also in its reflection on differences in style, approach, and design across aesthetic forms. In Moore's response to the exhibitions and paintings he saw and their contexts, we often find that aesthetic mergers create new idealized spaces of encounter between works and artists.

Beyond the painterly world, one of Moore's other great passions was the interface between words and music. With a keen interest in Wagnerism, Moore utilized the figure of the singer most notably in *Evelyn Innes* (1898) and *Sister Teresa* (1901). In chapter 3, Mary S. Pierse sounds out the multiple functions of musical engagement in his writing. Examining musical frameworks, references, and incantations across an extensive range of his texts, Pierse outlines the models of listening that are required to capture the complex meanings Moore sought to establish.

With chapter 4 we turn from art and aesthetics to reinterpretation of the wider *fin-de-siècle* parameters of cultural production. Jane Jordan positions Moore's attack upon the censorious role of the circulating libraries in relation to the popular novelist Ouida (Louise de la Ramée) and her own encounters with literary censorship. An alliance between these writers might at first glance appear startling, given that Ouida was one of the authors Moore indicted in his 1885 pamphlet on censorship, "Literature at Nurse." There, Moore made much of the fact that the immoralities of Ouida's populist works were freely available from Mudie's Select Library even as his own more serious novels were banned. While he drew on the cultural capital of writers like Ouida to expose the hypocrisy of any form of censorship, Ouida took inspiration from Moore's attack in her own publications on the book trade, although it would take until the mid-1890s for her to engage in a direct challenge to Mudie himself.

From the bookstall to the bar room, chapter 5 shifts emphasis to the figure of the barmaid as a contested site for a range of discourses about female literacy and literary censorship in the mid-1890s. Drawing on *Esther Waters* (1894) as a case study, Katherine Mullin suggests that Moore's interest in the barmaid, a character type he first examined in *Spring Days* (1888), reflects a changing social climate around female occupational roles, the ambiguity of sexual personae, and the presence of women in public places outside the strictures of high-Victorian moral codes. In her scrutiny of Moore's ambivalent portrayal of the barmaid, Mullin calls attention to the difficulties he faced in situating his approach within a literature that sought to challenge conservative morality while at the same time employing a code of representation that leaned toward constraint in the development of new models of female behavioral norms and respectable working patterns for women.

Moore's interest in exploring new roles for women is also central to chapter 6, which offers a new reading of *A Drama in Muslin* (1886) and its *Bildungsroman* protagonist Alice Barton in the context of feminist writing of the period. An artist figure, Alice illustrates aspects of Moore's engagement with cultural debates around the intellectual and socio-cultural awakening of women from the mid century onward and, in particular, the emerging literature of the New Woman at the approaching *fin de siècle*. Like Ibsen and the authors of New Woman fiction, Moore depicts his heroine's rebellion against the cultural, social, and religious conventionalities of her society; like them, he investigates the creative desire for, and failure, of artistic expression. Yet in enabling Alice to fulfill herself both professionally and in a happy marriage, Moore significantly departed from the script of New Woman writers. This came at a price, however, for Alice, for all her success with a popular audience, is not a "proper" artist. With its conflicted portrayal, Ann Heilmann and María Elena Jaime de Pablos point out, Moore's novel articulates considerable ambivalence toward the contemporary New Woman artist.

Nathalie Saudo-Welby takes these themes further in chapter 7 in her study of Moore's "Mildred Lawson" (published in *Celibates*, 1895). The story received immediate recognition by contemporary reviewers for its impressionistic method. As Saudo-Welby highlights, Moore's style and approach to the telling of the tale are responsible for the ambiguity of its commentary on the figure of the New Woman and for readers' interpretation of Moore's stance. The text's discursive invocation of the biological and social markers of instinct and degeneration sits uneasily alongside the indeterminacy of Mildred's character, raising questions about whether she is conceived as a parody or a critique of the New Woman.

Chapter 8 refocuses attention from Moore's literary response to feminist women and women writers to his writerly encounters with male contemporaries. In "Gossip, Art and the Public Secret," Elizabeth Grubgeld examines the ways in which Moore's frequently unpleasant remarks about fellow artists might be read as part of a reconceptualization of the notion of "gossip" as a literary genre. Moore's understanding of gossip as a form of art therefore can be seen to reflect back on the issue of (auto)biography, memoir, confession, and self-representation that we outlined at the start of this introduction. Moore's "fair game" approach to gossip about the people around him, in particular writers, artists, and other public figures, is transformed in his writing into a slippage between public and private, lived life and literary life, discretion and exposure.

Not all of Moore's male or Irish fellow artists, however, had to bear the brunt of his satirical gaze. Chapter 9 continues Grubgeld's inspection of Moore's cross-national influences and connections through the lens of Irish literary culture. Here, Michel Brunet considers the epistolary relationship between Moore and W. K. Magee (who wrote under the pen name John Eglinton) to investigate Moore's understanding of friendship, literary conversation, and cultural exchange. After crossing paths in Dublin in the 1890s, the two contrarian figures established a lifelong correspondence that explored questions of ideology, nationalism, and cosmopolitanism. That such conversations were conducted within close bonds of mutual respect proves an important corrective to ideas focused around Moore's general disloyalty toward his compatriots. It is through an awareness of a reciprocity fraught with contradiction, debate, and an acknowledgement of the divergence of opinion, Brunet argues, that we can recognize a different side to the persona of "George Moore," enabling us to identify an alternative perspective on his personal interaction with his contemporaries.

Moore's relevance for a wider sense of Celtic nationalism is the subject of chapter 10 on the cross-cultural influence of *The Untilled Field* on Welsh writer Caradoc Evans's *My People* (1915). As Kirsti Bohata outlines, Evans's short story collection was highly controversial in its depiction of a grotesque and depraved Welsh people, yet is now viewed as the foundational text of Anglophone Welsh fiction. This raises intriguing parallels with Moore's own Irish stories and their uncompromising sense of shared identity and collective experience. Bohata argues not for a simplistic comparison between the two writers, but for greater attention to be placed on the representative nature of their two collections. That both were conceived and published in a period that saw the dawn of two Celtic literatures in English manifested itself in the shared register of concerns about the repressive nature of priesthood (Moore was concerned about Catholicism, Evans about non-conformism), as well as in considerations of nationalism, language and identity.

The intellectual and artistic connections across cultures and nations that Moore's work stimulated are related back to friendship networks and artistic experimentation in the final chapter of part I. It is through Wagnerian composition, Stoddard Martin shows, that communications with French critic and writer Edouard Dujardin, Anglo-Welsh patron of arts T. E. Ellis, Lord Howard de Walden, and Italian novelist Gabriele D'Annunzio can provide a context for thinking about Moore's friendships and the shared spheres of cultural taste, value and influence they opened up. Martin's adoption of a lyrical wit in his own interrogation of a wide range of European and transcultural and trans-media allusion pays homage to the modernism of which he speaks. Drawing on unpublished correspondence, Martin appraises underexplored alliances between culturally significant figures of this period in an exercise in studying cross-influence through collaborative authorship and shared aesthetic intention.

Like the scholarly chapters, the second part of this book sets a new agenda for Moore studies, here by enabling access to heretofore unexplored source material. Following an introduction to Moore's collaboration with Craigie, part II provides annotated transcripts of the manuscripts of their first two co-authored plays, the three-act *The Fool's Hour* (hitherto considered a fragment, with only the first act being known, having seen publication in the *Yellow Book* in 1894) and the one-act *Journeys End in Lovers Meeting*. Both were composed in 1894; Craigie took the lead with the first, Moore with the second piece. In a wider sense, *Journeys End in Lovers Meeting* might be considered emblematic of Moore's impact, both short-term on his contemporaries and in the long term on the critical afterworld. For just as his strategic role in the construction of what proved to be a popular comedy fell victim to the acrimony of a failed love affair in which dismissal was accompanied by disavowal of co-authorship, so Moore remains largely under-recognized for the significance of his contribution to the definitional cultural movements of the *fin de siècle*. His literary recycling and satirical deflation of his contemporaries and their foibles, complemented as it was by his repudiation of groups and collectives when they stifled individuality and artistic independence, have made it too easy for too long to overlook the influence of the innovative drive, experimentalist mindset, and provocative imagination of George Moore.

NOTES

1. Matthew Potolsky, "Decadence, Nationalism, and the Logic of Canon Formation," *Modern Language Quarterly* 67, no. 2 (June 2006): 216.

2. Matthew Potolosky, "The Decadent Counterpublic," *Romanticism and Victorianism on the Net* 48 (November 2007), www.erudit.org/revue/ravon/2007/v/n48/017444ar.html (accessed February 22, 2014), and Michael Warner, *Publics and Counterpublics* (New York: Zone, 2005).

3. See Max Beerbohm's satirical portrait of self-styled "diabolist decadent" Enoch Soames, as discussed in N. John Hall's *Max Beerbohm: A Kind of Life* (New Haven: Yale University Press, 2002), 157. Beerbohm's sketch of his fictional decadent's features in *Enoch Soames: A Memory of the Eighteen-Nineties* (Privately printed, 1997) bears resemblance to his portrayal of Moore: "He was a stooping, shambling person, rather tall, very pale, with longish and brownish hair. He had a thin vague beard—or rather, he had a chin on which a large number of hairs weakly curled and clustered to cover its retreat. He was an odd-looking person . . . I decided that 'dim' was the *mot juste* for him" (5; for Soames's self-identification as a "diabolist" see 10). Compare with: "[There was] that quality of luminous vagueness which Moore's presence always had . . . He never seemed to enter or leave a room. Rather did he appear there, and in due time fade there. . . . He sat rather on the edge of his chair, his knees together, his hands hanging limp on either side of him. Limply there hung over his brow a copious wing of blond hair, which wavered as he turned the long white oval of his face from one speaker to another. He sat wide-eyed, gaping, listening. . . . His face was as a mask of gauze through which Nothing was quite clearly visible. And then, all of a sudden, there would appear—Something." David Cecil, *Max: A Biography* (Boston: Houghton Mifflin, 1965), 202. (See also the [equally fictitious and exquisitely constructed] *Bibliography of Enoch Soames*

[1862–1897], ed. Mark Samuels Lasner, with an afterword by Margaret D. Stetz [Oxford: Rivendale Press, 1999]).

4. Jean-Paul Sartre, *Gustave Flaubert, 1821–1857*, trans. Carol Cosman (Chicago: University of Chicago Press, 1989), 139.

5. George Moore, *Memoirs of My Dead Life*, Carra edition (New York: Boni and Liveright, 1923), 58.

6. George Moore, *Ave*, vol. 1 of *Hail and Farewell* (London: Heinemann, 1911), 27.

7. See Moore's imagined conversation with Robert Louis Stevenson in the "Advertisement" to *Celibate Lives* (1927), reproduced in *The Collected Short Stories of George Moore*, ed. Ann Heilmann and Mark Llewellyn, 5 vols (London: Pickering and Chatto, 2007), 5: 260–262.

8. Adrian Frazier, *George Moore, 1852–1933* (New Haven: Yale University Press, 2000), 468.

9. Charles Baudelaire, "The Painter of Modern Life" (1863), in *Baudelaire: Selected Writings on Art and Artists*, trans. P. E. Charvet (Harmondsworth: Penguin, 1972), 390–435; for a discussion of the *flaneur*, see especially 399–400.

10. Edouard Manet, as cited by Antonin Proust, quoted in Frazier, *George Moore*, 64.

11. George Moore, *Confessions of a Young Man* (London: William Heinemann, 1928), 25. First published in 1888 in book form after being serialized in 1886, *Confessions* was frequently revised.

12. Ibid., 26.

13. Adrian Frazier, "George Moore and Collaborative Authorship," in *George Moore: Across Borders*, ed. Christine Huguet and Fabienne Dabrigeon-Garcier (Amsterdam: Rodopi, 2013), 85.

14. R. B. Foster, *The Apprentice*, vol. 1 of *W. B. Yeats: A Life* (Oxford: Oxford University Press, 1997), 199.

15. Moore, *Confessions*, 28.

16. See the memoirs of Proust's housekeeper: Celeste Albaret, *Monsieur Proust: Souvenirs recueillis par Georges Belmont* (Paris: Robert Laffont, 1973), 270, 282.

17. Frazier, *George Moore*, 49.

18. Ibid., 98.

19. See Michael P. Farrell, *Collaborative Circles: Friendship Dynamics and Creative Work* (Chicago: University of Chicago Press, 2001), 17–26. For the case study of the Impressionists, see Chapter 2.

20. Joseph Hone, *The Life of George Moore* (London: Victor Gollancz, 1936), 378.

21. Moore, *Ave*, 206.

22. Ibid., 354.

23. Ibid., 68.

24. Foster, *The Apprentice*, 36.

25. Ibid., 453.

26. Ibid., 199.

27. Bennett to Moore, 24 December 1920, in *Letters of Arnold Bennett*, ed. James Hepburn, 4 vols (Oxford: Oxford University Press, 1970), 3:139. For a comparative reading of their work, see Ann Heilmann, "The Sublime and Satanic North: The Potteries in George Moore's *A Mummer's Wife* (1885) and Arnold Bennett's *Anna of the Five Towns* (1902)," in *The Literary North*, ed. Katharine Cockin (Basingstoke: Palgrave Macmillan, 2012), 56–72.

28. Frazier, "George Moore and Collaborative Authorship," 90. See also Charles Burkhart, "George Moore and *Father and Son*," *Nineteenth-Century Fiction* 15, no. 1 (June 1960): 71–77, and Peter Allen, "Sir Edmund Gosse and his Modern Readers: The Continued Appeal of *Father and Son*," *English Literary History* 55, no. 2 (1988): 487.

29. Frazier, *George Moore*, 406.

30. See Conor Montague, "A Class Apart: The Baptism of Stephen Dedalus," in *George Moore: Dublin, Paris, Hollywood*, ed. Conor Montague and Adrian Frazier (Dublin: Irish Academic Press, 2012), 123–136.

31. Frazier, *George Moore*, 317–318.

32. James Joyce, "The Day of the Rabblement" (1901), in *Occasional, Critical and Political Writing*, ed. Kevin Barry (Oxford: Oxford University Press, 2000), 51.

33. James Joyce, "Ireland: Island of Saints and Sages" (1907), ibid., 123.

34. Frazier, *George Moore*, 318.

35. Ibid., 318, 455.

36. Ibid., 244.

37. Charles Morgan, *Epitaph on George Moore* (London: Macmillan, 1935), 15–16; see also Frazier, *George Moore*, 468.

38. George Bernard Shaw, "A Letter as Postscript" (1934) in Geraint Goodwin, *Conversations with George Moore* (London: Jonathan Cape, 1940), 17.

39. Ibid., 18–19.

40. Ibid., 19.

41. Wilde to Reggie [Turner], in *The Letters of Oscar Wilde*, ed. Rupert Hart-Davis (London: Hart-Davis, 1962), 778, quoted in Frazier, *George Moore*, 268. See also Max Beerbohm's description of Moore's changeable face in Cecil, *Max*, 202.

42. See Frazier, *George Moore*, 278–281.

43. Ibid., 237. See Moore, *Memoirs*, 22. Hone (*Life*, 254) locates the event in the Isle of Wight, dating it to 1904, when the quarrel between Craigie and Moore flared up again about another collaborative play. For further details see Heilmann's "Co-authorship, Desire and Conflict" in this volume.

44. Moore in conversation with Vincent O'Sullivan, in Hone, *Life of George Moore*, 190.

45. Moore, *Memoirs*, 238.

46. See Ann Heilmann, "Deferred Desire and Textual Consummation in George Moore's *Memoirs of My Dead Life*: Beyond the Pleasure Principle?" *English Literature in Transition* 54, no. 3 (July 2011): 337–361.

47. *Memoirs*, 24–25. The latter phrase is adapted from Craigie's *The Sinners Comedy*; see Heilmann's "Co-authorship, Desire and Conflict" later in this volume.

48. Moore, *Memoirs*, 21.

49. Ibid., 19–20.

50. Hone, *Life*, 344.

51. Ibid., 182.

52. Moore to Clara Lanza, September 23, 1888, in "The Letters of George Moore, 1863–1901," ed. Robert Stephen Becker, 5 vols (PhD diss., University of Reading, January 1980), 2: 550.

53. Ibid.

54. Frazier, *George Moore*, 142.

55. Adrian Frazier, "On His Honor: George Moore and Some Women," *English Literature in Transition* 35, no. 4 (1992): 423–445, and Honor E. Woulfe, "George Moore and the Amenities," ibid., 447–461. For Cunard see Frazier, *George Moore*, 240.

56. Frazier, *George Moore*, 142.

57. Frazier, "George Moore and Collaborative Authorship," 93–97.

58. Lorine Pruette, "Leda and the Lion," *Story* 5 (July 1934): 3.

59. George Moore, *Avowals* (London: William Heinemann, 1924), 116.

60. Pruette, "Leda and the Lion," 12 (emphasis in original).

61. Ibid.

62. Frazier (*George Moore*, 421) quotes from Moore's 1921 letter to W. K. Magee (John Eglinton), where he refers to "the villager (Hardy), the sailor (Conrad), or the eunuch (James)."

63. Moore, *Confessions*, 157–158.

64. Ibid., 158.

65. Ibid., 67.

66. Ibid., 71.

67. Ibid., 149–150.

68. "Mr George Moore on America," *Observer*, December 17, 1916, quoted in Frazier, *George Moore*, 379.

69. Elizabeth Grubgeld, *George Moore and the Autogenous Self* (New York: Syracuse University Press, 1994); Mary Pierse, ed., *George Moore: Artistic Visions and Literary Worlds*

(Newcastle: Cambridge Scholars Press, 2006; pbk. edition 2014); Ann Heilmann and Mark Llewellyn, eds., *The Collected Short Stories of George Moore*, 5 vols (London: Pickering and Chatto, 2007); Conor Montagu and Adrian Frazier, eds., *George Moore: Dublin, Paris, Hollywood* (Dublin: Irish Academic Press, 2012); Christine Huguet and Fabienne Dabrigeon-Garcier, eds., *George Moore: Across Borders* (Amsterdam: Rodopi, 2013); María Elena Jaime de Pablos and Mary Pierse, eds., *George Moore and the Quirks of Human Nature* (Oxford: Peter Lang, 2014).

I

Influence

Chapter One

The *Fin de Siècle* Meets French Realism

*Moore, Balzac, and the
Peculiarity of Writers*

Adrian Frazier

For many years it appeared that George Moore had been utterly and completely buried, not just under a cairn on an island in Lough Carra, but under piles of ridicule, as if Thomas Hardy's deathbed wish for Moore had been fulfilled: "Heap dustbins on him . . ."[1] Chief among the gravediggers was W. B. Yeats, who went to work on *Dramatis Personae* as soon as he learned that Moore had died, but plenty of others lent a hand. Having embarrassed so many by turning their shortcomings into public entertainment, Moore was going to have to pay. And the penalty would come where to him it mattered most: in terms of his literary reputation.

A brilliant strategy of character assassination was deployed: his strengths were made into shortcomings. His detractors said the great stylist was unfamiliar with grammar and punctuation; that the comrade of Manet and Zola did not really know French; that the brazen truth-teller was just a liar; that the self-professed lover was actually incapable of the act of love; that the constantly invited guest at French salons and English country houses knew no etiquette. The point of the campaign was to make a fool of George Moore, and it temporarily succeeded, in that the crowd followed along. Even minor scholars attempted their own cheap jokes about Mcore. As an author, he was not taken seriously; as for being a great author, a man like him simply couldn't be. Didn't he himself say he was "peculiar?"[2] (As if writers ought to be otherwise.)

When Moore wasn't disrespected for being peculiar, he was diminished by being regarded as simply an English copy of Zola—just the same, but not as good. That was partly, no doubt, Moore's own fault. In a silly, youthful excess of enthusiasm, he called himself, in an 1884 letter to Zola, *"un reco-cher de Zola en Angleterre"*—a ricochet of Zola in England.[3] The phrase showed prescience about Moore's own immediate historical role with the publication of *A Mummer's Wife* in 1885, but how unhappy Moore became within ten years when the phrase had turned out to be prophetic of his own dependent role in the history of English fiction. "Ricochet of Zola?" "No one who knows anything would say such a thing."[4] Say instead, Son of Balzac. But many literary historians have not read any book written by Moore after 1885, so his achievement for them is not great, but minor, very minor.

In the process of conceptualizing what a great author is or might be, I think the example of Balzac, because of his own peculiarity, was useful to Moore, and it may be useful to us as well. Of course, Moore used Balzac in other ways too. First, he read Balzac's novels—apparently, all of them—with a view to learning how to write his own studies of the private lives of European people. Second, he profitably identified with the young heroes in Balzac novels who come from the provinces and set out to conquer the great city, men like Lucien de Rubempré and Eugène de Rastignac; he went from Mayo to London with a similar ambition. Third, he employed Balzac strategically as a protective influence, in order to keep at a safe distance the potentially dangerous and dominating influences of Flaubert, Zola, and Henry James. Fourth, and just as importantly, Moore noticed parallels between his own life and that of Balzac. These parallels enabled him to conclude that, peculiar though he found his own person to be, it might still have the makings of greatness, if only one could persuade the public that a great writer need not have the appearance and habits of life of a pope, a statesman, or a businessman.

It is difficult to know when Moore read which books by Balzac, but then it is difficult to know how, by 1884, he had read all of Zola, Goncourt, Gautier, James, Stevenson, Hardy, and most contemporary English novelists of note. It is clear that he had done so, because he surveys them all with penetrating familiarity in the 1884 pamphlet *Literature at Nurse*.

Nearly ten years earlier, in 1875, Maurice Moore visited his brother in Paris. The two, Maurice recalled, talked of Balzac.[5] In *Confessions of a Young Man*, Moore claims that he was first introduced to the work of the French novelist by Théophile Gautier's preface to Baudelaire's *Les Fleurs du Mal*, in which Balzac's story "Seraphita" is mentioned.[6] By early 1879, George Moore wrote to his mother that he was reading nothing but Balzac, Shakespeare, and the Bible.[7] What a good boy he was! But not that good. He also wrote that it was his aim to become the lover of the admittedly not very young Marquise d'Osmond. If he played his cards right, he confided to Mrs. Moore, he just might be lucky enough to succeed. This was necessary, for as he had learned from Balzac, "The first thing a young man who wants to get on in Paris must do is to get *under the wings* of some lady with a good name and in a high position[;] that done with tact he can wriggle anywhere."[8] That is indeed what Rastignac did, and Rubempré, and what Balzac did too. Moore even admits the cynicism of his strategy for success in the same laughing, laughable way that Balzac did.

Once the young Irish author began to develop a literary style, he acquired from French friends "new aestheticisms" week by week, unorthodox approaches to literature with which he experimented. It was the work of Balzac, Moore claimed, that saved him from losing his soul. Balzac was, Moore said, his Saint Peter, the rock upon which he would build, a Christological allusion that itself shows a ridiculous, Balzacian ambition.[9]

1886 appears to have been a key year in Moore's relationship to the French novelist. In March of that year, as Brendan Fleming has shown, Moore published an unsigned article in *The Freeman's Journal* on "Balzac and the Land League."[10] There, Moore argues that Balzac's *Les Paysans* tells the whole story of the Irish Land War decades before it occurred—including the boycotting, the assassination of bailiffs, and the redistribution of large estates. Moore then borrowed the ending of Balzac's novel to conclude *A Drama in Muslin*, published in the same year. When Moore's Parisian friend, art critic Théodore Duret, observed that the novel's heroine Alice Barton thinks and speaks a lot like George Moore, Moore defended himself by saying that Balzac "made his characters write letters they couldn't write, he made them speak as they couldn't speak." Flaubert would not have done so, of course; but Balzac was as "contradictory and as full of unexpected impulses as life itself." Balzac was, Moore concluded to Duret—and this is an early use of a key distinction in Moore—a "personal novelist," while Flaubert and Zola were "impersonal."[11]

Moore's loyalty to this new conception of the *personal* in prose narrative wavered in his next novel, *A Mere Accident* (1887). Everything wavered in that experiment. The book is a very Parisian enterprise, and seems a deliberate attempt to compete with, or go one better than, Huysmans's *A Rebours* (1884). At one extraordinary turn in Moore's novel, the vicar's daughter Kitty asks the aesthetically clerical John Norton if it had cost him much to give up his pessimism and republican politics for the Church: "John raised his eyes—it was a look Balzac would have understood and would have known how to interpret in some admirable pages of human suffering. 'None will ever know how I have suffered,' he said sadly. 'But now I am happy.'"[12] It is very strange in the course of a realistic novel for the narrator to butt in with a reflection on another novelist. It is not done. It is illusion-shattering. Stranger still, the passage could be read as a flat admission of ineptitude: the great Balzac could have expressed the emotion; Moore cannot. But in fact, it may be that Moore is speaking snidely, and saying, "Old Balzac would go on for pages here; I simply indicate the fact." That was the aestheticism of the moment, and it was not meant to be realistic.

However, if the allusion to Balzac in this novel is indeed partly self-serving, in *Confessions of a Young Man* (1888), Moore's next book, he veers sharply back in Balzac's favor. When telling of how he became a follower of Zola in the late 1870s, Moore says even then—in the heat of his disciple-ship—that he "did not fall into the fatal mistake of placing the realistic writers of 1877 side by side with and on the same plane of intellectual vision as the great Balzac."[13] When he spins out his comparison of Balzac with Shakespeare, and his personal preference for Balzac, it is clear that the novel-ist is meant to save him from Flaubert and Zola on the French side, and from the whole English tradition—from Shakespeare through George Eliot and Henry James—on the other side. Balzac is a kind of ideal naughty uncle, and very rich.

In addition to "Balzac and the Land League," there is another unsigned Balzac-focused article by Moore that appears not to have been formally attributed to him. This is "The Woman of Thirty," published in *The Hawk* in 1888. Of course, in *Confessions of a Young Man*, Moore had already spoken of Madame de Coëtlogon, his French-American mistress, as a "woman of thirty," deliciously cynical, morally tolerant, and physically passionate.[14] The author of the *Hawk* article would have us believe that women of this type and age went unnoticed—"lay under a ban"—"until the mighty Balzac eman-cipated her."[15] At the time of writing, the essayist pretends, every young man of style in London or Paris devotes himself to a divorcée or neglected wife. There is an anti-Victorian and anti-matrimonial program of shamelessness to the article that belongs to Moore, but it is true that the young Balzac did have a preference for older women, and that he published a long story entitled "The Woman of Thirty Years."

In 1889, Moore was invited by Frank Harris to bring together his thoughts on Balzac into a long article for the *Fortnightly Review*. The article was to serve as an introduction of the hitherto untranslated French master to English read-ers. "Some of Balzac's Minor Pieces," published that October, is not one of Moore's best essays. He returned to the essay a number of times—in *Impres-sions and Opinions* (1891), in an invited lecture in Paris in 1910 on Balzac and Shakespeare,[16] in *Avowals* (1919), and in *Conversations in Ebury Street* (1924)—but he never really got it right.

The essay begins with a stated fear of failure and ends with a cliché. Moore starts by saying that Balzac's *Human Comedy* is too large to be covered, and that no one—neither Sainte-Beuve, nor Zola, nor Henry James—has done justice to its author. The essay winds up by repeatedly saying that Balzac is like God because he created characters who live. In between this beginning and end, Moore needlessly insults William Makepeace Thackeray as trivial and George Eliot as both pedantic and, in a sexist gibe, un-virile.[17] Nonetheless, the original essay does capture a few of the aspects of Balzac that mattered to Moore.

First, he makes the interesting point that, prior to Balzac, painting and prose narrative were separate arts entirely; literature had hitherto been preoccupied with thoughts. Moore claims that Balzac pursued the pictorial in literature further than anyone had done before, and that all have followed in his path. Given that Moore's own strength was his capacity to do justice to the visible world, and to make that world suffice, this particular tribute is telling. There is in both writers a great appetite for life, and life is all that is required to satisfy that appetite. In the works of both Balzac and Moore, there is nothing of religion but priests and ceremonies, no belief. When people pray, they are represented as talking to no one, or to themselves. The invisible world is a non-existent world.

Second, Moore praises Balzac for having a unique capacity to imply a philosophical criticism of his own time by means of contrasting it with a representation of the immediate past.[18] He lived through a period of massive change—revolutionary France, Napoleon, his victories, his defeat, the Restoration, the Revolution of 1830—and saw individuals as defined by rapidly shifting values. This strengthened Moore's own sense that the writer was an antithetical figure, standing above or against the center, and seeing cultures in comparison—in the case of Moore, France versus England versus Ireland. Moore could reckon the velocity of modernity, but he took his own stand in the eighteenth century, just as Balzac arbitrarily insisted that a world of kings, courtiers, and Roman Catholicism was the best order of life, which for his novelistic purposes it certainly was.

Third, in his Balzac essay, Moore paints a little picture of the romance of creative composition: "Living as Balzac did in the giddiness and exaltation of an unceasing creation, I can imagine him lifting his face from the paper like one still under the influence of the dream, unable for a moment to bear the intensity of the enchantment."[19] To Moore, as to Balzac, writing itself was both toil and pleasure. It was at once drunkenness and the highest sobriety, love and a monkish solitude, glory and the annihilation of self, a higher wakefulness and outright somnambulism. In 1907, Moore would tell his friend Edouard Dujardin that he was deep into the composition of *Hail and Farewell,* writing eight hours a day, working, he said (using a slang word a half century before its offensiveness was to be acknowledged), "like a nigger or Balzac." He allowed that his own work was not so important as Balzac's, or maybe as the other fellow's, but the fact remained that prose composition was all he did with his days, and all he cared to do.[20]

Apart from these insights, most of "Balzac's Minor Pieces" is made up of careless translation of parts of three stories, and hasty paraphrase of the rest of them. And, as I said before, Moore never did succeed in writing a good essay on Balzac. In 1901, Edmund Gosse begged Moore to write a new five-thousand word article on the French novelist, but three months after agreeing to do so, Moore, when Gosse tried to collect the finished product, confessed that he had not yet begun: "The truth is that I knew from the beginning I had nothing further to say on the subject."[21] Putting a new style on the *Fortnight-ly Essay* on "Balzac's Minor Pieces" was hardly going to suffice. When invited to give a lecture in Paris in 1910, Moore turned his thoughts of 1889 into academic French. That made a poor essay worse. To say in England that Balzac was better than Shakespeare at least had the merit of being offensively unpatriotic; in France, it was just flattery from a foreigner.

There is one main reason for Moore's consistent failure to write well about Balzac. He tried to demonstrate the greatness of Balzac's work rather than the character of the writer. Moore was at all times an impressionist critic whose insights were rooted in biography, but the personal appeal of Balzac for him had to do with Balzac's character as much as with his works.

This interest in Balzac's life comes out as an aside in a review article on American women novelists that Moore published in *The Hawk* in 1890.[22] Moore complains that William Gladstone has poisoned the atmosphere for writing literature with his moralism. He spreads cant through the British Isles, Moore remarks, like a white man spreads smallpox in the Pacific Islands. Insincerity is pervasive in England. Moore remarks that in a biography of Balzac by Frederick Wedmore, on every page the author apologizes for something Balzac did: he was intimate with the Duchess de Castries, he was morbid, he was coarse, he did not marry until late in his life. Why, Moore asks, must a man marry, early or late, in order to write a great novel? Moore himself was constantly subjected to the tut-tut of the insincere and the condescension of the Protestant. He could not be admitted into the polite society of Tennysonian great literature, or even the country gothic of Thomas Hardy.

How differently from Frederick Wedmore he must have viewed the life and character of Balzac. There is a terrific and hilarious biography of the master in English by Graham Robb. It enables one to discover the many ways in which the Irish novelist resembles his French predecessor. In school, both were the despair of parents and schoolmasters. At one point, the headmaster wrote to Balzac's mother to fetch him immediately; he had passed from being alarmingly dull into something like a coma. Mental congestion was the diagnosis. He looked stupid, but he was really just thinking. Balzac said that such minds as his are like waterfalls from a distance; they only appear to be motionless.[23] Similarly, George Henry Moore got a letter from the Headmaster of Oscott suggesting that he take his oldest son back home. It was pointless to leave him at school; he was ineducable.[24] Yet, surely when Moore was a boy, his mind cannot have been a still and stagnant pool; his consciousness too was rushing and turbulent.

Both authors described themselves as gormless youths, thunderstruck by the charms of women. When Balzac's family moved to Paris, he was taken to his first ball. He sat on his own in wonderment at the ladies in their dazzling dresses. Then one sat down beside him: "I stretched up, trembling, to see the bodice and was utterly entranced by a bosom, chastely covered in gauze, but whose pale blue, perfectly rounded globes could be seen lying snugly in folds of lace."[25] He could not help himself, and lunged at the lightly veiled flesh. The woman naturally shrieked, and left the boy agape. Whether Moore ever did the like is in question; but he unquestionably could have written that he had, and in just Balzac's self-mocking spirit.

Balzac's shameless declaration that he thirsted for fame—and that by one means or another he would get it—was like Moore's blatant and premature ambition. Their motivations were also alike: fame would tempt women. "There was nothing attractive about *me*," Balzac wrote.[26] He was five foot two, had a big nose with a bulb on the end of it, black teeth in a large fat-lipped mouth, and long greasy hair—making him even less attractive, in short, than George Moore. Reputation, he wagered, would pull the women in his direction, and he was right. There came to him in later years, as there came to Moore, letters from young female readers addressed simply to the author's name and the city in which he dwelled. Ultimately, Balzac's actual image underwent a transformation, and he appeared to the public as ithyphallic. In Rodin's full-figure sculpture, Balzac is a penis personified. Max Beerbohm did the same favor for Moore, but made him appear limp.[27]

In his twenties, the young French writer plunged cheerfully into guerrilla journalism with the same comic gusto as Moore did seventy years later in the *Bat* and the *Hawk*. Neither shied away from fashionable flippancy or mad megalomaniacal philosophizing. A Balzac pamphlet from these years is "172 Honest Ways in Which to Acquire Other People's Property."[28] It is as eye-catching a title as that regular feature in *The Bat*: "Things We Ought Not to Have Done, By Those Who Have Done Them."

As was the case with Moore, when Balzac first enjoyed some success with his work, his acquaintances were flabbergasted. Him!? It can't be. Would you believe it—Balzac published an article in the newspaper.[29] Later accounts of Balzac's life would, as a result, be colored by envy and surprise. This reminds one of G. B. Shaw seeing *A Mummer's Wife* for sale in 1885. The author could not be the same George Moore he knew, but in fact he was. It all had to do with the terrible industry of the man, Shaw supposed.[30] Similarly, Baudelaire recalled of Balzac: "Nobody could ever possibly imagine how clumsy, silly, and stupid that great man was in his youth. And yet he managed to acquire, to get for himself, not only grandiose ideas, but also a vast amount of wit. But then he *never* stopped working."[31] When Balzac finished his first novel, even his mother was skeptical. She wanted to solicit a professional opinion. So she sent the manuscript to a tutor in the Polytechnic. "The author," he wrote, "should do *anything he likes but not literature*."[32] Even that does not match the brutality of Edmund Yates's review of *Pagan Poems*, which recommended that young George Moore be convicted of a crime and sentenced to a public whipping.[33]

Shared humiliations enabled Moore to identify with the great novelist. Even in later years, he sometimes enjoyed making silly comparisons between himself and the Frenchman. For instance, in 1909, he was engaging in a literary flirtation with one of his female readers, Emily Lorenz Meyer. As was often the case with such engagements, Moore was of two minds about whether or not he wished ever to see, or to be seen by, the woman at the other end of the exchange. In June, he wrote to Emily that it might be fun for him to go to Germany and walk down the alley of lime trees along which she lived, and wonder which of the women strollers she might be. But then he adds: "Only, remember Balzac who went to see Madame Hanska. She was reading one of his books and all the time she was saying to herself 'Good Heavens! I hope Balzac isn't that horrid little man walking up and down the street on the opposite pavement in such excitement.'"[34] That man was indeed Balzac.

Madame Hanska and Balzac met in 1833, and finally married after her husband's death in 1850, just five months before the end of the novelist's life. Balzac had traveled heroically across Europe to Russia in order to be with her, and then returned to Paris to set up a monumental city mansion for their establishment. If not chaste on either side, theirs was certainly a glorious, romantic, sincere love affair, the match of Wagner's with Mathilde Wesendonck. Moore liked to remind Lady Cunard that they had to live up to the glamour of these pairs of glorious lovers. To him, their affair, though extramarital, was not shabby and should not be secret. In France, and in Russia, it would be celebrated. While Lady Cunard was amused, she never forgot that it was England in which they made their homes.

There were, naturally, differences of character between the French and the Irish author. Balzac would plunge himself into debt in order to write himself out of it. After his early years in Paris, Moore was careful about money, and died a wealthy man. Balzac had a lot of madcap beliefs—like salvation through sexual intercourse, or the extension of life through retention of vital fluids (possibly contradictory beliefs?)—and Moore had no beliefs at all.

Balzac was a man of tremendous physical as well as mental energy. Nietzsche conceived of him, and Rodin sculpted him, as the very symbol of the life force and the will to power. Even if his stature was small, he had a larger-than-life presence, and the endurance of a military campaigner. Moore did not. One cannot imagine him climbing Mont Blanc. While he did make his way to the Holy Land in preparation for the composition of *A Brook Kerith*, he went by cruise ship. In *Elizabeth Cooper*, he allows the heroine to twit the George Moore figure on this very point:

> Countess: Balzac went to meet Madame Hanska. If you were really a great man you would have come to Vienna.
> Lewis: I suppose I should. The really great man can act as well as think. [35]

Balzac was truly Napoleonic; Moore was not in any way Napoleonic.

In his effort to leave to posterity a body of work that would always give pleasure to readers, Moore rewrote his books again and again, some of them up to five times. Critics, and sometimes friends too, would disparage him for this practice. It was, they said, an admission of the book's failure to rewrite it, and of the author's weakness of resolve. Moore's reply was that Balzac did it.[36] Nonetheless, he sometimes feared that all of his efforts to improve a work may have taken him nowhere. In particular, *Evelyn Innes* and *Sister Teresa* drove him mad. He was producing second and third editions even before their first editions went on sale. He kept up his efforts on this two-volume story for ten years. In the end, he felt that no one would read the books again until after he was dead, if then. He could not be sure that he had not spent a decade concocting an absurdity.

His own case reminded him of Balzac's story "Le Chef D'Oeuvre Inconnu" (1831), in which the famous painter Frenhofer has worked on a painting secretly for ten years, and finally is persuaded by a pupil to draw aside the curtain on it. When he does so, all that can be recognized of the work is a single foot, a delicious foot that has miraculously escaped from a slow and progressive decomposition wrought by over-painting. Perhaps, Moore concluded, what Balzac wrote had happened to him, and his own life was a realization of one of the master's fictions.[37]

This anecdote captures one final and important similarity between the two authors: it is, one might say, sad, and rich with a bewildered sense of life's mystery. But it is also cheerful—in that Moore stands outside his own experience, and smiles at it. He is enjoying the joke on himself, and knows we will enjoy it too. Graham Robb observes something comparable in Balzac. In any account of Balzac's behavior, he says, if cheerfulness fails to break through, the story is probably not accurate. Once in 1824, for instance, Balzac was standing on a bridge over the Seine and considering suicide. Two of his novels in a row had been savagely ridiculed in the press. He had no money. He had meant to conquer society, but society had crushed him. He was just about to jump into the freezing river when a friend, Etienne Arago, passed by and said, "Ah, Balzac, come along, I'll buy you dinner!" The novelist shrugged and fell into step alongside his friend.[38] Now this might happen to anyone—failure, thought of suicide, and a change of mind. But for Balzac and Moore, it was the kind of incident that gave them a tale to tell against themselves, and to produce a good and truly human laugh. There is a charm in the companionship of such authors that draws readers to them in all ages. George Moore, of course, is not like Balzac in the scale of his achievement. No novelist measures up to the author of the *Human Comedy*, but there are some that come closer than George Moore. The point of this chapter is that a number of features of Moore and his work that have been held against him—that he wrote too many books; that he wrote in too many styles; that he revised his books; that his love life was indecently complicated; that he was funny-looking; that he did not believe in God or the afterlife; that he relished nature as he found it; and that he was in love with fame—are all features that he shares with the greatest novelist of them all. Indeed, some of Moore's own strengths are the very powers that carried Balzac to the peak of human achievement: a capacity for work and a passion for the telling of tales.

NOTES

1. Thomas Hardy, "G. M.," in *The Complete Poems of Thomas Hardy*, ed. James Gibson (New York: Macmillan, 1978), 954.

2. George Moore to Mary Blake Moore; unreferenced, quoted in Tony Gray, *A Peculiar Man: A Life of George Moore* (London: Sinclair-Stevenson, 1996), 1.

3. George Moore to "*Mon cher Maitre*" [Zola], [February 1884], Shelbourne Hotel, Dublin, in Robert Stephen Becker, ed., "The Letters of George Moore, 1863–1901," 5 vols (PhD diss., University of Reading, January 1980), 1: 247.

4. Vincent O'Sullivan, *Opinions* (London: Unicorn Press, 1959), 36–37.

5. Joseph Hone, *The Life of George Moore* (New York: Macmillan, 1936), 51.

6. George Moore, *Confessions of a Young Man*, ed. Susan Dick (Montreal: McGill-Queens University Press, 1972), 97.

7. George Moore to Mary Blake Moore, [early 1879], in Becker, "Letters of George Moore," 1: 185.

8. George Moore to Mary Blake Moore, [Spring 1879?], in Becker, "Letters of George Moore," 1: 190 (emphasis in original).

9. Moore, *Confessions*, 100. See also 93–94.

10. Brendan Fleming, "'Balzac and the Land League': A 'New' Article by George Moore," *English Literature in Transition* 46, no. 4 (2003): 356–364.

11. George Moore to Théodore Duret, [c. Monday, August 16, 1886], in Becker, "Letters of George Moore," 1: 376.

12. George Moore, *A Mere Accident* (London: Vizetelly, 1887), 215.

13. Moore, *Confessions*, 97.

14. Ibid., see Chapters 5 and 8, 90–91, 118–126.

15. "The Woman of Thirty," unsigned, *The Hawk*, December 11, 1888, 521.

16. "Shakespeare et Balzac," February 18, 1910, Paris, later included in *Avowals*, see Edwin Gilcher, ed., *A Bibliography of George Moore* (Dekalb: Northern Illinois University Press, 1970), 103.

17. George Moore, "Some of Balzac's Minor Pieces," *Fortnightly Review*, n.s., 271, October 1, 1889, 492, 501.

18. Ibid., 503. Later adapted for Moore's "Balzac" chapter in *Impressions and Opinions* (New York: Brentano's, 1910), 16.

19. Moore, *Impressions and Opinions*, 6.

20. George Moore to Edouard Dujardin, April 25, 1907, in *Letters from George Moore to Ed. Dujardin*, ed. John Eglinton (New York: Crosby Gaige, 1929), 61.

21. George Moore to Edmund Gosse, May 9, [1901]; George Moore to Edmund Gosse, August 1, 1901; Brotherton Library, University of Leeds.

22. "Literature and Art," *The Hawk*, January 7, 1890, 14.

23. Graham Robb, *Balzac* (London: Picador, 1994, 2000), 23

24. Adrian Frazier, *George Moore, 1852–1933* (New Haven Yale University Press, 2000), 17.

25. Robb, *Balzac*, 32.

26. Ibid., 34.

27. Max Beerbohm, "Mr George Moore, Preacher to Lord Howard de Walden" (1907), reprinted in *George Moore: Letters to Lady Cunard 1895–1933*, ed. Rupert Hart-Davis (London: Hart-Davis, 1957), n.p.

28. Robb, *Balzac*, 38.

29. This incident refers to a pamphlet published in 1824 under the pseudonym M. D.; see Robb, *Balzac*, 109–110.

30. Quoted in Charles Morgan, *Epitaph on George Moore* (London: Macmillan, 1935), 16.

31. Robb, *Balzac*, 75 (emphasis in original).

32. Ibid., 60 (emphasis in original).

33. Edmund Yates, "A Bestial Bard," *The World*, 7, November 20, 1877, 18.

34. Helmut Gerber, ed., with the assistance of O. M. Brack, Jr., *George Moore on Parnassus: Letters (1900–1933) to Secretaries, Publishers, Printers, Agents, Literati, Friends, and Acquaintances* (Newark: University of Delaware Press, 1988), 152.

35. George Moore, *Elizabeth Cooper* (Dublin: Maunsel, 1913), 104.

36. George Moore to Filson Young, October 2, 1905, in Gerber with Brack, *George Moore on Parnassus*, 123.

37. George Moore, *Sister Teresa* (London: Ernest Benn, 1929), vii.

38. Robb, *Balzac*, 121.

Chapter Two

"A Visit to an Impressionist Exhibition" in Moore's *Confessions of a Young Man*

Anna Gruetzner Robins

In "Half-a-Dozen Enthusiasts" (1886), written for the *Bat*, George Moore reviewed the eighth and last Impressionist art exhibition, which opened May 15, 1886, in shop premises at 1 rue Lafitte, Paris. It was the only review to appear in English, and it was a serious review by a serious critic who was well-informed about the developments in the Impressionist movement.[1] Moore's assessment of Degas's canonical *Sequence of Nudes, of Women Bathing, Washing, Drying, Wiping Themselves, Combing Their Hair or Having it Combed*, a group of pastel nudes composed between 1884 and 1886[2] and of Seurat's large *A Sunday on La Grande Jatte* (1885–1886, The Art Institute of Chicago[3]), a manifesto picture for his newly invented *pointillist* technique, and Moore's appraisal of pictures by Guillaumin, Morisot, and Pissarro mark him out as a key player amongst French symbolist critics such as Felix Fénéon, Gustave Geoffroy, J. K. Huysmans, and Octave Mirbeau, all of whom also reviewed the exhibition. As his comments about the Degas pastels suggest, Moore had had a conversation with the artist about at least one of them. He wrote his review having taken part in the talk and gossip in and around the exhibition, after attending a few dinners with the artists and their critics, and after spending time in Degas's studio. This knowledgeable review with its *au courant* point of view could not have been written had Moore not mingled comfortably in this tightly knit Parisian art world. Moore was adept at recycling his writing on Impressionism, using a review as the basis of a fictional narrative, describing a picture in a novel, and expanding

39

on his first viewing in his reminiscences, so that his writings created multiple and overlapping impressions of the same painting.

Moore's first novel *A Modern Lover* (1883) contains descriptions of recognizable Impressionist pictures that he saw in Paris and London. Since the book was written before he turned his hand to art criticism, he relied on his memory of seeing these works for his descriptions. In *Confessions* (1888), the 1886 *Bat* review is recycled as the basis of a satirical account of a visit to an "*exposition*" (Moore uses the French word) of the Impressionists. That also had the purpose of serving as an indication of his most recent views on Impressionism. Descriptions of the same key pictures by Degas, Guillaumin, Morisot, Pissarro, and Seurat appear to make it a plausible account of the 1886 show but, significantly, Seurat's *Sunday on the Island of La Grande Jatte*, which Moore had treated seriously in the *Bat* review, now is the subject of mockery, while two more pastels by Degas from the 1886 show are added and, confusingly, one picture by Renoir and three by Monet exhibited in the 1876 and 1877 Impressionist exhibitions surface in this version of the later show. Moore's technique thus telescopes exhibitions that took place over a ten-year period into one fictive space and event. This is more than a careless indifference to historical accuracy. Moore the critic meets Moore the author in *Confessions* and speaks with more than one authorial voice as he draws on memories of his first viewing of Impressionist painting, recounts his response to the last exhibition of the movement, and adds his reassessment of Seurat's painting.

Moore recognized that the fabric of the Impressionist movement—its painters and their pictures, and the exhibitions they organized as an alternative to the Salon—was embedded in the spectacle of Paris. It is an unappreciated aspect of Moore's genius that he thought of using an Impressionist exhibition as a meeting point for several authorial voices from different time periods. He brings together memories of his younger self when he first saw pictures by Monet and Renoir as an uninformed art student with his more recent self as a professional critic. An analysis of the *Bat* review and the revisionary account of the exhibition in *Confessions* reveals different critical voices and assessments of Impressionism.

Moore discussed four artists—Degas, Guillaumin, Morisot, and Pissarro—who had taken part in the Impressionist exhibitions since their inception. Given that fifteen artists participated in the 1886 show, it may be odd to see the little-known Jean Baptiste Armand Guillaumin on Moore's list of subjects but for the fact that he was favored by the Symbolists, including Jean Ajalbert and Felix Fénéon. This suggests that Moore may have been led by their opinion. There is evidence that he had successfully infiltrated the Symbolist camp by spring 1886 and his critical support for Seurat confirms this to be the case. Seurat was a newcomer whom Pissarro, together with his son Lucien and Paul Signac, had brought into the exhibition. All three had taken up the *pointillist* technique that Seurat had developed the previous year of applying color in separate small *points*.

Few of the older Impressionists were sympathetic about Pissarro's defection to these younger artists, and his adoption of *pointillism* may explain why Moore focused on the dream-like quality of Pissarro's *La Cueillette de pommes* (*Apple-Picking*, 1886, Ohara Museum of Art, Kurashi), a utopian image of "girls in an orchard . . . beat[ing] the apples from the trees with long poles . . . [and] gather[ing] them into large baskets."[4] While he praised the luminosity of its "violet and red"[5] palette, he overlooked its technique, just as he ignored the luminous effect created by the miniscule *points* of separate color in Seurat's *Sunday on the Island of La Grande Jatte*. He preferred instead the social mix of the respectable and improper "children, nursemaids, dogs, young men, and cocottes," including the large-scale, fashionable courtesan in profile, who make up the flattened, hieratic figures of this allegory of modern Paris, which Moore said "looks like a modernised version of ancient Egypt."[6] Moore's review was one of the first to be published, and it comes as a surprise that Fénéon, the self-appointed spokesperson of the Neo-Impressionists, as he named them, cited Moore's comparison of Seurat's image of modern Paris with ancient Egypt in a lengthy theoretical piece that appeared at the end of June that same year.[7] The enigmatic Seurat provided virtually no explanation of any of his pictures. However, as Paul Smith suggests, he would have drawn on an established analogy between the decadence of ancient Egypt and modern Paris.[8] Moore must have heard the conversations that circulated amongst the Symbolist critics, many of whom were sympathetic to the anarchist ideals of several of the Neo-Impressionists. Clearly, he was no longer the newcomer who had stumbled across the Impressionists the previous decade.[9]

Edouard Dujardin's invitation to become a contributor to the Symbolist journal *La Revue indépendante* marked Moore's acceptance into the most avant-garde literary circle in Paris, and Moore made the most of this new contact, visiting the offices of the journal for the first time in February 1887.[10] He may have attended the housewarming for its new premises on the rue de la Chaisée d'Antin on November 26 of that year, which had hosted an exhibition by Anquetin, Manet, the Pissarros, Raffaelli, Seurat, and Signac. A rhymed verse by Stéphane Mallarmé summoned guests to this event.[11] Moore, Huysmans, Jacques-Emile Blanche, Téodor de Wyzewa, Jean Ajalbert, Maurice Barrès, and Paul Adam were invited.[12] This was far from Moore's only appearance at the journal's offices. Blanche remembered another banquet when he recalled that *"le brilliant causeur était entouré de Mallarmé, Villiers de l'Isle Adam, Huysmans, Francis Poitevin, Wyzewa— les convives de Edouard Dujardin"*[13] (the brilliant conversationalist was surrounded by Mallarmé, Villiers de l'Isle Adam, Huysmans, Francis Poitevin, Wyzewa—the companions of Edouard Dujardin); Paul Alexis also con-

firmed that Moore was a frequent visitor at these occasions.[14] Moore continued to view Neo-Impressionist paintings after 1886 as confirmed by his later
criticism, which contains references to pictures in subsequent exhibitions of
the Salon des Indépendants and at other venues including Alexis's collection.[15] These contacts should have buoyed up Moore's knowledge of the new
movement, but instead he became increasingly disillusioned with it, as is
confirmed by two 1892 articles in which he makes another confusing reference to the 1886 show and takes a swing at Pissarro, who until then had been
exempt from his criticism.[16]

It was not until *Confessions*, however, that Moore first attacked Seurat.
After stating in the *Bat* that "of the new-comers, Seurat strikes me as possess-
ing the most talent," he now wrote a satiric description of the "twenty foot
square" picture with "a lady walking in the foreground with a ring-tailed
monkey" with a tail "said to be three yards long" before giving a sampling of
the "clamour in the petite press," meaning those journalists whose comments
he had treated with derision in his original review.[17] Moore was not ever to
appreciate fully the experimental nature of the Impressionist palette. He mentions the glowing light effects in Impressionist painting without commenting
on its myriad of pure colors and their complements that replaced tonal
contrast. Probably Moore never overcame a widely held prejudice that color-
based painting and the complicated color theory of the Neo-Impressionists
was effeminate. He was deeply skeptical about the uniformity of the *pointillist* technique, which he compared to the manufacturing processes of capital-
ist society: "The world is dying of machinery; that is the great disease, that is
the plague that will sweep away and destroy civilisation," he warned in
Confessions.[18] The surface appearance of a picture could create a profound
uneasiness in Moore, who frequently expressed his dislike of the surface
effects of certain kinds of painting. There is an obvious equation between
surface and touch and we can imagine Moore's objection to the touch of the
hundreds of small points of pigment that make up Seurat's *La Grande Jatte*,
which he imagined were applied with machine-like regularity.

By 1887, Moore was straddling two groups: the Parisian Symbolist circle
and the Francophile British Impressionists who, with the exception of the
painter Phillip Wilson Steer, were suspicious of what they regarded as the
mechanical nature of the *pointillist* technique. This British group included
Walter Sickert, who formed a close friendship with Degas ("one of the greatest artists the world has ever known," as Moore described him), and who
must have persuaded Moore to abandon his interest in the Neo-Impressionists and turn his attention to Degas.[19] Out of the thirteen works Degas exhibited in 1886, Moore singled out three pastels in his review, all female nudes,
a focus that brought him close to the Symbolist critics, so preoccupied with
intimate views of women bathing while standing, bending, and squatting in
awkward positions, while hurling abuse at what they assumed were represen-

tations of prostitutes, living and working in the most abject conditions. Rarely has the sight of the female body incited such disgust and hatred, and though Moore was not without his own aversion to female flesh, he avoided any reference to prostitution in both his review and the fictionalized account in *Confessions*. Like his French peers, he reported that Degas was challenging the established canon of endless "Venus[es] with rosy finger-nails" for which the Salon audience had an unlimited appetite, questioning whether the middle-aged women who modeled for two of the works had much in common with these erotically charged female nudes. [20] Referring to *Young Woman Dressing Herself* (1885, National Gallery of Art, Washington DC), Moore pointed out that Degas chose to represent a "poor working woman . . . passing her chemise over her lumpy shoulders" because "the short, coarse, thick thighs of the poor working woman, deformed by the toil of modern days, have never been seen on canvas before."[21] He linked *Young Woman Dressing Herself* with "the short-legged lump of human flesh who, her back turned to us, grips her flanks with both hands"[22] in the pastel *The Baker's Wife* (1885–1886, Henry and Rose Pearlman Foundation, on loan to Princeton University Art Museum), which, he reported in *Confessions,* is "full of the malformations of forty years, of children, of hard work."[23]

Using an artist's intentions as an explanation of meaning is a suspect business; however, Moore seemed quite convinced about the age and class of these two models. He later fleshed out a complicated tale about the model for *The Baker's Wife*, where he identified her as the wife of the local butcher rather than of the baker:

> Degas more than once drew a creature as short-legged and as bulky, and the model he chose was the wife of a butcher in the Rue La Rochefoucauld. The poor creature arrived in all her finery, the clothes she wore when she went to Mass on Sunday, and her amazement and her disappointment are easily imagined when Degas told her he wanted her to pose for him naked. She was accompanied by her husband, and knowing her to be not exactly a Venus de Milo, he tried to dissuade Degas . . . Degas had assured the butcher that the erotic sentiment was not strong in him[.][24]

This is gossip but, as Elizabeth Grubgeld indicates elsewhere in this collection, Moore's is always interesting gossip. In this case it is intriguing because it suggests that the age and social identity of these models is an important aspect of Degas's project. We know that Degas approved of what Moore had written in *Confessions*, where all three Degas nudes have the same canonical importance as they did in the *Bat* review.[25] How do you distinguish between a critical reaction to an event and a later autobiographical account when looking at these different interpretations of the same picture that Moore claimed marked a "new phase" of Degas's "talent"?[26]

Just what this new phase consisted of was revealed in another throwaway comment when Moore linked these nudes (the third was probably *Woman Bathing in a Shallow Tub*, 1885, Metropolitan Museum of Art, New York) to the art of the Middle Ages, when "cynicism was one of the great means of eloquence," and claimed that Degas had "the pessimism of the early saint, and the scepticism of these modern days."[27] (In *Confessions*, he wrote, "Cynicism was the great means of eloquence of the middle ages, and with cynicism Degas has rendered the nude again an artistic possibility."[28]) Only one other critic, Huysmans, made a similar point about Degas's disinterested ascetic approach to the female nude when he observed that the nudes "even glorify the scorn of the flesh as no artist, since the Middle Ages, has dared to express it."[29] We cannot discount the possibility that Degas himself suggested this analogy with the Middle Ages to Moore and Huysmans, but, whatever the source, Moore wrote it down first; his review was published a year before Huysmans's commentary on the nudes appeared in print.[30]

The growing adulation for Degas in Britain explains why Moore included two more Degas pastels in *Confessions*, *The Little Milliners* (1882, Nelson Atkins Museum of Art, Kansas) and *At the Milliner's* (1882, Metropolitan Museum of Art, New York), which he would have remembered seeing at the 1886 exhibition although he did not mention them in the *Bat*. Writing from memory, he described the "fat, vulgar woman in the long cloak trying on a hat in front of the pier-glass" in *At the Milliner's* and connected her physiognomy with "her position in life. . . . [Y]ou know what the furniture of her rooms is like; you know what she would say to you if she were to speak."[31] This was not the last time Moore mentioned this picture. It crops up in the fascinating and informative "Degas: The Painter of Modern Life," in the *Magazine of Art* in 1890.[32] Two years later, an opportunity to revisit the picture at a London exhibition prompted Moore to write an extended and detailed narrative about the comings and goings of the female shopper incorporating a formalist analysis of Degas's inventive composition:

> there is a three-quarter length figure of a stout middle-class woman. She stands, leaning her head on one side, looking at herself in the glass. The back of the glass, seen in rapid perspective, is towards the spectator. See how well the glass swings in its frame!—it is slanted a little, and the space between the bamboo upright and the frame was observed by an eye of exceeding delicacy. Thus the glass cuts in twain the figure of the shop assistant; but the bonnets which she offers with both hands show on either side of the glass. How ingenious, how lifelike, how original, how well preserved, how well invented! And yet the figures are, in a sense, more written than drawn. It is terribly hard to express these things in English, but every painter will understand what I mean. Just now I used the word arabesque. I chose the word instinctively, but now it seems to me to have been an exceedingly well-chosen word, for if I had said silhouette I should have utterly failed to express my meaning. Apart from

this defect, the picture is superb, and is worth the eight hundred pounds that were paid for it. This middle class woman, will you ever forget her? I think not. Is she not of her class? Her mode of life, her manner of thought, her moral nature—all is there. You know what bourgeois comfort and bourgeois vulgarity she has lived in, still lives in, and will continue to live in, for she is especially adapted by nature to live the life that she lives so thoroughly, so fully, that she is the very type and epitome of it.[33]

In this lengthy passage, Moore abandons the fractured, pithy descriptions to be found in *Confessions*, which matched Degas's fragmented images of modern life, and offers a narrative that anticipates the endless British appetite for subject pictures with a story. There is always the possibility that his story about the picture was based in fact, just as his information about the model for *The Baker's Wife* must have come from Degas or someone else in his inner circle. Degas had a sharp eye for social detail and was a well-known snob who upheld conventional prejudice that class could be detected in a bodily type and who delighted in depicting the nuances of nineteenth-century deportment. It was left to Moore to tell the tale.

The addition of Monet's *Turkeys* (1877, Musée d'Orsay, Paris) and one of his Gare Saint Lazare pictures (Moore is probably describing *La Gare Saint Lazare*, 1877, Fogg Art Museum, Cambridge) to the fictive exhibition in *Confessions* confuses any expectation that the exhibition took place in a single moment in time because neither Monet nor Renoir contributed to the final Impressionist exhibition, although they were key figures in the early exhibitions. When Moore visited the 1877 show with Lewis Weldon Hawkins, a fellow student at the Académie Julian (fictionalized as Marshall in *Confessions*), he was probably finding the popularized academic painting practiced by Hawkins and other apprentice painters less than satisfactory; he had not yet acquired his later sophisticated understanding of Impressionism.[34] These two points of view are brought together in *Confessions*, where the young Moore stands beside Hawkins/Marshall as he and other students confront Monet's *Turkeys*. In response to their laughter of derision and disbelief, a common philistine reaction to Monet's pictures, another voice enters the narrative offering an appreciation of the innovatory painterly qualities of *Turkeys*:

Then we stood and screamed at Monet, that most exquisite painter of blonde light. We stood before the *Turkeys*, and seriously we wondered if "it was serious work,"—that *chef d'oeuvre!* the high grass that the turkeys are gobbling is flooded with sunlight so swift and intense that for a moment the illusion is complete. "Just look at the house! Why, the turkeys couldn't walk in at the door. The perspective is all wrong."[35]

By the time he wrote *Confessions,* Moore was no longer the belligerent, traditionally trained student of his Julian days, and his later appreciation of the original techniques and methods in Monet's painting creeps into this passage. The students "stood and screamed at Monet," but another voice informs us that Monet was an "exquisite painter of blonde light." They wondered if Monet's *Turkeys* was a "serious work," but Moore tells us it was a *"chef d'oeuvre."* They criticized the perspective for being "all wrong," but Moore tells us that the flattened space heightens the "illusion," that the "high grass . . . is flooded with sunlight."[36] Underlying this philistine reaction is a sophisticated understanding of Monet's radical experimentation with new brush techniques using pure color that ignored the traditional rules for modeling and perspective. Monet's *La Gare Saint Lazare*, which Moore also saw in 1877, prompts a similar response: "when we came to those piercingly personal visions of railway stations by the same painter,—those rapid sensations of steel and vapour,—our laughter knew no bounds. 'I say, Marshall, just look at this wheel; he dipped his brush into cadmium yellow and whisked it round, that's all.'"[37]

The visit to the Impressionist exhibition concludes with a conversation about Renoir's *Nude in Sunlight* (1876, Musée d'Orsay, Paris), and again, two different experiences of seeing are effectively telescoped. Moore and his friends "saw nothing except that the eyes were out of drawing" and did not "understand . . . Renoir's rich sensualities of tone; nor did the mastery with which he achieves an absence of shadow appeal to us. You see colour and light in his pictures as you do in nature . . . There was a half length nude figure of a girl. How the round fresh breasts palpitate in the light! Such a glorious glow of whiteness was attained never before."[38] Moore evokes the spectator experience in a gallery space, as Marshall and his companion move from one picture to another, stopping in conversation when a picture catches their attention. He concludes by assuring us that he no longer shares Marshall's opinion of Impressionist painting: "for art was not for us then as it is now,—a mere emotion, right or wrong only in proportion of its intensity." He no longer believes in the rules for "the grammar of art, perspective, anatomy, and *la jambe qui porte*" that he learned while studying at Julian's.[39]

This disavowal of his earlier training and his initial reaction to Impressionist painting does not explain how Moore provided a highly visual, sophisticated description of pictures that he had seen ten years previously. Why did he include the three pictures by Monet and Renoir? How did he come to appreciate the "high grass . . . flooded with sunlight" in Monet's *Turkeys* and Renoir's rich sensualities in *Nude in Sunlight*? Was the vivid image of Monet taking a brush "dipped . . . into cadmium yellow and whisked . . . round" written from his memory of seeing these works a decade earlier on? Did Moore, for that matter, even see the 1876 Impressionist exhibition? I suspect Moore was not writing from his memory of those 1870s events. Whenever he visited Paris, he would have seen *Turkeys* in the collection of his friend, Impressionist critic Théodore Duret. The two men probably first met in Manet's studio in 1879[40] and continued to see each other in London and Paris during the next decade, giving Moore ample opportunities to study Duret's paintings. When part of Duret's extensive collection of Impressionist works by Cézanne, Degas, Manet, Monet, Pissarro, Renoir, and Sisley was sold in 1894,[41] Moore made its importance clear in the *Speaker*: "I have said that this collection was *un point de repère* in my life. I never went to Paris without going to see it. Beside their beauty, which I never wearied of, the pictures brought back the old days. Is it strange, then, that I should feel sad at their dispersal? Another landmark gone!"[42] Moore's informed commentary on Monet's *Turkeys* grew out of one of his many conversations with Duret, an articulate and early advocate of the Impressionists, who identified Monet and Renoir as the archetypal landscape and figure painters. Duret owned several Renoir pictures including *Buste de Femme* (1875), a female nude included in his 1894 sale, now in the Barnes Collection, which lacked the Impressionist exhibition pedigree of Renoir's *Nude in Sunlight* and Monet's *Gare Saint Lazare*.[43] The latter two belonged to Impressionist painter and collector Gustave Caillebotte, a well-known figure on the Impressionist circuit who was on close terms with Duret. This suggests that Moore must have refreshed his memory of his earlier viewing of these pictures by visiting, on one of his later trips to Paris, the large Impressionist collection that Caillebotte kept in his third floor apartment at 31 Boulevard Haussmann.[44]

These pictures by Monet and Renoir serve to illustrate the avant-garde character of Impressionist painting that challenged popular opinion and tested the foundations of traditional representation by abandoning perspective and illusionist space. The twinning of ridicule and aggression in the face of avant-garde painting as a means of affirming its originality, as Moore does in *Confessions*, became a common trope in subsequent histories of the Impressionist movement, suggesting that *Confessions* had an influential role as a harbinger of the movement within the Anglophone world. Moore writes in *Confessions*, "The history of Impressionist art is simple" before proceeding to define it as a progressive, linear history that began with the great eighteenth-century giants Boucher, Fragonard, and Watteau, who begot Courbet, Millet, and the other so-called Barbizon landscapists,[45] and then pointing out that these in turn produced "Degas, Pissarro . . . Morisot, and Guillaumin."[46] Morisot is the wild card here. Although she was a stalwart participant in the Impressionist exhibitions, she remained excluded from subsequent histories until she was reinstated into the movement by feminist art historians in the 1980s. As Ann Heilmann and María Elena Jaime de Pablos outline in chapter 6, Moore was a great believer in a supposed gender division that marked the virile strength of art by male artists and the more delicate art of female artists.[47] But he would have known that Morisot was held in high regard by her Impressionist peers, and in his later piece "Sex in Art" credited her with "a style" of her own.[48] We can forgive him for writing that Morisot was "the only woman who has ever been able to infuse a trace of her sex into her art" for thinking to mention her at all.[49] He was complimentary about the "vision of nature" in her figures in landscape pictures, pointing out the "delicious . . . pale green and flesh colour" of *Jeune fille sur l'herbe* or describing *Le corsage rouge* (1886) as being as "fanciful and peaceful as a caprice by Chopin,"[50] praise which he turned into evocative Symbolist terminology in *Confessions*.[51]

The last Impressionist exhibition was a turning point for Moore. He was suspicious of the innovatory brush techniques that Monet introduced in the 1880s and, after seeing Monet's exhibition of the Grainstacks series in Paris in 1891, denounced it when it was shown in London the following year. Increasingly, Moore shared Théodore Duret's nostalgia for the initial phases of Impressionism, already evident in Duret's 1885 collection *Critique d'avant-garde*, a book that Moore wished he had written himself.[52]

Moore's history of Impressionism has been influential. John Rewald took it as a model when writing *The History of Impressionism* (1948), wherein *Confessions* is used as evidence of the 1886 exhibition.[53] Art historians accepted the simple trajectory of Rewald's book as a model for this history well into the later half of the twentieth century. The following passage, which Moore subsequently removed from *Confessions*, is usually taken as a comment on his preoccupations as a writer: "I was as covered with 'fads' as a distinguished foreigner with stars. Naturalism I wore round my neck, Romanticism was pinned over the heart, Symbolism I carried like a toy revolver, in my waistcoat pocket, to be used in an emergency."[54] This could equally describe the various art movements that made up his artistic education as he sat down to write *Confessions*.

NOTES

1. "Half-a-Dozen Enthusiasts," *Bat*, May 25, 1886, 185–186. While unsigned, the review is generally thought to have been authored by Moore; see Edwin Gilcher, ed., *A Bibliography of George Moore* (Dekalb, IL: Northern Illinois University Press, 1970), 179, who notes that "the section on Degas is strikingly similar to passages in the article 'Degas' in *Impressions and Opinions*." See also Kate Flint, ed., *Impressionists in England: The Critical Reception* (London: Routledge, 1984), 68. I provide conclusive proof of Moore's authorship in "Degas and George Moore: Some Observations about the Last Impressionist Exhibition," in *Degas 1834–1984*, ed. Richard Kendall (Manchester: Manchester Polytechnic, 1985), 32–41.

2. See Ruth Berson, ed., *Exhibited Works*, vol. 2 of *The New Painting; Impressionism 1874–1886. Documentation* (San Francisco: Fine Arts Museum of San Francisco, published with the assistance of The Getty Grant Program and The Andrew W. Mellon Foundation Endowment for Publications, 1996). Berson identifies six of these eight works (140–141).

3. Throughout this chapter the location of the paintings referenced by Moore has been given. This is the first time that many of the works Moore describes that he could only have seen in specific Impressionist exhibitions or private collections have been identified. This

evidence does much to counter the suggestion made by critics like Douglas Cooper that Moore made up his viewing of such works.

4. "Half-A-Dozen Enthusiasts," 186.

5. Ibid.

6. Ibid.

7. Felix Fénéon, "Les impressionists," *La Vogue*, June 13–20, 1886; see also Gustave Geoffroy, "Salon de 1886, VIII Hors du Salon, Les impressionists," *La Justice*, May 26, 1886, n.p.; J. K. Huysmans, *Certains,* 1889; Octave Mirbeau, "Exposition de Peintre," *La France*, May 21, 1886; all in *Reviews*, vol. 1 of Berson, *The New Painting: Impressionism 1874–1886*, 444, 457–458, 465–466.

8. Paul Smith, *Seurat and the Avant-Garde* (New Haven: Yale University Press, 1997), 14–18. Smith points out that Mirbeau and Paul Adam also made a connection between Seurat's picture and ancient Egypt.

9. Adrian Frazier, *George Moore 1852–1933* (New Haven: Yale University Press, 2000) does much to fill in the gaps of our knowledge about Moore's activities in Paris in the 1880s.

10. Edouard Dujardin, "Quand George Moore vient à Paris," *Les Nouvelles Littéraires*, November 10, 1922, 1.

11. For an account of this event and Mallarmé's invitation see Jean Ajalbert, *Mémoires en vrac: Au temps de symbolisme* (Paris: Albin Michel, 1938), 189.

12. Ajalbert, *Mémoires en vrac*, lists Moore's name amongst the frequent guests at the dinners that were later held in the offices of *La Revue indépendant* (189).

13. J. E. Blanche, "Les Quatre-Vingts ans de George Moore," *Les Nouvelles Littéraires*, February 27, 1931, 6.

14. See Paul Alexis, "Visite à la Revue Indépendante," *Le Cri du Peuple*, April 14, 1888, in *Naturalisme pas mort: Lettres inédites de Paul Alexis à Emile Zola, 1871–1900*, ed. B. H. Bakker (Toronto: University of Toronto Press, 1971), 513.

15. Paul Alexis, "Mon vernissage," *Le Cri du Peuple*, May 2, 1886, in Bakker, *Naturalisme pas mort*, 501. Alexis listed the following works in his collection: a Cézanne still life; a Signac landscape; two Seurat seascapes; two Manet watercolours; a Zandomeneghi portrait of Alexis; a Gustave Lasellaz watercolour; other works by Louis-Jules Dumoulin, Merwart, and Edouard Béliard; and a portrait in relief by Marguerite Syamour.

16. See George Moore, "Decadence" and "The Division of the Tones," *Speaker*, September 3 and 10, 1892: 285–286, 316–317. In "Decadence," Moore moves the date of the 1886 show back to "81 or 82" and suggests that it included "at least twenty pictures of yachts in full sail"; "only ten of these pictures were painted by the new man, Seurat" and "the other ten were painted by my old friend Pissarro" (286). In fact, Seurat exhibited two seascapes in 1886 while Pissarro made no seascapes using the *pointillist* technique. Moore also expressed his dissatisfaction with Neo-Impressionism in "Impressionism," *Hawk,* December 27, 1889, where he refers to Seurat and his cohorts indirectly: "A young man . . . paints a picture, which is, or seems to be, a slight variation on the current thought of the day . . . the pictures are exhibited in some 'bureau de la redaction,' and the originator of the new set is termed 'Jeune Maitre'" (670). The *Speaker* articles are a mixture of fact and error, and of learned explanation and serious observation combined with a silly humor. I suspect that Moore deliberately sought a method of presentation that matched what he construed to be the movement's puerile futility.

17. George Moore, *Confessions of a Young Man* (1888), ed. Susan Dick (Montreal and London: McGill-Queen's University Press, 1972), 68. All further references will be to this edition.

18. Ibid., 113.

19. "Half a Dozen Enthusiasts," 185.

20. Ibid.

21. Ibid.

22. Ibid.

23. Moore, *Confessions*, 69.

24. Moore tells the whole story in *Ave*, vol. 1 of *Hail and Farewell* (London: William Heinemann, 1947), 144.

25. See George Moore, "Memories of Degas," *Burlington Magazine* 32 (1918), where he remembered that, on a visit to Degas's studio, he found "Degas reading . . . my book in French translation" and that Degas was "highly pleased . . . with all I had said of him and that he had passages off by heart" (22).

26. Moore, *Confessions*, 69.

27. "Half a Dozen Enthusiasts," 185.

28. Moore, *Confessions*, 69.

29. Huysmans, *Certains*, 457.

30. See H. Jouvin, "Critique d'Art," *Bulletin de la Société J. K. Huysmans* XX (1947): 371, who suggests Huysmans did not publish any art criticism in 1886.

31. Moore, *Confessions*, 69.

32. George Moore, "Degas: The Painter of Modern Life," *Magazine of Art* X (1890): 424.

33. George Moore, "Degas in Bond Street," *Speaker*, January 2, 1892: 20.

34. In 1876, Mallarmé's tribute to Manet and the Impressionists appeared in English translation (the French original has not been traced). This important treatise, which explored the significance of the visual effects of Impressionism, must have influenced Moore's own thinking.

35. Moore, *Confessions*, 70.

36. Ibid.

37. Ibid.

38. Ibid., 71.

39. Ibid.

40. Frazier, *George Moore*, 57, cites Duret's reminiscences of Moore in Paris in 1879, which suggests this was the year they met; see Théodore Duret, *Manet and the French Impressionists*, trans. J. E. Crawford Flitch (London: Grant Richards, 1910), 85.

41. Théodore Duret, *Vente Théodore Duret* (Paris: Galerie Georges Petit, 1894) lists forty-two oils and pastels for sale. A copy of the catalog is held in the National Art Library, Victoria and Albert Museum. The sale included three Cézannes and eight Degas (*Danseuse en Rose; La Conversation; Danseuses à la barre et assises; Chevaux de courses; Danseuses; Chevaux de courses; Danseuse à sa toilette;* and *Femme au bain*). The first two are identified in P[aul-]A[ndré] Lemoisne, *Degas et son oeuvre* (Paris: Paul Brame and C. M. de Hauke, Arts et Métiers Graphiques, [1946–1949]), 1–4. Further included in the sale were: six Manets (*Le Port de Bordeaux; Torero salutant* [now known as *A Matador*, 1866–1867, Metropolitan Museum, New York], *Le Repos; Chez le père Lathuille; La femme au chapeau noir;* and *Portrait d'Albert Wolff*); six Monets (*Les Dindons* [*Turkeys*]; *La Chasse; Vétheuil vu de Lavacourt; Dans la prairie; Cabane à Sainte-Adresse;* and *Canal en Hollande*); one Morisot (*Jeune femme au bal*, Musée d'Orsay, Paris); four Pissarros (*Le printemps; La Gélée blanche; Rue de Village;* and *L'Âne du pasturage* [now known as *Donkeys at Pasturage*, 1862, private collection]); three Renoirs; and three Sisleys (*Vue de la Tamise à Hampton Court; Vue de la Seine;* and *Effet du Soir*). For the identification of pictures in the Duret sale see Merete Bodelsen, "Early Impressionist Sales 1874–1894 in Light of Some Unpublished 'Procès-verbaux,'" *Burlington Magazine* (June 1968): 344–346, and Yvon Bizardel, "Théodore Duret, An Early Friend of the Impressionists," *Apollo* XCX (August 1974): 146–155. See also John Rewald, in collaboration with Walter Feilchenfeldt and Jayne Warman, *The Paintings of Paul Cézanne: A Catalogue Raisonné*, vol. 1: *The Texts* (London: Thames and Hudson, 1996), which lists eight Cézannes in Duret's collection, including the three sold in 1894: *La Moisson*, c.1877 (301), *Pommes et Serviette*, 1879–80 (417), and *Le Quartier de Valhermeil près de Pontoise*, 1881 (489).

42. George Moore, "M. Duret's Collection," *Speaker*, March 17, 1894: 304–305.

43. François Daulte, *Figures 1860–1890*, vol. 1 of *Auguste Renoir: Catalogue raisonné* (Lausanne: Durand-Ruel, 1971), 144, lists four figure pictures in Duret's collection, including *Buste de femme* (144) and *Jeune soldat* (252), both sold in 1894. I have not identified the third picture in the sale, which was a landscape.

44. For a discussion of Caillebotte's collection, which was left as a bequest to the Luxembourg Gallery and is now housed in the Musée d'Orsay, see Anne Distel et al., *Gustave Caillebotte: The Unknown Impressionist* (London: Royal Academy of Arts in association with

Ludion Press, Ghent, c. 1996), 218–236. Caillebotte would later acquire Monet's *Turkeys* from the Duret sale in 1894, suggesting that it had a seminal importance for all three men.

45. Moore does not refer to the term Barbizon school because it was not used until David Croal Thomson's *The Barbizon School of Painters: Corot, Rousseau, Diaz, Millet, Daubigny, etc.* (London: Chapman and Hall, 1890). Thomson was an English art dealer and the manager of the London branch of the Goupil Gallery, which staged a series of exhibitions of the so-called Barbizon artists during the 1880s.

46. Moore, *Confessions*, 66–68.

47. See Moore's "Sex in Art," *Speaker*, June 18 and 25, 1892, reprinted in George Moore, *Modern Painting* (London: Walter Scott, 1897), 227–237.

48. Ibid., 235.

49. "Half-a-Dozen Enthusiasts," 185–186.

50. Ibid., 186.

51. See Moore, *Confessions*, where he wrote: "Here are two young girls; the sweet atmosphere folds them as a veil; they are all summer; their dreams are limitless, their days are fading, and their ideas follow the flight of the white butterflies through the standard roses" (70).

52. Ms letter, George Moore to Théodore Duret, July 5, 1885, Berg Collection, New York Public Library; Théodore Duret, *Critique d'avant-garde* (Paris: Charpentier, 1885). As the title of his book suggests, Duret recognized the innovatory aspect of early Impressionist painting and also its radical rupture with earlier convention. In fact, Duret was the first critic to apply "avant-garde" within an art context; traditionally it was a military term. By 1885, he was looking at early Impressionist paintings with a nostalgic eye.

53. John Rewald, *The History of Impressionism* (1948; New York: Museum of Modern Art, 1961), 401.

54. George Moore, *Confessions of a Young Man* (London: Swan, Sonnenschein, Lowrey and Co., 1888), 149. For a discussion of the deletion, see Dick's edition of the text, 2.

Chapter Three

Moore's Music

Reading the Notes, Knowing the Score

Mary S. Pierse

George Moore experimented with many art forms: drama, poetry, fiction, the memoir, painting, music. When music is mentioned in connection with Moore, it is most usually with reference to his conceptualisation of the "melodic line"[1] or his response to Wagner.[2] This chapter will adduce a much more varied and widespread preoccupation by Moore with music, the existence of that preoccupation from an early stage in his writing, and his ongoing determination to integrate music into text. The use of sound and music as enrichment for the written word was at the root of Moore's intentions, whether it is employed as backdrop, as a structural model, as reflective of mood, as a metaphor, or as suggestive of embracing an *à-la-mode* French synæsthetic trend. While his ambitious experimentation ranges from delicate restraint to wild excess, his awareness of, and responsiveness to, a broad range of music is always worthy of note. That Moore's complex engagement with music contributed to a vibrant debate concerning the constituents and boundaries of fiction reinforces his status as a literary innovator.

Exploration of musical connections, overlays, and patterns in Moore's writings has revealed fascinating links within the artistic world that traverse countries and decades. This is amply illustrated by the numerous associations noted by Stoddard Martin (a leading voice in Wagner-Moore studies) in his investigation in chapter 11 of the twentieth-century relationship between Moore and Howard de Walden: Maeterlinck, Wagner, Dylan Thomas, and settings such as Bavaria and Italy all join to add color, detail, and literary insights. With an expanded time frame, my chapter seeks to draw attention to a much earlier determination by Moore to engage with music, to use its forms, allusions, sounds, moods and memories as part of a highly ambitious

literary program that marks him out as a cultural pioneer, an author of excep-
tional skill and imagination. A wider scrutiny of novels and short fiction in
the period between 1850 and 1930 (in all languages) might furnish similarly
intriguing insights into the attitudes, practices, and synæsthetic achievements
of other authors.

Moore did not formulate a synthesis of his musical hopes and theories,
nor did he even present a mock debate on the subject as he did on the topic of
classical Greek literature in a preamble to *The Pastoral Loves of Daphnis
and Chloe* (1924). Nonetheless, a sprinkling of considered judgments and
obiter dicta emerges from the pages of his writings, as do several musical
comparisons and references. This chapter will trace some indications of
Moore's interest and practice from *A Mummer's Wife* (1885) and *A Drama in
Muslin* (1886) to *The Untilled Field* (1903) and *The Lake* (1905). A significant starting place must be *Confessions of a Young Man* (1887–1888),[3]
where Moore considers J. M. W. Turner's painting of Carthage using the
language of music. He says the painting is "nature transposed[4] and wonder-
fully modified. Some of the passages of light and shade there—those of the
balustrade—are fugues, and there his art is allied to Bach in sonority and
beautiful combination."[5] This blending of visual art, music, and literature is
remarkable: the visual image is invested with sound and with an additional
organizational structure; the prose is enriched by its appropriation of a vocabulary that seamlessly links to sister arts; and a nineteenth-century portrait of
ancient history is superimposed on Bach's fugues, thus suggesting ever-
reciprocal artistic relationships and intimating the timeless qualities of each
element.

Confessions also contains brief comments on the prose of Walter Scott
and Bulwer Lytton, which Moore delivers by means of musical analogy: "In
Scott leather jerkins, swords, horses, mountains, and castles harmonise completely and fully with food, fighting, words, and vision of life, the chords are
simple as Handel's, but they are as perfect. Lytton's work, although as vulgar[6] as Verdi's is, in much the same fashion, sustained by a natural sense of
formal harmony."[7] Moore's early reactions to Zola's *L'Assommoir* included
being impressed by "the immense harmonic development of the idea; and the
fugal treatment of the different scenes," by Zola's use of motive (motif) and
his working up to a *crescendo*.[8] On George Eliot's *The Mill on the Floss*,
Moore wrote of "Maggie Tulliver and all the many profound modulations of
that Beethoven-like countryside: the pine wood and the cripple; this aunt's
linen presses, and that one's economies; the boy going forth to conquer the
world, the girl remaining at home to conquer herself; the mighty river holding the fate of all, playing and dallying with it for a while, and bearing it on at
last to final and magnificent extinction."[9] The structure of that last comment
contains shades not just of Beethoven, but of Bedrich Smetana's "Moldau"
("Vltava").[10] When disparaging the account of Elly's marriage in Anne Isa-

bella Thackeray's "The Story of Elizabeth" (1863),[11] he finds "the jarring dissonance of her marriage is inadmissible; it cannot be led up to by chords no matter how ingenious."[12] Moore's verdict on what his friend Margaret Veley accomplishes in her first novel (*For Percival*) is that she "possesses an ear for the music of events" and he writes approvingly that "the suggestion is so perfect that we cease to yearn for the real music, as, reading from a score, we are satisfied with the flute and bassoons that play so faultlessly in soundless dots."[13] No matter how those individual assessments may be judged, the descriptive method leaves no doubt as to Moore's determination to weave notes into word and picture. The quotations from *Confessions* predate Moore's "music novels" (*Evelyn Innes* and *Sister Teresa*) by a decade, but they display an early preoccupation with sound and with music that will emerge and resound in much of his subsequent work.

Prior to publishing his critical assessments in *Confessions*, Moore had utilized music in his fiction, both in *A Mummer's Wife* and in *A Drama in Muslin*. In *A Mummer's Wife*, Kate Ede's unexpected stage career involves her in singing in operetta with a touring company; the minor nature of the works performed is indicated by the diminutive name forms of the roles she plays (Clairette and Serpolette). Moore's rendering of Kate's deterioration is conveyed with masterful musical touch in a deathbed scene that is depicted graphically, musically, off-key and in a cacophony: "she commenced to sing her famous song 'Look at me here, look at me there' alternately with the Wesleyan hymns. Sometimes in her delirium, she even fitted the words of one on to the tune of the other."[14] With their memorable conjunction of antithetical music hall[15] and chapel, the aural and musical components of that representation considerably augment the impact of the visual description.

The deployment of music and musically related language or structure in *A Drama in Muslin* is more widespread and, possibly on that account, artistically rather less successful. The musical program is more assorted than light opera and hymns: its overture is a French polka played by four duettists, on the obligatory Victorian pianos, to signal the arrival of a bishop for the opening of the school play.[16] That scene is plausible but simple in comparison with the blend of color and music employed by Moore to depict sea and sky at dusk in St. Leonard's:

> overhead the firmamental blue was stretched like a pall of turquoise-tinted silk. From the deeps of the sky the music of colour was chanted, and delicious but inaudible harmonies vibrated through the golden soul of the twilight. Soft and low and melancholy came the strain—it was the music of death, and the dark clouds that waited on either side, were as processional priestesses who, advancing, struck their lyres at each solemn step.[17]

Complete with its shades of Turner and echoes of Wagner, that attempt to yoke word, sound, and vision, appears to be an ill-judged romantic excess.

Nevertheless, since a surfeit of romantic notions is voiced by some members of the Barton family throughout the novel, there must be a possibility that Moore's verbal immoderation is an intentional reflection of their taste.

A less florid example is to be found in Moore's treatment of the tedium of playing postprandial music in the drawing room at Brookfield, a boring ritual that is rapidly communicated through mention of Mr. Barton's songs and the piano accompaniments that Alice is compelled to provide for dancing.[18] Alice's disinclination toward that task is a reflection of her unwillingness to conform to a prescribed and restrictive gender role, as discussed by Ann Heilmann and María Elena Jaime de Pablos in chapter 6. Pianos, those ubiquitous items of comfortable Victorian décor,[19] are also found in the genteel but impoverished home of the Brennans,[20] in Lord Dungory's castle where Cecilia plays Bach's Passions,[21] and in the house rented by Mrs. Barton in Dublin. However, none feature in the home of Alice and Edward Reed in London where they strike out on a new way of life. Mr. Barton's songs also deliver messages. In structural terms, Moore's allocation of a theme song to Mr. Barton[22] may be read as an embrace of a Wagnerian *leitmotif.* In content, the choice of song seems, initially, to be inappropriate as "Il Balen," the Conte di Luna's aria from *Il Trovatore,* provides a striking contrast between Barton's relative impotence and his ultimate fate (as a kept man), and the power and dramatic tragedy of di Luna. However, in light of Moore's association of Verdi and vulgarity, it can justifiably be said that Barton's Verdi arias underline the absurdity of the man and his illusions, and thus are perfect musical means by which to develop the character.

If a positive case can be made for an artistic, literary deployment of musical references in some parts of *A Drama in Muslin,* their wholesale distribution and disparate usages in that novel ensure that, in many of the situations to which they are applied, their net effects appear forced and disproportionate. Most flamboyantly, and with dubious taste, Moore resorts to musical terminology to support his portrayal of vision and odor in the crowded reception hall: "the sugary sweetness of the blondes, the salt flavours of the brunettes, and this allegro movement of odours was interrupted suddenly by the garlicky andante, deep as the pedal notes of an organ, that the perspiring arms of a fat chaperon slowly exhaled."[23] Faced with such prose, any commentator must be lost for words. Yet the representation is unforgettable and the author's determination to enrich the text with sound is unmistakable, even if it be to the point of overkill. Olive Barton's piano playing of "Dream Faces" inflicts considerable pain on Lord Kilcarney, the man she wishes to marry: "bang, bang, bang, the left hand pounded the bass into his stunned ears. . . . He gasped for words."[24] That same tune, "Dream Faces," reappears a year later with "doleful strains" when the second season of husband-hunting proves unsuccessful and Olive's only prospective partners in sight are "a dissipated young English lord and a gouty old Irish distiller."[25] The music underscores the message that Mrs. Barton's endeavor to procure an advantageous match for her daughter is either unattainable or repugnant.

There are over one hundred instances where music, in one way or another, is present in *A Drama in Muslin*. Amongst them are the debates on the qualities of a tenor,[26] Moore's diagnosis of amateur critics—"gossip and waltz tunes are all that they know"[27]—and repeated mentions of Liddell's orchestra at Dublin Castle.[28] In the middle of such plenitude, the absence of music takes on a greater import. Significantly, there is a prolonged silence after the unsuccessful ball is organized in a disused school by the Galway spinsters. The tone of the occasion is conveyed by Moore's description of "the melancholy harper and the lachrymose fiddlers" who supply the dance music: "the fiddler squeaks and scrapes, the harper twangs intermittently."[29] Scarcely a note is sounded for two chapters wherein the external political situation intrudes and scenes rapidly move from "threats, murders, and rumours of many murders" to Alice's black depression, Olive's doomed love-affair with Captain Hibbert, and the reduced rent payments of tenants.[30] Fittingly, the only musical intervention is a fleeting mention of Mr. Barton singing "A che la morte."[31] After that interlude, darkened by events in the real world, the focus returns to the search for a husband for Olive. Here, another glimpse of Mrs. Barton is provided: her laugh, we are told, is "artificial, irresistible, gleeful, birdlike as an opera by Offenbach."[32] As an aid to character assessment, the operatic simile is richer than it might initially appear; as a judgment on Offenbach, it would seem to confer quite a degree of favor, and reflects Moore's recognition of that composer's popular appeal in France.[33] It is clear that he situates both Barton and Offenbach in the world of operetta rather than of serious opera. The underlying verdict is that found in *Confessions*: "the mass can only appreciate simple and *naïve* emotions, puerile prettiness, above all conventionalities."[34]

In *A Drama in Muslin*, Moore's intention to integrate music, literature, and visual art meets with varying degrees of success. His education in this regard is conducted very publicly.[35] In places, the roots of his strategies are too clearly visible, and his efforts to emulate J. K. Huysmans and René Ghil in linking color, sound, and texture are astoundingly exaggerated. The nadir—or the apex—is reached in the litany encompassing such gems as "tender green velvet, pastoral as hautboys heard beneath trees in a fair Arcadian vale," "the tinkling of a guitar twanged by a Watteau shepherd," and "scarves and trains of midnight-blue profound as the harmonic snoring of a bassoon."[36] Even if the overindulgence is intended and the aim is to convey the false associations and empty promises of the expensive fabrics, that would not be the first interpretation by today's readers.[37] And yet, the incorporated sounds—and then their absence—can still enhance and deepen the reading experience, if only because they stimulate reaction.

Moore's treatment of music in the 1890s and later differs considerably from the jumbled notes sounded in the 1880s. In the tale of *Esther Waters* (1894), the emphasis is more on musical form, with an apposite *da capo* return at the end of the novel to the depiction of Esther's initial arrival at Woodview. Beginning with "she stood on the platform watching the receding train," the opening paragraph of that first chapter is repeated at the start of chapter XLVI as her life appears to come full circle.[38] This is not an isolated incident of the technique as, in *Celibates* (1895), Mildred Lawson appears on a warm, flower-scented night, and the exact phraseology of the initial chapter is repeated in the final one: "As she tossed to and fro, the recollections of the day turned in her brain, ticking loudly; and she could see each event as distinctly as the figures on the dial of a great clock."[39] This is but one illustration of Moore's symphonically related organization of prose. As Jean C. Noël has pointed out, the repetition in *Esther Waters* is complex: "*Elle se prolonge en résonances. Decrescendo, les chapitres XLVII, XLVIII et XLIX brodent dessus plusieurs variations*" [It is continued through echoes, with chapters XLVII, XLVIII and XLIX elaborating several ever-waning variations].[40] A slightly different usage of music in *Esther Waters* indicates that Esther and Fred (one of her suitors) are aware of the music of life whereas William, father of Esther's child and later to be her husband, is deaf to it, seeing only opportunities to make money. This presents a complication for Esther in deciding which man would make the better husband. By refusing to present a crystal-clear musical affirmation of character, Moore again seizes the opportunity to reflect the diversity of real life rather than the cardboard cut-outs of the novelette or operetta.

The Untilled Field offers yet another variation on Moore's synæsthetic approaches. From that collection of short stories, he had four favorites: "Homesickness," "The Exile," "A Letter to Rome," and, the one he liked best, "So on He Fares."[41] In the "Épître Dédicatoire" to *The Lake* in 1905, Moore opined that while an orchestra would be needed to replicate the flow of the River Seine through the countryside, "*une seule flute*" [a solitary flute] would suffice to reflect "*la tristesse de mon pauvre pays là bas*" [the sadness of my poor country over there].[42] This would seem to be borne out in his preferred stories. Certainly, "The Exile" and "A Letter to Rome" are entirely bare of sound and music, as though he deemed it appropriate that bleak times and pathos should be represented in a two-dimensional account shorn of accompaniment. "So on He Fares" only provides one "chirrup" of a bird[43] and little Ulick's scream when his mother makes a bee sting him. In "Homesickness," the musician is a lone piper. Any other music is not orchestral, operatic, or instrumental but is provided by the sounds of nature, and they are few. However, they illuminate the contrasting choices faced by the protagonist Bryden: rural Ireland or New York. On one side of the Atlantic, there is "the cackling of geese and a dog howled," and just a single reference to the sharp cries of the snipe. There are also tones of the pleasant lakeside, "a delicious breeze rustled in the trees, and the reeds were talking together, and the ducks were talking in the reeds."[44] On the other side of the Atlantic, the counterpoint is in "the din of voices and strange accents" and "the clang of money."[45] Unable to settle, suffering homesickness and exile in both places, Bryden exemplifies the woes of his native land.

In the other stories of *The Untilled Field*, Moore maintains the minimalist approach to musical involvement. There is total silence in town and country in "Julia Cahill's Curse," "A Playhouse in the Waste," "Almsgiving," and "The Clerk's Quest." Fleeting mention is made of a melodeon in "Some Parishioners" and in "Patchwork," and a similarly brief reference to "the piper" appears in "The Wedding Feast."[46] In "The Wedding Gown," an old woman hears church bells ringing in her mind; the bells are not identifiable by anyone else in the tale as they ring out in joy for her and then toll at her gentle and peaceful passing from this life. Positioning such joyous music in the imagination and in an afterlife emphasizes the lack of melody or harmony in the present moment; the inclusion of the bells constitutes a poignant, delicate, and restrained touch by Moore. A somewhat similar message emerges from "The Window," a story in which the figures in a stained glass window in a church come alive for Biddy M'Hale. She sees them with harps and hears them plucking the strings. The words "notes," "music," "harp," "strings," and "singing" sound over again in the tale as Biddy tells of a little tune of six notes played by the saint in the window, the ethereal nature of which is made apparent from Moore's conversion of sound into color: "it grew white like snow and remote as star fire and yet Biddy heard it more clearly than she had heard anything before."[47] In this story, heavenly music is heard by the poor and the uneducated while mercenary clerics are deaf to harps and blind to visions. With the few notes and the light from the stained glass, Moore creates another world and allows the comfort of miracles.[48]

In "The Wild Goose," the penultimate story of *The Untilled Field*,[49] music takes yet another turn. Ned's sophistication is conveyed not only by his familiarity with fugues, preludes, Beethoven, Mozart, Bach, and orchestras, and by his ability on the violin, but also by his writing down a musical score that takes up the majority of one page, with the crotchets, quavers, and minims ostensibly constituting the notation of a tune played on the flute by a shepherd in the mist, which he then interprets as "the song of the exile, the cry of one driven out into a night of wind and rain, a prophetic echo."[50] For Ned, this is music that represents the primitive. He calls it "raw and unintellectual,"[51] and it is what he wishes to leave behind him in Ireland. In this story, his choice is neither affirmed nor repudiated by music; the conjunction of music and man is suggestive rather than prescriptive.

The Lake, originally intended for inclusion in *The Untilled Field*, departs considerably from the pared-down, almost music-free state of that volume.

After reading *The Untilled Field*, meeting the lyrical prose of *The Lake* is rather like emerging from grayness into the sunshine. While the 1905 "Épître Dédicatoire" had mentioned "*une seule flute*," the new "Preface" for the 1921 edition puts an even greater emphasis on the aural and the auditory but this time with repetition of the word "hear" and with the suggestion that when it comes to "the mysterious warble that abides in the heart," "it may be that all ears are not tuned, or are too indifferent or indolent to listen."[52] Nature and birdsong are significant accompaniments to this story and Father Gogarty's internal reverie yields up his belief in the linkage between the beauty of nature and music: "a Mass by Mozart must sooner or later inspire belief in the friendliness of pure air and the beauty of flowers . . . there is nothing more entirely natural or charming in the life of man than his love of flowers; it preceded his love of music"; "Very often the wood was like a harp; a breeze touched the strings, and every now and then the murmur seemed about to break into a little tune."[53] The gentle rambling progress of the novel is accomplished through a succession of styles, in letters, musings, folk tales, and a back-and-forth of conscious and unconscious voices that exemplifies the approach that, as Moore later explained, resulted from his concert-going and "returning home thinking how a story might be woven from start to finish out of one set of ideas, each chapter rising out of the preceding one in suspended cadence always, never a full close."[54] The music of *The Lake* unfolds in its *legato* passages more than in its references to sounds, whether natural or instrumental. It is as Moore had analyzed in his description of Wagner: "the form is ceaselessly changing, but the melody of narration is never interrupted."[55] Also without interruption or discordance, Moore's abiding feminist sympathies emerge in the proud and resourceful character of Nora (called Rose in the first edition),[56] who is a music teacher, a profession that allows her to be independent and to carve out a life for herself despite being a single mother in a hostile environment. In structure and language, in character and reference, the musicality of *The Lake* is simultaneously superficial, profound, and pervasive. Aptly, a 1906 review of the book was entitled "Mr. Moore's Symphony in Gray and Black."[57]

When he was approached by Heinemann about a Uniform edition of his writings, Moore's initial choice was to omit both *Evelyn Innes* (1898) and *Sister Teresa* (1901), although he later reversed that decision. They were, he wrote, "two of my most successful books," but "they do not correspond with my aestheticism."[58] Since both books are unmistakably "music novels," it is unnecessary in the context of this chapter to dwell on the many aspects of their portrayal of musical life and ambition, or on their references to composers and their works. Their Wagnerian resonances have been the subject of several studies.[59] However, the widespread acknowledgment of Moore's achievement in those novels suggests that his passion for music in literature was much more than that of an enthusiastic amateur. Joseph Hone praises

Evelyn Innes as a most convincing musical novel: "there are many passages which persuade the reader that he really understood something of the subject."[60] The verdict of music specialist Elizabeth Roche on *Evelyn Innes* is that it is "one of the most authentic-seeming of English musical novels," and that "even the knowledgeable can read it with enjoyment."[61] Roche considers the passages dealing with Mr. Innes's musical opinions to be of great interest for "their erudition"[62] and for the accuracy with which they reflect general attitudes toward early music at the time.[63] Some sixty years earlier André Cœuroy had praised Moore's "fine Bayreuth romances."[64] W. Wright Roberts, while critical of the "softness" and "incessant slipping flow" of Moore's English, extolled his representation of the music world in *Evelyn Innes* as "an astonishing *tour de force*": "the expertness of understanding matches the quiet precision of the technical language"; "Moore brings treasures for the antiquarian and the connoisseur."[65] Moore's later disaffection from his two novels did not arise in reaction to criticism by music experts[66] but rather from his ever-modulating aesthetic tastes, the expression of which swung radically in the course of the few short years between *Sister Teresa* and *The Untilled Field*, as it had done in the period from *A Drama in Muslin* to *Esther Waters*.

For Moore, the changes in his literary style were merely part of an inevitable evolution in the development of any thinking artist, and perhaps reflective of the fashionable phases through which literature passes:

> One generation of *littérateurs* associates itself with painting, the next with music. The aim and triumph of the Realist were to force the pen to compete with the painter's brush and the engraver's needles in the description, let us say, of a mean street, just as the desire of a symbolistic writer was to describe the vague but intense sensations of music so accurately that the reader would guess the piece he had selected for description, though it were not named in the text.[67]

And yet, it seems abundantly clear that Moore himself did not order his transmedial word pictures sequentially, nor necessarily confine himself to using just one sister art in any work. However, his inclusion of music as a novelistic norm is an acknowledgment of its importance for him, as it was for others in the later nineteenth century. The intention to communicate atmosphere through musical reference and description may be discerned on occasion, with the descriptive purpose perhaps being, as Michael Riffaterre claims, "not to offer a representation, but to dictate an interpretation."[68] A contemporaneous example of this occurs in Kate Chopin's *The Awakening* (1899), where Frédéric Chopin's *Fantaisie Impromptu* becomes an erotic trigger and the blending of Wagner and Chopin at twilight corresponds sinuously with Edna's desire.[69] With more connection to topical debates, George Eliot's *Daniel Deronda* (1876) put a spotlight on music and the musician as artist, as did George Meredith's *Sandra Belloni* (1864); Samuel Butler caught the interwoven associations of music, gender, and social maneuvering in *The Way of All Flesh* (1882); and, at a slightly earlier period, and with more emphasis on psychology, Wilkie Collins interwove many musical clues and allusions into *The Woman in White* (1859–1860).[70] The topicality of musical issues was indisputable, but the ability to render musical text (for instance, in the manner of Moore's melodic line), or meaningfully to structure a prose work on symphonic lines, was more rare.[71]

Is it possible to ascertain the point at which music entered Moore's life? Some of his first practical encounters with music antedated much of the writing in which his visual art components and references are most usually identified. As early as 1883, he had, with his brother Augustus, written the libretto for *Les Cloches de Corneville*.[72] In the same year, he combined with Paul Alexis to produce the French version of W. S. Gilbert's *Sweethearts*.[73] Even before that, he had surely absorbed the music and music/art debates that permeated the Parisian artistic scene—and some echoes of those arguments, discussions, and plans surface in 1883 in *A Modern Lover*. His acquaintance with Stéphane Mallarmé dated from the 1870s and evidence points to the fact that Moore met Débussy at Mallarmé's Tuesday salons.[74] Moore also knew Ludovic Halévy, co-writer[75] of the libretto for Bizet's *Carmen*, and Paul Dukas, composer of *The Sorcerer's Apprentice*.[76]

Most importantly of all, the topic of music in literature and painting was very much alive in Paris at that time. As Elizabeth McCombie points out, "Wagner's influence challenged writers to reclaim language as the supremely expressive medium to rival the power of music."[77] Mallarmé's qualified dissent from the Wagnerian position could only increase discussion. The embrace of musical titles by poets and painters, and the literary references apparent in the names of musical compositions, bear testimony to the energy of the period's discourse. The intertwining or reciprocity of the arts was in the air and Moore absorbed it all. How the indications of his musical education remained almost invisible to critics for a long period is somewhat puzzling. In all probability, the popularity of paintings, the fame or infamy of painters, and the focus on the visual aspects of the artist novel may have distracted from, or obscured, the musical features in Moore's prose up to the point when they swept the stage in *Evelyn Innes*. Looking back, it is apparent that many of Moore's musical notes were not heard—and they were definitely not recognized by his brother Maurice, who asserted that George was unmusical, could not hum a tune correctly, and that what he wrote about music was what he heard others say. Maurice allowed that "Perhaps he had some taste, but he had no ear."[78] Joseph Hone's summation of Moore and music is that "his interest in the art was genuine as well as discerning."[79]

In 1901, considerable musical discernment and artistic courage were required to commission Edward Elgar to write the incidental music for Moore and Yeats's play *Diarmuid and Grania*. Great daring was involved in featuring English composition at the time, either in Britain or in Ireland, and Elgar's music is startling in its modern form. W. H. Reed, later to be leader of the London Symphony Orchestra, first heard the funeral march from that work in 1902 and reacted enthusiastically: "I was so thrilled by the music, and by what was to my ear the newness of the orchestral sound."[80] The reaction of a professional musician was not that of the general audiences at the time. Even today, Elgar's score has a freshness and originality that is far from the raw and unintellectual music despised by Ned in "The Wild Goose," and even further removed from the hackneyed waltzes that were played and replayed in *A Drama in Muslin*. Moore's pursuit of Elgar underlines his sophisticated appreciation of new trends in music, his determination to include music in prose and drama, and his commitment to augmenting cultural experience in every way possible. The choice of this composer could not be attributed to following a musical herd; it was definitely not part of the Wagnerite program.

If most of the critical focus on Moore and music has concentrated on the significant presence of Wagner, it should now be recognized that the Wagnerian influence was productive because Moore was alert and receptive when other notes sounded. While Wagner would continue to provide signature tunes and important reference points, Moore drew on music hall songs, Debussy, and everything from Palestrina, Bach, and Beethoven to Elgar and Delius via Verdi and Strauss. For him, and in his writings, music is always more a treasury of notes awaiting new arrangements and performances, and less a limited and restricted Wagnerian repertoire. From his earliest writings, there is music in the backdrop, the simile, the metaphor, the symbolism, the form, and the allusion. With such a plenitude of music and notes in much of Moore's writings, it remains for us to read the score.

Figure 3.1. This Siegfried fragment was the communication code between Moore and Maud Cunard. *George Moore, Vale, in Hail And Farewell!* (London: Heinemann, 1925), vol. 2, chapter XII, 381.

NOTES

1. Graham Owens, "The Melodic Line in Narrative," in *George Moore's Mind and Art*, ed. Graham Owens (Edinburgh: Oliver and Boyd, 1968), 99–121.

2. See William F. Blissett, "George Moore and Literary Wagnerism," in Owens, *George Moore's Mind and Art*, 53–76; Richard Allen Cave, "Wagner and the Novel," *A Study of the Novels of George Moore* (Gerrards Cross: Colin Smythe, 1978), 133–469; and Stoddard Martin, "Moore," *Wagner to "The Wasteland": A Study of the Relationship of Wagner to English*

Literature (London: Macmillan, 1982), 99–120. For further details see note 59 and Stoddard Martin's chapter in this volume.

3.   *Confessions of a Young Man* was first published in installments in *Time* in 1887 and by the publisher Swan, Sonnenschein, Lowrey and Co in 1888. This chapter uses the annotated critical edition produced by Susan Dick (Montreal: McGill-Queen's University Press, 1972).

4.   Earlier in the text, in praising the poem "Contralto" by Théophile Gautier, Moore remarks particularly on the word "transpose": "a word never before used except in musical application, and now for the first time applied to material form, and with a beauty-giving touch that Phidia might be proud of" (*Confessions*, 80).

5.   Ibid., 158–159.

6.   This anti-Verdi stance was common in France, and it may be from there that Moore absorbed the prejudice. As Katharine Ellis has documented in *Music Criticism in Nineteenth-Century France* (Cambridge: Cambridge University Press, 1995), the ongoing and partly successful campaign against Verdi by *La Revue et Gazette musicale de Paris* was an element in their ambitions for canon construction but also a commercially based effort to damage a rival music publisher. However, Moore's mixed feelings concerning the Italian composer persisted and, over twenty-five years later, he wrote to Maud Cunard about *Falstaff*: "We have only to think of *Pelléas* to apprehend the Italian vulgarity of Verdi; very like Dickens; yet there are good things in it," November 7, 1919, in Rupert Hart-Davies, ed., *George Moore: Letters to Lady Cunard 1895 – 1933* (London: Hart-Davis, 1957), 103.

7.   Moore, *Confessions*, 159.

8.   Ibid., 97.

9.   Ibid., 162.

10.   It is utterly in keeping with Moore's mold-breaking artistic patterns that Smetana's 1874 *Ma Vlast* (of which "Vltava" is the second symphonic poem) would vigorously and successfully challenge the prevalent contemporary notion that programmatic music was incapable of symphonic integrity.

11.   Anne Isabella Thackeray was a daughter of William Makepeace Thackeray.

12.   Moore, *Confessions*, 162.

13.   Ibid., 162–163.

14.   George Moore, *A Mummer's Wife* (New York: Brentano's, 1903), 466.

15.   In fact, the song is more accurately placed in the category of light operetta than music hall repertoire, but Kate's drunken renditions remove from it any respectability that accrues to operetta, and associate it rather with the clientele and vulgarity of the music hall, if not the gutter. Moore's interest in, and enjoyment of, music hall culture did not prevent him from recognizing the disapproval of it in some circles.

16.   George Moore, *A Drama in Muslin* (Gerrard's Cross: Colin Smythe, 1981), 8.

17.   Ibid., 16.

18.   Ibid., 28, 29, 236.

19.   See *Spring Days* (1888; New York: Brentano's, n.d.), third impression, identified by Gilcher as taken from the 2nd English edition (London: T. Werner Laurie, 1912); Edwin Gilcher, ed., *A Bibliography of George Moore* (Dekalb: Northern Illinois University Press, 1970), 29 (entry A13/2a2/b3). Frank Escott considers a grand piano to be "indispensable" for "its appearance in the studio" (*Spring Days*, 169). Later, in *Confessions*, Moore ties the piano to a deplored concept of respectability: "a suburban villa, a piano in the drawing-room, and going home to dinner." These he identifies as not promoting "intensity of feeling, fervour of mind" (*Confessions*, 138). In fact, pianos had become so ordinary by the 1890s that periodicals such as *The Young Woman* recommended that the "thousands of nice girls who are lost in the crowd of our surplus female population" should change to the violin in order to "stand out and shine" in social gatherings. Paula Gillett, *Musical Women in England, 1870–1914* (New York: St. Martin's Press, 2000), 100.

20.   Moore, *Drama in Muslin*, 56.

21.   Ibid., 59.

22.   Ibid., 22, 37, 276.

23.   Ibid., 173.

24.   Ibid., 212.

25. Ibid., 269.

26. Ibid., 155.

27. Ibid., 159.

28. Ibid., 162, 176, 178, 192.

29. Ibid., 87, 89.

30. Ibid., chapters VI and VII, 94–130.

31. Ibid., 107; from Verdi's *Il Trovatore*.

32. Ibid., 131.

33. *La Revue et Gazette musicale de Paris* promoted Offenbach and other French composers (Ellis, *Music Criticism*, 203–204).

34. Moore, *Confessions*, 112.

35. The accusation that Moore conducted his education in public was attributed by Frank Harris to Oscar Wilde, and the allegation took wings, being repeated innumerable times in various publications, usually without any source being quoted. Harris, a notoriously unreliable informant and not friendly to Moore, published his book on Wilde in 1918, some eighteen years after Wilde's death. The import of the phrase about Moore's public self-education was to disparage Moore's ability and popularity. Frank Harris, *Oscar Wilde: His Life and Confessions* (New York: Harris, 1918), vol. 2, 475.

36. Moore, *Drama in Muslin*, 162.

37. It might be supposed that while some reactions are instantaneous, a number of antipathetic and unfavorable verdicts on Moore's musical ventures in this novel arise from fashionable prejudice. What can be viewed as a similar but later overload by Proust, for instance in *Du côté de chez Swann*, has not met with the same antagonism.

38. George Moore, *Esther Waters* (London: Walter Scott, 1894), 359.

39. George Moore, "Mildred Lawson," reprinted in *Celibates (1895)*, ed. Ann Heilmann, vol. 1 of *The Collected Short Stories of George Moore*, ed. Ann Heilmann and Mark Llewellyn (London: Pickering and Chatto, 2007), 7. For a discussion of the flower symbolism in the text see Nathalie Saudo-Welby's contribution to this collection.

40. Jean C. Noël, *George Moore: L'homme et l'œuvre* (Paris: Marcel Didier, 1966), 254, my translation.

41. This was the preference he expressed when he wrote a new preface for *The Lake* in 1921. That "Preface" is reproduced in a (Gerrards Cross: Colin Smythe, 1980) edition of the text, ix–xi. The 1905 "Épître Dédicatoire" is reproduced in the same edition (vii–viii). All subsequent references to *The Lake* are to that edition, which has an afterword by Richard Allen Cave.

42. Moore, "Épître Dédicatoire" to the 1905 edition, *The Lake*, viii, vii.

43. George Moore, "So on He Fares," *The Untilled Field* (Gloucester: Alan Sutton, 1991), 138.

44. Moore, "Homesickness," *The Untilled Field*, 27–28.

45. Ibid., 32.

46. Moore, "The Wedding Feast," *The Untilled Field*, 64–65.

47. Moore, "The Window," *The Untilled Field*, 84.

48. In a letter to "Gabrielle" in December 1903, Moore states that Biddy M'Hale is intended to represent Ireland but he does not expand on that point. See *George Moore's Correspondence with the Mysterious Countess*, ed. David B. Eakin and Robert Langenfeld (Victoria, BC: University of Victoria, 1984), 29. See also Kirsti Bohata's discussion of Moore and Caradoc Evans in chapter 10.

49. As arranged by Moore in the 1914 edition.

50. Moore, "The Wild Goose," *The Untilled Field*, 190–191.

51. Ibid., 191.

52. Moore, 1921 "Preface" to *The Lake*, x.

53. Moore, *The Lake*, 54, 136–137.

54. George Moore, "The Nineness in the Oneness," *The Chesterian* 1 (September 1919): 4–10.

55. Moore, *Confessions*, 158.

56. See also Stoddard Martin's comment on the change of name in chapter 11.

57.   Not all reviews were in agreement with Carolyn Shipman Whipple in *Critic* 48 (May 1906), quoted in entry 356 of Robert Langenfeld, ed., *George Moore: An Annotated Secondary Bibliography of Writings about Him* (New York: AMS Press, 1987), 82. The *New York Times Saturday Review of Books* ("Topics of the Week," November 25, 1905) called *The Lake* "another intimate study of animalism" (Langenfeld, *George Moore*, entry 340, 80), while the reviewer in the *Bookman* (London) accused Moore of "gratuitous unpleasantness" ("Novel Notes," February 29, 1906, Langenfeld, *George Moore*, entry 348, 81).

58.   Moore, 1921 "Preface" to *The Lake*, x.

59.   See, for example, Martin's *Wagner to "The Wasteland"* and chapter 11. See also Grace Kehler's "Artistic Experiment and the Reevalutation of the Prima Donna in George Moore's *Evelyn Innes*," in *The Arts of the Prima Donna in the Long Nineteenth Century*, ed. Rachel Cowgill and Hilary Poriss (Oxford: Oxford University Press, 2012), 147–166; Christine Huguet's "The Prima Donna and the Convent: Border Crossings in *Evelyn Innes* and *Sister Teresa*," Stoddard Martin's "George Moore and Literary Wagnerism: A Revisitation," and Ann Heilmann and Mark Llewellyn's "The Quest for Female Selfhood in *Evelyn Innes* and *Sister Teresa*: From Wagnerian *Künstlerroman* to Freudian Family Romance," in *George Moore: Across Borders*, ed. Christine Huguet and Fabienne Dabrigeon-Garcier (Amsterdam: Rodopi, 2013), 15–41, 139–159.

60.   Joseph Hone, *The Life of George Moore* (London: Victor Gollancz, 1936), 131–132.

61.   Elizabeth Roche, "George Moore's 'Evelyn Innes': A Victorian 'Early Music' Novel," *Early Music* 11, no. 1 (January 1983): 71.

62.   Ibid., 72.

63.   Ibid., 73.

64.   André Cœuroy, "Musical Inspiration in English Literature of the Nineteenth Century," trans. Theodore Baker, *The Musical Quarterly* 10, no. 3 (July 1924): 317.

65.   W. Wright Roberts, "Musical Parlance in English Literature III," *Music & Letters* 6, no. 1 (January 1925): 3–4.

66.   For instance, the critic writing in the *New York Times* on June 18, 1898 ("George Moore's Evelyn Innes: A Curious and Perhaps Deplorable Example of the Modern Psychological Novel"), talked of *Evelyn Innes*'s "audacity and elegant depravity" and described Moore as "interminably wordy and prosy, insufferably pedantic, and grotesquely eccentric and illogical in some of the 'appreciations' of art with which his new psychological novel is laboriously padded."

67.   George Moore, *Vale*, in *Hail and Farewell: Ave, Salve, Vale*, ed. Richard Allen Cave (Gerrards Cross, Washington DC: Colin Smythe; Catholic University of America Press, 1985), 531.

68.   Michael Riffaterre, "Descriptive Imagery," *Yale French Studies* 61 (1981): 125.

69.   Kate Chopin, *The Awakening and Selected Stories*, ed. Sandra M. Gilbert (New York: Penguin, 1986), 116.

70.   Nicky Losseff's article "Absent Melody and *The Woman in White*" provides a fascinating reading. Losseff says that "Collins evokes powerfully a type of musical language and texture which functions not only as apparitional sound but also as a symbol through which we gain access to Laura's precarious state of mind," *Music and Letters* 81, no. 4 (November 2000): 534.

71.   In *The Presence of the Present: Topics of the Day in the Victorian Novel* (Columbus: Ohio State University Press, 1991), Richard Altick refers to George Eliot and Wilkie Collins as authors particularly interested in, and knowledgeable about, music.

72.   See Entry A4 in Gilcher, *Bibliography of George Moore*, 6.

73.   Gilbert's play had been produced in London in 1875. Arthur Sullivan subsequently wrote the theme song, and, presumably, that song was part of the Moore/Alexis version *Le Sycamore* (Gilcher, *Bibliography*, 236; Noël, *George Moore*, 80, 129, 221–222) later produced at the Théâtre de l'Odéon, Paris. Noël renders the title as *Le Sycomore*.

74.   Edward Lockspeiser draws attention to the similarity between the discussions amongst the young artists in *A Modern Lover* and those in a similar grouping in *Frères en Art*, a work by Debussy in which Lockspeiser identifies the character Redburne as representing George

Moore, and moreover deems him "*le héros de la pièce*" [the hero of the piece]; "Frères en art, pièce de théâtre inédite de Debussy," *Revue de musicologie* 56e, no. 2e. (1970): 173.

75. Henri Meilhac was the other writer. The premiere of *Carmen* took place in Paris in March 1875. "George Bizet," *Encyclopedia Britannica*, vol. 3 (1951), 675.

76. George Moore to Maud Cunard, March 30, 1908, in Rupert Hart-Davis, *George Moore: Letters to Lady Cunard*, 56.

77. Elizabeth McCombie, *Mallarmé and Debussy: Unheard Music, Unseen Text* (Oxford: Clarendon Press, 2003), 2.

78. Quoted in Hone, *The Life*, 131.

79. Ibid., 132.

80. W. H. Reed, *Elgar as I Knew Him* (London: Victor Gollancz, 1973), 21.

Chapter Four

"Literature at Nurse"

George Moore, Ouida, and Fin-de-siècle
Literary Censorship

Jane Jordan

In his 1885 pamphlet *Literature at Nurse; or, Circulating Morals*, George Moore asked why the works of the popular novelist Ouida had for years been included in Mudie's Select Library while his own first two novels, *A Modern Lover* (1883) and *A Mummer's Wife* (1885), were rejected for circulation on moral grounds.[1] Ouida was one of several contemporary novelists Moore referred to in his pamphlet, but his interest in her was by no means casual. Ouida, like Moore, published a number of articles attacking the moral censorship of British literature. A careful reading of their polemical assaults on Mudie's circulating library not only suggests that the two writers read each other's work, but also reveals the manner in which they responded to each other in public, through the periodical press. Moore's essay "A New Censorship of Literature," published in the *Pall Mall Gazette* on December 10, 1884, attributes "the mock-moral quagmire into which our literature is sinking"[2] to the interference of the circulating libraries, but he also responds to an earlier essay by Ouida, "Romance and Realism," printed in *The Times* on October 12, 1882, in which she had first expressed her own disgust with the state of the contemporary British novel. Both writers then issued more lengthy anti-censorship articles in 1885, Moore's pamphlet *Literature at Nurse; or, Circulating Morals*, and Ouida's essay "The Tendencies of English Fiction" (*North American Review*, September 1885), in which they kept up their campaign against Charles Mudie's self-appointed role as "custodian of the national virtue" and his policy of circulating only those new novels unlikely to give offence to unmarried women readers.[3] That same year,

Moore's second novel, *A Mummer's Wife*, was issued as a low-cost (6s.) single volume for private purchase and rapidly went through several editions. Moore was at last recognized as "the coming novelist with a new manner of writing."[4] Meanwhile, Ouida continued to berate the two main commercial libraries, Mudie's and Smith's, in her 1895 *North American Review* essay "Literature and the English Book Trade." Echoing Moore, she argued that librarians "are not Popes or police officers, nor is the public a child or a ward in Chancery."[5]

The contributions made by Moore and Ouida to a public debate about the decline of the English novel provide a significant context for understanding the growing concern at the time about the debilitating effects of literary censorship. Their essays anticipate by some years the debate conducted in the *New Review* under the title "Candour in English Fiction" (1890), now remembered solely for Thomas Hardy's own contribution.[6] Moore and Ouida almost certainly never met and appear not to have corresponded. As novelists they were opposites: Moore saw himself as an ambassador of French realism, or naturalism, a disciple of Zola; Ouida was, as fellow novelist Marie Corelli called her, "a *romancer*," and precisely the kind of popular novelist derided by Zola and Moore—as one of those women writing for the circulating libraries "who produce their two or three books a year."[7] It was Moore's and Ouida's frustration with the literary censorship conducted by libraries like Mudie's and W. H. Smith's that made them improbable allies.

That Moore also read Ouida's fiction is indicated by the similarities in plotline between his second novel, *A Mummer's Wife* (1885), the story of an unhappily married young woman who falls in love with an operetta singer, and Ouida's *Moths* (1880).[8] In Ouida's novel, sixteen-year-old Vere Herbert is married against her will to libidinous Russian Prince Zouroff ("He had all the vices, and had them all in excess"[9]), but is loved from afar by the celebrated tenor Corrèze, who sends Vere roses, comes no closer than kissing her hand, rescues her from drowning (twice!), and finally, in defense of Vere's unblemished moral character, challenges her husband to a duel. Vere (meaning "truth"), is scrupulously moral and unworldly (her own mother despairs that she is "puritan").[10] Indeed, Vere is so unworldly that one wonders whether Ouida intended her heroine, in part, as a satirical representation of the girl reader she and Moore so scorned as the English novel's reading public. Ouida's treatment of her young heroine is nothing short of sadistic: Vere not only endures marital rape and beatings while her husband maintains three mistresses, but she also discovers that her mother was his lover when Vere was a child.

A Mummer's Wife provides a critique of the romantic excesses of Ouida's *Moths*. In his biography of Moore, Adrian Frazier makes the point that it is Kate Ede's reading of romantic fiction that brings about her downfall (her adulterous affair with a mummer, her prosaic second marriage, and her subsequent descent into alcoholism): Kate's problems begin with "the sort of novels M. E. Braddon wrote and Mudie circulated."[11] Moore seems to have specifically targeted *Moths* in his handling of Kate's relationship with Dick Lennox, the singer-manager of a traveling opera company. On the eve of her elopement with Lennox, the draper's wife accounts for the relative ease with which she has been seduced by Lennox, telling him that he was "so much more like what I imagined a man should be, so much more like the heroes in the novels. You know in the books there's always a tenor who comes and sings under the window in the moonlight, and sends the lady he loves roses."[12] Once they've run away together, Kate reflects, "she had done what she had so often read of in novels, but somehow it did not seem at all the same thing. . . . She had to admit that nothing had turned out as she had expected; even her own power of loving appeared feeble in comparison to the wealth of affection she had imagined herself lavishing upon Dick. . . . The past was still reality, and the present a fable. It didn't seem true."[13] Frazier argues that in his exposure of Kate's impoverished romantic fantasies through the medium of realistic fiction, whilst "borrowing from Flaubert, Moore showed his originality as a controversialist it turned his novel not only into a provocation of Mudie's, courting censorship, but also an indictment of Mudie himself as the real author of immorality."[14]

Moore was absolutely right to complain that Ouida's novels were more sexually suggestive than his own. As one critic ruefully reflected, plain adultery was not sufficiently sensational material for Ouida, but "she must needs hint at something worse."[15] Even the French regretted Ouida's "lack of good taste" in her insistence upon writing about incestuous relationships, saying that "she plunges into the most brutal situations with astonishing careless-ness."[16] The fact that Ouida wrote romances rather than realist fiction of the kind espoused by Moore explains in part why her novels were deemed fit for circulation. In its 1880 review of Henry Vizetelly's series of English translations of "Popular French Novels," *Lloyd's Weekly Newspaper* pointed out the lengths to which British publishers had to go in "carefully selecting [French] books" in order "to avoid disfiguring works by shrinking and expurgating to suit the British public, which, by the way, can read Ouida . . . with equanim-ity."[17] Ouida's romances, with their often exotic (distinctly un-English) settings and exaggerated heroes and heroines, gave her a certain license to introduce morally dangerous situations, while Moore's focus on "real" people in realistic settings confronted such situations head-on. In *Moths*, the sensational aspects of the novel are framed by a conventional romance in which the virtuous heroine is won by her chivalrous lover (Zouroff survives the duel and divorces Vere, leaving her free to marry Corrèze). The couple retreat to the French Alps, where "the air is pure and clear as crystal," and live "in heaven's light!"[18] It was the novel's exotic backdrop (Zouroff's palaces in France, Russia, and Poland) and its characters (drawn exclusively

from members of the British and European aristocracy), as well as its romantic denouement, that Moore set out to rewrite in *A Mummer's Wife*. His
response to Ouida's *Moths* was to render the extramarital love between Vere
and Corrèze within the context of French realism and, through Kate's alcoholism, to produce instead an English version of Zola's *L'Assommoir*.

Yet Ouida, like Moore, courted controversy through her fiction; when
reviewers claimed to find offense in her writings she felt vindicated, as can
be seen by her reaction to the press reception of *Moths*: "The English press is
never so absurd as when it has, as Macaulay said, one of its periodical fits of
morality."[19] In her exposure of the sexual mores of the ranks of the upper
classes, Ouida was to claim that she had out-Zolaed Zola. When Lady Dolly
reveals to Prince Zouroff that she got her daughter to marry him by deception
(Dolly tells Vere that Zouroff has it in his power to expose Vere's affair with
another lover), even Zouroff is taken aback: "Miladi, I never did you justice . . . Zola will want a lower deep before long, I suppose; he will do well to
leave his cellars for the drawing-rooms."[20] Since the 1860s, the name of
Ouida had been associated with the "literature of marital infidelity," but it
was the publication of "the unspeakable" *Moths* that confirmed her association with Zola.[21] Published a matter of days before Zola's *Nana*, Ouida's
novel was apparently Zola's "chief rival on the fashionable bookstalls."[22]
The *North American Review*, which reviewed the two novels together, concluded that Ouida (an "adventuress of no nationality," who has "no claim to
the title of English-woman") was as French as Zola in her view of life.[23]
Anglo-Saxon literature, it went on, was a "powerful agency of reform and
purification," while the literature emanating from France (here, the reviewer
makes no distinction between romance and realism) had the power to corrupt
and was akin to a contagious disease. Ouida and Zola were together damned
as "foreign purveyors of infection."[24] It was probably this association in the
public mind of Ouida's name with that of Zola that upset Moore's equanim-
ity and threatened his own unique identity in the literary world as the "English Zola," or to use his own expression, "*un ricochet de Zola en Angleterre.*"[25]

Even though she had French paternity ("Ouida" was christened Marie
Louise Ramé, a name she would later refashion as Louise de la Ramée),
unlike Moore she never lived in France (she was brought up in England and
moved to Italy at the age of thirty-two). Moore had studied in Paris from
1873–1880, intending to train as an artist, and had met leading French artists
and writers, including Zola, whom he continued to visit and correspond with
in the early 1880s. Ouida's identification with French writers was as cultivated as Moore's. Central to this identification was their rejection of English
"unwritten literary laws" that judged literature by moral standards alone.[26]
Two particular confidences Ouida made to fellow writers make her position
clear. Flattered at the comparison of her 1875 novel *Signa* to works by

George Sand, Ouida declared that it was "the French brain in me which has always rendered me so utterly indifferent to the 'prurient Puritanism' of the English hostility to all forms of genius."[27] In 1890, she told Marie Corelli that she felt herself to be "so very little English that my words and expressions must be often alien to the English mind, whilst many an English fetish, social and moral, is in my sight an absurdity to be destroyed as so much rubbish."[28]

Given the fact that Ouida was taught French from an early age, she was able to read a wide range of contemporary French novelists in the original. Besides Zola, she refers to her reading of Alphonse Daudet, Alice Durand, Guy de Maupassant, "J. H. Rosny," Paul de Heyse, Pierre Loti, "Gyp," Anatole France, and the brothers Paul and Victor Margueritte.[29] This was a very different set of authors to that recommended by the *Morning Post* in its article on "New French Novels" in 1880. British readers curious to read French novels were advised to confine themselves to morally safe examples, most of them by women (Madame Charles Reybaud, Elle Berthet, Zenside Fleuriot, and "Raoul de Navery," the pen-name of Eugénie-Caroline Saffray): "Several of Balzac's novels are as pure in tone as any by Miss Austen . . . George Sand's pastoral stories can be placed with impunity in the hands of any schoolgirl."[30] Like Moore, who published his interviews with Zola and de Maupassant in the *Pall Mall Gazette* and *St James's Gazette* (May 1884) and worked on Zola's behalf to get *Germinal* serialized in a British paper, Ouida championed French literature, reviewing Victor Cherbuliez's *Le Secret du Précepteur* (June 1893) and J. H. Rosny's *L'Impérieuse Bonté* (May 1894) for the *Fortnightly Review*.[31] She was herself a celebrated author in France. She was published there first by George Sand's publishers, Michel Lèvy Frères, in 1874, and from 1880 onward her works were issued by Hachette.[32] *Moths*, which had "electrified" English readers, was translated as *La Princesse Zouroff* in 1882.[33] From early on in her career, the *Revue des Deux Mondes*, in which she would have read many of the novelists listed above, commissioned translations of many of her shorter works. The *Revue* often likened Ouida to George Sand, and noted that British readers found her frank discussion of sexual morality unpalatable: "Ouida has never been one of those novelists, who abound in England, whose works can be put into all hands."[34] Of Ouida's story "A Branch of Lilac," a tale of sexual betrayal, the *Revue* observed that it "seems to give us the measure of the influence which our literature has had on that of our neighbours for several years, and which a critic has compared to a blood transfusion. No-one has undergone this influence more than the novelist known as Ouida."[35]

English reviewers, too, identified the French influence in her work. Thus, *The Times*'s review of *Moths* read: "'Ouida' shows little of the scrupulous sensitiveness which makes most English male novelists hesitate to *aborder* [tackle] subjects which are delicate or something more; and she has the knack of insinuating with eloquent suggestiveness what it would be bad taste and false art to express."[36] It became a commonplace of Ouida criticism to liken her work to that of contemporary French novelists—not that she was, by any means, a French realist, but she treated sexual morality with French candor. In the opinion of the *Saturday Review*, Ouida's novels embodied "many of the characteristics of the worst kind of French literature."[37] The *Athenaeum*, too, observed that she "betrays some acquaintance with some of the more disreputable of modern French novels."[38]

As has been noted, both Moore and Ouida challenged British attitudes toward sexual morality, not just through their fiction but through polemic. In fact, Ouida's several essays on the book trade owe a great deal to Moore's campaign, and it was a significant failure on Moore's part not to recognize that he and Ouida were fighting on the same side. It could even be said that it was Ouida, rather than Moore, who initiated public debate of the issue of literary censorship. On October 12, 1882, she published an attack on English realism in *The Times*. This essay, republished in much briefer form the following year under the title "Romance and Realism," functions a little like Zola's thesis *The Experimental Novel* (1880, published at the same time as *Nana*), as both a literary manifesto and a statement of intent.[39] In defending her choice of the romance genre, Ouida argued that, owing to the censorship of literature on her side of the Channel, "the realistic novel of English or English-writing authors is [not] real." Only in France, where writers were "not afraid to grapple with vice and depravity in its worst form," could the novel truly be said to be realist.[40]

Since English realism belied its name, Ouida rejected the realist mode of fiction for romance, a literary form that gave her greater freedom with which to portray the vital human passions that she insisted were a "legitimate centre of interest."[41] She was not alone. Fellow romancer H. Rider Haggard, in a slightly later article, "About Fiction" (1887), similarly describes his disgust with English realism, which is "at the mercy of the Young Person," and hence "utterly false as a picture of life." Unable to stomach French naturalism (which he describes as "an accursed thing"), Haggard urges, "surely there is a middle path?"[42] Moore's own position was not to reject English realism, but to reform it from within, upon French principles of candor—to effect "the transplantation of a French style to the English novel."[43] Moore's first foray into the question of moral censorship, "A New Censorship of Literature," appears to question Ouida's "manifesto" in his concluding remarks: "the literary battle of our time lies not between the romantic and realistic schools of fiction but for freedom from the illiterate censorship of a librarian."[44]

That Ouida read Moore's article carefully is demonstrated by her next article, "The Tendencies of English Fiction" (1885), the first of a series of essays she was commissioned to write for the *North American Review* in the succeeding decade. This, of course, was the same journal that had so criticized *Moths* for its French candor. In "A New Censorship of Literature," Moore had blamed Mudie's circulating library for what he regarded as the emasculation of British fiction. In a stirring passage, Moore outdid Ouida's description of English realism as "spineless" in suggesting that under Mudie's censorship, "humanity becomes headless, trunkless, limbless, and is converted into the pulseless, non-vertebrate, jelly-fish sort of thing."[45] Ouida's tack was rather different (perhaps because she was an author who had never actually suffered from Mudie's policies). To her mind, the fault lay with a bourgeois readership careful to protect the innocence of its young people, whereas Mudie, a mere shop-keeper, was obliged to cater to his subscribers. As she remarked in her essay on Charles Reade, a novelist whose works were "written for men and women," "Most English novels always appear to me to be written either for school-children or police-sergeants."[46] But she was united with Moore in warning of the consequent harm done to contemporary literature. In what was either a gesture of solidarity with Moore or an example of lazy plagiarism, Ouida repeated Moore's satirical description of the second-rate fiction to be found in Mudie's boxes, fiction stripped of all likeness to reality, calling it a "vast invertebrate, jelly-like mass [in which] the reader searches in vain for any knowledge of human nature."[47]

Ouida's article was published in the September 1885 issue of the *North American Review*. Thus, she would not have had time to amend her proofs in order to respond to Moore's pamphlet *Literature at Nurse*, which came out in early August, and in which, as we have seen, Moore distanced himself from female popular novelists, mentioning Ouida, Florence Marryat, and Mrs. Campbell Praed. Indeed, the timing of the two essays was doubly unfortunate. Moore's pamphlet, like his earlier essay, rebuked Ouida, conceiving of her as a favored Mudie author—not as an ally in the late-Victorian campaign against literary censorship, but as a popular novelist shaped, even enslaved, by the demands of the market, a "bonds-woman" as he put it in "A New Censorship of Literature."[48] In fact, Ouida and Moore made very similar criticisms of contemporary British fiction. In *Literature at Nurse*, Moore imagines the censorious librarian's defense: "I cater for the masses, and the masses are young unmarried women who are supposed to know but one side of life," to which Moore replies, "And so it comes to pass that English literature is sacrificed on the altar of Hymen. . . . Let us renounce the effort to reconcile those two irreconcilable things—art and young girls."[49] In similar spirit, Ouida writes in "The Tendencies of English Fiction" (this could not have been a borrowing), "The imbecile English boast that their novels may all be read by school-girls indicates at once the intellectual and psychological level on which they are composed. They are quite 'pure'; but as human nature is not 'pure' in this sense, and never will be, of what use are they then as pictures of human nature?"[50] Given their shared opposition to literary censorship, Moore would have enjoyed Ouida's assessment of the state of the English novel:

> There is a tacit arrangement on the part of the [English] nation to regard itself as chaste and immaculate in a wholesome manner which is very curious, and has never had any parallel in any other nation. The favourite English illusion is that the English people are without senses or passions, and as no art can exist without recognition of both senses and passions, the effect on English litera-ture is fatal. Natural love, unblessed by the priest, or at least by the registry-office, must never be written up; so that the story-teller is grotesquely fettered at starting, and this obligation to obey the canon of English ethics leads to grotesque results . . . everybody must be married that the English public is to be invited to read about.[51]

The interesting question is: why were Ouida's novels issued by the two leading circulating libraries yet Moore's first novels turned down by those same libraries? Moore later regretted that he had not stayed in France and written his novels in French for a French readership unfettered by questions of sexual morality.[52] Yet perhaps this was mere posturing. Ouida's publish-ers made no quarrel with the sexual content of her fiction. Indeed, the spirit in which she frequently complained to Chatto and Windus (her publishers from 1877–1894) about the baneful moral influence of librarians and review-ers suggests that she had their sympathy.[53] And while Moore claimed that it had been necessary to issue *Literature at Nurse* through Vizetelly as a three-penny pamphlet, because "for purely commercial reasons, it would be impos-sible for any English magazine to print it," Ouida's articles on censorship were all published by major newspapers and periodicals: *The Times*, the *Fortnightly Review*, and the *North American Review*.[54]

Yet, for all the relative license she enjoyed throughout her career, Ouida continued to assert that, "Of all countries, France remains the land in which it is possible to tell the most truth . . . In France alone its pictures of the most terrible facts pass unarrested, by right of that literary liberty which the *esprit gaulois* has always awarded, however much government and law may have been alarmed."[55] She is writing here about George Darien's politically con-troversial semi-autobiographical novel *Biribi* (1897). That she does not dif-ferentiate between political and moral censorship gives some indication of the seriousness with which she regarded the issue of authorial freedom. Her article on Darien is also worth noting because of its opening reference to the second trial in 1889 of Moore's publisher, the "martyrised" Vizetelly,[56] on the charge of publishing inadequately expurgated English translations of novels by Zola.[57] Ouida regarded the case against Vizetelly as an absurdly English way of dealing with morally sensitive literature, and the *Pall Mall Gazette*, commenting on the original sentence passed on Vizetelly on October 31, 1888, claimed to be astonished "at the unexpected zeal which our contemporaries display in the cause of decency. No one ever suspected them of so delicate a sense of modesty."[58] That Ouida was affected by Vizetelly's treatment is indicated in a private communication of hers to Marie Corelli in April 1890. A matter of months after Vizetelly's release from Holloway Prison, where he had served a three-month sentence for the crime of selling French novels written in English, Ouida drew to Corelli's attention an article in a French paper that had described Ouida's novels as *"Romans français écrits en anglais."*[59]

In 1885, the year that Moore's pamphlet was published, Moore acted independently of Mudie's by publishing *A Mummer's Wife* as a one-volume edition through Vizetelly ("The 'select' circulating libraries can no longer injure me; I am now free to write as I please").[60] Ouida did not break free from the demands of the three-volume library edition for another five years, after writing *Syrlin*, her last three-decker for Chatto and Windus in 1890.[61] She might be thought to have done quite well from her library editions, but like Moore she consistently advocated that British publishers drop library editions and offer the reading public new novels that were affordable. At the close of "A New Censorship of Literature," Moore advertises the fact that *A Mummer's Wife* was now available for sale at 6s. (or "4s. 6d. at a discount bookseller's"), and concludes, "I shall now, therefore, for the future enjoy the liberty of speech granted to the journalist, the historian, and the biographer, rights unfortunately in the present day denied to the novelist."[62] His high spirits are, though, tempered by concern for the purse of the common reader: even 6s., he says, is "still too high a price, in my opinion."[63]

In a similar manner, Ouida concludes "The Tendencies of English Fiction" with an attack on the library system, "which induce[s] hasty and undigested reading": "The English public, as a rule, does not read; it skims a little, that is all . . . nobody in England ever buys a book if he can borrow it."[64] The answer, she suggests, again echoing Moore, lies in "One simple, plain and well-printed edition issued from first to last."[65] Ouida consistently urged British publishers to bring down the price of the standard one-volume edition. Like Moore, she maintained that six shillings was "too dear to be suitable for private purchase," and in her later essay, "Unwritten Literary Laws" (1899), called for all new novels to be issued at two shillings and sixpence.[66] But here she shows no understanding of publishing as a business in which a range of differently priced editions were offered to suit the taste of different readers. "If the [cheaper] price be sufficient to pay expense of production," she argued, "why not start with it?" Chatto recognized that he could appeal to either end of the book market, issuing her backlist in the 5s. uniform edition (dropped to 3s. 6d. in 1887), the 2s. yellowback (introduced in 1879), and, in the case of *Moths*, a 6d. paperback edition in 1896.[67] What Moore's troubled early career demonstrates is a shift in the balance of power between the circulating libraries' monopoly over the distribution of new novels and the growing diversification and economic confidence of younger publishers, such as Chatto and Windus.

When, back in 1883, William Tinsley had wanted to issue an expurgated version of Moore's first novel, *A Modern Lover*, he warned Moore of the power of Mudie and W. H. Smith to reject unsuitable new novels: "A novelist is turned down for very little."[68] He also advised the young writer not to think of taking on the libraries single-handedly: "some two or three successful novelists, if they combined, could do it."[69] "A New Censorship of Literature" concludes with Moore's plea that "a higher name than mine [undertake] to wave the flag of Liberalism . . . to denounce and to break with a commercial arrangement that makes of the English novel a kind of advanced schoolbook, a sort of guide to marriage and the drawing-room."[70] He evidently considered Ouida not to be the kind of ally he was looking for. Her own essays on the book trade, and her correspondence with her publishers, provide an important context for understanding the significance of Moore's battle against literary censorship and, also, the significance of his assault on the dictatorial power wielded by Mudie and Smith. The action taken by publishers as diverse as Vizetelly and Chatto and Windus in their several attempts to bypass the library system were not always coherent and were certainly driven by different motives, but taken together they contributed toward the system's demise, and, more importantly, fueled the late nineteenth-century public debate about whether sexual morality was a legitimate center of interest for the English novel. Vizetelly's one-volume edition of *A Mummer's Wife* was, at the very least, a symbolic break with the library system. It was not until the later commercial success of Moore's finest work, *Esther Walters* (1894), however, that he was able to declare, "The censorship of the librarians has come to an end . . . I had served the cause of humanity."[71]

NOTES

1. George Moore, *Literature at Nurse; or, Circulating Morals* (London: Vizetelly and Co., 1885), 17. The circulation of the library edition was essential to the livelihood of British novelists. In the early 1880s, Ouida was paid at least £1,500 by her publishers Chatto and Windus for rights to the expensive three-volume library edition of her novels. (See, for example, Ouida's negotiations over the copyright for her 1885 novel *Othmar*, during which she reminded her solicitor that "with serial rights it should not be less than £1,500," Ouida Correspondence with J. Anderson Rose, Wolff Uncat., Harry Ransom Humanities Research Centre, University of Texas at Austin, 6 October 1884.) Chatto's practice was to print 1,500 copies of this edition, which was largely bought up by Mudie's and W. H. Smith's, who supplied many of the lesser commercial libraries (Chatto and Windus ledger books [1877–1890], Reading University Library).

2. George Moore, "A New Censorship of Literature," repr. in *Literature at Nurse; or, Circulating Morals. A Polemic on Victorian Censorship*, ed. Pierre Coustillas (Hassocks: The Harvester Press, 1976), 31.

3. Moore, *Literature at Nurse*, 16.

4. So Moore recalls his publisher Vizetelly telling him in 1885, in George Moore, "A Communication to My Friends," *A Mummer's Wife* (London: William Heinemann, 1933), xliv.

5. Ouida, "Literature and the English Book Trade," *North American Review* 160 (February 1895): 162.

6. "Candour in English Fiction," *New Review* (January 1890): 6–21. Hardy's fellow contributors were Walter Besant and Eliza Lynn Linton.

7. Quoted in Adrian Frazier, *George Moore, 1852–1933* (New Haven: Yale University Press, 2000), 104. Corelli's description of Ouida comes from her essay "A Word about Ouida," *Belgravia Magazine* (April 1890): 370. In view of Moore's subsequent campaign against the moral censorship of literature, it is perhaps remarkable that his first choice of publisher for *A Modern Lover* was William Tinsley. As Moore knew well, many popular novelists published their works with the Tinsley Brothers (Mary Braddon, William Black, Charles Reade, Mrs. Henry Wood), and it had been the Tinsleys who published Ouida's first novel, *Held in Bondage*, in three volumes in 1863, for the sum of £50. (When Edward Tinsley died in 1866, his brother William carried on the business.) Moore would later realize how fortunate he was to have been so briefly associated with the "commonplace" Tinsley, a "huckster" of the three-volume novel, whose only interest in Zola was in his sales figures ("A Communication to My Friends," xxi, xi).

8. Ironically, given Moore's rewriting of Ouida's *Moths*, he was later accused of plagiarizing her worst excesses of style. The *Pall Mall Gazette* identified Ouida's influence in Moore's 1886 novel *A Drama in Muslin* on July 14, 1886, 5–6.

9. Ouida, *Moths*, ed. Natalie Schroeder (Ontario: Broadview Press, 2005), 123.

10. Ibid., 112.

11. Frazier, *George Moore*, 114.

12. George Moore, *A Mummer's Wife* (London: William Heinemann, 1918), 173.

13. Ibid., 194–195.

14. Frazier, *George Moore*, 114.

15. Harriet Waters Preston, "Ouida," *Atlantic Monthly* 58 (July 1886): 50, repr. in Ouida, *Moths*, ed. Schroeder, 560.

16. "*Il y a là un défaut de délicatesse . . . elle aborde avec une insouciance surprenante les situations les plus brutales,*" Th. Bentzon [Marie-Thérèse Blanc], "Les Romans Italiens d'un Auteur Anglais," *Revue des Deux Mondes*, July 15, 1877, 378. These remarks come from the reviewer's commentary on Ouida's earlier novel *Signa* (1875), in which a father and son unknowingly have sexual relations with the same woman. I am grateful to Elizabeth Dreyer for her translation of this article.

17. "Literature," *Lloyd's Weekly Newspaper*, August 15, 1880, 5.

18. Ouida, *Moths*, ed. Schroeder, 540–541.

19. "'Proverbial Philosophy' at Home. An Interview with Mr Martin Tupper," *Pall Mall Gazette*, July 24, 1889, 1–2. Martin K. Tupper (1810–1889) was the author of *Proverbial Philosophy*. In this interview he recalled a letter Ouida wrote to him from Italy in 1880 at the time of the publication of *Moths*.

20. Ibid., 431.

21. *Literary World*, March 3, 1880, 90.

22. A. K. Fiske, "Profligacy in Fiction: Zola's 'Nana,' Ouida's 'Moths,'" *North American Review* 285 (July 1880): 79–88, repr. in Ouida, *Moths*, ed. Schroeder, 551.

23. Fiske, in ibid., 553.

24. Ibid.

25. Quoted in Frazier, *George Moore*, 104.

26. "Unwritten Literary Laws" was the title of an essay Ouida published in the *Fortnightly Review* LXVI (November 1899): 803–814.

27. Ouida to Signor Gallenga, November 11, 1875, University of Texas at Austin, Harry Ransom Humanities Research Centre, Wolff 5343a.

28. Ouida to Marie Corelli, April 4, 1890, The Shakespeare Centre, Stratford-upon-Avon, DR 777/55.

29. Ouida refers to her knowledge of French writers in her articles "Literature and the English Book Trade," *North American Review* CLX (February 1895): 157–165, and "Unwritten Literary Laws," mentioned earlier.

30. "New French Novels," *Morning Post*, February 5, 1880, 6.

31. For details of Moore's interviews and his efforts on Zola's behalf, see Frazier, *George Moore*, 105–106 and 109. The two reviews referred to were reprinted in Ouida's second collection of essays, *Critical Studies*, published by T. Fisher Unwin in 1900. A further article on Georges Darien, also reissued by Unwin, first appeared in the *Fortnightly Review* LXII (September 1897): 341–357.

32. Michel Lèvy Frères bought the translation rights to *Two Little Wooden Shoes* (*Deux Petits Sabots*, 1874) and *In a Winter City* (*Dans une Ville d'hiver*, 1876). For further details, see Jane Jordan, "The English George Sand? Ouida, the French Novel and late Victorian Literary Censorship," *Anglistica Pisana* VI, no. 1 (2009): 107–116.

33. Ouida to Chatto & Windus, June 7, 1880, New York Public Library, Berg Collection, 1880 folder.

34. "*Ouida n'a jamais été de ces romanciers, nombreux en Angleterre, dont les œuvres peuvent être mises dans toutes les mains,*" Anon., "La Branche de Lilas," *Revue des Deux Mondes*, September 1, 1873, 64. It is noted in this editorial that "George Sand has often inspired Ouida," and in the article "Les Romans Italiens d'un Auteur Anglais" referred to earlier, Ouida's 1873 novel, *Pascarel*, described as "dense, whimsical, fantastic and poetic," is likened to "certain stories by George Sand" (383).

35. "*Ce récit . . . nous paraît donner la mesure de l'influence qu'exerce depuis quelques années notre littérature sur celle de nos voisins, et qu'un critique a comparée à la transfusion du sang. Personne n'a subi cette influence plus vivement que le romancier connu sous le nom de Ouida,*" Anon., "La Branche de Lilas," 65.

36. Anon., "Recent Novels," *The Times*, Saturday, March 27, 1880, 12.

37. Anon., "Signa," *Saturday Review*, June 26, 1875, 831.

38. Anon., "Othmar," *Athenaeum*, December 19, 1885, 803. This was a familiar criticism. In its review of her late novel *Guilderoy*, the *Athenaeum* stated that it was derivative of "second-rate French fiction" (June 1, 1889, 694).

39. Ouida, "Romance and Realism," *Frescoes* (1883; London: Chatto and Windus, 1884), 301–310.

40. Ibid., 307.

41. Ibid., 303.

42. H. Rider Haggard, "About Fiction," *Contemporary Review* (February 1887): 177.

43. Frazier, *George Moore*, 99.

44. Moore, "A New Censorship of Literature," 32.

45. Ibid., 28.

46. Ouida, "Charles Reade," *Gentleman's Magazine* (October 1882): 494. Reade had successfully adapted Zola's *L'Assommoir* as *Drink* for the English stage in 1879.

47. Ouida, "The Tendencies of English Fiction," *North American Review* CXLI (September 1885): 214.

48. Moore argues that novelists of the day are incapable of producing good art until they "break their bonds first . . . it will be time when they are free men to consider the possibilities for formulating a new aestheticism" ("A New Censorship of Literature," 29).

49. Moore, *Literature at Nurse*, 21.

50. Ouida, "The Tendencies of English Fiction," 220.

51. Ibid., 218.

52. Moore, "A Communication to My Friends," xlv.

53. See, for example, Ouida's letter to Andrew Chatto, n.d. [c. June 1880], in which she writes of Charles Mudie's "pompous silly ways of trying to pass as a Mentor to the public," or that of July 5, 1878 (in response to the reception of her scandalous novel *Friendship*): "I am so used to the slanderous pettiness of the English Press that I never think about it." New York Public Library, Berg Collection, 1880 folder and 1878 folder.

54. Moore, *Literature at Nurse*, 3. Besides "Romance and Realism," Ouida published two further articles in *The Times*: "English Novels" on the issue of dramatic copyright (June 2,

1882, 3), and "New Literary Factors" on the rise of the literary agent and the subsequent decline of literary standards (May 22, 1891, 3).

55. Ouida, "Georges Darien," *Critical Studies* (London: T. Fisher Unwin, 1900), 50.

56. Ibid.

57. At the first of these, in October 1888, Vizetelly was fined £200. At the second, in May 1889, he was sentenced to three months' imprisonment (see *Times*, May 31, 1889, 12). Moore himself was implicated in these cases, having, as Katherine Mullin points out in chapter 5, contributed prefaces to two of Vizetelly's editions. Moore petitioned the Home Secretary for Vizetelly's release, but to no avail (see *Pall Mall Gazette*, June 26, 1889, 7).

58. "Abating a Literary Nuisance," *Pall Mall Gazette*, November 1, 1888, 1. This editorial, which commented on the sentencing of Vizetelly on October 31, also made a clear distinction between Ouida's (uncensored) romances and the "unrivalled . . . graphic force and photographic detail" of works by Zola, arguing that the former "has probably done much more to corrupt the imagination and deprave the hearts of our young people than M. ZOLA." (Ibid.)

59. Ouida to Marie Corelli, April 4, 1890, The Shakespeare Centre, Stratford-upon-Avon, DR 777/55.

60. Moore, *Literature at Nurse*, 4.

61. Her last three novels were each issued as one-volume editions: *The Massarenes* (London: Sampson Low, Marston and Co., 1897), *The Waters of Edera* (London: T. Fisher Unwin, 1900) and *Helianthus* (London: Macmillan, 1908).

62. Moore, "A New Censorship of Literature," 32.

63. Ibid.

64. Ouida, "The Tendencies of English Fiction," 216, 224.

65. Ibid., 224.

66. Ouida, "Unwritten Literary Laws," 182.

67. Ibid., 183.

68. Moore's conversation with Tinsley is recounted in "A Communication to My Friends," xvii.

69. Ibid., xvi.

70. Moore, "A New Censorship of Literature," 32.

71. Moore, "A Communication to My Friends," liv. The novel was a commercial and critical success. Moore calculated that Smith's had lost as much as £1,500 in refusing to stock it.

Chapter Five

"The sort of girl I'd like to see behind the bar at the King's Head"

Barmaids and Censorship in George Moore

Katherine Mullin

A key scene in *Esther Waters* (1894) sees the servant heroine returning from an errand to fetch beer from a nearby pub, colliding with the long-lost father of her child and spilling her brimming jug. William Larch is immediately smitten. Now a man of the world, with "half a share in a public-house" and "plenty of money to treat you," he appreciates Esther's attractions not only for themselves, but as a prospective asset to his business: "when I saw you coming along with the jug in your 'and [. . .] I said, 'That's the prettiest girl I've seen this many a day; that's the sort of girl I'd like to see behind the bar of the "King's Head."' You always keeps your figure—you know you ain't a bit changed."[1] William's reaction is not simply an indication of his own particular predilections. It also speaks to *Esther Waters*'s wider cultural moment as, by 1894, barmaids were firmly established as the ubiquitous "It-girls" of the urban scene. In initially titling the novel *Travellers' Rest*, then the name of Larch's pub, and in eventually placing Esther behind its bar, George Moore participates in this fascination. This chapter will argue, however, that the voguish figure of the barmaid acquires a particular and cumulative significance during the years leading up to *Esther Waters*'s publication.

Curiously, Esther is fetching a jug of beer not for herself, but for her employer, the genteel lady novelist Miss Rice—one small indication of how Moore persistently entangles barmaids with creative practice. That association is initially borrowed from Moore's mentor Edouard Manet, whose barmaid paintings leave traces on Moore's early fiction. His first novel, *A Modern Lover* (1883), identifies artistic value not with the protagonist Lewis

83

Seymour, who specializes in meretricious pictures of mythologized beauties, but with his rival, the leader of "The Moderns," Thompson and his dazzlingly new paintings of "bar girls serving drinks to beery looking clerks."[2] Thompson's work suggests several of Manet's barmaid paintings, most notably *Corner of a Café-Concert* (c. 1878–1880), and Manet's presence is similarly felt in *Spring Days* (1888), where the glamorous Lizzie Baker captivates Frank Escott from behind the bar at the Gaiety Theatre.[3] Moore's portrait of Lizzie serving amorous customers against a backdrop of "shelves charged with glasses and bottles, gilt elephants and obelisks" blatantly evokes Manet's 1882 sensation, *Un bar au Folies-Bergère*.[4] Sure enough, Lizzie eventually becomes both model and muse. Yet, in aligning barmaids with aesthetic innovation, Moore does more than share Manet's interest in this disconcerting icon of sexual modernity. By 1894, the occupation's fraught contemporary reputation would play a strategic role in his highly public campaign against censorship. In repeatedly returning to this culturally loaded figure, Moore enacts a subtle and highly effective revenge against those moral conservatives who had, for over a decade, both the barmaid and "pernicious literature" in their sights. The terms of this struggle will be the subject of this chapter.

By the early 1880s, the barmaid had become a distinct sexual persona. In 1881, a *Times* editorial noted that "the bar, in its present form, is a modern institution of an essentially new type," introducing "new splendours," chiefly "young women who have quite obviously been chosen for their good looks." Alongside new opportunities came new perils:

> The young women are apt to become a little too forward. Too much modesty would disqualify them for their situation, as well as rob them of its attendant diversions. Of the men, no small number mean mischief, and they have a very fair chance of doing mischief. An acquaintance across the bar may end where it began, or it may be followed up elsewhere. This is the sequel of the perpetual half-flirtation to which the modern bar system lends itself, and which it seems positively intended to promote.[5]

The Times summarized an ambivalence that was sustained over the next two decades. To many, the barmaid was a quotidian sexual celebrity, her flirtatious accessibility personifying the eroticization of everyday life.[6] By the early 1890s, "barmaid fever" had reached such heights to inspire the launch of *The Barmaid: An Illustrated Journal*, a pictorial guide to "the many fascinating young ladies who are to be found ensconced behind the mahogany of the innumerable palaces of refreshment in England."[7] She was celebrated in music hall songs, from Alec Hurley's "The Barmaid, or, She Was a Nice Little Innocent Thing" (1891) to Marie Lloyd's "masher" hit "The Barmaid (Awf'lly Jolly Girl, Don't You Think So?)" (1894). She would eventually feature in her own sell-out transatlantic stage sensation, *The New Barmaid: A Musical Vaudeville* (1897). Yet, to some, barmaids were the root cause of particularly acute instances of demoralization since, in adding a sexual frisson to the purchase of drink, their occupation intensified two kinds of vice.

Temperance and social purity leagues joined forces with evangelicals to condemn the "modern bar system" as symptomatic of a sexualized, degraded urban culture. Social reformer Edward Watherston spoke for many in 1881 when he pleaded for urgent action to halt "the rush on the part of young girls to the terrible life of the barmaid, with all its temptations and evil influences."[8] A British Women's Temperance Association pamphlet approvingly quoted a Salvation Army report that found "young men filling drunkard's graves or living out ruined lives" because of "the seductive, winsome ways of some barmaid who fascinated them and lured them to their ruin. By the barmaid system, the girl is not only sinned against, she is made to be a sinner."[9] To J. W. Horsley of the National Temperance League in 1887, "[t]he white slaves of the bar are infinitely worse off as regards hours of labour, unpleasant surroundings, temptations to evil and the impossibility of discharging their religious duties as ever were the negroes we freed."[10] The National Vigilance Association argued that it was "unwholesome and unhealthy for girls and young women to administer to public needs behind the bar of a public house."[11]

These pressure groups collected information on working conditions and distributed tracts in pubs, seeking both to dissuade new barmaid recruits and to "rescue" those already established. By 1889, a London club for barmaids had been set up by the Young Women's Christian Association, followed by Lady Wolverton's Barmaids' Guild and the Church Army Barmaids' Rest Home.[12] By March 1890, these anxieties had inspired the creation of a committee of "influential ladies" drawn from purity and temperance circles. The Joint Committee on the Employment of Barmaids was dedicated to "the banishment of the barmaid from the bar" but, as a first step, proposed "A Bill for the Barmaids" to ameliorate their working conditions. Introduced into the House of Commons by one of the National Vigilance Association's most supportive Members of Parliament, William Caine, the bill was unsuccessful but did much to publicize the cause.[13] In 1893, the Royal Commission on Labour employed Eliza Orme to investigate allegations that barmaids suffered from long hours, overwork, "temptations" in the twin forms of drink and predatory men, and a "noxious atmosphere" comprised of smoke and risqué conversation.[14] While Orme's report did not recommend abolition of the occupation, instead suggesting how conditions could be improved, it nonetheless formalized the barmaid's status as a target for social concern.

What animated this widespread unease is extensively illustrated in *Spring Days*:

Lizzie had her bar manners and her town manners, and she slipped on the
former as she would an article of clothing when she lifted the slab and passed
behind. They consisted principally of cordial smiles, personal observations,
and a look of vacancy which she assumed when the conversation became
coarse. From behind the bar she spoke authoritatively, she was secure, it was
different—it was behind the bar; and she spoke with a cheek and a raciness
that at other times were quite foreign to her. "I will not sleep with you to-night
if you don't behave yourself," so Frank once heard her answer a swaggering
young man. She spoke out loud, evidently regarding her words merely in the
light of gentle repartee. [15]

As reformers feared, the barmaid's sexual identity is precarious and slippery.
A curious mixture of the chaste and the brazen, Lizzie is neither "fallen" nor
"respectable," but somewhere in between, as Frank's first encounter with her
underlines. Meeting Lizzie at the theatre, where she is enjoying a night off
with a friend, he is initially puzzled as to what class of women his new
acquaintances belong. They are "evidently not prostitutes," but still "not
quite ladies," and eventually he "got it out of them at last: they're at the bar at
the Gaiety Restaurant." [16] Frank's confusion attests to the barmaid's border-
line sexual status, and he increasingly frets over the demoralizing effects of
her trade. Quizzing her about her "long weary hours of standing, politeness,
washing glasses, and listening to filthy jokes," [17] he soon recoils at how
barmaids become "the subjects of hideous flirtations," forced into "the little
comedy, the effort to appear as virtuous young ladies—'young ladies of the
bar.' It is very pitiful. In such circumstances how do you expect a girl to keep
straight?" [18]

Frank's fears are confirmed in *Spring Days'* sequel, *Mike Fletcher*
(1889), where he pursues Lizzie through London's purlieus, eventually discovering her "in straitened circumstances" and on the brink of the "down-
ward path." [19] "How can a girl remain respectable," she asks him, when "the
landlady used to tell me to go out and get my living?" [20] *Spring Days* and
Mike Fletcher together form a drama of surveillance, rescue, and redemption
as Frank tracks Lizzie from bar to bar, watches anxiously over her risky
career and whisks her away to become his mistress, later his wife, and eventually the mother of his child. Though self-consciously bohemian, Frank
nonetheless shares contemporary disquiet about the "white slaves" behind
the bar. Both novels extensively illustrate the source of that disquiet, together
producing an unexpectedly conservative story of a barmaid compromised,
coarsened and imperiled, only to be ultimately restored to the domestic
sphere.

A first reading of *Esther Waters* in 1894 would have disclosed how Moore
continued to weave his fiction from the raw material of these moral crusades.
Yet, whereas in *Spring Days* and *Mike Fletcher* contemporary anxieties are

relatively straightforwardly voiced through Frank, *Esther Waters* offers a more intriguing mediation of cultural unease. In 1894, Esther's decision to exchange domestic service for a new life behind the bar of the King's Head would have been immediately recognizable as a troubling aspect of the much-discussed "servant problem." Although servants' wages were steadily rising from the 1870s onward, observers nonetheless complained of a "growing distaste to going into service," frequently ascribed to "a growing spirit of independence and general insubordination."[21] Young women desired to "seek other openings instead—anything rather than be servants": top of the list of alternatives was bar work, which was better-paid, available to the unskilled and, crucially, glamorous.[22] Despite perils ranging from "the fatal sin of drink" to men leaping across the bar for a kiss, "the girls prefer this life to domestic service—they think it more genteel to be a barmaid than a servant."[23] Many organizations attempted to counter such attitudes: the National Vigilance Association, the Salvation Army, the Young Women's Christian Association, the Metropolitan Association for the Befriending of Young Servants and the Ladies Association for the Care of Friendless Girls all set up servants' registries for unemployed young women, often recruiting the destitute from workhouses.[24] The Joint Committee on the Employment of Barmaids similarly insisted that "clever, neat-handed girls can always get work as parlourmaids, and wages are largely on the increase in domestic service."[25] Service was thus vigorously promoted as an occupation that protected young women by placing them under close moral supervision within the domestic sphere. However, women like Esther were increasingly reluctant to submit to such supervision.

Esther Waters maps out the process of its heroine's dissent. Initially, Esther is grateful to Lady Elwin, who has "rescued" her from her compromising job with the "bad woman" Mrs. Dunbar and passed her on to her devout friend, Mrs. Barfield.[26] Yet, once she has left Woodview, such interventions are repeatedly interrogated. The kindnesses of Lady Elwin and Mrs. Barfield are balanced against the later callousness of Mrs. Rivers and meanness of Mrs. Bingley, who resorts to the workhouse for servants because the indigent provide cheap labor. When Mrs. Bingley demands an account of how Esther spends her wages on the grounds that she is "responsible for your moral welfare," Esther retorts with "There ain't much chance of temptation for them who work seventeen hours a day."[27] Meanwhile, the novel persistently associates service with a sexual fall. Despite the supervision of the exemplary Mrs. Barfield, Esther nonetheless proves susceptible to those "illicit desires and furtive ambushes" that characterized life below stairs for many young servants.[28] Her career following her illegitimate son Jackie's birth underlines her vulnerability: she is first dismissed after telling her mistress of the advances of her schoolboy son; then, unemployed and sinking into destitution, becomes acutely conscious of her precarious state when she sights the prostitutes promenading through Piccadilly Circus. Their "elegant disguise" fails to conceal their origins: "Esther could pick out the servant girls. She thought how similar their stories were to her own."[29] The fate of Esther's two comrades at Woodview, Margaret Gale and Sarah Tucker, further confirms the porous boundary between service and prostitution. Esther meets Margaret as the latter sways unsteadily through a red-light district, and, over a repast of sausages and brandy in a nearby pub, hears that "one of her masters had got her into trouble, . . . and what was she to do?"[30] Sarah similarly drifts into prostitution while in service, becoming entangled with Bill Evans, a criminal pimp who forces her onto the streets when the pair are lying low in that notorious center of "white slavery," Brussels.[31] In repeatedly associating service with sexual catastrophe, the novel draws attention to an inconvenient truth minimized by many reformers: throughout the closing decades of the nineteenth century, it was former servants, not former barmaids, who made up the majority of prostitutes and unmarried mothers.[32] *Esther Waters* provocatively undermines contemporary pieties about women, work, and sexuality, repeatedly pointing out the faultlines in the moral valorization of domestic service.

Esther's transition from servant to barmaid thus shadows an established narrative of young women "tempted" away from domestic service toward the public house. However, Moore uses Esther's change of occupation to set up contemporary readerly expectations only to undercut them. Esther herself is influenced by those expectations when attempting to decide between evangelical Fred Parsons and raffish publican William Larch:

> If she were to marry William, she would go to the "King's Head." She would stand behind the bar; she would serve the customers. She had never seen much life, and felt somehow that she would like to see a little life; there would not be much life in the cottage at Mortlake, nothing but the prayer meeting. She stopped thinking, surprised at her thoughts.[33]

This yearning to "see a little life" succinctly condenses the motives of the thousands of young women who, to philanthropic dismay, were choosing the lively heterosociality of the bar room over the drab loneliness of the scullery. Esther, however, is disappointed, for her experience of bar work is a long way from Lizzie Baker's. Unlike the voguish Gaiety Bar or the Criterion on the Strand, where Moore carefully places Lizzie, the King's Head is "a humble place in the old-fashioned style . . . not an up-to-date public house."[34] Whereas moral crusaders imagined the barmaid at the center of erotic intrigue, Esther is simply "the missus," sitting sewing in the afternoon "with these empty bars staring you in the face morning and afternoon" and selling only "a dozen pots of beer" to a few passers-by.[35] No wonder Esther "envied the painted tiles and the brass lamps in the other public houses." There, she might have more fun. Instead, the King's Head is tamely domestic, far from the den of vice imagined by social purists. The bar adjoins the family parlor, where Esther gives her son a nursery tea and her husband his evening meal. Milk is even served alongside champagne, whisky, and beer: it is the solace William calls for when his consumptive symptoms become apparent, and it sustains the starving gambler John Randall. These incongruously anodyne glasses of milk do more than reinforce the King's Head's homely atmosphere; they recall Esther's earlier occupation. As wet-nurse for Mrs. Rivers, Esther also sells liquid refreshment, but the parallel emphasizes the gulf between the two occupations. Wet-nursing involves the hiring out of the servant's body, a trade that borders on prostitution.[36] Safely behind her bar, respectably married and raising her thriving son, Esther has put such indignities behind her.

Esther Waters thus meticulously assembles the constituent parts of a familiar cautionary tale, only to disturb its moral coordinates. As Nina Auerbach has observed, Esther is "the bouncy heroine who is able to fall up," and her inverted trajectory is emphasized through the contrast with Moore's previous representations of barmaids.[37] *Spring Days* and *Mike Fletcher* directly portray contemporary unease in plotting Lizzie's "rescue" and rehabilitation through domesticity. In *Esther Waters*, however, the King's Head proves to be, however briefly, redemptive—ironically enough, a refuge of domestic legitimacy for the besieged heroine. At one level, the increasing complexity of Moore's mediation of this contemporary controversy might be ascribed to the respective merits of his novels themselves. For, as Moore himself admitted, *Spring Days* and its sequel were hastily written and published, allowing him little time for critical reflection. As a result, both were critical failures: reviews castigated "the artist-hero's love for the worthless barmaid," deploring the compound of "senseless gossip of the bars mixed up with aimless ravings about art," and damning them as vulgar, poor work.[38] Moore's preface to the 1912 edition of *Spring Days* indicates his subsequent embarrassment: "Never mention that book again . . . I wonder how I could have written it."[39] He did not publish another novel in the five years dividing *Mike Fletcher* from *Esther Waters*. Moore's slow, careful composition of *Esther Waters*, begun in 1888, offers one explanation for the greater sophistication of his creative response to barmaid anxieties in that work. However, another context also lies behind Moore's apparent about-face: his ongoing battle with censorship during the decade leading to *Esther Waters*'s publication. That battle came to a head during the period of *Spring Days* and *Mike Fletcher*'s publication, which coincided with the National Vigilance Association's successful prosecution of Moore's publisher Henry Vizetelly. By early 1889, as Adrian Frazier notes, Moore's publication of his "Don Juan Trilogy in the age of the National Vigilance Association" had branded him "a man of criminal association."[40] It is in this light that Moore's sustained yet shifting interest in the barmaid takes on polemical force.

In December 1884, *The Pall Mall Gazette* published "A New Censorship of Literature," Moore's attack on the acquisitions policies of the two principal circulating libraries, Mudie's and W. H. Smith. Later expanded into *Literature at Nurse, or Circulating Morals* (1885), it argued that, in defining their readership as "young unmarried women who are supposed to know but one side of life," the libraries treated novels as "circulating corals whereon young ladies are supposed to cut their flirtation teeth."[41] Demanding that "We must give up once and forever asking that most silly of silly questions, 'Can my daughter of eighteen read this book,'" Moore urged the abandonment of "this effort to reconcile those two irreconcilable things—art and young girls."[42] As Moore well understood, in declining to stock novels like *A Modern Lover* and *A Mummer's Wife* (1885), the libraries participated in creating a broader anxiety over the sexual vulnerability of young women. Ironically enough, the chief architect of that anxiety was the editor of the *Pall Mall Gazette*, W. T. Stead. In July 1885, Stead published "The Maiden Tribute of Modern Babylon," a sensational exposé of juvenile prostitution in London. The subsequent hasty passage of the Criminal Law Amendment Act, raising the age of consent for girls to sixteen, was soon followed by Stead's founding of the National Vigilance Association. One aspect of the Association's crusade to protect young women was its campaign against the barmaid. Literary censorship was another significant tactic, as the prosecutions of Henry Vizetelly under charges of obscene publication would make notoriously clear.

In May 1888, the National Vigilance Association initiated the first of these two successful prosecutions. Vizetelly had issued Moore's *Literature at Nurse* and his novels *A Mummer's Wife*, *A Drama in Muslin*, *A Mere Accident*, and *Spring Days* in cheap "one-volume" editions designed to circumvent the controlling influence of the circulating libraries by making books affordable to the private purchaser. However, the volumes concerning the court were translations of Zola's *La Terre*, *Nana*, *La Curée*, and *Pot-Bouille*, the latter two polemically prefaced by Moore. Advised by his counsel to plead guilty, Vizetelly was fined and bound over not to reissue the novels "in their present form."[43] When, in early 1889, he reissued slightly expurgated editions of them, the Association initiated its second prosecution, which resulted in Vizetelly being fined and imprisoned for three months, a punishment that ensured his bankruptcy and eroded his health.

In the aftermath of the second trial, the Association issued a pamphlet, *Pernicious Literature*, to underscore the implications of its triumph. Deploring "the rapid spread of demoralising literature in this country," it placed the prosecution of Vizetelly in the context of its wider moral crusade, drawing a direct correlation between Stead's exposé of juvenile prostitution and the selling of "demoralising" fiction:

> It had become the rule with a class of low booksellers in London to provide indecent literature for young girls, to offer them every inducement to come into the shops and read the books, to provide them with private rooms stocked with the vilest class of literature. In many cases these shops were in league with houses of the worst class, to which these girls when their minds had become sufficiently polluted and depraved were consigned. [44]

Pernicious Literature not only offered a retort to *Literature at Nurse* by reasserting the primacy of "the young girl" as the imagined reader of fiction; it also compared sexually daring fiction to other forms of vice. Borrowing the language of temperance, it imagined the "indecent" book playing a role akin to that of the spiked drink in its melodramas of seduction. [45] "Vile literature" was an intoxicating draught weakening the virtue of the nation's youth. It questioned "whether at the present time the people of this country were suffering more from the effect of an excessive use of strong drink than they were from the more subtle poison of vile and obscene literature. There was nothing that so corroded the human character, or sapped the vitality of the nation." [46] This rhetoric not only indicates how temperance and social purity campaigns were mutually supportive, but, most importantly, it also signals the extent to which the National Vigilance Association associated reading with those other notorious routes to demoralization, sex and drink.

In both of the novels composed and published during the months of Vizetelly's trials, Moore also associates reading with sex and drink, and he does so through the figure of the barmaid. [47] Frank's first glimpse of Lizzie behind the Gaiety Bar in *Spring Days* may suggest Manet's *Un bar au Folies-Bergère*, but Frank himself "remembered having read a description of the place somewhere, he thought for a moment, and then he remembered that it was in one of Harding's novels." [48] Frank soon attempts to write his own novel about her, *Her Saviour*, and these metafictional associations cumulate when, struggling to free himself of his obsession, he imagines Lizzie as a compelling read: "He went to sleep, certain he had torn this page out of his life, and he awoke to find it still there; and day after day he continued to brood upon it, and still unable to understand its meaning, he longed to turn it over and read, for there were other pages; but they were sealed, and he might only read this one page." [49] This labored metaphor epitomizes the ways in which both *Spring Days* and its sequel connect barmaids with reading. In *Mike Fletcher*, the polemical implications of this connection are spelled out through Frank's role as the editor of *The Pilgrim*, an iconoclastic literary journal. Its contributors ridicule the "national tendency towards chaste literature," deploring the "prurient purity of the 'English' novel" and its implied reader, "the society girl." [50] They not only rehearse the argument of *Litera-*

ture at Nurse, but also self-consciously highlight the difference between such novels and Moore's own work, with its earthy, compromised heroine. The barmaid acquires a talismanic force as the inspiration and icon of creative experiment, in ways that seem designed to challenge contemporary interrelated crusades against drink, promiscuity, and "pernicious literature." If *Spring Days* and *Mike Fletcher* retaliated against the tyranny of the "young girl" archetype by presenting the barmaid as naturalism's muse, then *Esther Waters* complicates these polemical associations.

Moore's battle with moral conservatives casts a long shadow over *Esther Waters*, published two months after Vizetelly's death. Campaigns to cleanse the public sphere are openly acknowledged in William Larch's complaint: "There's a temperance party, a purity party and a hanti-gambling party, and what they is working for is just to stop folk from doing as they like."[51] Those forces are personified in William's rival Fred Parsons. A member of the Plymouth Brethren and the Salvation Army, Fred is a committed member of all three of William's "parties," a teetotaller who declines to "frequent public houses," an opponent of gambling who inveighs against "drunkenness and debauchery" from a Salvation Army tent on Derby Day, and a man who boasts during his courtship of his ability to "fly from temptation," even though "Esther did not like him better for his purity."[52] Fred is thus representative of those behind the campaign against "pernicious literature," and his organization's crusade against the King's Head deploys tactics reminiscent of those used against Vizetelly. In December 1887, Stead had approached Vizetelly, requesting information about his stock of Zola's fiction and giving him advance warning of the danger of possible prosecution.[53] In *Esther Waters*, Fred similarly calls into the King's Head to warn Esther "that the law will be set in motion" if the gambling is not stopped.[54] Vizetelly's trial was precipitated by a visit from an agent provocateur: "The Vigilance Society's man has been here purchasing one of our translations of Zola's novels," Vizetelly warned Moore in early 1888.[55] William is likewise trapped when "a tall, clean-shaven man dressed in broadcloth," "suspicious" in his respectability, places a bet across the bar.[56] Even the rhythm of William's trials and punishments suggest Vizetelly's: after the first offense, William is merely fined and discharged, but after the second, he is deprived of his livelihood, financially ruined and in broken health. Behind the unlikely form of William Larch, who never reads a book, stands the ghost of Henry Vizetelly.[57] Yet Moore's engagement with the purity crusades is more ingenious than these parallels might first suggest.

Specifically, long before Esther takes her place behind the bar at the King's Head, the novel persistently associates fiction with drink, in ways that slyly parody the favorite rhetorical trope of *Pernicious Literature*. The association is present from William's ice-breaking anecdote about the suggestively named footman Jim Story, sacked for tipsily "chattering over the bar in the

Red Lion."[58] It continues during the servants' dinner, when Esther is shocked by the lavish provision of both beer and romantic fiction. While she abstains from the former, her attempt to resist the latter is less successful. As Sarah reads aloud an installment from her *Family Reader* story of actresses, moonlit trysts, and elopements, Esther's response is akin to intoxication: "fascinated against her will, Esther could not but listen," temporarily overwhelmed by this "imaginative stimulant."[59] A key temperance term, "stimulant" underlines the conjunction of drink and fiction imposed by Esther's memories of her Plymouth Brethren childhood: "She had often been told the story of how one day the fumes of the beer [her father] had drunk over-powered him as he sat in the sun on his derrick, and that he had called upon God to relieve him of his suffering in the hospital, and that a Plymouth Brother who occupied the next bed had answered him."[60]

The framing words "she had often been told the story" were added to the 1899 second edition. The change not only reinforces Esther's status as an absorbed listener, but also calls attention to its own intertextuality, since her father's account of how he "in early youth had been led into intemperance by some wild companions" borrows both plot and language from temperance tracts.[61] For the young Esther, bedtime stories were cautionary tales: as she grows into womanhood, "imaginative stimulants" and intoxication will continue to be intertwined. Esther's seduction is effected while she is under a doubled sense of influence:

> One evening, putting his pipe aside, William threw his arm round her and whispered that she was his wife. The words sounded delicious in her ears, but she could hardly hear what he said after; a sort of weakness seemed to come over her. It must be the beer she had drunk. She wished she had not taken the last glass. She could not struggle with him.[62]

Beer and romantic fantasies thus play a twinned role in Esther's fall, as William's "delicious" words, their reception primed by Sarah's before them, merge with that fatal "last glass" to break down her resistance.

In combining fiction and drink so persistently, Moore deftly undermines parallel conservative crusades against barmaids and against "pernicious literature." His most eloquent retaliation is to make his heroine both a barmaid and the author of her own story. The novel opens with the spectacle of Esther, struggling up from the station to Woodview under the dead weight of her mother's parcel of books—a strange burden, since she cannot read. Yet Esther's illiteracy only emphasizes her curious propensity to take control of her own tale. To read *Esther Waters* is to be faced, again and again, with dramatized scenes of narrative disclosure or withdrawal.[63] Esther and her "story" are so thoroughly entwined that her novelist employer Miss Rice comes to imagine her as "this rough page torn out of life."[64] This focus on

Esther as author can simply be seen as a natural extension of Moore's earlier interest in the barmaid as naturalism's muse. Yet *Esther Waters* nuances this association to oblique polemical effect. Moore's assault on the purity crusaders does not simply repudiate, through Esther's redemptive journey into domesticity, their anxieties about her compromised and compromising occupation. More subtly, it presents Esther as the mediatrix of two suspect commodities—stories and drink—only to depict her as unsullied by their influence. William's remark as she drops her brimming jug, "You always keeps your figure—you know you ain't a bit changed," in one sense proves grimly ironic, since Esther ends the novel back where she began. Yet, William's recognition of her integrity also summarizes how the novel resists master-narratives of demoralization. Answering the reproaches of her former suitor with "No, I've not changed, Fred, but things has turned out different," Esther herself reminds us how her goodness endures. [65]

Esther's integrity helped, finally, to seal Moore's triumph. For the most potently rebellious aspect of *Esther Waters* inheres in the queasy accuracy with which it mimicked contemporary crusades, while disputing their catastrophic trajectories. Moore's decision to serialize parts of the novel as "Pages from the Life of a WorkGirl" in Stead's *Pall Mall Gazette* set up a latent tension between that newspaper's agenda and his own. [66] If Stead believed that Moore was contributing to his paper's ideological program, it was not the first time that their positions had been confused, for in 1885, Moore was rumored to be the real author of "The Maiden Tribute" articles. [67] When *Esther Waters* finally appeared in March 1894, only for W. H. Smith to refuse to circulate it, reviewers competed to defend Moore by attesting to its uplifting effects. *The Athenaeum* found it "eminently moral," while *The Sketch* suggested that "anti-gambling societies should circulate the book by the thousands" and that "Esther Waters Homes for Girl Mothers" should be founded. [68] As the temperance paper *The Woman's Signal* noted, while the novel appeared to be "a tract against betting," Esther's seduction "is ascribed far more truly, and indeed more instructively also, to strong drink—the true source of danger to good, pure-minded yet reckless and headstrong girls of the working-class." [69] One of the many ironies behind these misreadings is that a particular species of "reckless and headstrong girls," synonymous throughout the period with both "strong drink" and sexual peril, is crucial to Moore's final triumph over the National Vigilance Association and its supporters. In Moore's early fiction, barmaids are associated both with sexual danger and aesthetic innovation, acting as a counterweight to the imperiled innocent of the censor's imagination. Yet, in *Esther Waters*, Moore puts the barmaid controversy to far more sophisticated polemical use by raising expectations of sexual danger and disgrace, only to dismantle them. Through

Esther Waters's teasingly unstable engagement with these discourses of moral reform, Moore accomplishes an enduring revenge.

NOTES

1. George Moore, *Esther Waters* (London: Walter Scott, 1894), 190, 203.
2. George Moore, *A Modern Lover* (London: Tinsley Brothers, 1883), 115.
3. Manet's influence on Moore is more thoroughly explored in Anna Gruetzner Robins, "George Moore's *A Modern Lover*: Introducing the French Impressionists to London," *French Studies: A Quarterly Review* 61, no. 1 (2007): 47–56. See also Gruetzner Robins's chapter 2.
4. George Moore, *Spring Days* (New York: Brentano's, 1912), 110. The novel's debt to Manet has been observed by Adrian Frazier, who notes that Lizzie displays "just that look of vacancy that Manet represented in his final masterpiece; it is the stunned look of a person who is becoming an urban commodity," *George Moore, 1852–1933* (New Haven: Yale University Press, 2000), 177–178.
5. *The Times*, December 30, 1881, 7d.
6. See Peter Bailey, "Parasexuality and Glamour: The Victorian Barmaid as Cultural Prototype," *Gender and History* 2, no. 2 (1990): 148–172.
7. "Editorial," *The Barmaid: An Illustrated Journal*, December 17, 1891, 2.
8. Edward Watherston, "The Industrial Employment of Women," *Reynolds News*, Friday, December 30, 1881, 7.
9. Sarah Reid Perkins, *Should Women Serve in Drinking Bars?* (London: National British Women's Temperance Association, n.d.), 12.
10. Rev. John William Horsley, *Jottings from Jail* (London: T. F. Unwin, 1887), 166.
11. "Annual General Meeting," *The Vigilance Record* (April 1900): 135.
12. The British Weekly Commissioners, *Toilers in London. An Enquiry Concerning Female Labour in the Metropolis* (London: Hodder and Stoughton, 1889), 213; Gifford Lewis, *Eva Gore-Booth and Esther Roper* (London: Pandora, 1988), 104; "Gilded Cages," *Church Army Quarterly Paper* (Summer 1903): 10–11.
13. "A Bill for the Barmaids," *Pall Mall Gazette*, March 12, 1890. The Bill proposed limitations to 72 hours of labor per week and the enforcement of stricter sanitary regulations, thereby bringing barmaids some of the protections already granted to other women workers under the terms of the 1878 Factory Act.
14. Eliza Orme (Assistant Lady Commissioner), "Conditions of Work of Barmaids, Waitresses and Book-Keepers Employed in Hotels, Restaurants, Public Houses and Other Places of Employment," *Royal Commission on Labour*, vol. 4, *The Employment of Women, Parliamentary Papers* 37, 4, no. A (1893–1894): 197–211.
15. Moore, *Spring Days*, 264.
16. Ibid., 49.
17. Ibid., 128.
18. Ibid., 135.
19. George Moore, *Mike Fletcher* (London: Ward and Downey, 1889), 41.
20. Ibid., 108. Moore revisited the theme in a later short story, "In Blue Silk and Brass," published in *Hawk*, April 22, 1890, 463–464, reprinted in *The Collected Short Stories of George Moore*, ed. Ann Heilmann and Mark Llewellyn, 5 vols (London: Pickering and Chatto, 2007), 2: 57–61. A prostitute nostalgically recalls her former marital happiness in her "beautiful 'ome, it was all in blue silk and brass" (59) and explains how, her husband having failed to support her through novel writing, she now disguises that she has returned to her former trade to save his pride while supporting them both: "I told him I was going to take a situation as a barmaid. He is so innocent he'd believe anything I told him" (61). Moore was clearly highly conscious of the barmaid's cultural proximity to the prostitute.
21. Mrs. Eliot James, *Our Servants: Their Duties to Us and Ours to Them* (London: Ward, Lock and Co, 1882), 3.

22. Miss Kenward, "Girl Life in an Industrial Centre," *Women Workers: The Quarterly Magazine of the Birmingham Ladies Union of Workers among Women and Children* 4, no. 2 (September 1894): 3.

23. The British Weekly Commissioners, *Toilers in London*, 211, 206.

24. Ibid., 133; Metropolitan Association for Befriending Young Servants, *Annual Report* (1885): 5; Ladies Association for the Care of Friendless Girls, *Friends in Need* (London: Hatchard, 1889), 5.

25. The Joint Committee on the Employment of Barmaids, *The Employment of Barmaids*, undated flyer, HD6 / 79, London School of Economics Library, London, UK.

26. Moore, *Esther Waters*, 24.

27. Ibid., 158.

28. Francoise Barret-Ducrocq, *Love in the Time of Victoria*, trans. John Howe (London: Verso, 1991), 50.

29. Moore, *Esther Waters*, 168.

30. Ibid., 171.

31. Since Alfred Stace Dyer's investigation into the traffic of women to Brussels in 1881, the capital had become associated with "white slavery." See Katherine Mullin, "Dyer, Alfred Stace (1849–1926)," *The Oxford Dictionary of National Biography* (Oxford University Press, 2008), accessed June 25, 2014, 0-www.oxforddnb.com.wam.leeds.ac.uk/view/article/94647.

32. For instance, the 1880 Annual Report of Queen Charlotte's Maternity Hospital, where Esther herself is admitted, disclosed that 71.3 percent of its inmates were servants. See John Gillis, "Servants and the Risks of Illegitimacy in London, 1801–1900," in *Sex and Class in Women's History*, ed. Judith Walkowitz, Mary Ryan and Judith Newton (London: Routledge and Kegan Paul, 1983), 116.

33. Moore, *Esther Waters*, 225–226.

34. Ibid., 236. Both the Gaiety Bar and the Criterion on the Strand were owned by Spiers and Ponds, a company that prided itself on only hiring young women it deemed "the pick of the basket"; "Social Sketches: The Barmaid," *Table Talk*, October 6, 1893, 10.

35. Moore, *Esther Waters*, 236.

36. Tess O'Toole has elsewhere noted the connections between prostitution and wet-nursing in the novel, observing that "The most rapacious pursuit of Esther's body is that performed by Mrs Rivers, who seeks to claim and confine it as a resource for her child." See Tess O'Toole, "The Servant's Body: The Victorian Wet-Nurse in George Moore's *Esther Waters*," *Women's Studies* 25 (1996): 338.

37. Nina Auerbach, *Woman and the Demon: The Life of a Victorian Myth* (Cambridge: Harvard University Press, 1982), 158.

38. "Literature," *The Glasgow Herald*, September 8, 1888; "Spring Days," *Pall Mall Gazette*, October 18, 1888. *Mike Fletcher* fared no better: *The Graphic* commented that "clean minds will instinctively avoid" this "biography of a particularly feeble and vulgar Don Juan of the music halls, with a morbid taste for Schopenhauer" ("New Novels," *Graphic*, December 21, 1889).

39. Moore, "Preface," *Spring Days*, vii.

40. Frazier, *George Moore*, 199.

41. George Moore, *Literature at Nurse, or Circulating Morals* (London: Vizetelly and Co, 1885), 21, 16.

42. Ibid., 21. For further details see Jane Jordan in chapter 3.

43. Frazier, *George Moore*, 175.

44. The National Vigilance Association, *Pernicious Literature* (London: National Vigilance Association, 1889), 7.

45. W. T. Stead emphasized the role of drink in procuring young girls for prostitution in "The Maiden Tribute of Modern Babylon": "He asked us to have some wine and something to eat, and we sat eating and drinking. I had never tasted wine before, but he pressed it on me, and I took one glass and then another, until I think I had four glasses. My head got very queer, and I hardly knew what I did" (*Pall Mall Gazette*, July 7, 1885; the other articles in Stead's undercover investigation were published on July 6, 8, and 10, 1885).

46. National Vigilance Association, *Pernicious Literature*, 10.

47. *Spring Days* was begun in December 1887, serialized in May and June 1888 in daily supplements in the *Evening News*, and then issued by Vizetelly in September. *Mike Fletcher* was written with similar briskness, begun that August and published by Ward and Downey in November 1889, Vizetelly being by then in prison and out of business.

48. Moore, *Spring Days*, 109.

49. Ibid., 311.

50. Moore, *Mike Fletcher*, 55.

51. Moore, *Esther Waters*, 324.

52. Ibid., 182, 230, 263. Intriguingly, Stead's "Maiden Tribute" articles claimed that the underclass was more willing to sell its children into prostitution around Derby Day in order to fund drinking and gambling. See *Pall Mall Gazette*, July 7, 1885.

53. Frazier, *George Moore*, 168. Stead's newspaper, the *Pall Mall Gazette*, had been running a campaign against the "nastiness" and immorality of Zola for some months. See, for example, a letter to the editor protesting that, though Zola's *La Terre* was considered "too vile" for publication in France, "it is being brought out with impunity here in English" (December 16, 1887, 12); or the article "Why French Novels Sell," which argued that both Moore and Zola were popular because "anything which is nasty will always sell" and "young ladies dote on anything naughty" (March 9, 1888, 13).

54. Moore, *Esther Waters*, 289.

55. Frazier, *George Moore*, 168.

56. Moore, *Esther Waters*, 321.

57. Vizetelly died on January 1, 1894, shortly before *Esther Waters* was published.

58. Moore, *Esther Waters*, 4.

59. Ibid., 20.

60. George Moore, *Esther Waters* (1899 edition), ed. David Skilton (Oxford: Oxford University Press, 1983), 22. In the 1894 first edition version, see 21.

61. Moore, *Esther Waters* (1894 edition), 21.

62. Ibid., 69.

63. "[S]he could tell a very different story if she wished it"; "One word led to another, and soon Esther was telling her mother the whole tale of her misfortune"; "the lady, although unswervingly faithful to her principles, seemed not indifferent to Esther's story, and asked her many questions"; "my story is not one that can be told to a lady such as you"; "Esther told Fred the story of her betrayal and he was interested in the story, and sorry for her"; "Why go back on that old story"; "It ain't an old story, it's the story of my life, and I haven't come to the end of it yet"; "Esther gradually told Mrs. Barfield the story of her life"; "It is quite a romance, Esther." Ibid., 99, 102, 110, 175, 170, 222, 366.

64. Ibid., 231.

65. Ibid., 289.

66. "Pages from the Life of a WorkGirl" appeared in the *Pall Mall Gazette* daily from October, 2–14, 1893.

67. Frazier has speculated that Stead "would not realise the ways in which he was being had" (*George Moore*, 228).

68. *Athenaeum* 3470, April 28, 1894, 537–538; *Sketch* 5, no. 64, April 18, 1894, 630. These and similar reviews of the novel are quoted in Frazier, *George Moore*, 234–235. There, were, however, also disparaging voices: an article entitled "Brandy and Soda" in the *Sporting Times* (July 21, 1894) derided *Esther Waters* as "a novel which the Anti-Gambling League Johnnies have claimed as their text-book and whose great moral lessons appear to be 'Never catch cold on a racecourse' and 'Never visit a lying-in hospital if you want fun.'" The sporting fraternity got their own back: on April 11, 1896, *Horse and Hound* carried a report of the Derby Spring Meeting, which listed a horse named Esther Waters owned by Lord Ellesmere. Sadly, the equine Esther failed to distinguish herself at fixtures later that year at Newmarket and Kempton.

69. Mrs. Fenwick Miller, "Books Worth Reading," *The Woman's Signal*, May 3, 1894, 237. *The Woman's Signal* was primarily a temperance paper and was vigorous in its opposition to barmaids.

Chapter Six

Alice Barton

*A Portrait of the Artist
as a Young (New) Woman?*

Ann Heilmann and
María Elena Jaime de Pablos

George Moore's "girl-novel"[1] about a female artist, *A Drama in Muslin* (1886), might be considered a singular about-face to his polemic call, in *Literature at Nurse* (1885), to "renounce the effort to reconcile those two irreconcilable things—art and young girls."[2] Twenty-year-old Alice Barton is introduced as a fledgling author and the narrator's depiction of her public success frames the beginning and end of the text. In the course of her journey, Alice develops from provincial Irish schoolgirl playwright to professional metropolitan writer. Her ultimate destiny as a fashionable novelist in the British capital enabled cosmopolitan Moore, not yet stirred by early rumblings of the Irish Renaissance,[3] to intimate that there was no place for the creative imagination in Ireland. At the same time his choice of a female middlebrow writer served to explore questions of gendered authorship and invoke his own superior position as a more high-cultured and challenging, hence censored, artist. As Jane Jordan notes in chapter 4, Moore's response to popular women writers was considerably conflicted; the complex tensions in his approach are encapsulated by this novel about young women, art, and marriage. Such tension can also be found in the unstable relationship the text establishes with contemporary feminist thought. With its female-centered artist plot conceived to underscore the text's indictment of middle-class girls' objectification in the marriage market,[4] *A Drama in Muslin* makes a contribution to the emerging New Woman genre of the 1880s–1890s even as it cautions (women) readers against the "undercurrent of hatred and revolt" exhibited by "the leaders of the movement."[5] In a similarly ambivalent vein, Moore's woman writer gains public recognition and a living while falling short of the higher standards of art as defined by the narrator. Arguably, the sharp differentiation between "women's writing" and "men's art" was of such importance to Moore because he was still in the process of establishing himself. Preceded by two novels that were banned and thus less likely to reach a broad public, *A Drama in Muslin* predates the stir of *Confessions of a Young Man* (1888), and the breakthrough success of *Esther Waters* (1894) was a decade away, while his failure as a painter and poetaster was painfully imprinted on his memory. It is this anxiety about the value of his own art that drives the instability of his portrait of the artist as a young woman.[6]

Our chapter applies what Elizabeth Grubgeld has called Moore's "discourse of repudiation"[7] to his approach toward the female *Künstlerroman*. Grubgeld draws attention to the way in which the contrapuntal rhetorical strategy that shapes *A Drama in Muslin* among other novels is sustained by "a narrative voice that addresses the reader, comments upon, condemns—and on rare occasions, praises—what it displays."[8] While particularly prominent in the construction of the artist plot, this rhetoric also bears on the concurrent slippage between the Irish nationalist and women's rights causes, the former being consistently associated with the latter. The Darwinian doom of the landowners corresponds to the condition of the middle-class spinster,[9] just as the insurgent spirit of the peasant population awakening from age-old oppression resembles rising levels of discontent among Alice and her friends. Female Irish dissidence features most conspicuously in Alice's nationalist sympathies and deviation from conventional standards of "proper" (male-focused, husband-chasing) femininity, but is also explored in the sexual psychosis of the lesbian hysteric and Roman Catholic convert Cecilia Cullen and the libidinal-cum-social anarchy of her counterpart, Mrs. Lawler, a woman cold-shouldered by her neighbors for her reputed past as a streetwalker. If Cecilia represents an Ireland in the grasp of Catholic religion, Mrs. Lawler's nighttime holdup of the Barton heiress[10] parallels League-inspired nocturnal forays on the landlords. As Brendan Fleming points out, however, Moore vocalizes Ireland's grievances through the voice of the evolving New Woman only to "compromise" both nationalist and feminist liberation discourses "within a less subversive image of femininity" by ending his heroine's struggle for independence with her maternal domestication.[11]

And yet, in contradistinction to female-authored New Woman novels, it is precisely her matrimonial and maternal experience of self-actualization that sustains Alice's career as a writer. In attaining all she desires in both the domestic and the professional spheres, Alice embodies the feminist ideal: the eminently successful woman who has seized "both sides of the apple of life": a privilege that, as the New Woman writer Mona Caird complained, remained the preserve of men, whereas women had to contend with "the choice of the halves" or more likely were "offered neither."[12] Here, then, Moore draws the picture of a female all-rounder who, in the face of considerable obstacles, demonstrates women's ability to "have it all." That Alice's vision and creative faculties do not extend to the aesthetics of the "true" artist, on the other hand, serves to qualify her achievement. Moore's politics of equivocation constructs a heroine who is permitted to flourish for the very reason that she will never pose an actual challenge to the male artist. If, as outlined in the Introduction to this book, Moore's collaborative ventures with women were always eroticized, the implications of such sexual aesthetics are here filtered through the lens of the aspiring female author who is inducted into writerly as sensual arousal by a male mentor figure who acts as Moore's *alter ego*. In focalizing the encounter through a female consciousness that is given agency but whose creative authority remains circumscribed by the aesthetic value judgments of the author-narrator, *A Drama in Muslin* thus offers a doubly refracted perspective on Moore's conceptualization of "George Moore's" influence on his contemporaries.

The first chapter of *Drama in Muslin* presents Alice as the author and director of the play *King Cophetua*, an adaptation of Tennyson's 1842 ballad of "The Beggar Maid" (the subject of Edward Burne-Jones's Pre-Raphaelite painting of 1884, which is conjured up in Moore's description of Alice's idealized character conceptualization). The play is performed in a convent school where Alice, her younger sister Olive, and their friends Violet Scully and May Gould (Pre-Raphaelite beauties, ethereal and voluptuous) have just completed their studies. Alice's authorial accomplishment is comically deflated by her dismay at the misrepresentation of her characters: May's King, his dignity already impaired by the dress code imposed by the nuns (trousers being replaced by a dressing gown), struts the stage in quest of sensual rather than aesthetic gratification, while Violet's beggar maid "looked upon her lover . . . as a clever huckstress at a customer who had bought her goods at her valuing"[13]—an intimation of the amateur actresses' personalities as much as their prospective destinies (May will plunge headlong into an affair with Fred Scully, whereas Violet will seize her opportunity for social advancement through a prestigious marriage). That at graduation Alice is awarded a complete edition of the works of Cardinal Newman adds a further sardonic note, given her closet atheism. The irony of this particular prize offering will not be lost on readers familiar with Moore's ferocious disparagement of Newman's style in *Salve* (1912).[14] Even if Alice does not discard her edition in the manner of Thackeray's Becky Sharp, Newman is anything but a choice gift for a secular artist-in-the-making.

However unlikely a context for a girl's intellectual growth, the convent school provided scope for Alice to direct her studies, enabling her to educate herself well beyond conventional confines. It is with her return home and entry into the world that her problems begin. The girls are formally launched into society, with the expectation that they will enjoy a life of idleness and sensuality, devoted to balls and flirtation, in order to fulfill their ultimate purpose, that of securing a suitable husband. This is where Moore's novel most closely intersects with the Victorian feminist *Bildungsroman*. Alice's sister and most of her friends throw themselves into the new regime with energy and passion: Olive immediately becomes infatuated with a handsome officer, May starts a romp with a neighbor's son that will end in illegitimate pregnancy, and Violet, Mrs. Barton's greatest adversary if her only true heir in spirit, bides her time until the most profitable match moves within her reach. Alice, however, equipped as she is with a "keen, . . . yearning, . . . inquiring, . . . doubting mind," feels alienated at the thought of the "wasted" existence of such "awful mummery in muslin."[15] Her reflections on girls' defective education, which imposes as its single, and soul-destroying, object in life "a little French, a little music, a little water-colour painting—for this, and only this: . . . to cajole . . . any man who would condescend to . . . keep them," are reminiscent of the (also twenty-year-old) artist-heroine's denunciation of women's intellectually stultifying and degrading "cage-bird life" in Elizabeth Barrett Browning's verse novel *Aurora Leigh* (1856).[16] Like Aurora, who, contemptuous of conventional expectations of femininity, nevertheless declares herself "hungry . . . for man's love"[17] and complements her artistic career with an emotionally fulfilling marriage, Alice is anything but the confirmed "*type de vieille fille*" for which her mother mistakes her because of her love of reading.[18] In contradistinction to humpbacked Cecilia, whose physical disability Moore constructs as a visual marker of psychic and sexual deviance, Alice "trembled to think of her life pure from end to end"; "a husband had always formed part of her thoughts . . . she had always joyed in things relating to motherhood."[19] Profoundly disheartened by a sense of her own superfluity in the face of both Mrs. Barton's transparent disdain for "this gawk of a girl" and Olive's great promise as a society beauty, and with a keen desire to start "acting independently and living an individual life," she retreats within herself and, again like Aurora, finds in books the intellectual company that she has to forgo among family and friends.[20]

A skeptic from the age of sixteen, Alice's development is grounded in autodidactic reading. Her iconoclastic schedule—"Darwin on the Origin of Species, a History of the French Revolution, Byron, Shelley's Satires on the absurdity of Revelation, the Immaculate Conception, and belief in God"— retraces Moore's own literary diet.[21] In contradistinction to Moore, however, who rejected any kind of religious faith, Alice is drawn to nature religion and regards humanity as part of an all-pervasive organic world. As the narrator notes, Alice "in an obscure and formless way divined the doctrines" of the German philosopher Eduard von Hartmann (1842–1906).[22] In his *Philosophy of the Unconscious* (1869), von Hartmann diagnosed the death of Christian religion, "artificially and violently preserved as a mummy," and advocated its substitution by pantheism: a "synthesis of Naturalistic Monism and Theism."[23] Like von Hartmann, and in contrast to Schopenhauer's teachings (which so adversely affect some of Moore's protagonists elsewhere),[24] Alice believes that even if individual happiness should be out of reach, life must be affirmed: that social evolution can be achieved by discovering and following the "ordinary and simple laws of nature." This implies "the entire and unconditional resignation of personal existence into the arms of the cosmic process."[25] Her pantheistic principles are reflected in her conviction that the "ideal life" consists in "making the ends of nature the ends also of what we call our conscience."[26]

Moore goes to some lengths to establish his heroine as an intellectual, a seeker after philosophical truths like himself. For all her unorthodoxy, it is Alice, not her environment, who is in harmony with the "ordinary . . . laws of nature." She does not wish to starve her senses in feeding her mind, whereas the other girls seem content to live for their physical appetites alone. Alice's difference from her friends marks her out as a "new" type of woman, singular and yet characteristic of the period that saw the rise of first-wave feminism. Her desire for an active as well as emotionally fulfilled life and the independence of thought that underpins her religious skepticism are complemented by her growing political awareness of class injustice. At a time when the Land League is at its most active and violent, killing landlords and agents, she recognizes the exploitation involved in "each big house being surrounded by a hundred small ones, all working to keep it in sloth and luxury."[27] The contrast between her own life and that of others is forcefully brought home to her during a ball: "look at all those poor people staring in at the window. Isn't it dreadful that they, in the dark and cold, should be watching us dancing in our beautiful dresses, and in our warm bright room?"[28] The irony is, of course, that the dancers are every bit as much enslaved mentally as the impoverished villagers are materially—an analogy conveyed through animal metaphors[29]—and that both (with the exception perhaps of Mrs. Barton, who does not suffer defeat lightly) are in equal measure disenfranchised and excluded from processes of power.

Conceived as "a representative woman of 1885,"[30] one of the New Women the age has brought into being, Alice arrives at a recognition of the mental and physical damage the patriarchal system has inflicted on women ("she realised how men have bought women, imprisoned women, kept women as a sort of common property"), and reaches the conclusion that "[u]ntil we are free to think, until we are their sisters in thought, we cannot hope to become the companions, the friends, the supports of men."[31] Of immediate concern for her emerging feminism is the pervasiveness of the social constraints that limit the intellectual, cultural, and professional development of young women, condemning them, in the name of a misconceived ideal of femininity, to physical and mental confinement:

> How horrible, how narrow, how indefensible, how unintelligent did the laws
> that guarded a young girl's life from the living touch of the world appear to her
> to be! and, as a prisoner will raise his arms to beat down the walls of his cell,
> she appealed against them all: "Give me a duty, give me a mission to perform,
> and I will live!" she cried despairingly; "but, oh! save me from this grey dream
> of idleness!" [32]

Just as Alice's indignation at the inadequate and pointless education meted
out to girls resembles that of Barrett Browning's artist-protagonist, so her
sentiments on the condition of women invoke the voices of Victorian women
writers and their feminist characters. Her desperate quest for a purpose in
life, echoed by the heroine in Moore's first "Mildred Lawson" version two
years later, [33] is strongly evocative of Florence Nightingale's passionate out-
cry in her novel-fragment *Cassandra* (1860):

> Give us back our suffering, we cry to Heaven in our hearts—suffering rather
> than indifferentism; for out of nothing comes nothing. But out of suffering
> may come the cure. Better have pain than paralysis! A hundred struggle and
> drown in the breakers. One discovers the new world. But rather, ten times
> rather, die in the serf, heralding the way to that new world, than stand idly on
> the shore! [34]

Alice's words also resonate with contemporary New Woman fiction such as
Olive Schreiner's enormously popular *The Story of an African Farm* (1883),
a novel Moore read during the composition of *A Drama in Muslin*. [35] Moore
admired and, for a few months in 1885, courted Schreiner. [36] Her heroine
Lyndall, a failed artist who once hoped to become an actress, chafes against
the social law denying women an education, professional training, and mean-
ingful occupations, instead conspiring to drive them into mercenary mar-
riages as their only means of survival (the equation of marriage and prostitution arguably had a long tradition dating back to Mary Wollstonecraft's 1792
Vindication of the Rights of Woman). Invoking Chinese footbinding as a
metaphor for the injuries wreaked on women, Lyndall declares that the "parts
we are not to use have been quite atrophied, and have even dropped off. . . .
A little bitterness, a little longing when we are young, a little futile searching
for work, a little passionate striving for room for the exercise of our powers,—and then we go with the drove. A woman must march with her regi-
ment." [37] Lyndall's self-inflicted downfall proves her point. By according
Alice a happier fate, Moore challenges Schreiner's pessimistic outlook in the
figure of a protagonist whose superior common sense always keeps her passion in check. Too rational to deceive herself into believing that her feelings
for John Harding might be requited, too conventional to visit a man in his
home without a chaperon, Alice resists the physical temptations to which the
freethinking Lyndall succumbs, while May, whose sensuality and sexual

appetite more closely resemble that of Schreiner's heroine, fails to crumble under the impact of her short-lived experience of single motherhood and the loss of her baby. (Indeed, while Lyndall's fatal illness appears to be a manifestation of an extreme urge for self-punishment borne from crippling guilt about not having loved and thereby somehow having brought about the death of her child, May, far from being haunted by her failure to develop "those maternal sentiments," confesses to being relieved by the turn of events).[38]

If Alice (and to a lesser extent May) is constructed as a counterpart of Lyndall, she is also juxtaposed to Henrik Ibsen's Nora, whose door-slamming exit at the end of *A Doll's House* (1879) electrified British feminists when the play premiered in London in 1889.[39] In his 1915 preface to the revised version of his novel, *Muslin*, Moore emphasizes that, while not directly inspired by Ibsen's play, the first translation of which was read out to him when he was "half through his story," he was motivated by "a hatred as lively as Ibsen's of the social conventions that drive women into the marriage market," but that he covered "the same subject from an entirely different point of view."[40] His novel's comedic[41] depiction of the battle lines drawn up for the marriage season at the Shelbourne Hotel (Moore's own favorite haunt)[42] and Mrs. Barton's vain endeavor, on behalf of Olive, to entrap an ever more resistant marquis, offer light relief to Ibsen's more solemn tone. Unlike Nora, Alice finds personal liberation in a congenial marriage that enables her to fulfill her professional aspirations. His heroine, Moore claims, is cast "in one of Nature's moulds"; the implication is that Nora is unnatural when she decides to leave her family and live by herself.[43] Indeed, Nora's abandonment of her children was considered not unproblematic by contemporary feminists.[44]

An artist-protagonist's right to unshackle herself from her maternal as well as her marital ties was a conflicted issue in New Woman fiction, not least because the genre also heralded modern women as the mothers of national renovation. Whatever the regenerative power ascribed to women in socio-political terms, however, feminist literature by women on both sides of the Atlantic threw into sharp relief the difficulties faced by individual heroines in their struggle to combine childcare responsibilities with professional, specifically artistic trajectories. Elizabeth Stuart Phelps's American artist-novel *The Story of Avis* (1877) and Charlotte Perkins Gilman's haunting story about madness, "The Yellow Wallpaper" (1892), dramatize the incompatibility of domesticity with artistic production. Mona Caird's *The Daughters of Danaus* (1894) posits family desertion (and, like Moore, invokes exile, here in France) as the precondition for a successful composer's career. The novel's unequivocal indictment of motherhood as a patriarchal bond to be severed scandalized *fin-de-siècle* supporters of feminism like W. T. Stead.[45] Sarah Grand's *Ideala* (1888, the first in her feminist trilogy) was more fortunate in appealing to a wider readership with a moral-purist protagonist who abjures marriage and a sexual life for social rescue work and political authorship. This, however, is precisely what Alice does not want. As a "puritan . . . but not a sexless puritan," Moore takes care to stress, his heroine "represented her sex better than the archetypal hieratic and clouded figure of Nora" and, by inference, other feminist characters of the time, on the grounds that, "if women cannot win their freedom without leaving their sex behind they had better remain slaves, for a slave with his sex is better than a free eunuch."[46] *A Drama in Muslin* thus offers, Judith Mitchell argues, a "modified," male-oriented version of feminism.[47] Alice is explicitly dissociated from feminist activists (particularly of the social purist kind, as embodied in the sexually repressed and dysfunctional Cecilia) who, afflicted with "physical defect" and outraged by "the abasement of their sex . . . forget the immutability of the laws of life, and with virulent virtue and protest condemn love . . . and proclaim a higher mission for women than to be the mother of men."[48] Here, then, Moore performed the virtuoso act of liberating his heroine from the social law that "a woman can do nothing without a husband"[49] and depicting her gradual evolution into selfhood, independence, and an artistic voice of her own from within a conceptual discourse that insisted on the biological inevitability of her urge for marriage and motherhood.

The maternal ethic Alice comes to embrace is arguably a broad-minded, intellectually productive, and responsible model and as such is placed in stark contrast to the failing system represented by the older generation of mothers in the novel. Thus Mrs. Gould remains blissfully ignorant of her daughter May's near-ruin; Mrs. Scully has never given a moment's thought to instilling a sense of accountability in her son, to May's detriment; above all, Mrs. Barton has made a career of pleasing men and therefore can only conceive of her daughters as goods for barter, with disastrous consequences for Olive (who at the end of the novel has faded into a depressed hysteric). Rather than acknowledge Alice's quiet industry, Mrs. Barton responds to her love of books with vehement disapproval. In her eyes, "reading and moping"—the two being coterminous—will make her daughter "fit for nothing."[50] Above all, it will disable her for her primary function in life, marriage: "Don't waste your time thinking of your books, your painting, your accomplishments; if you were Jane Austens, George Eliots, and Rosa Bonheurs, it would be of no use if you weren't married. A husband is better than talent, better even than fortune . . ."[51]

With the sole purpose of finding suitable quarry for her daughters (Olive's love interest, Captain Hibbard, is sacrificed to the ambition of capturing a title), Mrs. Barton takes them to Dublin. There, Alice meets Harding, a Moore look-alike,[52] writer and journalist, the first person to share her religious, political, and social views. Harding takes her seriously and their conversations open up new ideas about literature and life: "His fearless speech was what the sea-wind and the blue and white aspects of a distant mountain range are to the convict. Her life seemed suddenly to have grown larger, clearer; she felt as if the breathing of the dawn were on her face."[53] Inevitably, given Alice's cerebral disposition, Harding is a dual object of desire: the "light, freedom, and instruction" of the mentor combine with the "intellectual sensualism"[54] of the man, making his company as irresistible as balls, dancing, and flirtation are to her friends. Discussing books and, later, writing them thus becomes a mental substitute for courtship. It is Harding, not her own impetus, that steers her toward writing as a vocation. Now at last Alice sees herself entrusted with "a duty to perform . . . an occupation to which [she] can turn with pleasure,"[55] the very purpose she had so despaired of discovering. Harding even predicts a dazzling future for her: "you'll be writing novels one of these days in Kensington, I wouldn't mind betting."[56] Though he "spoke with a view to effect" rather than with inner conviction (Alice is aware that "Harding was not quite sincere"),[57] his words present her with the possibility of an alternative, self-determined career.

It is significant for Moore's portrait that, unlike New Woman artist figures such as the composer Hadria in Caird's *Daughters of Danaus*, or the musical performer Angelica and the writer Beth in Grand's *The Heavenly Twins* (1893) and *The Beth Book* (1897) respectively, Alice is not propelled by an overpowering impulse to give expression to herself and her vision (the mark of the "true" artist), but is motivated by intellectual purpose. Her writing is not inspirational so much as aspirational; it is informed by her "clear, concise intelligence"[58] and the need to do something with her life. With Harding's guidance, she succeeds in gaining an income. While Moore's avatar of the male writer displays a degree of condescension toward the emerging woman intellectual and popular author, the older male mentor figure was a plot device also employed in female-authored New Woman novels. In Grand's *The Heavenly Twins*, the physician Dr. Galbraith acts in this capacity (before reinventing himself as Evadne's second husband), and Caird's Professor Fortescue and Monsieur Jouffroy provide emotional and professional support in *The Daughters of Danaus*, urging the protagonist to follow her career, whereas—as in *A Drama in Muslin*—it is older, male-identified women, above all mothers, who seek to impose traditional and stifling lifestyles on resisting daughters.

Alice's literary trajectory of self-liberation begins with autobiography. Her first book draft, *The Diary of a Plain Girl—Notes and Sensations*, carries echoes of *Jane Eyre* and also anticipates the New Woman writers, who would often veil personalized accounts with generalist titles (examples of third-person fictionalized autobiographies that reflect on the authors' experiences are Ella Hepworth Dixon's *Story of a Modern Woman* and Edith Johnstone's *A Sunless Heart*, both published in 1894). As Kimberley Reynolds and Nicola Humble have argued, Victorian female authors of fictionalized autobiography demonstrated considerable courage in exposing themselves and their unorthodox views to public scrutiny: "this use of fiction makes a political statement about the role of women in Victorian society and the ways in which that society regarded attempts by women to construct independent identities as subversive."[59] The emphasis on "sensations" in Alice's title also draws attention to the importance of tackling the emotional fallout resulting from the clash between personal imperatives and social expectations. Reynolds and Humble note that these "fictionalised autobiographies are . . . works of healing, restoration and shared experience."[60] The benefit the auto-biographical genre afforded women was thus twofold: while the author, in the act of writing, experienced a cathartic process that helped to restore her confidence in herself, her readers were likely to identify with the heroine and feel relief on recognizing the thoughts, frustrations, and longings of the pro-tagonist as their own. In New Woman autobiography this further served to encourage female readers to sympathize with the protagonist's rebellion and endorse feminist demands for wider social change.[61]

In another parallel with New Woman protagonists (like Hepworth Dix-on's Mary Erle) whom material conditions impel to abandon "high" art for the economic benefits of the marketplace, Alice sets her autobiographical novel aside in order to concentrate on generating revenue from shorter writ-ings, stories and newspaper articles. This retraces Moore's own steps when, faced with the mismanagement of his Irish estate and the loss of his rents, he had to fall back on journalistic work. In contradistinction to Moore's experi-ence, however, Alice is not troubled by any concern for the literary merit of her writing, and instead prides herself exclusively on her ability as a woman to earn a living: "Joy bubbled in her brain. To know that she could do something, that she would not prove a drag, a hindrance upon the wheel of life, was an effervescent delight."[62] Her newfound economic independence saves May from certain ruin when, having discovered her advanced stage of pregnancy, Alice is able through relentless hack work, ironically of the senti-mental kind ("penny journal fiction of true love and unending happiness"),[63] to fund her prolonged stay away from home during and after confinement. Alice's surrender of higher aesthetic ambitions for commercial considera-tions reflects the juxtaposition" of "woman of genius" and "woman of Grub Street" that Penny Boumelha has identified as constitutive of late-Victorian representations of the woman artist in the works of male and female (includ-ing New Woman) writers.[64] The toll that Alice's feverish activity takes on her health is further evocative of the New Woman *Künstlerroman* in which, as Lyn Pykett points out, the protagonist is "[t]ypically . . . engaged in a complex negotiation of various forms of self-sacrifice" by means of which "authenticity in art" is associated with suffering.[65] Alice's trajectory thus resembles a secular female pilgrim's progress through adversity toward pur-ification.

Crucially, Alice also undergoes a course in vocational training. The experience of working under intense pressure to meet tight deadlines has the effect of professionalizing her writing practice. Moore projects a measure of his own journalistic discipline onto his heroine's apprenticeship. Moreover, in having Alice establish her workspace in a corner of the sitting room she shares with her sister and enabling her to reach the public and draw an income from her writing, he offers an outlook significantly different from Virginia Woolf's famous later dictum, in *A Room of One's Own* (1929), that "a woman must have money and a room of her own if she is to write fiction."[66] Alice has neither and nonetheless develops into a published author, whereas her indolent and bombastic father has an entire studio to himself and yet fails to bring anything to completion, and her grandfather "had spent fifty years in his study, imagining himself a Gibbon, and writing unpublishable history and biography."[67] More important even than physical space, Moore implies, is the inner space Alice carves out for herself in the parental home. As Fabienne Gaspari points out, this is a moral rather than a geographical site of emancipation and independence.[68]

Extending the concept of spatial autonomy within the constraints of family life, Moore sends Alice on a journey abroad, as a consequence of which she attains greater personal and professional maturity, thus anticipating the novel's conclusion that Ireland's oppressive atmosphere obstructs the development of the rational and imaginative faculties and therefore that a writer must choose exile.[69] What Paris did for Moore, a trip to Europe accomplishes for Alice: it brings a sense of liberation and introduces her to new social and artistic outlooks that directly benefit her work:

> she had picked up ideas of the variety of life, and now with these ideas germinating in her, a time of quiet, a time for reading and thinking, came after the noise of casinos and the glitter of fireworks as a welcome change. The liberty she had enjoyed, the sense it had brought with it that she was neither a doll nor a victim, had rendered her singularly happy. The plot of a new story was singing in her head, the characters flitted before her eyes.[70]

No longer haunted by the idea of her failing femininity or the futility of her life, Alice works steadily at her writing and, with the professional's eye to new material, finds inspiration in personal impressions and experiences. Her ultimate success appears unequivocal: once she has come into her own and acquired a public voice, she also gains emotional contentment with the physician Edward Reed. Their marriage brings to fruition her early vision of the "ideal couple, journeying with a firm step through life" in shared companionship.[71]

In rewarding Alice with a congenial working partnership—Reed is an author in his own right, though of a scientific work, and supportive of her writing career—Moore's novel conveys the same message that mid-Victorian women writers like Charlotte Brontë and Elizabeth Barrett Browning embedded in their feminist blueprints of female liberation, *Jane Eyre* and *Aurora Leigh*: that if women are only determined enough to place their self-development above conventional gender expectations and even above their immediate emotional longings, they will ultimately achieve both public and private fulfillment, while those who follow traditional paths risk failure on all counts. Alice's sister is a case in point: a feeble imitation of her male-centered mother, albeit without the latter's personality, intelligence, and drive, Olive is a vain and silly girl bereft of backbone, who falls victim to Mrs. Barton's over-ambitious schemes and ends up with impaired health, frazzled looks, and no husband.[72] In *A Drama in Muslin*, Moore thus invokes an earlier feminist script, whereas *fin-de-siècle* New Woman writers, intent on challenging the romance and marriage plot, favored what Tess Cosslett calls a "woman-alone ending"[73] (Grand's *Ideala*, Hepworth Dixon's *The Story of a Modern Woman*) or dramatized the failure of protagonists who endeavored to combine marriage, motherhood, and a career (Caird's *The Daughters of Danaus*, Phelps's *Story of Avis*). As Schreiner put it, "In the ideal condition for which we look men and women will walk close, hand in hand, but now the fight has . . . to be fought out alone by both."[74] In contrast, by the end of Moore's novel, Alice appears to have it all. Harding's prediction has come true, and we see a thriving writer in a comfortable London suburb surrounded by her family and in possession not only of a study, but also of a literary salon of her own.

And yet Moore's narrator strains to contain the scorn in his depiction of Alice's achievements. There is first her neighborhood, revealed in all its bourgeois primness and "homely vulgarity":[75]

> Each house has a pair of trim stone pillars, the crude green of the Venetian blind jars the cultured eye, and even the tender green of the foliage . . . seems as cheap and as common as if it had been bought—as everything else is in Ashbourne Crescent—at the Stores. . . . [T]here is neither Dissent nor Radicalism, but general aversion to all considerations which might disturb belief in all the routine of existence. . . . To some this air of dull well-to-do-ness may seem as intolerable, as obscene in its way as the look of melancholy silliness which the Dubliners and their dirty city wear so intermittently. . . . Ashbourne Crescent, with its bright brass knockers, its white-capped maidservant, and spotless oilcloths, . . . is certainly . . . in all its cheapness and vulgarity, more than anything else representative . . . of . . . typical England. Neither ideas nor much lucidity will be found there, but much belief in the wisdom shown in the present ordering of things, and much plain sense and much honesty of purpose. Certainly if your quest be for hectic emotion and passionate impulses you would do well to turn your steps aside, you will not find them in Ashbourne Crescent; there life flows monotonously . . . but it is built upon a basis of honest materialism . . .[76]

Even if the passage carries on by assuring us that "No. 31 differs a little from the rest of the houses,"[77] the damning impression that is conveyed of the overriding traditionalism, priggish atmosphere, commercialist spirit, lack of originality and refinement, monotony, and banality of the locale does not augur well for Alice's artistic development. How did a couple united in their sympathy for Irish nationalism and sympathetic to the underdog (their last act before departing from Ireland was to pay the rent arrears of a peasant family in the process of being evicted) choose as uninspiring a locality as this, one so contrary to "the cultured eye" of the author-narrator and, by implication, his reader? The reference to Dublin is significant, since throughout the novel the woman question is conceptualized in analogy with the Irish question (in one particularly telling scene, Mrs. Barton is shown dismissing Captain Hibbard with the vague promise of a later review of his suit, while her husband negotiates rent payments with the villagers).[78] Alice may have left Ireland behind, but traces of its conservative mindset remain ingrained in her psyche. She is, Moore writes in his preface to *Muslin*, "a creature of conventions and prejudices, not her mother's but her own."[79] Ultimately the reader is left wondering whether "honest materialism," "plain sense" and "much honesty of purpose" can make up for the absence of a more sophisticated, intellectually and aesthetically refined environment.

Moore's rhetorical strategy of dealing out faint praise in a tone of high-cultural condescension continues in the description of the Reeds' home, whose "interior is as orderly, commonplace and clean as we might expect at every house in the crescent," thus countering the earlier promise of difference.[80] There is the same "irreproachable" air of middle-class prosperity tempered with prudent materialism, as indicated in the second-hand origins of a mahogany table.[81] The dining room is "rigid and bare,"[82] if adorned with respectable classical and contemporary paintings—albeit those one would be unlikely to find in Moore's home. As George Hughes points out, the Victorian Academician William Powell Frith is "not quite the taste of the man who introduced Monet, Degas, and Renoir to the English public"[83] (and indeed, in *Modern Painting* [1897], Moore was to launch an attack on the Royal Academy as "a mere commercial enterprise protected and subventioned by Government").[84] Alice's study, however, offers a brighter and artistically more enlightened outlook, as represented by her reading, where Romantic and Victorian poetry (Shelley, Keats, and Browning, gifts from her husband) is complemented by art criticism (Walter Pater, much admired by Moore) and *fin-de-siècle* decadence (Swinburne and yellow-backed French novels).[85] These "traces of new artistic impulses," reflected also in decorative pottery by William Morris and Pre-Raphaelite engravings by Burne-Jones, lift the otherwise "essentially provincial" ambience.[86] And yet, even as he praises her achievements, the narrator casts doubt over Alice's qualities as an artist:

> Her mind being simple, logical, direct—so unblinded by sidelights that it often
> touched, if it did not merge in, the commonplace—found, without difficulty,
> words that were at least the appropriate equivalents of the thoughts she wished
> to express: not being possessed of that supreme power of seeing more than one
> aspect of her subject, which is genius, her execution was facile and sure as the
> conception was moderate and well balanced. Her choice of subject was always
> healthy and practical, and she wrote . . . unfalteringly: her work as it unfolded
> itself was an image of the writer's own integrity and good sense. And if her
> writings excited neither nervous surprise nor any subtle emotion, they did not
> provoke contempt by stupidity or vulgarity.[87]

In an exemplary piece of discursive ambiguity, Moore condemns the artist
for the very virtues for which he commends the woman: Alice's "integrity"
and "good sense" (a mirror image of her home) save her from the pitfalls of
either insipidity or geniality.

Anne Higonnet and Penny Boumelha have drawn attention to the gendered definition of genius in the nineteenth century, a concept that was
exclusively reserved for men. Edmond and Jules de Goncourt quipped that
"t[h]ere are no women of genius; the women of genius are all men."[88] In its
female incarnation, genius was closely associated with sexlessness at best,
and abnormality at worst: "idiocy, convulsions, dementia, and criminality."[89]
The former is exemplified in Moore's *Modern Painting* chapter on "Sex in
Art" with the dismissal of George Eliot as an artist "in whom sex seems to
have hesitated."[90] Alice's happy marriage and the narrator's reference to her
"well-balanced" mind protect her against the charge of sexlessness while
firmly confining her talent to the "commonplace." Hers is the realm of the
"simple" and "facile," not the aesthetic. We never witness her expressing any
anxiety about or labor over the quality of her work, suffering indecision or
even writer's block, revising and fine-tuning her style the way Moore did.
Instead, her pen always appears to "ru[n] on without a perceptible pause.
Words come to her easily."[91] It is her very ease of writing that disqualifies
her from the category of the "true" artist. As Moore proclaims in "Sex in
Art," the female artist's "nature is more facile and fluent than man's. Women
do things more easily than men, but they do not penetrate below the surface."[92] Alice thus represents the typical woman artist as Moore envisages
her, who is accomplished in what she does within the limits of her sex, and
whose strength is not to be found in any genuine originality of approach,
stylistic experimentation, or "the peculiarity or the keenness of her vision,"[93]
but, rather, in her "extraordinary powers of assimilation":[94] hence, Harding's
importance as a catalyst. Ultimately, "the artistic question troubled her little."[95] In other words, Alice may enjoy professional success as a middlebrow
author whose works speak to a wide (presumably predominantly female)
audience, but a literary writer of great merit she is not.

In a further twist to his intensely conflicted representation, Moore depicts a woman professional who, in contradistinction to a plethora of artist-heroines in feminist New Woman fiction, does not fall victim to domestic constraints but continues to devote herself to her writing even after her marriage and the birth of her son. She follows a rigorous work schedule, from which her family responsibilities do not distract her. Her career runs parallel to and is supported by that of other women writers, providing a sense of the literary community of New Women that was, at the time, in the process of formation: "Every Thursday afternoon numbers of ladies, all of whom write novels, assemble here to drink tea and talk of their work."[96] Here, Moore portrays Alice and other women engaged in the kind of exchange enjoyed by male writers, invoking the get-togethers he hosted himself in Dublin and London, while at the same time implying that Alice's salon is an extension of the feminine "At Home."

By emphasizing that a woman could develop her career with no detriment to her identity as wife and mother, Moore challenged traditionalist as well as feminist tenets that held either that any woman aspiring to a professional life of her own betrayed her biological destiny,[97] or that marriage killed the artist (a view to which Moore subscribed in his personal artistic practice). Alice is depicted as achieving a balance between being a writer and spending private time with her son (who is otherwise looked after by a nursery-maid):

> It is now eleven o'clock in the morning. Alice enters her drawing-room. You see her: a tall, spare woman with kind eyes, who carries her arms stiffly. She has just finished her housekeeping, she puts down her basket of keys, and with all the beautiful movement of the young mother she takes up the crawling mass of white frock, kisses her son and settles his blue sash. And when she has talked to him for a few minutes she rings the bell for nurse: then she sits down to write.[98]

Moore's portrait of the professional woman writer as a homemaker who is as proficient in household management as she is affectionate toward her son has a markedly programmatic and even mechanical edge (Alice's "stiff" body posture shifting into movement carries echoes of Miss Skiffins's initially "wooden appearance" and sudden animation in *Great Expectations*).[99] Significantly, however, this passage mimics the representational politics of the contemporary woman writer's interview. Moore's adaptation of this model introduces important modifications that account for the impression of semi-automatism created in his depiction of the way in which Alice discharges her domestic responsibilities before settling down to her writing, which is accorded the greatest share in her day's work. Where Moore calls attention to Alice's happy family life as boost rather than obstruction to her focus on her career, real-life women writers often sought to soften and diminish their professional persona. Helen C. Black's interview of Helen Mathers (author of *Comin' thro' the Rye*, 1875) in *Notable Women Authors of the Day* (1893) is particularly striking in this respect.[100] The popular novelist is introduced in terms that highlight her intense femininity within the context of masculine settings and traditional furnishing styles that have been transformed by her influence. In entering, Mathers "seems to bring [a] . . . sense of the fitness of things. She carries a big basket of China tea-roses" and is dressed in a flowing "white cashmire and silk tea-gown"[101] evocative of a Whistler paint-ing.[102] More prominently than Alice's self-made middle-class home, Math-ers's ancestral estate marries patrilinear grandeur with aesthetic opulence, with the hall displaying coats of arms alongside "great velvet shields of china and brasses on . . . gold leather walls, and quaint old oak chairs, cabinets, and [a] high old-fashioned clock."[103] Where Alice draws inspiration from the Arts and Crafts movement, Mathers stamps a distinctly female monumental-ism onto the masculine spaces of her home. A "very old cathedral glass partition" opens on a room dominated by a sepia portrait of the author, and in the "banqueting hall" a "vast" looking-glass is framed by "colossal winged female figures" that "reflected . . . the caryatides who . . . hold up the massive carvings above the door."[104] While references to her decorative style serve to highlight her "refined and artistic taste,"[105] in her self-construction as "a lady author at home," Mathers appears determined to dilute the threat posed by the career woman by accentuating a femininity marked by a singular feeble-ness of purpose, with the result that her agency as a writer is neutralized. Her diminution to mere muse and vessel, a conduit for text that passes through her almost without volition, is reflected in the effortlessness of her writing. Like Alice's, Mathers's compositional speed is "very rapid": "my ideas seem to run out of my pen."[106] Another parallel is Mathers's husband, Henry Reeves, an orthopedic surgeon who, like Alice's Dr. Reed, has authored scientific books and supports her career. But here the similarities between the two women end. Mathers is at great pains to downplay her authorial identity: "Often, just as I have settled down to do a good morning's work, and have perhaps finished a page, . . . my boy Phil rushes up . . . or my husband brings in some little commission . . . and often [the story] is not touched again for a week."[107] For all the sumptuousness of her surroundings, she has "no writ-ing-room and no particular table. Indeed, I can't say . . . how my books get written."[108] That the interview culminates in a Wilde-inflected anecdote about a parcel containing several novel manuscripts being left behind in a cab[109] confers the status of an amateur on Mathers. Moore, by contrast, is intent on authenticating his protagonist as a professional writer who is seri-ous about and dedicated to her work.

In presenting an affirmative image of a woman who is both a successful writer *and* a fulfilled mother, Moore deconstructs gender stereotypes in the manner of Schreiner's *From Man to Man* (published posthumously in 1926), whose central protagonist Rebekah is a rare example in New Woman fiction of an artist able to draw inspiration from taking care of a large family. Similarly, in her 1898 article on "The New Woman and the Old," Grand features a busy New Woman hastening not away from but back to her home "to put my baby to bed, and get my husband's tea."[110] Like these New Woman writers, Moore contested conservative attitudes in society that held literary women in suspicion and considered their professional aspirations a danger to the well-being of the family. In its challenge to Victorian gender norms, *A Drama in Muslin* explores a holistic vision that presents contemporary readers with an early version of successful New Womanhood: to rephrase Barrett Browning's mid-Victorian portrait of the artist as a young woman, Alice Barton, at the end of her fictional *Bildung*, is "woman and female artist, both complete."[111]

The gender qualification is significant here. For while constructing a positive portrait of a young woman professional who rebels against the religious, political, and social constraints that atrophy nineteenth-century Ireland, Moore evidently struggled with the concept of the female artist as artist rather than as professional author. In his entire oeuvre there are only two "genuine" women artists, the opera singer Evelyn Innes (the titular heroine of his 1898 novel) and the actress Rose Massey (a minor character in *Vain Fortune*, 1891). Their professions represent the realm of the "inferior" arts in which, as he concedes in "Sex in Art," women were able to excel because the performative nature of these arts facilitated self-expression. Both Evelyn and Rose channel their femininity, passion, and sexuality into their work and thus create authentic art, as Moore saw it.[112] In *A Drama in Muslin*, Alice achieves all of her aspirations, realizes her full potential (the conclusion being conceived as "a fulfilment of the beginning"),[113] and is never unduly concerned about her artistic shortcomings. She is Moore's answer to the "poor muslin martyrs" condemned to waste their lives in pointless self-abasement, but she is not the "worthy predecessor for Joyce's Dedalus" that Alexander Gonzalez sees in her.[114]

While engaging with the themes of the emerging genre of New Woman fiction and moving beyond many feminist works of the time by granting his heroine an even share of personal and professional success, Moore's "discourse of repudiation" signals his conflicted response to the contemporary woman writer in his reluctance to recognize her claim to equal status as an artist. Yet even as he disavowed women's ability to attain the lofty heights of masculine art, by holding their professional achievements up for praise Moore struck out on a course different from those of his fellow male authors who, as Boumelha notes, associated women's writing "with trash: with commerce, with the values of the marketplace" and therefore also with cynicism and vulgarity.[115] Alice is no Lady Carbury, the hack writer of Anthony Trollope's *The Way We Live Now* (1875) who dashes off poorly researched historical novels to nourish the tastes of a popular readership but "would have written a volume of sermons" if it stood a chance of generating sales; in her supreme pragmatism, "[s]he had no ambition to write a good book, but was painfully anxious to write a book that the critics should say was good."[116] Nor is Alice in any danger of producing the crude and tasteless fare, set in exotic locations, that Henry James parodies in his Ouida/Corelli-inflected "Greville Fane" (1893), whose eponymous *romancière*, for all her delusion of "resembl[ing] Balzac," "could invent stories by the yard, but . . . couldn't write a page of English."[117] In both cases, the protagonist's incompetence as a writer is coupled with her failure as a mother: each woman breeds a monstrous progeny who threatens her very survival (indeed, Greville Fane's son is cast as a quasi-vampiric predator who even after his mother's death still feeds on her textual remains). The target of James's and Trollope's satirical images of sexual and literary malfunction, the romance writer is also subjected to attack in *Literature at Nurse*; but here Moore includes an equal number of male and female writers. It is not so much the author as the reader of "light literature"[118]—the "British Matron," the provincial "lad[y] in the country," and the commercial intermediary between reader and author, the tradesman-librarian with his "motherly" stranglehold—who is feminized and held to account for the decline of the erstwhile "virile" tradition of English literature.[119] As discussed in Jane Jordan and Katherine Mullin's chapters, this is a battle about realism in art, and Alice is a realist, not a sentimentalist. The conflation of masculinity, realism, and art in James and Trollope is rendered more complex in Moore's work, which acknowledges the contribution women can make to literature, if only they lead rounded, (hetero)sexually grounded lives and accept the constraints their sex places on their artistic powers. *A Drama in Muslin* presents us with an authentic writer figure genuinely committed to and good at her work, whose greatest distinction as a woman and a professional is her ability to derive satisfaction from her feminine artisanship without being unduly concerned about her limitations, and who harbors no desire to contest the superior qualities of the male artist. Perhaps the reason why the walls in Alice's home pay tribute to male painters rather than a portrait of herself and why we do not find the monumental mirror or display of statuesque matriarchal authority that mark out Helen Mathers's creative space is that Alice herself assumes the role of a looking-glass vis-à-vis the male narrator. The portrait of the artist as a young woman thus ultimately turns out to be a self-reflection on the artistic achievements of "George Moore."

NOTES

1. George Moore, "Defensio Pro Scriptis Meis," *Time*, March 1887, 278. See also A. Norman Jeffares, "A Drama in Muslin," in *George Moore's Mind and Art*, ed. Graham Owens (Edinburgh: Oliver and Boyd, 1968), 5. Jeffares's reference to "young girl's book" is to

Moore's "*Mon roman sur les jeunes filles*" in his letter to Jacques Emile Blanche [October 4, 1885], see Robert Stephen Becker, ed., "The Letters of George Moore, 1863–1901," 5 vols (PhD diss., University of Reading, January 1980), 1: 311. Moore started to gather material for *A Drama in Muslin* in January 1884, during his unsuccessful courtship of Maud Browne, with whom he attended the Castle Ball in Dublin described in Book 2 chapter 4 (see Adrian Frazier, *George Moore, 1852–1933* [New Haven: Yale University Press, 2000], 103).

2. George Moore, *Literature at Nurse, or Circulating Morals* (London: Vizetelly, 1885), 21. For further discussion of Moore's denunciation of the censorship of the circulating libraries see Jane Jordan's and Katherine Mullin's chapters in this volume (chapters 4 and 5).

3. The Gaelic League was not formed until 1893, and the Irish Literary Theatre, in which Moore was to take a prominent if typically provocative part, was founded in 1898.

4. See Moore's 1915 "Preface" to the revised version of his novel, *Muslin*, Uniform edition (London: William Heinemann, 1936), viii.

5. George Moore, *A Drama in Muslin: A Realistic Novel*, introduction by A. Norman Jeffares (1886; Gerrards Cross: Colin Smythe, 1981, reprinted 1993), 196.

6. That Moore did not adjust his portrait when he revised the novel at a much later stage suggests that his attitude towards "women's writing" remained in place.

7. See chapter 1 of Elizabeth Grubgeld's *George Moore and the Autogenous Self: The Autobiography and Fiction* (Syracuse: Syracuse University Press, 1994), 1–35. Grubgeld focuses on how this rhetoric shapes Moore's response to Ireland in *A Drama in Muslin* and *Parnell and His Island* (1887) but also notes the former novel's ambivalent and condescending representation of Alice's artistic endeavors.

8. Ibid., 3.

9. See the following passage about the landlord class, which could with equal force be applied to the novel's surplus community of spinsters: "they saw themselves deprived of their only means of existence. . . . [N]ow they saw that which they had taken to be eternal, vanishing from them even as a vapour. An entire race, a whole caste, saw themselves driven out of their soft, warm couches of idleness, and forced into the struggle for life. The prospect appalled them. . . .What could they do with their empty brains? What could they do with their feeble hands?" (Moore, *Drama in Muslin*, 95).

10. The Bartons have no wealth of their own and Olive is the younger daughter, but Mrs. Barton cajoles her lover of twenty years' standing, Lord Dungory, to settle £20,000 on Olive to force the hand of an impoverished marquis.

11. He further notes that Moore excluded any references to the Ladies' Land League, and both Cecilia and Mrs. Lawler are marginalized. Brendan Fleming, "Re-Gendering the Nation: Representations of Ireland and the Figure of the New Woman in George Moore's *A Drama in Muslin* and George Meredith's *Diana of the Crossways*," *Bells: Barcelona English Language and Literature Studies* 11 (2000): 44, 46.

12. Mona Caird, "A Defence of the 'Wild Women,'" *The Morality of Marriage and Other Essays on the Status and Destiny of Woman* (London: George Redway, 1897), 171. Caird's essay was originally published in the *Nineteenth Century* 31 (1892): 811–829.

13. Moore, *Drama in Muslin*, 13.

14. As Moore asserted, "Newman could not write at all"; "a man of weak intellect cannot write a fine style." George Moore, *Salve*, vol. 2 of *Hail and Farewell*, Uniform edition (1933; London: Heinemann, 1947), 181, 185.

15. Moore, *Drama in Muslin*, 33, 83, 99.

16. Ibid., 98–99; Elizabeth Barrett Browning, *Aurora Leigh* (1856; London: Women's Press, 1993), 1, l.305.

17. Ibid., 5, l.487–488, 498.

18. Moore, *Drama in Muslin*, 132 (emphasis in original).

19. Moore, *Drama in Muslin*, 100.

20. Ibid., 178, 67.

21. Ibid., 66. For Moore's reading habits see *Confessions of a Young Man*, ed. Susan Dick (Montreal: McGill University Press, 1972), 53.

22. Ibid., 229. A "metaphysician," Hartman "attempted to provide an ontological rationale for . . . historical realism" in the second half of the nineteenth century; see Robert J. Rubanow-

ice, *Crisis in Consciousness: The Thought of Ernst Troeltsch* (Tallahassee, FL: University Presses of Florida, 1982), 75.

23. Eduard von Hartmann, *Philosophy of the Unconscious: Speculative Results According to the Inductive Method of Physical Science*, trans. William Chatterton Coupland (1869; London: Routledge, 2003), 270, 345.

24. See the eponymous heroes of *Mike Fletcher* (1889) and "John Norton" (*Celibates*, 1895).

25. Moore, *Drama in Muslin*, 229.

26. Ibid., 228.

27. Ibid., 68.

28. Ibid., 87.

29. See Catherine Smith, "'A Nice Little Covey of Love Birds': Animal Imagery and Female Representation in *A Drama in Muslin*," in *George Moore: Artistic Visions and Literary Worlds*, ed. Mary Pierse (Newcastle: Cambridge Scholars Press, 2006), 197.

30. Moore, *Drama in Muslin*, 229.

31. Ibid., 101.

32. Ibid., 98.

33. The overpowering inner need Alice feels for a purpose in life is also articulated by Mildred Lawson in the first (1888) version of Moore's novella (*Lady's Pictorial*). The later adaptation for *Celibates* (1895) is discussed by Nathalie Saudo-Welby in the next chapter. See "Mildred Lawson," *Lady's Pictorial*, February 18 to March 17, 1888, reprinted in *The Collected Short Stories of George Moore: Gender and Genre*, ed. Ann Heilmann and Mark Llewellyn, 5 vols (London: Pickering and Chatto, 2007), 1: 265–300.

34. Florence Nightingale, "Cassandra," in *Cassandra and Other Selections from Suggestions for Thought*, ed. Mary Poovey (London: Pickering and Chatto, 1991), 208. The text was written in the early 1850s and published privately in *Suggestions for Thought* in 1860; see "Chronology of Florence Nightingale's Life," ibid., xxxi.

35. Grubgeld, *George Moore and the Autogenous Self*, 10.

36. Frazier, *George Moore*, 126.

37. Olive Schreiner, *The Story of an African Farm* (1883; London: Virago, 1989), 172.

38. Moore, *Drama in Muslin*, 260.

39. For an account of the "breathless . . . excitement" with which the play was received see Edith Lees, "Olive Schreiner and her Relation to the Woman Movement" (1915), in *Olive Schreiner*, ed. Cherry Clayton (Johannesburg: McGraw-Hill, 1983), 46.

40. Moore, "Preface" to 1915 edition of *Muslin*, ix. In a letter to his mother, Mary Blake Moore, of February 17, 1884, Moore expressed his indignation about "the horrible system of terrorism" to which young middle-class Irish women at marriageable age were subjected: "The poor girls [*sic*] life is one of those unknown tragedies . . . in which the history of nations is written in as much as in the chronicles of battles and conquests"; Becker, "The Letters of George Moore," 1: 214.

41. The "author's design," Moore wrote in his preface to *Muslin*, "was a comedy" (x).

42. As Moore wrote to his mother [January 1884], life in this Dublin hotel exceeded the powers of the imagination: "if I introduce it [the Shelbourne] into my girl novel . . . I shall fail to describe it. The scenes that pass here defy description. . . . Marriage is of course the ruling topic of conversation. . . . I think that I shall this time knock *l'ecole sentimentale* head over heels"; Becker, "The Letters of George Moore," 1: 240.

43. Moore also castigates Ibsen for creating an implausible heroine, whose abrupt change from a sensual to an educational outlook enabled him to "thunder out a given theme" ("Preface," *Muslin*, ix).

44. For details, see Sheila Stowell, *A Stage of Their Own: Feminist Playwrights of the Suffrage Era* (Manchester: Manchester University Press, 1992), 33–34.

45. W. T. Stead, "The Novel of the Modern Woman," *Review of Reviews* 10 (1894): 66–67, reprinted in *The Late-Victorian Marriage Question: A Collection of Key New Woman Texts*, ed. Ann Heilmann, 5 vols. (Bristol: Routledge Thoemmes, 1998), 5.

46. Moore, "Preface," *Muslin*, x.

47. Judith Mitchell, "*A Drama in Muslin*: George Moore's Victorian Novel," *English Literature in Transition* 25, no. 4 (1982): 221. Mitchell's comparison with Grant Allen is too damning on Moore, however. Author of *The Woman Who Did* (1895), a bestselling novel about a (pseudo-)feminist who becomes a martyr to her ideas, Allen embraced feminism as a rhetorical strategy in order to lecture female readers about their maternal duties; see his "Plain Words on the Woman Question," *Popular Science Monthly* (1889): 170–181, reprinted in Heilmann, *The Late-Victorian Marriage Question*, 5.

48. Moore, *Drama in Muslin*, 196.

49. Ibid., 58.

50. Ibid., 132.

51. Ibid., 137.

52. As Grubgeld notes, however, Harding is not conceived as Moore's *alter ego*: he is "not a simple figure of wish-fulfilment or self-justification; rather, he is held up to prosecution and judgment" (*George Moore and the Autogenous Self*, 17).

53. Moore, *Drama in Muslin*, 151.

54. Ibid., 196.

55. Ibid., 180.

56. Ibid., 198.

57. Ibid., 197.

58. Ibid., 187.

59. Kimberley Reynolds and Nicola Humble, *Victorian Heroines: Representations of Femininity in Nineteenth-Century Literature and Art* (London: Harvester Wheatsheaf, 1993), 148.

60. Ibid., 148–149.

61. For details of New Woman autobiography see Ann Heilmann, *New Woman Fiction: Women Writing First-Wave Feminism* (Basingstoke: Palgrave Macmillan, 2000), 71–76.

62. Moore, *Drama in Muslin*, 233.

63. Ibid., 260.

64. Penny Boumelha, "The Woman of Genius and the Woman of Grub Street: Figures of the Female Writer in British *Fin-de-Siècle* Fiction," *English Literature in Transition* 40, no. 2 (1997): 164–180.

65. Lyn Pykett, "Portraits of the Artist as a Young Woman: Representations of the Female Artist in the New Woman Fiction of the 1890s," in *Victorian Women Writers and the Woman Question*, ed. Nicola Diane Thompson (Cambridge: Cambridge University Press, 1999), 142, 146.

66. Virginia Woolf, *A Room of One's Own* (1929; London: Hogarth Press, 1931), 6.

67. Moore, *Drama in Muslin*, 38.

68. Fabienne Gaspari, "More than Dramas of Sterility: Portraits of the Artist in Moore's Fiction," in Pierse, *George Moore*, 21.

69. Interestingly, as Fleming has suggested, Alice may be modeled on the Irish romantic writer Margaret Hungerford, who did not opt for emigration. Fleming argues that Moore adapted Hungerford's story "Ugly Barrington" for his play, staged as "The Honeymoon in Eclipse" in April 1888. Brendan Fleming, "*Mrs Gardiner. A Comedy in One Act* (1888): A Play by George Moore," *English Literature in Transition* 48, no. 3 (2005): 259–260, 263.

70. Moore, *Drama in Muslin*, 270.

71. Ibid., 101.

72. The contrast between the sisters' emotional trajectories is hinted at in Moore's choice of the same first name for their love objects (Edward).

73. Tess Cosslett, *Woman to Woman: Female Friendship in Victorian Fiction* (Atlantic Highlands: Humanities Press International, 1988), 138.

74. Olive Schreiner to Havelock Ellis, April 8, 1884, in *The Letters of Olive Schreiner 1876–1920*, ed. S. C. Cronwright-Schreiner (London: T. Fisher Unwin, 1924), 15.

75. Moore, *Drama in Muslin*, 324.

76. Ibid., 325–326.

77. Ibid., 326.

78. Richard Allen Cave argues that Moore adapted his technique of themed parallelism from Flaubert's *Madame Bovary*; see *A Study of the Novels of George Moore* (Gerrards Cross: Colin Smythe, 1978), 56.

79. Moore, "Preface," *Muslin*, x.

80. Moore, *Drama in Muslin*, 326.

81. Ibid., 326.

82. Ibid., 326.

83. George Hughes, "Writer and Artist in George Moore's *A Drama in Muslin*," *Barcelona English Language and Literature Studies* 11 (2000): 138.

84. George Moore, "Our Academicians," *Modern Painting* (London: Walter Scott, 1897), 99. The chapter is based on two articles published in the *Fortnightly Review* in June 1892; see Edwin Gilcher, ed., *A Bibliography of George Moore* (Dekalb, IL: Northern Illinois University Press, 1970), 39.

85. Moore, *Drama in Muslin*, 327.

86. Ibid.

87. Ibid., 223.

88. Quoted in Havelock Ellis, *Man and Woman: A Study of Human Secondary Sexual Characters*, 6th edn. (London: A. and C. Black, 1930), 488; see also Boumelha, "The Woman of Genius and the Woman of Grub Street," 168.

89. Boumelha, "The Woman of Genius and the Woman of Grub Street," 173; see also Anne Higonnet, "Las mujeres y las imágenes: Apariencia, tiempo libre y subsistencia," in *Historia de las mujeres* (*Storia delle Donne*), ed. George Duby and Michelle Perrot (1990; Madrid: Taurus ediciones, 1993), 276.

90. One of the few women artists to escape Moore's censure, as Anna Gruetzner Robins indicates in chapter 2, was Berthe Morisot. Moore, "Sex in Art," *Modern Painting*, 227. The article was first published in the *Speaker* on June 18 and 25, 1892; see Gilcher, *Bibliography*, 40. Its title evokes Henry Maudsley's notorious *Fortnightly Review* article of 1874, "Sex in Mind and in Education," a repudiation of women's claim to higher education.

91. Moore, *Drama in Muslin*, 328.

92. Moore, "Sex in Art," 226.

93. Moore, *Drama in Muslin*, 233.

94. Moore, "Sex in Art," 232. Ironically, of course, as noted in this volume's introduction, Moore prided himself on his own aptitude for assimilation vis-à-vis artistic friends and movements.

95. Moore, *Drama in Muslin*, 233.

96. Ibid., 327.

97. Higonnet, "Las mujeres y las imagines," 276–278.

98. Moore, *Drama in Muslin*, 327–328.

99. Charles Dickens, *Great Expectations*, ed. Janice Carlisle (Boston: Bedford Books of St Martin's Press, 1996), 275.

100. See also Pykett, "Portraits of the artist as a young woman," 143, and Margaret Diane Stetz, "New Grub Street and the Woman Writer of the 1890s," in *Transforming Genres: New Approaches to British Fiction of the 1890s*, ed. Nikki Lee Manos and Meri-Jane Rochelson (New York: St. Martin's Press, 1994), 28–30. For the "self-crafting" of the later Victorian woman professional, see the essays in Kyriaki Hadjiafxendi and Patricia Zakreski's *Crafting the Woman Professional in the Long Nineteenth Century: Artistry and Industry in Britain* (Farnham: Ashgate, 2013). For the wider context see Linda Peterson's *Becoming a Woman of Letters: Myths of Authorship and Facts of the Victorian Market* (Princeton: Princeton University Press, 2009).

101. Helen C. Black, "Helen Mathers (Mrs. Reeves)," *Notable Women Authors of the Day* (1893; Brighton: Victorian Secrets, 2011), 83. Black's interviews, first published in the *Lady's Pictorial* in 1890–1891 (Troy J. Bassett, "Preface," ibid., 6), postdate *A Drama in Muslin*. While the similarities in the representation of Mathers and Alice are therefore coincidental, Moore evidently drew on the feminine tropes that female interviewers and authors alike sought to reinforce in their endeavor to pre-empt charges of unwomanliness. For women writers' expert manipulation of their periodical press image, see the examples of Marie Corelli and

Sarah Grand: Annette Federico, *Idol of Suburbia: Marie Corelli and Late-Victorian Literary Culture* (Charlottesville: University Press of Virginia, 2000), 14–52, and Ann Heilmann, *New Woman Strategies: Sarah Grand, Olive Schreiner, Mona Caird* (Manchester: Manchester University Press, 2004), 13–26.

102. See James McNeill Whistler, *Symphony in White, No. 1: The White Girl* (1862). The tea roses with their hint of Orientalism are also reminiscent of *The Princess from the Land of Porcelain* (1863–65) later exhibited in the Peacock Room, now in Washington's Freer Gallery of Art, www.asia.si.edu/exhibitions/current/peacockRoom/pano.asp (accessed March 18, 2014).

103. Black, "Helen Mathers," 84.

104. Ibid.

105. Ibid., 83.

106. Ibid., 86.

107. Ibid., 86.

108. Ibid.

109. Ibid., 89–90.

110. Sarah Grand, "The New Woman and the Old," *Lady's Realm* (1898), 466, reprinted in Heilmann, *The Late-Victorian Marriage Question*, 2.

111. Barrett Browning, *Aurora Leigh*, Book 2, 1.4–5 (the original quotation reads: "Woman and artist—either incomplete, / Both credulous of completion").

112. Moore, "Sex in Art," 229, 235.

113. Moore, "Preface," *Muslin*, x.

114. Moore, *Drama in Muslin*, 329; Alexander G. Gonzalez, "Paralysis and Exile in George Moore's *A Drama in Muslin*," *Colby Library Quarterly* 20, no. 3 (Sept. 1984): 152.

115. Boumelha, "The Woman of Genius and the Woman of Grub Street," 177.

116. Anthony Trollope, *The Way We Live Now* (1875; Ware: Wordsworth Classics, 1995), 677, 14.

117. Henry James, "Greville Fane" (1893), in *Henry James: Complete Stories 1892–1898*, ed. David Bromwich and John Hollander (New York: Library of America, 1996), 220–221. See also Boumelha, "The Woman of Genius and the Woman of Grub Street," 167.

118. Ibid., 233.

119. Moore, *Literature at Nurse*, 16, 3, 18.

Chapter Seven

"Not fitted for marriage"

"Mildred Lawson" and the New Woman

Nathalie Saudo-Welby

Mildred Lawson, the heroine of George Moore's eponymous *Celibates* story of 1895,[1] is a woman of many flaws, but as a literary character she has one great quality: she is very much alive. Her voice rings true. One reason for this is that the 1895 version of the text grew out of Moore's doomed affair with American heiress Pearl Craigie.[2] Mildred is also the product of many literary influences. Given that Moore was a great admirer and reader of Balzac (as explored more fully by Adrian Frazier in chapter 1), Mildred owes something to Sylvie and Denis Rogron, the destructive siblings in *Pierrette* (1840).[3] The unpleasantness of "Mildred Lawson" led some critics, such as that of the *Bookman*, to argue that it was a clinical study in the style of Zola or the Goncourts, "a book that tortures every sensitive mind, that wounds, and keeps the wounds open for scrutiny."[4] Moore's contemporaries were quick to find in Mildred's coldness and her fierce belief in chastity a form of frigidity denoting mental degeneracy. Mildred constantly analyzes herself and is particularly conscious of what she calls her instincts, but clinical terms are almost entirely absent from the novella. If Moore is indeed "do[ing] the Zola act,"[5] as a critic put it in *Harper's Weekly*, he does so without letting narrative commentaries predominate. The analysis is done from within the story.

Mildred also resembles the heroine of a pessimistic "novel with a purpose" reflecting the difficulty modern women had adjusting to their time.[6] Her failed attempts at painting recall the artist protagonist in Ella Hepworth Dixon's *Story of a Modern Woman* (1894). The caricature is so cruel that there seems to be a purpose behind it. Yet, once readers overcome their emotional response to the heroine's repulsive personality, their reaction to the story is likely to resemble the doubt and wonder expressed by Moore's contemporaries. "Mildred Lawson" reads like a "novel[la] with a purpose" without a purpose. In its unstable use of a recognizable contemporary genre, the text reflects the ambiguity of the central character.

The difficulty of how to read "Mildred Lawson" was noted as a puzzle by reviewers. A critic of the *New York Times* wrote in 1895:

> Here are three queer stories by the author of *Esther Waters*, the reading of which suggests a number of questions. For instance: Why did the publishers accept these things, which are certainly not nice, and seem to have no serious purpose whatever? *Esther Waters* was not a pleasing book, but was at least a truthful one, which seemed to have a sound moral purpose underlying it.
>
> It was useful, too, in defining a position for Mr. Moore in the literary world. He was exhibited clearly as a stern moralist using the naturalistic novel as his medium of expression. But now Mr. Moore seems to have abandoned that position, and he leaves us in a worse state of doubt in regard to his forte than we were before . . . in *Celibates* we do not know how to take him. It cannot be that these are further essays in the naturalistic style, and that Mr. Moore really believes he is telling the honest truth about humanity. If he does, we fear he has made a sad mistake, for he will not even convince the most credulous reader. [7]

Even though the storyline and themes of "Mildred Lawson" closely correspond to the formulae of contemporary problem novels on the marriage question, no critic called Mildred a "New Woman," and neither this nor related terms (such as "womanly" or "feminine") appear in the story. Many New Woman novels were wordy and almost all of them served a didactic purpose, which was fully explored by the narrator or the heroine in the course of the text. Mildred is frequently argumentative and "vocal," like a New Woman, but it is impossible to gather a feminist message from the novella as a whole. "Mildred Lawson" thus partakes of several genres and clearly subverts the codes of New Woman fiction, a genre which was fully established by 1894.

As the story opens, Mildred is in open rebellion against her brother Harold and her fiancé Alfred. In their conversations, the two men appear conservative, and life in Sutton is so dreary that the reader is encouraged to side with Mildred. But toward the close of the text, Mildred openly admits to herself that her mentor, Mrs. Fargus, a recognizable type in New Woman fiction, "had said enough to make her understand that it were possible to rebel against marriage; and that in proclaiming antipathy to marriage, she would win admiration, and would in a measure distinguish herself." [8] The meaning of Mrs. Fargus's speech on marriage is thus subverted by Mildred, who focuses not so much on the message as on the effect the attitude expressed would produce in others.

Mildred initially claims that she would "like to see more of [her] own sex," have a female companion, and go to Girton because women are more stimulating, but when given the choice of a studio in Paris, she opts for the men's (despite the fact that the fees are higher) on the grounds that, as she puts it, "there are cleverer pupils there than in the ladies' studio."[9] Similarly, while she desires independence and freedom, she cannot imagine her life in Paris without a chaperon. She is incapable of overcoming her psychological dependence on the admiration and gaze of others. While most New Women are intent on changing the order of things by becoming agents of their destiny, Mildred remains locked in the feminine paradigm of appearances. She can only conceive of the women around her as rivals. Her financial independence is illusory, for she never manages to complete a single painting, let alone sell one. She is unwilling to marry, on the face of it because "At Oxford they say that marriage is not the only mission for women—that is to say, for some women."[10] She is also reluctant to give herself sexually, another feature familiar to readers of New Woman fiction. But while in Grand's *The Heavenly Twins* (1893) Evadne withholds herself from her previously profligate officer-husband to protect herself and her children against potential syphilitic infection (a precaution her friend Edith fails to take, to the detriment of her health), Mildred's choice of celibacy and chastity seems to reside in a mental obstacle, as in the case of Thomas Hardy's Sue Bridehead (*Jude the Obscure*, 1895), with whom she has much in common. Yet when she looks at herself in the mirror, she perceives herself as "a dainty morsel," something to be admired and consumed by men.[11] The image we see in the mirror is that of a woman who is anything but a feminist.

Finally, New Woman novels generally ended badly, betraying their antifeminist stance by proving either the absurdity of the New Woman's cause or the fact that the social conditions were not yet ready for her advent and the realization of her convictions. Lyndall, the heroine of the first New Woman novel, Olive Schreiner's *The Story of an African Farm* (1883), dies in misery as a result of her disastrous theories. We have to wait until 1909 for H. G. Wells's *Ann Veronica* for a New Woman to live happily hereafter—albeit in the shelter of a patriarchal marriage. The heartless pessimism of Moore's inconclusive ending, leaving Mildred seemingly reconciled to marriage and suburban life, can best be appreciated in light of Balzac's commentary on his own ending of *Pierrette* in the preface to his novel: "*si Rogron se marie, il ne faut pas prendre son mariage comme un dénouement, il reste Rogron, il n'a pas longtemps à vivre, le mariage le tue.*"[12] [Rogron gets married, but this should not be taken as a resolution. He remains Rogron and marriage will kill him.] Moore's open ending leaves the question of Mildred's marriage in suspense and marks a departure from the conventions of romance as much as from New Woman fiction.

Courted by and flirting with several men, Mildred is torn between her desire to be a modern woman and her feminine training, which predestines her for marriage. Middle-class women were brought up to turn men's heads, but they were never told how to select a congenial spouse, except money-wise. Mildred has come to consider her chastity as "a safeguard,"[13] the limit she must not cross unless she brings down her value on the marriage market. She is unable to complete her artistic education, not so much because she lacks talent, as because she lets herself be distracted by men. Yet Mildred is not free to choose her future husband. Her brother objected to her first love, Alfred, on financial grounds, but Alfred ends up proposing to her at the end of the novel for his own monetary reasons. As Mildred turns down one lover after another, the cruelty and coldness she can perceive in herself might therefore be the result of culture rather than nature. Her personal fight against marriage has no effect in averting what appears to be her inescapable fate: "After all her striving she found herself back at the point whence she had started; she had accomplished the circle of life, or nearly so. To fulfil the circle she had to marry."[14] By concluding just before the point where traditional novels end and many New Woman novels start, Moore implies that a solution to the marriage question might reside in a girl's education rather than in the nature of her marriage contract.

Another original feature of Moore's treatment of the New Woman theme is focalization. New Woman novels generally have an omniscient narrator; short stories tend to let a woman's own voice be heard. Moore's use of internal focalization resembles George Egerton's in her collections of short stories *Keynotes* (1893) and *Discords* (1895), where frame narratives allow the central heroines to express their thoughts to friendly women. Many fictional New Women are skilled public speakers, but Egerton's and Moore's New Women are private speakers. The omniscient narrator of "Mildred Lawson" is so discrete as to be almost absent. In his introduction to the fifth volume of *The Collected Short Stories of George Moore*, Mark Llewellyn writes of "Henrietta Marr" (*In Single Strictness*, 1922), the final version of "Mildred Lawson" later reproduced in *Celibate Lives* (1927): "Like sketches of a moment rather than minute accounts of a life, Moore's narratives are not really about condemnation or criticism of the individual under the reader's eye; rather, they are about understanding and interpretation. Moore is the teller of the tale but not to the extent that he prescribes our reading of it."[15] This can also be applied to a reading of "Mildred Lawson." The unobtrusive narrator shows the characters in conversations and situations that are for the reader to judge, and the story mainly consists of a mixture of dialogues and internal monologue, with descriptive narratorial passages leading to free in-direct style. The reader is never given an omniscient view of the characters. We are not told what to think of them. This effect can be found to a greater degree in "Henrietta Marr" because the suppression of all of the quotation marks in the dialogues has the effect of blurring point of view. This narrative organization comes very close to stream-of-consciousness technique, allowing us to feel the contradictions inherent in Henrietta's and Mildred's characters. Mildred is pitilessly shown to expose herself as a flirt who passes as a New Woman to protect and advance her own interests. She is vaguely aware of her dual nature, but the reader often gains better insight into her than she does into herself. She constantly plays a part, but she also has difficulty accounting for what she experiences mentally and physically.

Mildred is the archetypal liar, [16] uncharacteristic of New Women, who are known for their outspokenness to the point of bluntness. Herminia, Grant Allen's eponymous heroine of *The Woman Who Did* (1895), is a great believer in "the truth." [17] Schreiner's *Story of an African Farm* contains an embedded story that tells an allegory about the Bird of Truth: a metaphor for the search for knowledge on which the protagonist embarks on his solitary journey through life. Far from worshipping truth, Mildred breaks all her promises and engagements, says one thing and does another. Our appreciation of Mildred is made more complex by the fact that she always acts a part and never expresses what she thinks, even to herself. When the unobtrusive narrator draws back and moves into free indirect representation of thought, Mildred is shown lying to herself by staging a sort of melodrama for her own sake:

> Then the desire to weep overcame her, and, so as to be able to surrender herself wholly to grief and tears, she took off her gown and released herself of her stays. She put on an old wrapper and threw herself upon the floor. She threw herself over to this side and that; when she got to her feet her pocket-handkerchief was soaked, and she stood perplexed, and a little ashamed of this display of grief. For she was quite conscious of its seeming artificiality. Yet it was all quite real to her, only not quite as real as she would have had it be. She had wept for herself and not for him! But no, it was not so; she had wept for them both. And she had taken off her gown, not because she was afraid of spoiling it, no such thought had crossed her brain; she did not care if she spoilt her dress or fifty dresses like it; no, it was not on account of the dress, but because she felt that she could find a fuller expression of grief in a loose wrapper than in a tight dress. That was the truth, she could not help things if they did seem a little incongruous. It was not her fault, she was quite sincere, though her grief to a third person might seem a little artificial. [18]

By the time Mildred has finished justifying herself, the reader is wholly unconvinced by her line of reasoning, and in fact, the more she seeks to defend herself against potential accusations, the guiltier she sounds. In this long passage, the third-person omniscient narration gradually shifts into free indirect speech, thus creating a realistic representation of bad faith in process. The thought Mildred denies being guilty of ("not because she was afraid of spoiling it") is more fully developed than the others, and she further betrays herself in her use of the verb "seem." Her mind is engaging in a dialogue with those who observe her. Given that Mildred is alone, to whom could things "seem a little incongruous?" Far from finding her attitude incongruous, we are confirmed in our initial impression that Mildred is play-acting; that she constantly imagines herself under the gaze of others. Thus, when her brother visits her in Paris, she instantly recognizes an "excellent opportunity for acting" and, "determined to act up" to the situation, she "compos[es] her most demure air," "improvising the words of her part."[19] The narrator comments that "Mildred was only happy when she could get outside herself."[20] Mildred's taste for striking poses becomes an opportunity for Moore to problematize the performances in which the characters engage.

Besides getting outside herself when acting out a part, Mildred also realizes that her thoughts are not truly hers. She often imagines herself as she would like others to see her. When Moore writes, "But in the morning she was, as she put it herself, better able to see things from a man's point of view,"[21] the irony lies in the fact that Mildred has always excelled at seeing herself with a man's eyes, but she does not perceive this as a limitation. Ideas that might compromise her[22] are attributed to unwanted external influences, as if she were "the victim of a wandering thought."[23] Her inner dialogue reflects a sense of estrangement: "'Few women have inspired such a love as that . . . If it were known—if'—she pushed the thought angrily aside as one might a piece of furniture over which one has stumbled in the dark. It was shocking that thoughts should come uncalled for, and such thoughts! the very opposite of what she really felt."[24] Mildred's consciousness is spatialized, turned into a dark room where she cannot find her way, and where thoughts arrive unbidden. The narrative structure of the novella brings us close to a heroine who (pretends that she) does not know herself. Mildred ultimately appears unreliable but this judgment is not imposed upon us, in contradistinction to Balzac's descriptions of the Rogrons.[25] Since Mildred is never judged for what she really is, the part of us that is familiar with unwanted thoughts can sympathize with her. Her selfishness, cruelty, and coldness are damning features, but she is redeemed by her awareness of those faults, and by her realization that her feelings are at odds with what she should be experiencing. Either Mildred has the physical signs of sadness but is pursued by incongruously selfish thoughts, or she is sad in mind but her body gives no indication of it. This contradictory state can be observed in the carefully slow passage that follows: "How sad it all was. But she did feel sorry for him, she really was sorry, though she wasn't overcome with grief."[26] The use of "but" and of the superfluous "did" implies that her sadness is not authentic. The reinforcing sentence that follows confirms that her sorrow is not truly felt and also suggests that she is fully aware of that fact. The last clause of the quoted passage shows that her thoughts are at odds with her feelings.

Mildred's experience of dissociation extends to the domain of language. Not only is she prey to strange thoughts, but she also carries in her mind words that belong to the world of the New Woman novels that she inhabits. Such is the case with the word "instinct," a keyword of biosocial discourse of the time.[27] Instinct drives women away from unfit men and toward worthy lovers. Instinct tells a woman to give herself sexually against common prejudice. In *Esther Waters*, the word "instinct" is used by the narrative voice, commenting on Esther from a naturalist perspective. In "Mildred Lawson," almost all thirteen occurrences of the word can be attributed to Mildred herself, who conveniently formulates her motives in terms of the instincts that speak to her.[28] This is clearly apparent in the following passage: "The desire to see her dead lover was an instinct."[29] Significantly, desire comes first and instinct second. The voice that Mildred mistakes for her instinct is sometimes that of respectability and at other times that of vindication, as on the last page of the text: "Why cannot I live in natural instinct?"[30] Mildred uses the tautological expression "natural instinct" because the instincts that have governed her life are nothing but half-formulated desires.

The expression "not fitted for marriage" is another interesting case of the subversion of the expected use of language in the context of New Woman novels. References to fitness are part of the eugenic message frequently found in such fiction. The expression "not fitted for marriage" was part of the rhetoric of the New Women who evaluated the potential of their prospective spouses (as in Menie Muriel Dowie's *Gallia* [1895]), or were judged to be unwomanly and incapable of bearing children (as in Arabella Kenealy's *Dr Janet of Harley Street* [1893]), but one would hardly expect a New Woman to pass upon herself a diagnosis of unfitness.[31] Yet this is exactly what Mildred does: "I don't think I shall marry at all. There are other things besides marriage . . . I'm not fitted for marriage. I'm not strong. I don't think I could have children. It would kill me."[32] While the doctor's examination was a stock scene of New Woman fiction, Mildred is made to pass a diagnosis upon herself. Her appreciation of her own unfitness associates the New Woman's reluctance to marry and bear children with contemporary fears that clever women were becoming unable to bear children.

Such reluctance to marry and have children recalls Sylvie Rogron's panic, which turns into ridicule in Balzac's *Pierrette*. Halfway through the novel, Sylvie and her brother both become bent on marrying out of financial interest. Sylvie, who is in her forty-second year, grows hesitant because she is afraid of dying in childbirth and arranges for a friend of hers called Céleste to see a doctor for her, unaware that Céleste is intent on marrying Sylvie's brother so that her children can inherit the Rogron fortune. Hidden in her friend's private bathroom, Sylvie overhears Céleste's manipulative discourse and Monsieur Martener's frightening verdict:

> *"Un accouchement heureux est alors un de ces miracles que Dieu se permet, mais rarement."*

"Et pourquoi?" dit Céleste Habert.
Le médecin répondit par une description pathologique effrayante; il expliqua
comment l'élasticité donnée par la nature dans la jeunesse aux muscles, aux
os, n'existait plus à un certain âge, surtout chez les femmes que leur profes-
sion a rendu sédentaires pendant longtemps, comme Mlle Rogron. . . .

Enfin il résulta de cet entretien, clairement, sérieusement, scientifiquement
et raisonnablement, que, passé quarante ans, une fille vertueuse ne devait pas
trop se marier. Quand M. Martener fut parti, Mlle Céleste Habert trouva Mlle
Rogron verte et jaune, les pupilles dilatées, enfin dans un état effrayant. [33]

["In such a case, a happy delivery is a miracle, which God sometimes allows,
although rarely."
"And why ?" asked Céleste Habert.
The doctor then delivered a frightening pathological account, explaining
how the flexibility that nature gives to muscles and bones no longer exists at a
mature age, especially in women whose occupation has made them sedentary,
like Mlle Rogron. . . . What came out of this interview, in a clear, scientific and
reasonable sense, was that a virgin over forty ought not really to get married.
When M. Martener left, Mlle Céleste Habert found Mlle Rogron green and
yellow in the face, her eyes wide open, in a frightening state, in fact.]

The nastiness of Balzac's characters (with the sole exception of Pierrette and
her lover) is only matched by Balzac's own cruelty toward them. Unwilling
to write a novel as long as "that wonderful poem called Clarissa Harlowe,"[34]
Balzac explains that he has chosen not to depict in every detail the vile
calculations of his characters, preferring to insert a commentary on the base-
ness of the human heart or an ironical sign of authorial presence into his text
(like in "*pas* trop *se marier,*" literally not to get "too much" married). What
grew into a small comical episode in Balzac consists in a series of disjointed
allusions in Moore's story, in which Mildred is depicted less cruelly, and in a
style that reflects a modern woman's mixed feelings toward pregnancy.
Moore's early representation of a New Woman in *A Drama in Muslin* (1886)
allowed her to be portrayed as an able mother and writer (see Ann Heilmann
and María Elena Jaime de Pablos's discussion in chapter 6). Mildred, by
contrast, resembles the later, more pessimistic Hadria from Mona Caird's
Daughters of Danaus (1894): marriage and motherhood interfere with her
creative aims, forcing her into exile. Mildred's reasons for not wanting to
marry and bear children are perfectly valid. In her study of Sarah Grand,
Olive Schreiner, and Mona Caird, Ann Heilmann writes that New Woman
writers rarely "create[d] successful female artist figures who are also mothers. . . . Only in dreams and in allegory . . . can [they] conjure up the vision of
a woman who is both a nurturing mother *and* a productive artist."[35] Considering that Mildred excels at self-absorption rather than self-realization, we
come to have doubts about her feminist leanings.

Moore's subversion of the traditional features of New Woman fiction is so systematic that the reader may wonder whether "Mildred Lawson" is not a parody. But, as Mary Pierse has shown, Moore depicted a New Woman with "much credit and humanity" in the character of Mrs. Fargus.[36] Besides, the energy invested in subverting the tradition is less playful than aesthetic, less satirical than experimental. This appears a purposeless text pervaded with aimlessness, failure, and repetition. Mildred is incapable of producing anything approaching a work of art and she is not a source of inspiration for men but a "disintegrating influence."[37] George Du Maurier's novel *Trilby* (1894), which had been a tremendous success the year before "Mildred Lawson" was written, is also a novel about celibates set in bohemian Paris, whose heroine becomes a disintegrating influence on the life of the young genius Little Billy. The omniscient narrator is a merry man who constantly injects his sense of humor and energy into the tale. In Moore's novella, the narrative voice is neutral; it neither participates in the characters' failures, in contradistinction to Flaubert, nor distances itself from them, in contradistinction to Balzac. Its main positive and invigorating element lies in the aestheticization of Mildred's life.

One of the reasons for Mildred's dissociated consciousness is precisely that her existence is largely aestheticized. The product of influences acting on her, she strives to "exist beautifully."[38] Her sensitivity has been warped by artistic works and various other forces, some of which are described as mesmeric.[39] Her aesthetic experiences contribute to the construction of her own persona rather than to the creation of an artistic work. Mildred poses as a New Woman. As a female dandy, her identity is shaped by external factors. Some passages read like a toned-down version of *The Picture of Dorian Gray* (1890), another great novel of celibate lives and the impact that subtle and sometimes poisonous influences, whether intellectual, artistic, moral, or sensory, have on these lives. Like Dorian, Mildred has forged for herself a mask of purity, the object of her narcissistic gaze; and like Wilde's anti-hero, she grows "more and more enamoured of [her] own beauty, more and more interested in the corruption of [her] own soul."[40] A dirty dress makes her feel "quite ill."[41] Recognizing that "her faults at all times had especially interested her," she is "delighted" when she discovers that she is "a cruel woman" and "thrill[s] at the thought that she could make a man so unhappy."[42] Her former lover's grief becomes an intense source of fascination, like Dorian's obsession with Sybil: "His grief was wonderful to witness, and involuntary remarks had escaped her admirably designed to draw it forth, to exhibit it."[43] Similarly, "[l]ying sleepless in his own delicately-scented chamber," Dorian "would think of the ruin he had brought upon his soul, with a pity that was all the more poignant because it was purely selfish."[44] Mildred "wished to feel, she longed for the long ache of regret which she read of in books, she yearned for tears. Tears were a divine solace, grief was beautiful. And all along the streets she continued to woo sorrow."[45] Like the hero of the absorbing yellow book given by Lord Henry to Dorian, she "lov[es] for their mere artificiality those renunciations that men have unwisely called virtue."[46] In the words of Norbert Kohl writing about the dandy, she engages in a "narcissistic flirtation with [her] own depravity."[47]

Having been taught by Ralph that the "artificiality [of trees] is their beauty,"[48] Mildred becomes a perfect artificial type. Her extreme sophistication in dress, her obsession with her appearance, and her relentless efforts to fascinate can easily be attributed to her performance of femininity, but they are also the characteristics of the dandy. Selfish, solipsistic, useless, ornamental and witty, creative yet unproductive, independent and uncommitted, never saying a right thing and never doing a wrong thing, busy with filling up her leisure time, lacking sincerity and constantly playing a part for the effect it will create in observers, Mildred displays many of these characteristics.[49] Critics have noted that the best description of Mildred is the one that she gives herself: "the soul of a courtesan in the body of a virgin."[50] Significantly, this description is inspired by a painting by Greuze[51] that she tries to copy without success. In Wildean style, she copies art and, failing in it, turns art into her life.

While avoiding all kinds of mannerism, Moore's style emulates aestheticism. His use of floral motifs in depicting this "unnatural" woman is again reminiscent of *The Picture of Dorian Gray*. The first lines of Moore's story—"The tall double stocks were breathing heavily in the dark garden; the delicate sweetness of the syringa moved as if on tip-toe towards the windows; but it was the aching smell of lilies that kept Mildred awake"[52]—are strongly evocative of Wilde's novel, where conversation, art, dress, and the fascination theme also take pride of place: "The studio was filled with the rich odour of roses, and when the light summer wind stirred amidst the trees of the garden, there came through the open door the heavy scent of the lilac, or the more delicate perfume of the pink-flowering thorn."[53] In the original version of "Mildred Lawson" published in the *Lady's Pictorial* in 1888, Mildred already relished tending flowers, "mourn[ing] for the beautiful Gloire de Dijon that had only lived a day,"[54] and the syringa is an aesthetic motif developed at strategic moments in Mildred's life.[55]

In her study of dandyism, Ellen Moers makes an interesting connection between the New Woman and the dandy in her section on decadence. Masculinized, the New Woman took on the attributes and cultivated the powers of the dandy: independence, distance, amorality, sophistication, and creativeness. Moers regrets the fact that the New Woman put an end to the dandy's long career and was never able to replace him. In her view the part played by the New Woman is not an honorable one:

A figure which had survived so much succumbed in the *fin de siècle* to the domination of the New Woman—not because she fought against him (she had her own uses for the dandified male) but because she pushed him from the centre of the stage. Without centrality the dandy could only retreat into nostalgia; he languished in the midst of his revival. [56]

Moers observes that novels started being peopled by the counterpart of the New Woman, the kept man, who was very willing to marry in order to be protected by a woman. [57] This could explain what is probably the most unlikely element in "Mildred Lawson": the enthusiasm with which men who might otherwise need to be reminded of marriage by their lovers are willing to marry unpleasant Mildred (Alfred, Ralph, and Morton are all ready to make her their wife or mistress, as she wishes). [58] Moore put a lot of effort into the characterization of Mildred, but his male characters are more loosely sketched and not very distinctive, which is reflected in the names he gave them (Ralph, Harold, and Alfred all sound like variations on a single male figure). Such indistinctiveness is instructive. Moore's men are creative, good, passionate, and incredibly keen to get married; they contrast with the brutish and selfish men of New Woman fiction.

At the time when Moore was writing, the New Woman had a well-defined role in literature and culture that could be impersonated at will [59] and dissociated from her socio-political commitments. By feigning to espouse the cause of the New Woman, Mildred escapes her middle-class fate and constructs an alternative personality for herself. Moore's interest in drama can once more be felt. His aesthetic achievement lies in bringing out the thematic and structural resemblances between the artificiality of the artistic world he depicts, the duplicity in Mildred's mental life, and the cause of the so-called unnatural woman. Mildred thus remains a complex figure, who, despite her tragic condition, often elicits a smile.

NOTES

1. The original text of "Mildred Lawson" was published in *Lady's Pictorial* (February 18, 1888, 156–157; February 25, 1888, 196–197; March 3, 1888, 212; March 10, 1888, 241–242; March 17, 1888, 274–275), reprinted in *Celibates*, ed. Ann Heilmann, *The Collected Short Stories of George Moore*, ed. Ann Heilmann and Mark Llewellyn, 5 vols. (London: Pickering and Chatto, 2007), 1: 265–300. This chapter, however, explores a reading of the 1895 version: George Moore, "Mildred Lawson," *Celibates* (1895), ed. Heilmann, 7–114. All references to "Mildred Lawson" are to this edition.

2. Adrian Frazier, *George Moore, 1852–1933* (New Haven: Yale University Press, 2000), 250–252; Heilmann, "Introduction" to *Celibates*, xxxvi–xliii. The *Lady's Pictorial* version could not possibly have been inspired by Pearl Craigie since Moore met her five years after its publication.

3. In this short novel, later included in the part of *La Comédie Humaine* entitled *Les Célibataires*, Denis and Sylvie adopt their orphaned niece only to turn her into their servant and martyr. The plotline of *Pierrette* is thus closer to that of Moore's story of a young girl in "Agnes Lahens" (the third *Celibates* story), but Mildred's and the Rogrons' psychologies have

much in common. In calling his main character Mildred, Moore might have tried to reproduce the unpleasantness of the name "Rogron" to both French and English ears.

4. "Celibates," *Bookman* 5 (July 1895): 114, in *Celibates*, ed. Heilmann, 221.

5. W[illiam] D[ean] Howells, "Life and Letters," *Harper's Weekly* 39, July 27, 1895, 701, in *Celibates*, ed. Heilmann, 223.

6. "Novel with a purpose" was a term used at the time for problem novels discussing social issues. Such work was often opposed to fiction written "for art's sake." In Sarah Grand's *The Beth Book* (1897), the aesthete Alfred Cayley Pounce tells Beth: "It is hardly likely I shall write a novel with a purpose. I leave that to the ladies." Sarah Grand, *The Beth Book*, ed. Elaine Showalter (New York: Dial, Virago, 1980), 455.

7. "George Moore at his Worst; *Celibates*," *The New York Times*, June 2, 1895, 31.

8. Moore, "Mildred Lawson," 103.

9. Ibid., 11, 31.

10. Ibid., 8.

11. Ibid., 40. The feminist doctor called in to examine Jessamine in Emma Frances Brooke's *A Superfluous Woman* (London: Heinemann, 1894) observes disapprovingly that "she never thought of herself save as a dainty piece of flesh which some great man would buy." (21) Mere femininity was often denigrated in New Woman novels. Thus in Arabella Kenealy's *Dr Janet of Harley Street* (London: Digby, 1893, reprinted in vol. 5 of *Anti-Feminism in the Victorian Novel*, ed. Ann Heilmann [Bristol: Thoemmes Continuum and Edition Synapse, 2004]) the titular protagonist, a female physician, distinguishes between "femininity" and "womanliness," decrying the former and valorizing the latter: "That is just what [contemporary women] are not. . . . [M]any of them, with their slim forms and little heads, are distinctly *feminine*; but feminine is a kind of spurious womanliness, a sort of degeneration which is no more womanliness than feebleness of mind is refinement of brain. . . . How many women nowadays have any of the instincts for home, and wife, and motherhood, which are the crown of their lovely sex? No! believe me, those of us who are not distinctly masculine are feminine, but very few are womanly" (125; emphasis in original).

12. Translation mine. Honoré de Balzac, Préface de la première édition de *Pierrette* (1840), *Les Célibataires* (Paris: Nrf/Gallimard, La Pléiade, 1976), 26, part 4, *Etudes de Moeurs: Scènes de la vie de province*, of *La Comédie Humaine*.

13. Moore, "Mildred Lawson," 91.

14. Ibid., 232–233.

15. Mark Llewellyn, Introduction to George Moore, *In Single Strictness*, ed. Llewellyn, vol. 5 in Heilmann and Llewellyn, *Collected Short Stories*, x.

16. Mildred lies about Ralph's death, suggesting that Ellen poisoned her, while it is she who is the cause of his death; she also pretends that Morton tried to assault her ("Mildred Lawson," 85).

17. As Herminia protests, "I believe in the truth . . . and I'm never afraid of it. I don't think even a lie, or even a suppression can ever be good in the end for any one. The Truth shall make you Free. That one principle in life can guide one through everything." Grant Allen, *The Woman Who Did* (Oxford: Oxford University Press, 1995), 131.

18. Moore, "Mildred Lawson," 110. A similar episode can be found at the beginning of chapter 12 (54).

19. Ibid., 90, 91.

20. Ibid., 90.

21. Ibid., 54.

22. Mildred seeks to absolve herself by saying, "But I don't know why every base thought and calculation enter my head. I don't know why such thoughts should come into my head, I don't know why they do come, I don't call them nor do their promptings affect me." (Ibid., 49.)

23. Ibid., 46.

24. Ibid., 47.

25. "Mildred Lawson" appears more of an independent text than *Pierrette*, whose commentaries often read like general laws about human categories of behavior. Balzac clearly diagnoses Denis's and Sylvie's flaw as a "*défaut d'affection*" (emotional defect) and uses the term

"affection" repeatedly so as to build up a coherent psychological analysis of his human specimens (*Pierrette*, 91).

26. Moore, "Mildred Lawson," 47.

27. Discussion of the New Woman often revolved around the question of her innocence and knowledge, and consequently, around intuitive knowledge and instinct. Anti-feminist literature described modern women as deprived of the "home instinct," "sex instinct," or maternal instinct. When two female mentors try to reclaim Perdita in Eliza Lynn Linton's *The Rebel of the Family* (1880), the reader is informed that she has "the natural woman's instinctive admiration for masculine strength—the loving woman's instinctive glory in acknowledging her own comparative inferiority—and she had the modest maiden's vague desire to love and be beloved. Her nascent maternal instinct was beginning to manifest itself in a greater love for children than heretofore." Reprinted in vol. 1 of *Anti-Feminism in the Victorian Novel*, ed. Ann Heilmann (Bristol: Thoemmes Continuum and Edition Synapse, 2004), 299. New Woman novels often engaged directly or indirectly with the heroine's instincts. In Hardy's 1895 novel *Jude the Obscure* (Oxford: Oxford University Press, 2002), Sue is described as an "ethereal, fine-nerved, sensitive girl, quite unfitted by temperament and instinct to fulfil the conditions of the matrimonial relation with Phillotson, possibly with scarce any man" (210), whereas Jude later asserts that her instincts are healthy and natural. In the last novel of that genre, H. G. Wells's 1909 *Ann Veronica* (London: Dent, Everyman, 1993), Ramage and the eponymous protagonist discuss what is meant by female instincts (136–137).

28. For examples see "Mildred Lawson," 43: "An imperative instinct was drawing her back to England, but another instinct equally strong said: 'As soon as I am rested, nothing shall prevent me from returning to Paris'"; 54, "suddenly she decided that Ralph was not worthy of her. Her instinct had told her from the first that something was wrong. She had never known why she had refused him. Now she knew"; 55, "she had been to see him! She knew that she ought not to have gone. Her instinct had told her not to go."

29. Ibid., 56.

30. Ibid., 114.

31. In George Gissing's *The Unclassed* (1884), Maud Enderby writes to Waymark to release him from his engagement because she has had some "warnings" and is worried about her heredity. George Gissing, *The Unclassed* (New York: Fenno, AMS, 1968), 305–306.

32. Ibid., 14.

33. Translation mine. Balzac, *Pierrette*, 102.

34. Ibid., 101.

35. Ann Heilmann, *New Woman Stategies: Sarah Grand, Olive Schreiner, Mona Caird* (Manchester: Manchester University Press, 2004), 145.

36. Mrs. Fargus "has the much-mocked external appearance of the stereotypical intellectual woman but her actions reflect the solid virtues that were so lauded by the Victorian age. . . . [T]he reader is deftly steered towards questioning convention and attitude." Mary Pierse, "His Father's Son: The Political Inheritance," in *George Moore: Artistic Visions and Literary Worlds*, ed. Mary Pierse (Newcastle: Cambridge Scholars Press, 2006), 108–109.

37. Moore, "Mildred Lawson," 80.

38. Maudle's ideal lifestyle in George Du Maurier's caricature of Oscar Wilde, "Maudle on the choice of a profession," *Punch*, February 12, 1881, reprinted in *The Cambridge Companion to Oscar Wilde*, ed. Peter Raby (Cambridge: Cambridge University Press, 1997), 202.

39. To justify her sexual resistance to Morton's advances, Mildred refers to "mysterious occult influences which she could neither explain nor control [that] were drawing her away from him." (Moore, "Mildred Lawson," 84).

40. Oscar Wilde, *The Picture of Dorian Gray* (New York: Norton, 1988), 99.

41. Moore, "Mildred Lawson," 35.

42. Ibid., 103, 104.

43. Ibid., 104.

44. Wilde, *Dorian Gray*, 99–100.

45. Moore, "Mildred Lawson," 47.

46. Wilde, *Dorian Gray*, 97.

47. Norbert Kohl, *Oscar Wilde: The Works of a Conformist Rebel* (Cambridge: Cambridge University Press, 1989), 217.

48. Moore, "Mildred Lawson," 25.

49. For a discussion of the female dandy, see chapter 3 of Miranda Gill's *Eccentricity & the Cultural Imagination in Nineteenth-Century Paris* (Oxford: Oxford University Press, 2009). The New Woman's dandyhood is explored in anti-feminist New Woman fiction such as Eliza Lynn Linton's *The New Woman: In Haste and at Leisure* (New York: Merriam, 1895).

50. Moore, "Mildred Lawson," 47.

51. In her introduction to *Celibates* Heilmann suggests that the painting could be *The Broken Pitcher* or *The Broken Jug* (xl).

52. Moore, "Mildred Lawson," 7.

53. Wilde, *Dorian Gray*, 7.

54. Moore, chapter 7 of "Mildred Lawson," *Lady's Pictorial*, March 17, 1888, reprinted in *Celibates*, ed. Heilmann, 292.

55. See ibid., 265, 299, 300.

56. Ellen Moers, *The Dandy: Brummell to Beerbohm* (New York: Viking, 1960), 308.

57. Moers notes that "[f]or the amusement and gratification of the New Woman, the best-selling novelists created a new kind of masculine foil which combined the aesthete, the decadent and the dandy. The resulting species was disturbingly rather than gracefully effeminate. More playthings than heroes, these gentlemen are actually 'kept men'" (*The Dandy*, 311).

58. These men are nevertheless fully aware that Mildred would make a bad wife. In "Henrietta Marr," Mildred makes that argument herself: "Besides, you don't want to marry me. If I am as false as you say—your falsehood being my truth and vice versa—you cannot want to marry me. Think what the marriage would be of such an ill-assorted couple." See "Henrietta Marr," in *In Single Strictness*, ed. Llewellyn, vol. 5 of Heilmann and Llewellyn, *Collected Stories*, 156.

59. In 1894, Sidney Grundy's play *The New Woman* exploited the potential of the New Woman figure for drama and comedy. See *The New Woman and Other Emancipated Woman Plays*, ed. Jean Chothia (Oxford: Oxford University Press, 1998), 2–59.

Chapter Eight

Gossip, Art, and the Public Secret

George Moore on his Contemporaries

Elizabeth Grubgeld

Discussing the role of gossip in George Moore's writing could be a disagreeable pursuit, given that when George Moore talked about his contemporaries, he was often disagreeable. Throughout his later essays and in interviews, Moore repeatedly denigrated the efforts of most of his competitors in the realm of fiction: Joseph Conrad, Thomas Hardy, Henry James, Robert Louis Stevenson, and Rudyard Kipling. By the time of *Hail and Farewell* (1911–1914), Moore had also dismissed William Butler Yeats as a poet in decline, although he was by no means alone in this assessment. Neither was he alone in casting his critical eye on the personage of the author as well as on his or her work. Literary criticism at the turn of the century was highly personalist, with evaluation and ranking its preeminent task. That evaluation and ranking frequently derived from a judgment of an author's manners, morals, and even bodily appearance. Like other writers of fiction, Moore transformed his contemporaries into characters but customarily retained so much of the original models that the reader's knowledge of the origins of certain characters played a significant part in the effect of the works in which those characters appeared, as in the case of Yeats as the model for Ulick Deane in *Evelyn Innes* (1898) and its sequel *Sister Teresa* (1901), or of Edward Martyn repeatedly acting as model for the pious and deeply repressed homosexual in *A Mere Accident* (1887), "John Norton" (*Celibates*, 1895), and "Hugh Monfert" (*In Single Strictness*, 1922).

The degree to which Moore traversed the boundaries of biography and fiction was matched by a similar fusion of the genres within his autobiographies. Readers of Moore's many autobiographies recognize as a predominant feature the recounting of memories—reveries, he called them—in an oral style that effectively produces a sensation of intimacy between speaker and reader. Moore confesses to his reader his desires, his lost loves, and his multiple failings as a son, sibling, lover, and friend. This careful development of a discourse of intimacy also allows Moore to use the whispered secrets of gossip. In creating the illusion of intimacy, Moore talks about his contemporaries so as to straddle the boundaries between spoken and written discourse and between private and public speech. By so overtly and extensively fusing orality with textuality and nonfiction with invention, and by voicing private information and public secrets about his contemporaries, Moore not only represents but engages in acts of gossip.

Gossip can make us generically and morally ill at ease, drawing as it does from observation, hearsay, speculation, and invention, much as did the novel when it first emerged in English as a mongrel genre. Also like the early novel, gossip has been further denigrated as a characteristically feminine genre. Practiced by "matronly middle-aged women, chatty maids, little girls, and effeminate fops," gossip is "womanish, low, slavish, servantish, silly, pert, loose, wanton, jiggety, mean."[1] Yet, gossip is also a tool of satire, and, like other great satirists, Moore uses gossip both to create memorable literary characters and to express his most fundamental criticisms and convictions concerning human life. Moore appears most willing to use gossip in writing when depicting persons whose friendship he had left behind, such as W. B. Yeats or Edward Martyn, people whom he never liked to begin with, such as Augusta Gregory, or those against whom he bore some grudge, such as Pearl Craigie. Still, it was one thing to talk, and another to publish hearsay about one's friends and acquaintances. As Moore remarked in a letter to Maud Cunard, "As for the news and gossip, that too is amusing but one cannot often write it . . . ink is an adjuvant which develops a dangerous quality in harmless ingredients."[2] In some cases, ink signed the death warrant on a friendship, while others of Moore's contemporaries, like Oliver Gogarty, for example, understood the game and volleyed back and forth with their own often caustic speculations and revelations. Some—like W. K. Magee, as discussed by Michel Brunet in the next chapter—appear to have escaped unscathed from this game, although there may have been many occasions of spoken gossip of which we are unaware. And although Moore was often able to extract confidences from his partners in conversation, they also dreaded that their words might one day appear in print.[3]

If, in *Hail and Farewell*, the imputations of homosexuality to Ethel Walker and Edward Martyn, transvestism to Hugh Lane, and the role of adulterer to George Russell verge on the explicit, few of the men and women on whose friendship Moore depended during his later years in London drew his attention as a subject of writerly gossip. Moore's reasons for writing little gossip about his London friends may be twofold. His satiric method was sophisticated in its focus on the discrepancies between an idea and its incarnation, aspiration and reality, or what could be said and what was. Gossip thrives on such disjunctions also, depending for its power on a cloak of silence and secrecy around reality until the gossiper makes his privileged revelation of a secret. Although the imprisonment of Oscar Wilde and subsequent persecutions of homosexuals had necessitated caution in the early years of the twentieth century, the private lives of English acquaintances like Max Beerbohm, Aubrey Beardsley, or Robert Ross were neither hidden nor at odds with who they purported to be. Secondly, while others of his English acquaintances would have provided intriguing material for literary gossip, Moore left their secrets alone for reasons that may have been more personal than literary.

Edmund Gosse provides a case in point. An acquaintance of Moore's since 1877 and a source of good dinners and literary conversation since the 1890s, Gosse figures as a dull if dignified interlocutor in *Avowals*, Moore's 1919 venture in "imaginary conversations," and in *Conversations in Ebury Street* five years later. Gosse was long married and apparently happily so, yet as we now know from his correspondence, he battled with an intense passion for other men, and for one man in particular. No definitive evidence confirms that he ever acted on his desires despite, or perhaps because of, his long struggle with what he called in a letter to John Addington Symonds "the wild beast" within him, "this volcanic force, ever on the verge of destructive ebullition."[4] It was Gosse who, as literary executor, severely censored Symonds's posthumously published memoir and effectively obscured what he did not eliminate from Symonds's final defense of homosexual practice. Richard Dellamora calls Gosse "a heterosexual by choice rather than by inclination,"[5] and when one considers the kind of private agony that such a choice entails, we see a far more complex picture than that of the staid pillar of British literary culture that Moore gives us in *Avowals* and *Conversations in Ebury Street*. Perhaps Moore was unaware of this facet of Gosse's inner life, yet his intuition was keen about such matters, and the secret was sufficiently well-known that Lytton Strachey, Rupert Hart-Davis, and Siegfried Sassoon all remarked on it after Gosse's death.[6] Perhaps Moore feared that the kind of gossip he had practiced on other subjects would alienate these men whose companionship and connections he valued and might close avenues to the pleasant meals and the conversation he craved. When Gosse expressed irritation with what he took to be a condescending representation of him in an early draft of *Avowals*, Moore sent three frantic letters of apology over the subsequent forty-eight hours.[7] Although often stubborn and overly sensitive himself, he clearly was willing to go to considerable lengths to avoid offending his friend. With his particular talent at textually realizing the incongruities between the desires of the body and the aspirations of the mind, had Moore built a portrait of Gosse from the same kind of innuendo and hearsay he employed throughout his other portraits, he might have created a figure as rich and compelling as that of *Hail and Farewell*'s "Dear

Edward." That he did not suggests that, in some situations, there were human bonds that might trump even the possibilities of art.

Although as a writer he refrained from exploiting gossip about friends in his later years, were Moore to have done so, he would have likely targeted the repressed sexuality of a man like Gosse. Moore would have understood this as the key to Gosse's character, literature and literary pronouncements, and perhaps even as a significant measure of the tensions within upper-middle-class English Protestant life, just as he offered the shape of Edward Martyn's apparently celibate life, like the shape of his body, as symptomatic of what he believed to be the disease of Irish Catholicism and the weakness of the Irish mind. In Moore's hands, cultural critique, as a function of gossip, tended to center on matters of appetite. The disconnection between what one is thought to be (or even thinks oneself to be) and the secret of what one is generally forms the subject matter of gossip, and these disconnections frequently derive from problems of appetite. Thus, we gossip about uncontrolled spending, eating, drinking, displays of emotion, and uncontrolled behaviors of all kinds, most particularly those sexual in nature. As Michel Foucault argued, now famously, in *The History of Sexuality*, "what is peculiar to modern societies is not that they consigned sex to a shadow existence, but that they dedicated themselves to speaking of it *ad infinitum* as *the* secret." This secret we are "henceforth doomed to always speak about precisely because it is secret."[8] If we are going to inquire as to why gossip figures so prominently in Moore's investigation of the forces that shape personality and, in shaping personality, shape art and national culture, we are necessarily going to discuss this preoccupation with other people's sexual lives and gender identities, as well as with his own. Although Moore may have been reluctant to gossip in print about the friends of his elder years, he was by no means hesitant to do so about his former colleagues in Dublin.

As a morally precarious endeavor, the use of gossip in autobiography requires some consideration of its ethical effects. The character of those effects depends entirely on rhetorical context: who is speaking and who is listening. Read in the twenty-first century, a work like *Hail and Farewell* provides a highly subjective insight into persons such as W. B. Yeats and Augusta Gregory who, being long dead, are immune from its satire and incapable of answering its tales and insinuations—although both made sharp retorts during their lifetimes, and the latter threatened a lawsuit.[9] As Patricia Meyer Spacks remarks, "moral uneasiness may rise to consciousness when one reads published letters or journals . . . if they mention the living; records of the dead feel less troubling. Death fictionalizes everyone."[10] From the standpoint of the present, *Hail and Farewell* is exactly what Moore himself called it: "a novel about real people."[11] Interest in the details of their lives derives less from any additions Moore makes to the historical record than from the insights into complex human behavior afforded by his portraits.

Most readers of *Hail and Farewell* know Maurice Moore, Clara Christian, and even Edward Martyn and George Russell, primarily as literary characters who come to life on the pages of Moore's book. In its own time, however, *Hail and Farewell* was also a speech act: that is, speech that functions as an action or produces an action. *Hail and Farewell* was written by, about, and for living persons to be read by those same living people and by those who knew them, with the understanding that they might well wish to answer back. As I have noted, many did, whether to say that they were untroubled by its gossip or to deliver their own judgments and disseminate their own gossip concerning the man who had rendered them literary characters and put their secrets into print.

Much of the gossip of *Hail and Farewell* goes far beyond the tit-for-tat tales that traveled back and forth between various literary men. One such instance also tells us much about both the limits of Moore's emotional understanding and, at the same time, the extent to which he was dedicated to principles that went beyond even his avowed dedication to art. George Russell, called throughout *Hail and Farewell* by his pseudonym AE, was Moore's friend throughout his Dublin years, but as Adrian Frazier has explained, their friendship cooled after Moore made oblique references in *Hail and Farewell* to Russell's less than satisfactory marriage and long relationship with journalist and poet Susan Mitchell. Mitchell, in turn, satirized Moore mercilessly in her 1916 study of the man and his work.[12] Many of their common acquaintances were aware of the connection between Russell and Mitchell, but no one spoke in public about it and certainly never wrote about it, any more than they wrote about Moore's relations with the painter Clara Christian, who was liked and respected by those who knew her.[13] What does this incident of gossip tell us about how and why Moore engages in such an exposure? What possible effects could be expected from writing about a public secret like the Russell-Mitchell relationship?

A little more than halfway through *Vale*, the last volume of *Hail and Farewell*, Moore begins to turn a penetrating glance toward Russell, who had hitherto been an amiable if excessively idealistic companion in the literary movement from which Moore was becoming increasingly estranged during the period recalled in *Hail and Farewell*'s final volume. AE, Moore tells us, has protested that the portrait given of him is inhuman in its goodness. Moore, he complains, has "represented him in *Ave* and *Salve* as a blameless hero of a young girl's novel": "Why have you found no fault with me? If you wish to create human beings you must discover their faults."[14] The narrator responds to this challenge in the following passage:

> Wherefore I am put to discovering a stain upon his character. I cannot accuse him of theft, and he never speaks of his love affairs; he may be a pure man; be that as it may, it is not for me to cast the first stone at him; lying and black-

mail—of what use to make charges that no one will believe? If he will not sin, why should he object to my white flower in his buttonhole? And feeling that humanity was on the whole very difficult and tiresome, I fell to thinking. . . . But of what I cannot tell; I only know I was awakened suddenly by a memory of a young painter in London, one who brought imagination and wit and epigram and laughter into our midst, and when he left us we rarely failed to ponder on the unmerited good fortune of his wife, for to live with him always seemed to us an unreasonable share of human happiness. But one day I made the acquaintance of this woman whom I had only known faintly during her married life, and heard from her that her husband did not speak to her at dinner, but propped a book up against a glass and read; and after dinner sat in his chair composing, and often went up to bed forgetting to bid her goodnight. If she reproached him, he assured her there was no other woman in the world he loved as much as her; but being a man of genius his mind was away among his works. But what proof have I, she said, that he is a man of genius? Of course, if I were certain, it would be different. . . . All the same, it is a little trying, she added. And her case is the case of every woman who marries a man of genius. A trying tribe, especially at meal-times; ideas and food being apparently irreconcilable. I have often regretted that our good friend did not leave some of his ideas on the landing with his hat and coat, for it is distressing to hear a man say that he could not tell the difference between halibut and turbot when you have just apologized to him for an unaccountable mistake on the part of your cook. This painful incident once happened in Ely Place; and I reflected, duly, that if he were indifferent to my food he might show scant courtesy to the food that his wife provided. [15]

Here, Moore employs a battery of rhetorical skills to drive home his speculations about Russell while retaining the innocent persona of Russell that he has manipulated throughout the book. He has made Russell rather than himself the one who seeks a flaw or "sin" in the representation that appears in *Hail and Farewell*. He then suggests that his friend "*may* [my emphasis] be a pure man," thereby implying that he might not be, while the reference to "casting the first stone" echoes the story from the Gospels concerning adultery and thus narrows the field of implication in the discussion of "purity." Then, using a syntactical construction akin to zeugma, Moore glides almost imperceptibly from the story of a London painter to that of Russell in that interim epithet, "our good friend," which might refer to the London painter or to Russell. Suddenly the London painter has become Russell, and it is Russell then, who thus becomes indifferent to his wife and an artist of uncertain genius.

The narrator next begins to imagine the "man of ideas" at home at 17 Rathgar Avenue (the home of George and Violet Russell), "and saw him picking a little from his plate, and then, becoming forgetful, his eyes would rove into dark corners." [16] Later in the passage, Moore defends him against those who would prefer to picture him "domesticated," bringing "home to a little house in the suburbs a reel of office chit-chat to unwind for his wife's pleasure, the poet on one side of the hearth, the wife on the other, the cat between them. Jane and Minna would listen attentively, but Violet's thoughts would stray. . . ."[17] Unlike Jane Carlyle or Minna Wagner, who attempt to engage their husbands, Violet pays no more attention to Russell in this invented scenario than he paid to her in the prior invented scenario. Moore has chosen his analogy artfully, for there is more comparison than contrast to be had among the three wives. Like Jane and Minna, he implies without saying anything directly, Violet is unloved. The problems of the Carlyle marriage were well known through James A. Froude's biographies, the fourth of which was most explicit in describing Thomas Carlyle's sexual dysfunction and created a scandal when published in 1903. Moore had long been an attentive reader of Carlyle, but in light of the vocal response to Froude's *My Relations with Carlyle* in the press, almost anyone interested in literature would have held the sexual disaster of the Carlyle marriage in fairly recent recall. As for the third wife in this trio, Moore was likely recalling that Minna Wagner's husband carried on a passionate affair with Mathilde Wesendonck, whose correspondence with the composer Moore knew well and considered a model of the love letter. Wesendonck was also an accomplished poet—as was Susan Mitchell. Thus, Violet Russell is both contrasted with the dutiful wife of the genius and paralleled with two women whose husbands were either celibates or adulterers.

All of this subtle insinuation has gone on solely in the speaker's mind. Not so indiscreet as to speak or write such speculations, the narrator has simply thought them. Only a reader who actually knew the persons involved would sense the shock of public disclosure, as the staging of the reverie allows for the dramatic illusion that private matters have remained private, neither written nor spoken about with anyone but the reader, the narrator's most intimate boon companion. Finally, the veil is rent when Moore's friend W. K. Magee, who appears under his pseudonym John Eglinton, drops by Ely Place and engages in a bit of gossip himself, relaying to Moore the information that "somebody had said that AE was an unhappy man." As he leaves, Eglinton admonishes his friend to "be very careful what I said about AE's home life."[18] Having first turned responsibility for the whole exposure over to his subject, who had requested a more humanized characterization, here Moore distances himself from the source of the secret, as well as from its utterance. It is Eglinton who first breaks into speech and repeats to the narrator a story that someone else has related. By this point in the narrative, the stage has been effectively set with painted props of speculation, so that Eglinton's gossip seems immensely plausible. A reasonable degree of plausibility, if not a basis in truth, distinguishes gossip from rumor in the taxonomies of speculative discourse generated by those social scientists who study the phenomenon.[19] The fictional fantasy of the Russells at home that precedes Eglinton's remark establishes enough imaginative plausibility that

Moore's tale has the power of possibility that comes with gossip, instead of the uncertainty that comes with rumor. Although the source of the gossip is many steps away from Moore, he has set the scenario in such a way as to indicate the gossip's truth value. Similarly, the admonition to be careful regarding Russell's home life takes on by context, but only by context, a suspicious tenor. Instead of a reminder to respect the privacy of Russell, or anyone for that matter, the remark allows us to assume that something is indeed rotten on Rathgar Avenue.

The meaning of this gossip also shifts according to its audience. To a modern reader, or even a contemporary who didn't know George Russell particularly well, the story says little more than that he may be, at the least, a bit distracted and, at the most, a bit unhappy. And as a writer, Moore's instincts are correct: the suggestion of some failure of attention or tact as a husband, even the suggestion of unhappiness, adds dimensionality to the blandly pleasant AE we have come to know in *Hail and Farewell*. But to those who are more in the know than the average reader, Moore has uttered a public secret: that Russell has for some time been the companion and lover of Susan Mitchell. He has created a more satisfying literary character, but he has also articulated a public secret about one of his readers. The latter produces a very different effect than the former and serves very different purposes.

The first of these effects—the creation of a better character—is a substantial motive for a writer. Almost every one of Moore's contemporaries, even in the press and those who were pilloried in the text, admired the comic brilliance and strange truthfulness of *Hail and Farewell*. Could the quality of his book have been the sole motive for putting into print the gossip that others uttered only in private? Moore declares it so, and his devotion to art above all else is the abiding dominant theme of his self-description ever since *Confessions of a Young Man* (1888) put to death the wastrel dilettante Landlord M. of *Parnell and His Island*, published in English only a year before. In *Salve*, for instance, the narrator complains to George Russell that Dublin doesn't appreciate the "sacrifice" he is making for art in "throwing everything into the flames" by returning to Ireland:

> You understand, but the others don't, so I'll tell you something that I heard Whistler say years ago. It was in the Old Grosvenor Gallery. . . . Nothing, he said, I suppose, matters to you except your writing. And his words went to the very bottom of my soul, frightening me; and I have asked myself again and again if I were capable of sacrificing brother, sister, mother, fortune, friend, for a work of art. One is near madness when nothing really matters but one's work.[20]

Despite the narrator's moral concern, this is exactly the image Moore assiduously promoted of himself through his essays, his autobiographies, and even conversation. It is integral to his consciously constructed and controlled self-portraiture. And yet again, he was later unwilling to sacrifice his friendship with any of the many English friends whose complicated private lives he might have exposed.[21] It is possible that Moore simply did not understand that revelations concerning Russell's domestic life might be harmful; he once expressed astonishment at the claim that some men practice fidelity to their wives. For his part, Russell seems to have taken it in stride and made efforts to continue the friendship.

But if we put aside for a moment the declared, but not entirely credible, motive of "all for art" and the remote possibility that Moore failed to realize that he had crossed the line, we might consider the question in light of the paradoxical nature of gossip itself. Near the conclusion of *Conversations in Ebury Street* (1930), Moore laments that his theory that Charlotte Brontë plagiarized her sister Anne cannot be published under his own name: "Were I to write it," he says, "it would be looked upon as one of my paradoxes, or a desire to tread upon somebody's corns."[22] Moore's gossip about the Russell-Mitchell affair has elements of both. It arises in part as a concession to the temptation of bedevilment: that is, treading on corns (along with a willful obtuseness about the feelings of neglected wives and the reputations of single women like Susan Mitchell). Moore was also capable of using gossip to wound people, revenge a perceived slight, make himself appear witty and worldly at others' expense, or, as he acknowledges, to tell a good story. But this episode also falls within the realm of paradox, and its rhetoric is characterized by a multiplicity of paradoxical motives and effects.

Among those motives and effects must be counted gossip's regulatory action. Gossip, like satire, often shores up a conservative norm. As the early twentieth-century sociologist Emile Durkheim writes,

> Crime brings together upright consciences and concentrates them. We have only to notice what happens, particularly in a small town, when some moral scandal has just been committed. They stop each other on the street, they visit each other, they seek to come together to talk of the event and to wax indignant in common. . . . If, then, when [crime] is committed, the consciences which it offends do not unite themselves to give mutual evidence of their communion, and recognize that the case is anomalous, they would be permanently unsettled. They must re-enforce themselves by mutual assurances that they are always agreed.[23]

On one hand, people may repeat a story in horrified fascination, but the fascination exploits the act of telling in private as a tool that enforces the mandate of public silence. On the other hand, several recent studies of gossip's role in communities lacking fundamental human rights conclude that gossip may also act as a counter-hegemonic and potentially curative form of speech providing alternatives to authoritarian discourse.[24] Moore's more privileged use of gossip also counters the silence imposed by accepted norms, particularly in the realms of religion and sex. "It would be a sad thing indeed," he wrote to Hildegard Hawthorne in his old age, "if love were limited to the mere act which grocers and their mates perform at midnight in the middle of a four posted."[25] In context, he was simply counseling Hawthorne as to heterosexual practices that would relieve her from the worry of pregnancy, but in a wider sense, this old man's advice speaks to his appreciation of human diversity and his conviction that one must be true to what he called "instinct." Ethel Walker (the Florence of *Hail and Farewell*) might be a lesbian, Hugh Lane a transvestite, and Edward Martyn a homosexual tragically distorted by his inability to live according to his nature, and Moore in turn speaks to that truth with interest, curiosity, even fascination, but without horror.

Yet is doing so justifiable in an ethical sense? In an essay concerning the ethics of writing about others, Claudia Mills has argued that the revelation of certain secrets may be justified, in that "by protecting one person's secret, we contribute to a climate of false shame surrounding that secret. The greater the climate of shame surrounding a secret, the more costly its revelation is to the subject of the secret. But the more some individuals are willing to, or forced to, bear those costs, the less those costs become for future others."[26] As cultural critic Henry Abelove suggests in his analysis of Allen Ginsberg's elegy for New York poet Frank O'Hara—an elegy by one gay American poet for another that describes O'Hara as the "curator of funny emotions" with an ear "for our deep gossip"—gossip can be of great service to those who experience "funny emotions," that is, emotions "likely to be made fun of— mocked, derided, trivialized, even stigmatized." "Gossip," Abelove continues, "is illicit speculation, information, knowledge. It is an indispensable resource for those who are in any sense or measure disempowered, as those who experience funny emotions may be, and it is deep whenever it circulates in subterranean ways and touches on matters hard to grasp and of crucial concern."[27]

It is possible that Moore understood George Russell's relationship with Susan Mitchell as a matter of "funny emotions" as he understood the public secret of homosexuality with Walker, Lane, and Martyn. Much earlier in *Hail and Farewell*, he queries his willingness to "lift the veil" on his cousin Dan's love for a pretty country girl who worked as his housekeeper. The narrator briefly considers the objections of their relatives, "the prejudices of our time being that a man's frailties should not be written about." Dismissing such reservations, he asserts that "It is difficult to understand why a mistress should be looked upon as a frailty . . . Bridget was a pretty girl, and beauty in a woman is all that a man like Dan could be expected to seek. Whoever amongst you has bought an Impressionist picture or a Pre-Raphaelite picture let him first cast a stone."[28] We may well have some qualms about an analogy between homosexuality and adultery, or as in the case of Cousin Dan, cohabitation without marriage. Even Richard Mohr, who has written extensively in defense of the phenomenon of gay "outing," distinguishes between sexual orientation as a matter of public policy and sexual behavior between adults as a private matter. [29] But although Moore knew Russell would be embarrassed, this "outing" of the man with a mistress is consistent with his deepest beliefs in the necessity to live in accordance with one's "nature," with Edward Martyn his book's most devastating example of what happens when one does not.

The conservative nature of gossip may be thus undermined rather than reinforced, but even this reversal of expectation is not the foremost of Moore's paradoxes. The utterance of a public secret breaks a taboo and releases a knowledge whose articulation he appears to see as liberating: why should Dan not have Bridget, or George have Susan, or Hugh Lane his extravagant costumes, or Edward Martyn—at least in his fictional incarnation—find some satisfaction, as in the final ending of the much-revised "Hugh Monfert"? However, at the same time as it liberates a secret, gossip reinscribes the taboo of the secret by marking it as scandalous and drawing much of its electric power from the scandal of exposure. Whether the energy of scandal acts in service to liberatory articulation or to the huddle of gossipers praying the Pharisee's prayer, "I thank God that I am not like other men," depends upon the historical moment in which the utterance is made. Whether the community will close or open its arms to the object of gossip depends on forces far beyond anything within a single speech act, oral or written. Unlike the London of 1895, when the debacle of Oscar Wilde's trials came to its terrible conclusion, Dublin did not respond with fear and loathing to what *Hail and Farewell* implied about anyone's private life. Perhaps Moore sensed that far from driving his subjects to suicide, his malicious but accurate and, in some cases, affectionate insinuations and revelations might draw vitality from the power of a desecrated taboo, while comically, and even gently, assisting the demise of that power.

And lastly, we might consider one final paradox. In his book about secrecy as a tool of political repression, anthropologist Michael Taussig draws upon Walter Benjamin's distinction between *exposures* that *destroy* secrets and *just revelations* that *illuminate* them: "Truth is not a matter of exposure which destroys the secret, but a revelation which does justice to it." Taussig asks whether "defacing" a "public secret" destroys it while simultaneously rendering it more powerful and mysterious, as a ritual unmasking might unleash the magical force of what lies beneath the mask. "Defacement is like Enlightenment," he writes, "It brings insides outside, unearthing knowledge, and revealing mystery. As it does this . . . it may also animate the thing defaced and the mystery revealed may become more mysterious." [30] By defacing that which is private, Moore, who was criticized both fondly and bitterly as being unable to distinguish between public and private, articulated the essential and necessary privacy of human relationships in all of the various desires, failings, accommodations, and mercies they encapsulated.

NOTES

1. Blakey Vermeule, "Gossip and Literary Narrative," *Philosophy and Literature* 30, no. 1 (2006): 102.

2. George Moore to Maud Cunard, October 12, 1898, in *Letters to Lady Cunard, 1895–1933*, ed. Rupert Hart-Davis (London: Rupert Hart-Davis, 1957), 29.

3. For discussion of the responses Moore's real-life models made to both the possibility and the reality of their appearances in *Hail and Farewell* and other texts, see Adrian Frazier, *George Moore: 1852–1933* (New Haven: Yale University Press, 2000), 367–371 and Elizabeth Grubgeld, *George Moore and the Autogenous Self: The Autobiography and Fiction* (Syracuse: Syracuse University Press, 1994), 118–120, 161–173.

4. Edmund Gosse to John Addington Symonds, 1890, in Richard Dellamora, *Masculine Desire* (Chapel Hill: University of North Carolina Press, 1990), 23.

5. Dellamora, *Masculine Desire*, 214.

6. Ann Thwaite, *Edmund Gosse: A Literary Landscape, 1849–1928* (Chicago: University of Chicago Press, 1984), 194.

7. Charles Burkhart, "The Letters of George Moore to Edmund Gosse, W. B. Yeats, R. I. Best, Miss Nancy Cunard, and Mrs. Mary Hutchinson" (PhD diss., University of Maryland, 1959), 132–136.

8. Michel Foucault, *The History of Sexuality*, vol. 1, *An Introduction*, trans. Robert Hurley (New York: Vintage, 1980), 50.

9. Frazier, *George Moore*, 390–391.

10. Patricia Meyer Spacks, *Gossip* (New York: Knopf, 1985), 205.

11. Grubgeld, *Moore and the Autogenous Self*, 97.

12. After the fashion of its time, Susan Mitchell's study, *George Moore* (New York: Dodd, Mead, 1916), is as much about the man as it is about his work. Her satiric, if insightful, portrait infuriated Moore.

13. See Frazier, *George Moore*, 367–368, 558 n. 236.

14. George Moore, *Hail and Farewell*, ed. Richard Cave (Gerrards Cross: Colin Smythe, 1985), 582.

15. Ibid., 582–583.

16. Ibid., 583.

17. Ibid., 584.

18. Ibid., 585.

19. See particularly Glen A. Perice, "Rumors and Politics in Haiti," *Anthropological Quarterly* 70, no. 1 (1997): 1–10; and Nicholas DiFonzo and Prashant Bordia, *Rumor Psychology: Social and Organizational Approaches* (Washington, DC: American Psychological Association, 2007).

20. Moore, *Hail and Farewell*, 269.

21. The discrepancy between Moore's treatment of Russell (and other Irish friends and acquaintances) and his general reticence regarding his English friends is even more striking because, according to Frazier, the exposure of Russell and Mitchell in *Hail and Farewell* was written in October 1913, almost three years after Moore had been settled in London (*George Moore*, 558 n. 234). Frazier notes that the painter William Orpen expressed fears that Moore might expose his homosexuality as Moore had done with Martyn and Lady Gregory's nephew Hugh Lane, but Moore published nothing on the subject (369–370).

22. George Moore, *Conversations in Ebury Street* (London: William Heinemann, 1930), 223.

23. Emile Durkheim, *The Division of Labor in Society*, trans. George Simpson (Glencoe: Free Press, 1960), 102–103.

24. See Perice, "Rumors and Politics in Haiti," and DiFonzo and Bordia, *Rumor Psychology*, as well as Henry Abelove, *Deep Gossip* (Minneapolis: University of Minnesota Press, 2003), and Richard D. Mohr, *Gay Ideas: Outing and Other Controversies* (Boston: Beacon, 1992).

25. George Moore to Hildegard Hawthorne, November 16. 1907, in *George Moore on Parnasssus: Letters (1900–1933) to Secretaries, Publishers, Printers, Agents, Literati, Friends, and Acquaintances*, ed. Helmut E. Gerber, with the assistance of O. M. Brack, Jr. (Newark: University of Delaware Press, 1988), 143.

26. Claudia Mills, "Friendship, Fiction, and Memoir: Trust and Betrayal in Writing from One's Own Life," in *The Ethics of Life Writing*, ed. Paul John Eakin (Ithaca: Cornell University Press, 2004), 108.

27. Abelove, *Deep Gossip*, xii.

28. Moore, *Hail and Farewell*, 69.

29. See Mohr, *Gay Ideas*, 11–38.

30. Michael Taussig, *Defacement: Public Secrecy and the Labor of the Negative* (Stanford: Stanford University Press, 1999), 2, 3.

Chapter Nine

Readers, Writers, and Friends

George Moore and John Eglinton

Michel Brunet

Literary influence can be difficult to determine. There is most often no clear evidence that an author read precursor works or even became vicariously acquainted with them. Identifying correspondences and spotting thematic resemblances and related formal patterns between literary texts so as to establish direct influence can therefore prove to be an adventure, if not a contentious critical enterprise. As Kirsti Bohata argues in the next chapter, what can be too readily construed as direct influence may boil down to a matter of sheer coincidence or, more probably, to the influence of comparable social and cultural circumstances or the spirit of the age in which the authors composed their works. However, critical or essayistic works by novelists, and what biographical study can glean from those novelists' letters, memoirs, and related writings, can provide oblique though informative material to aid tracing the generic and thematic lineage of their oeuvre.

A one-time avowed and fervent admirer of Zola, George Moore acknowledged his indebtedness to the French master of naturalism in his letters and autobiographical writings and liked to present himself as Zola's English disciple, cultivating the author's influence in *A Mummer's Wife* (1885) and *Esther Waters* (1894). Similarly, Adrian Frazier, in chapter 1, explores the importance of Balzac on Moore's textual aesthetics. But one's direct textual exposure and allegiance to leading writers and key aesthetic movements cannot solely determine literary influence. Lesser-known bonds of friendship and elective literary associations with independent, so-called minor authors also constitute sources of pervasive influence through mutual critical appraisals and such intangibles as casual conversations gone unrecorded. By charting the history of Moore's relationship with Anglo-Irish essayist William

Kirkpatrick Magee, better known by his pen name John Eglinton, this chapter argues that Moore scholarship, when addressing the issue of literary influence, should not exclusively focus on his affiliations to aesthetic schools or movements or on his putative connections with a core of prominent canonical authors, but should also be mindful of the complex symbiotic nexus of influences sometimes more enduringly, though less conspicuously, embodied and sustained by minor literary figures. Shifting the angle of the critical approach to Moore may contribute to reframing current understandings of his achievement, while also providing a context for his successive endorsements of diverse ideological and aesthetic positions on the future of Irish letters.

A withdrawn figure in the group of writers commonly associated with the Irish Literary Revival, Eglinton did not stand out as a charismatic actor in the prevailing cultural debate although he made thought-provoking interventions with reference to the necessity to forge a new literary consciousness in Ireland. Eglinton was an intellectual in the full sense of the word—one who was to leave his imprint on Moore and serve as a constant and stimulating critical reference. He was a scholar well-versed in European culture and, as such, probably steered the course of Moore's creative development by introducing him to non-Irish canonical literary masters. But, most importantly, he was of a somewhat rebellious disposition, if wary of partisan passion, and his uncompromising independence of thought probably encouraged Moore to dispute the aesthetic choices of the Irish literary movement. As is borne out by their lifelong personal bond, Moore was responsive to Eglinton's intellectual alertness and propensity to challenge prevalent mainstream ideology.

In his introduction to the selection of letters he received from Moore, Eglinton recalls that the man of letters "kept his friendships in compartments, writing with almost equal intimacy to people who knew little or nothing of one another."[1] The remark is probably well-founded, given the great number of people with whom Moore exchanged letters in different countries at various stages of his long life. His relationship with Eglinton, at least at its inception, was, however, neither altogether exclusive nor entirely personal. Moore came to make Eglinton's acquaintance amidst a circle of literary personalities who had achieved a small measure of public recognition in the early days of the Irish Renaissance, when Moore had moved his residence from London to Dublin. Some of the members of this intelligentsia, such as Edward Martyn and George William Russell (or AE), already numbered among his close friends. Moore's new home in Dublin at 4 Upper Ely Place had become the locale where they would all meet for subsequently institutionalized "Saturday evenings." As he was to recall later, Eglinton initially kept his distance: "out of a ridiculous diffidence I shrank for a long time from presenting myself at the gatherings."[2] As time passed, Moore and Eglinton forged a friendship that was to last until the former's death in 1933.

The vast quantity of letters Moore addressed to Eglinton[3] could certainly serve as an objective criterion to bear out the longevity of their association. But their correspondence also reveals that their friendly bond was subjected to the ebb and flow of two wayward personalities. It often leaves the impression that the temperaments between the Presbyterian-born Eglinton and the mercurial, iconoclastic Moore were barely compatible. I am interested in exploring the complex nature of this intricately woven relationship by trying to disentangle some of its threads in light of the prevalent debates that took place within the broader context of the Irish Revival and its aftermath. In doing so, I show how mutually influential both men of letters might have been, whatever their blatant divergences. The chapter's main focus, however, will be on examining Moore and Eglinton's literary and personal association as encapsulated in Moore's injunction to outgrow their respective roles of "reader and writer" in order to secure their friendly bond when it was most imperiled in the early 1920s.

In many respects, Moore's association with Eglinton is similar to that which he developed with Edouard Dujardin, a lifelong bond founded on shared literary preoccupations, with undisguised streaks of interest on Moore's part, and disrupted by occasional spells of disagreement, with quarrels and squabbles resulting in prolonged periods of silence. Admittedly, the relationship with Eglinton did not prove to be quite as tempestuous as the one Moore had with Dujardin. It did not start under the most pleasant auspices, either. We know that they first met at a picture show at Leinster Hall in 1900,[4] where they were introduced to each other by Lady Gregory. Eglinton retrospectively recalls:

> He looked me up and down, rapidly as it seemed to me comparing me with the probably favourable accounts he had heard from AE. and in a strong harsh voice which impressed me disagreeably, told me that he had read my articles in the *Daily Express*. He did not say what he thought of them, and I for my part could think of nothing to say, so that he turned off at once to catch Lady Gregory's eye and to be introduced to some other hole-and-corner man of letters.[5]

Having read Eglinton's articles, Moore was conversant with the debate about what constituted the proper subjects of a national literature. Eglinton had triggered the controversy by asserting, provocatively, in the early days of the Irish Literary Revival, that the ancient legends of Ireland "obstinately refuse to be taken out of their old environment and transplanted into the world of modern sympathies."[6] In his view, the old myths could not address modern realities. Even worse, they were bound to encourage a nostalgic discourse leading to escapism and a petty form of *belles lettres*. Eglinton consequently advocated a thought movement looking forward to the future rather than the language movement that the Gaelic League was then propounding.

While Moore was sensitive to Eglinton's intellectual integrity and appreciative of his prose as well as his talent for controversy, he could not possibly condone anyone opposing the promotion of the Irish language and the literary movement for which he displayed so much enthusiasm and had decided to champion. Unlike George William Russell, the mystic poet better known as AE, who idolized the old Celtic mythological deities, Eglinton did not "commune with the Gods" and was "at liberty to deny their speech,"[7] in other words, he did not shy away from questioning the doctrines of the Irish Literary Revival. For his part, Eglinton knew about Moore, the established man of letters, and how he had been urged by that "daemonic man W. B. Yeats"[8] to return to Ireland; he also remembered that one of his relatives had warned him against Moore, this "child of Hell."[9] No two people could have been more at odds than these two as regards their origins, their age, their situations in life, and their ideological convictions in the early years of the twentieth century. That Moore and Eglinton should become friends was, nevertheless, not altogether surprising as the former was "in the habit all his life of contracting friendships with men totally dissimilar from himself; and his whim, while in Dublin, of contracting a particular friendship with the present writer," wrote Eglinton, "puzzled and amused our circle."[10]

The fact remains that they came to appreciate each other over the course of time, Eglinton gradually yielding to the dominance that Moore exercised over the small literary circle gathered around him. Naturally enough, Moore's friendship was not altogether disinterested. As discussed in this book's Introduction, Moore often had ulterior motives when he struck up friendships, as these could be mined for his work. This most blatantly applied to Eglinton, who in his capacity of assistant librarian at the National Library of Ireland, could both supply him with the information he needed for his books and advise him on his reading. Moore's early enthusiasm for all things Irish as expounded by the Gaelic League was starting to abate and disenchantment was beginning to set in, as his subsequent works and correspondence indicate. His ultimate about-face in his critical appraisal of the Irish Literary Revival could therefore partly be ascribed to the pervasive influence of his friend's censorious stance.

Exploring the paradigms of literary friendships is a rewarding endeavor as it is likely to shed light on the works of the respective partners and on the cultural and sociological context in which those works were produced. As such, Moore's association with Eglinton, though a less productive author, deserves attention. Their friendship was not simply set against the backdrop of the Irish Literary Revival, but it wrote its own page in the narrative of this outstanding period in Irish literary history. Although both men of letters were parties in the ongoing cultural debate and their ideological stances certainly bore upon the development of the Revival and what is best remembered of it, their relationship had its most evident impact on each other's personal literary production. What is particularly fascinating about such an association from a purely literary standpoint is that not only were both men writing during an intensively productive period and its aftermath, but they were writing also of each other. In other words, they were not merely "reader and writer" in the seemingly restricted sense that Moore suggested in one of his letters,[11] casting Eglinton in the role of the reader and himself in that of the writer. As a matter of fact, they were both reader and writer and both wrote of one another. Moore opted for fictionalized autobiography and Eglinton for nonfiction writing or, to be more precise, for reviews and essays, the latter being the genre in which he specialized with the most success. They also exchanged a huge amount of private correspondence, which is no less arresting for being as casual as it is highly informative on the way they perceived each other and their respective works, making it possible, retrospectively, to chart the progress of their relationship.

In *Hail and Farewell*, which Eglinton aptly described as a "series of scenes and episodes opening one into the other like the rooms of a picture gallery,"[12] Moore offers a vivid though succinct portrait of his friend. Admittedly, one must make allowances for the specific genre of the trilogy, supposedly written at the outset as an autobiography but certainly more akin to a novel, blending fact and fiction, and not therefore claiming utter veracity. As early as 1907, Moore wrote to Edouard Dujardin: "You know the title and subject of my book *Hail and Farewell*. It is taking the form of a novel with no women in it."[13] In a letter to Emily Lorenz Meyer, he went even further, explaining that the book was in a light-hearted satirical vein: "It is written very lightly: the subject is serious enough, but I am laughing all the while and turn myself and my contemporaries into ridicule."[14] While Eglinton could not escape the butt of Moore's mordant wit any more than his companions could, the literary treatment Moore meted out to him was inspired by an underlying sympathy, rendered all the more important as Moore wrote his book with the benefit of hindsight at a time when both writers already held one another in high esteem. As a result, the portrait of Eglinton in *Hail and Farewell* is ambivalent, both gently critical and endearing, as if the author did not mean to hurt his friend's feelings or as if he were honest enough to recognize his intellectual merits and integrity behind a not-so-appealing facade.

Admittedly, Moore's physical description of his prospective friend is not flattering: "I noticed a thin, small man with dark red hair growing stiffly over a small skull; and I studied the round head and the high forehead, and the face somewhat shrivelled and thickly freckled."[15] The portrait, however, ends on a more sympathetic note as the author grows more sensitive to the loneliness of the character:

> A gnarled, solitary life, I said, lived out in all the discomforts inherent in a bachelor's lodging, a sort of lonely thorn tree. One sees one sometimes on a hillside and not another tree near it. The comparison amused me, for John Eglinton argued in a thorny, tenacious way, and remembering his beautiful prose, I said: The thorn breaks to flower, and continued to discover analogies. A sturdy life has the thorn, bent on one side by the wind, looking as if sometimes it had been strangled by the blast. John Eglinton, too, looked as if he had battled, and I am always attracted by those who have battled, and who know how to live alone. [16]

Subsequent notations scattered all through the trilogy insistently point to the physiognomy of the character: Moore often depicts Eglinton as plunged into a state of perplexity and confusion, frowning, puckering his face and looking nonplussed. On reading all these details, one is left with the impression of a withdrawn personality—Austin Clarke incidentally described Eglinton as "a writer of retiring disposition"[17]—who is prone to engage in debate, though most of the time for debate's sake. Moore's literary treatment made him a somewhat predictable character, easily identified by a natural penchant toward contradicting his companions, hence his nickname, "Contrairy John." Moore derived great enjoyment from casting him in the role of the constant opponent, to the point of ridicule: "Contrairy John was confused and round about, and at the end of many an argument found himself defending the very principles that he had started out to contravene."[18]

Even though this characterization verges on caricature, Eglinton seems to fare better than the other protagonists in the trilogy.[19] Abiding by the determined principle of his writing project to stage not "personalities" but "human types," as he explained to George Birmingham,[20] Moore ascribed Eglinton the role of the skeptic, but far from being disparaging, the classification has positive connotations. Eglinton, a minor figure, is gradually defined as someone real, "boiled down" like "a sort of Liebig extract of himself"[21] by the pervasive Catholic atmosphere of Dublin. Eglinton stands out all the more forcibly because the other protagonists are made to look unreal, such as AE being carried away by his mystic visions, or paltry figures such as Douglas Hyde. If AE stands for "belief," Eglinton embodies "unbelief."[22] Thus, Moore's final assessment of Eglinton in *Vale*—"I shall never find a better model than Eglinton. It seems to me that I understand him"[23]—provides, as it were, an answer to his initial interrogation: "And I wondered if we should ever become friends."[24]

If Moore generally showed himself to be appreciative of Eglinton's writings in a somewhat flattering way, systematically praising his "beautiful prose" but occasionally taking him to task for disputable lapses in the purity of the English language, Eglinton, for his part, as a critic then as a "writer," displayed less enthusiasm for his elder companion's writings, though he relented in the course of time, revising some of his most severe critical judgments.[25] While he regarded Moore's Irish adventure as marking the heyday of the author's literary production, at least retrospectively, Eglinton seemed to be much more critical of Moore's post-Dublin period, considering his subsequent works as "very artificial affairs," on the basis that "Moore himself was not in them."[26] We must bear in mind some of the critical yardsticks against which Eglinton was measuring or "reading" Moore's works of fiction. Under the mixed influence of Emerson, Thoreau, Arnold, and Wordsworth, Eglinton was probably more of a philosopher and social historian than a literary critic in the strictest sense, at least by modern standards, his writings being more essayistic and personal than scholarly. Wary as he was of abstractions and of vain, contrived, aesthetic effects, his approach to literary matters was informed by his interest in the individual perceived as a human consciousness and through humanist values. His own biographical-critical portraits, which he called "stories," are representative of this biased critical outlook.[27] It seems as if the essayist never totally emancipated himself from his romantic concept of literature, which held that art is the expression of personality: "There are many ways of being interested in literature, but I will confess to the belief that the vitality of a work of literary art is in proportion to the interest which it excites in the author."[28] Eglinton accordingly thought that Moore was at his best in *Hail and Farewell*, in full command of his art, just because he managed to achieve therein "the art of reminiscence in which he is wholly himself and in which he truly excels."[29]

Conversely, he harshly criticized Moore's subsequent novels whenever the author lapsed, in his view, from this line of conduct and when his style supposedly reflecting his personality did not come up to Eglinton's critical standards, even as he praised Moore's sense of language and diction:

> A prose style as masterful as his, is in itself a positive achievement . . . I am speaking here of the style into which he threw himself personally. Of the style practised with deliberate monotony in the long semi-historical narratives on which he chiefly valued himself, highly praised by not a few authoritative critics but I fancy, more praised than read, it was understood between us that I was an imperfect admirer.[30]

To put it bluntly, few of Moore's books seemed to find favor in Eglinton's eyes. Moore was not affected (or pretended not to be) by this lack of critical recognition from his friend, probably because he felt grateful for the wise emendations Eglinton suggested when proofreading his typescripts. Moore once sent a signed book to Eglinton with the provocatively humorous line, "To John Eglinton, who likes me better than he likes my books."[31] Moore would usually bear no lasting grudge, though he energetically defended him-

self and vehemently justified his literary choices. He maintained some kind
of composure, but only up to a point, as he was hurt by the critical indifference displayed and prolonged silences suffered during their correspondence.
As if to give the lie to the obituary that Eglinton wrote for *The Observer*, to
the effect that "He was never angry when I expressed my indifference to
them [his novels],"[32] Moore occasionally flared up. In one particular case, he
grew indignant when Eglinton granted less place and importance to his book
Héloïse and Abélard than to Yeats's poem "about his daughter"[33] and to
AE's "lofty silences."[34] Tension built up in a drawn-out silence that Moore
finally broke for fear that their bond of friendship might dissolve. The unusually long-winded, dramatically orchestrated letter that he wrote on August
16, 1923, sheds light not so much on the circumstances of the rift between
the two friends as on the foundations of their association. Moore dismissed
their literary differences, making a list of the books Eglinton did not like and
mischievously going to the length of asserting that Eglinton's likeable "misunderstandings of [his] writings"[35] could serve as a sound basis for their
friendship. At that stage, Moore's blind spot may have been to ignore the fact
that Eglinton was probably resentful at being cast in the role of a reader and,
what is more, a very obtuse reader.

However, the letter of summer 1923 had a sort of cathartic effect on the
relationship and subsequent letters depicted Moore making amends, showing
more consideration and trying to patch things up, culminating in a declaration of exclusive friendship six months later: "You were never an external,
and had it not been for you I should not have stayed so long in Ireland; of that
I am sure, and now we are both out of Ireland."[36] The ideological arguments
that Moore threw into the balance to justify their friendship may appear to
have even greater importance than such declarations:

> We are friends because we are animated by a dislike of the Irish character and
> Papistry. No country is so foreign to me as Ireland, but I am not sure if this last
> sentence represents you. I think it does; you will never be at home in Ireland,
> and since the burning of my house I don't think I shall ever be able to bring
> myself to set foot in Ireland again. . . . Our dislike of Ireland is a sufficiently
> broad basis for us to rear a noble fane of friendship; dislike of Ireland is deep
> enough in us, strong enough, close enough, intimate enough, for us to scorn
> our literary differences.[37]

Stylistically speaking, these lines afford a glimpse of Moore's strategic epistolary rhetoric. Besides the conventionally derogatory mention of the word
"Papistry," much in keeping with the vehemence of his all-too-frequent anti-
Catholic diatribes, his use of the first-person plural, either as a pronoun or as
a possessive, points to his determination to achieve a rapprochement, in an
attempt to win over his correspondent's approval in anticipation. His letters
usually rest on a more clear-cut division between an "I" and a "you," the first

person appearing more often than the second. Equally noteworthy, the chain of adjectives—"deep," "strong," "close," and "intimate," here associated with Moore and Eglinton's shared loathing of Ireland—is what we would expect to define the more positive feeling of friendship.

Regarding the ideological reasons Moore puts forward in the hope of renewing the interrupted relationship, it must be borne in mind that the wished-for reconciliation was based more on a contextual convergence of views than on an actual communion or personal identification premised on similar religious persuasions. There were differences in sensibility between Moore and Eglinton and in their motivations for rejecting Catholicism and their native country at large, some of which were personal. Moore was still outraged by the upsetting news of the recent burning of Moore Hall, allegedly by Republican forces, and Eglinton had prematurely resigned from the National Library of Ireland, unwilling to serve the Free State Government and only too happy to escape the all-pervasive Catholic sway and leave his share of "clerical drudgery"[38] behind.

More fundamentally, as the son of a Northern Irish Presbyterian minister, Eglinton was probably not culturally immune from the "traditional Protestant aversion for the more demonstrative type of Catholic,"[39] though he claimed to be an agnostic, keeping out of all forms of organized religion and preferring to support transcendentalist tenets and humanist values. In Moore's eyes, the circumstances of Eglinton's life had favored the seed of Puritanism in him. For Moore, on the other hand, whose "cradle was rocked in the Nouvelle Athènes"[40] in Paris, his anticlerical bias stemmed from his personal experience of censorship as an author. He blamed the Roman Catholic Church for its narrow-mindedness and the restricting influences it exercised on artistic freedom and on private lives. Moore aimed his attack at Irish Catholicism in particular: "We have a black Catholicism which begins at the North wall and ends at Galway Bay—a Catholicism that exists nowhere else and that is the ruin of Ireland."[41] But whatever the origins of their grievances, what both men condemned in the first place was obscurantist sectarianism, which they saw as responsible for the cultural stagnation, if not the degradation, of Ireland. Both also shared a dissatisfaction with the Irish Revival's incapacity or lack of real determination to curb "the recrudescence among us of religious bigotry."[42]

Coupled with this was also Moore's implied realization, a few years before, that the advancement of the virginal Irish language was of no real use—all the less so as it would remain inaccessible to him—and, moreover, was potentially dangerous, given that it was politically and ideologically loaded since the Catholic Church dominated the language movement through the Gaelic League.[43] His loathing of Catholicism and the Irish Revival as expressed in his 1923 letter to Eglinton incidentally recalls what he wrote to Edouard Dujardin as early as 1902 and 1903: "For the moment I have enough of the Gaelic League and of Ireland," and "I have absolutely renounced all my Celtic hopes. Of the race there is now nothing but an end left over, a tattered rag, with plenty of fleas in it, I mean priests."[44] Unlike Moore, Eglinton had never supported the language movement, nor had he believed in its capacity to assert an Irish national identity and to foster cosmopolitan ambitions. In that respect, his influence on Moore's ideological turnabout should not, perhaps, be underrated. Whether Moore somehow rallied to his friend's firmly established ideas on the question or came to a similar conclusion on his own is open to debate,[45] as is the extent to which Eglinton came to bear on Moore's literary production in terms of stylistics and literary directions.[46]

In the course of time, Moore and Eglinton discovered that they held similar views on a number of issues related to Ireland as an infant nation-state. As Eglinton was to sum it up after Moore's death: "We found indeed many points of agreement, particularly in our confabulations about Ireland, its literature, its religion and politics."[47] The moot question of nationality versus cosmopolitanism certainly occupied a place of prime importance in their eyes. Although they did not altogether reject the notion of a national literature, they did not subscribe to the narrow conception that those upholding the Irish Revival propounded, inasmuch as it imposed sectarian cultural views and denied diversity in ideological opinions and artistic expression. As a Protestant-born member of the Anglo-Irish community claiming to be "still there," Eglinton resented the community being "left a good deal out of account in recent years," and could not therefore accept a purely "Irish Ireland" favoring a partisan discourse.[48] Advocating a more inclusive national mingling of identities—in his case, a recognition of the hyphenated Irishman—and probably under the influence of his family background and its ideological legacy,[49] he openly declared himself a Unionist,[50] but one with definitely progressive and cosmopolitan views. Eglinton envisaged the ultimate avatar of the Anglo-Irishman as the "Modern Irishman, the Irishman, namely, who accepts as a good European the connection with Great Britain" and yet, in his ideological and cultural specificity, "feels himself to be far more distinct from the Anglo-Saxon than he is from the Mere Irishman."[51] In a similar way, Moore proved to be equally supportive of the Unionist cause when he contemplated publishing a pamphlet in 1919 "to show how necessary England was to Ireland." But his stance also evinced a particular brand of Unionism, leaving out "all contentious matter—principles of government and such like"[52] to reflect a more cosmopolitan orientation. Thus, while both authors defensively combated ideological and religious zealotry, and their Gaelic exclusiveness united them in dissidence, their confirmed cosmopolitan literary sensibility also contributed to ensuring their intellectual rapprochement and sealed their association.

The two men of letters not only dreaded that the "Irish Ireland" movement and obscurantist forces might culturally cut off the emerging nation
from the rest of Europe, but they also shared a manifest interest in European
culture, fostered by first-hand experience of living on the Continent. In a
practical way, they both enjoyed a good command of the French language
(Eglinton also mastered German and classical languages); both undertook
some translation work and were well-read in European literatures, Eglinton
more often than not acting as an influential literary advisor to Moore. His
own writings are replete with references to foreign authors and it was part of
the editorial policy of the short-lived review *Dana*, which he co-edited with
Fred Ryan, to address contemporary foreign intellectual thought.[53] Moore,
for his part, while settled in Dublin and then in London, kept on corresponding with and visiting lifelong friends from his Parisian period, such as Dujardin and Jacques-Emile Blanche, who enabled him to remain cognizant of the
Continental European literary and artistic scene.

Whatever the differences in their itineraries and their dissensions with
each other, it appears that there was ample common ground for their association to thrive on. However, if Moore and Eglinton seemed to hold similar
views on a number of subjects, somehow falling in line with each other or
getting close to doing so, it is probably not so much because they went
through similar experiences as because they were prone to take a consistently
critical stance on any ideological or artistic matters, which resulted in a
characteristically ironic detachment. This was the first overall impression
Eglinton reminisced about when paying a last tribute to Moore: "The general
feeling one had about Moore personally, specially during the later period of
his life, was that he was extraordinary aloof and separate."[54] For his part,
Moore had always welcomed Eglinton's independence of mind and his capacity to call into question the literary doxa inherent in the Irish Revival. For
instance, he had readily supported Eglinton's *Dana* (aptly subtitled "An Irish
Magazine of Independent Thought") by contributing work himself, and defined the journal as "somewhat on the lines of the *Revue des Idées*, that is it
has an anti-clerical bias."[55] Transgressing codes and asserting their individuality certainly served Moore and Eglinton as a sounder line of conduct than
conformity and compliance with the mainstream of any intellectual movement would have done. Adversity and their instinctive leaning towards rebellion against any forms of orthodoxy contributed to bringing them together.

Moore's association with Eglinton was founded not only on purely intellectual and ideological affinities and a sustained collaboration over the years, but
also on a genuine bond of affection that proved stronger than any cause of
dissension. It certainly grew deeper as both men concluded their lives far
from Ireland and their erstwhile common friends. The quality of their friendship resulted from each maintaining his own intellectual integrity within the

bond, their strong personalities paradoxically keeping them apart and binding them together at the same time. Eglinton probably feared that the powerful personality of his elder by sixteen years might influence his creative develop-ment. He did not readily respond to Moore's encouragement to write and to publish more. He certainly also nursed some resentment at being cast in the role of literary consultant, and at not being regarded as a widely recognized author, but he was equally sensitive to the constancy and exclusiveness of Moore's friendship until the end: "This man, whom I judged at first to be completely alien to me, was to be the most familiar of my acquaintance, peering curiously into my privacy, and opening his soul to me more than I believe than to others: a soul in contact with some perennial source of caustic insight and salutary disillusionment, yet one that craved for affection."[56]

If Moore's correspondence often relates to his own literary work and the books that he read, it is also peppered with complimentary remarks on Eglin-ton's writings[57] and more personal considerations. As in the case of his correspondence with Dujardin, Moore's letters frequently recall past "happy disputation[s]"[58] and look forward to some prospective reunion. References to talks with Eglinton are characteristically associated with recollected "long walks"[59] in Dublin by lamplight, or rambles in the Welsh countryside or along the seaside in Bournemouth. Moore and Eglinton both regarded walks as intellectually stimulating, artistically productive, and propitious to friendly communion.

Some of Moore's final letters strike a note of genuine pathos, though, as they came from an aging and ailing author sensing the approaching end of his creative powers. They show a Moore in high demand of friendship with an Eglinton whom he confirmed in his role of reader while Moore claimed the status of the Grand Old Man of Letters. If Eglinton's untold story of bitter resentment and frustration put a strain on their association, there remained "something better": "a spiritual kinship."[60] More than ten years after Moore's death, Eglinton recalled that there were "moments of mutual under-standing in which beat the pulse of true friendship."[61] If their association thrived on marked differences and misunderstandings, it also brought out certain affective affinities providing just as much intellectual stimuli in the course of time. We may therefore venture to surmise that such an uneasy rapport somehow left its mark on their respective creative development and literary achievements.

NOTES

1. John Eglinton, ed., *Letters of George Moore* (Bournemouth: Sydenham, 1942), 5. For the titular quotation see 61.
2. John Eglinton, ed., *Letters from George Moore to Ed. Dujardin, 1886–1922* (New York: Crosby Gaige, 1929), 8.

3. There were in total 540 according to George H. Ford, ed. *Victorian Fiction: A Second Guide to Research* (New York: The Modern Language Associat on of America, 1978), 348.

4. John Eglinton specifies "around 1898" twice, in "Recollections of George Moore" in his *Irish Literary Portraits* (London: Macmillan, 1935), 85, and in his introduction to *Letters from George Moore*, 6. Adrian Frazier more accurately situates the meeting in 1900 in *George Moore, 1852–1933* (New Haven: Yale University Press, 2000), 288.

5. Eglinton, introduction to *Letters from George Moore*, 6–7.

6. John Eglinton, "What Should be the Subjects of National Drama?," in *Literary Ideals of Ireland* (1899), ed. John Eglinton, W. B. Yeats, A. E., W. Larminie (New York: Lemma Publishing Corporation, 1973), 11.

7. George Moore, *Ave*, vol. I of *Hail and Farewell*, ed. Richard Cave (1976; Gerrards Cross: Colin Smythe, 1985), 143.

8. John Eglinton, "George Moore and His Story," *The Dial* 81, no. 2 (August 1926): 97.

9. Eglinton, introduction to *Letters from George Moore*, 8, and *Irish Literary Portraits*, 88.

10. Eglinton, "St. Winifred's Well," *Irish Literary Portraits*, 115.

11. August 16, 1923, in Eglinton, *Letters of George Moore*, 61.

12. Eglinton, introduction to *Letters of George Moore*, 7–8.

13. George Moore to Edouard Dujardin, April 25, 1907, Eglinton, *Letters from George Moore*, 61.

14. George Moore to Emily Lorenz Meyer, August 2, 1909, in Helmut E. Gerber, ed., with the assistance O. M. Brack, Jr., *George Moore on Parnassus: Letters (1900–1933) to Secretaries, Publishers, Printers, Agents, Literati, Friends, and Acquaintances* (Newark: University of Delaware Press, 1988), 171.

15. Moore, *Ave*, 143.

16. Ibid.

17. Austin Clarke, *Reviews and Essays of Austin Clarke*, ed. Gregory A. Schirmer (Gerrards Cross: Colin Smythe, 1995), 118.

18. Moore, *Vale*, vol. III of *Hail and Farewell*, 581.

19. Susan L. Mitchell dedicated her book on George Moore to "'A. E.' and John Eglinton who alone were treated mercifully by the author of 'Ave, Salve and Vale'" (Dublin and Cork: The Talbot Press Limited, 1917).

20. George Moore to George Birmingham, October 27, 1911, Correspondence of Rev. James Owen Hannay (pseud. George A. Birmingham (Dublin: National Library of Ireland), MSS. 8271, quoted in W. B. Yeats, *Memoirs*, ed. Denis Donoghue (London: Macmillan 1972), 269 n5.

21. Moore, *Vale*, 585.

22. Moore, *Salve*, vol. II of *Hail and Farewell*, 434.

23. Moore, *Vale*, 586.

24. Moore, *Ave*, 144.

25. Moore expected Eglinton, the reviewer, to be more lenient after his marriage in 1921: "Now that you are married I hope you will apply yourself to literary criticism and discover for your readers the qualities to be found in the books you write about, not forgetting the qualities that are absent," January 14, 1921, in Eglinton, *Letters of George Moore*, 57.

26. Eglinton, "George Moore and His Story," 99.

27. Some of these "stories" previously published in *The Dial* were collected in one volume entitled *Irish Literary Portraits* in 1935. In many respects, they prove to be markedly influenced by Edward Dowden's critical approach. Eglinton wrote of Dowden: "in all literature he sought above all things to discover the soul of the author" (*Irish Literary Portraits*, 76).

28. Eglinton, "George Moore and His Story," 92.

29. Ibid., 93.

30. Eglinton, *Letters of George Moore*, 12. Eglinton is probably referring to *The Brook Kerith* (1916), *A Story-Teller's Holiday* (1918), *Héloïse and Abélard* (1921), *Ulick and Soracha* (1926) and *Aphrodite in Aulis* (1930).

31. Eglinton, "George Moore and His Story," 99.

32. John Eglinton, "A Personal Sketch, Monk-Like Devotion," *The Observer*, January 22, 1933, 17.

33. November 1921, Eglinton, *Letters of George Moore*, 59.

34. April 4, 1922, ibid., 60. Their friendship was also dampened in 1922 by Eglinton's disapproval of the subject of "Hugh Monfert" (in which the protagonist, modeled on Edward Martyn, comes to a recognition of his homosexuality), published in *In Single Strictness*; see Frazier, *George Moore*, 446.

35. August 16, 1923, in Eglinton, *Letters of George Moore*, 62.

36. January 8, 1924, ibid., 64.

37. August 16, 1923, ibid., 61.

38. John Eglinton, *Confidential or Take it or Leave it* (London: The Fortune Press, 1951), 6.

39. Declan Kiberd, *Inventing Ireland* (London: Jonathan Cape, 1995), 159.

40. August 16, 1923, in Eglinton, *Letters of George Moore*, 63.

41. George Moore to Virginia Crawford, May 11, 1903, in Gerber, *George Moore on Parnassus*, 111.

42. John Eglinton, "The Weak Point of the Celtic Movement," *Dana* 11 (March 1905): 321. Moore must have disappointed Eglinton as the latter expected Moore to become the Irish Cervantes. He estimated that *Hail and Farewell* had only partially fulfilled his hopes. See the appendix to the chapter "Irish Books" in *Anglo-Irish Essays* (Dublin: The Talbot Press Ltd, 1917), 89.

43. For the ideological dimension of the use of the Irish language, see Timothy G. McMahon, *Grand Opportunity* (Syracuse: Syracuse University Press, 2008).

44. George Moore to Dujardin, September 24 and June 1903, in Eglinton, *Letters from George Moore*, 44–45, 47.

45. For instance, Moore's declaration that Irish "seemed to me a language suitable for the celebration of an antique Celtic rite, but too remote for modern use" (*Ave*, 139) sounds highly reminiscent of Eglinton's words: "The ancient language of the Celt is no longer the language of Irish nationality," in *Bards and Saints* (Dublin: Maunsel & Co., 1906), 11.

46. Moore regularly asked Eglinton to proofread his writings and to correct him so as to hone his style.

47. Eglinton, introduction to *Letters of George Moore*, 6.

48. Eglinton, "Preface" to *Anglo-Irish Essays*, 3.

49. Eglinton's father, Hamilton Magee, was a staunch Unionist. See his book *Fifty Years in "The Irish Mission"* (Belfast: Religious Tract and Book Depot, n.d.), 188, n1: "But I feel constrained . . . to express the ever deepening conviction that the setting up of an 'Independent Parliament,' in College Green, or anything that might lead to an Independent Parliament, would not only be fatal to the highest and best interests of Ireland, but would be full of the gravest peril to the stability of the British Empire, and to the cause of Protestantism and real liberty throughout the world," accessed June 16, 2014, archive.org/details/intheirish missio00mageuoft.

50. Austin Clarke defines him as "a sentimentalist Unionist," *Reviews and Essays of Austin Clarke*, 79.

51. Eglinton, "Preface" to *Anglo-Irish Essays*, 4. Edward Dowden's international literary outlook must have been influential in shaping Eglinton's political and literary leanings. In his essay on the Anglo-Irish scholar, Eglinton wrote: "in insisting that literature, like religion, is essentially international, Dowden was certainly right"; *Irish Literary Portraits*, 66.

52. George Moore to T. Werner Laurie, May 28, 1919, in Gerber, *George Moore on Parnassus*, 419. The pamphlet was to be entitled "Ireland's Chances; Substance or Shadow" and to include letters he had sent to *The Times* and an article for the *Sunday Chronicle*. See ibid., 418.

53. Essays in *Dana* frequently mentioned or dealt with British and Continental authors and philosophers. See Fabienne Garcier, "*Dana*: A Contribution to Irish Modernism," in *The Book in Ireland*, ed. Jacqueline Genet, Sylvie Mikowski and Fabienne Garcier (Newcastle: Cambridge Scholars Press, 2006), 276–289.

54. Eglinton, "A Personal Sketch, Monk-Like Devotion to Letters," 17.

55. George Moore to Edouard Dujardin, March 17, 1904, in Eglinton, *Letters from George Moore*, 49.

56. Eglinton, *Irish Literary Portraits*, 86.

57. These remarks were often unfortunately interwoven with encouragements to write and to publish more essays, which could only irritate Eglinton.

58. January 8, 1924, in Eglinton, *Letters of George Moore*, 63.

59. Eglinton, introduction to *Letters from George Moore*, 14.

60. Moore to Eglinton, January 8, 1924, ibid., 63.

61. Eglinton, introduction to *Letters of George Moore*, 10.

Chapter Ten

Celtic Cousins?

George Moore's The Untilled Field *and*
Caradoc Evans's My People[1]

Kirsti Bohata

George Moore's role in the Celtic Renaissance is well known. Already famous for his nineteenth-century novels with their decadent influences and
risqué topics, in 1901 Moore turned his back on *fin-de-siècle* London and
Europe. Answering what he later satirically depicted as a messianic call, he
set up home in Dublin and remained there for the next ten years.[2] Newly
enthused by the Irish Renaissance, Moore looked toward the literary future,
producing a collection of proto-modernist short stories, *The Untilled Field*
(1903), which was reissued in a substantially revised edition in 1914.[3] The
linked stories therein and their focus on religious oppression and the "authentic" Irish peasantry can be seen as anticipating an iconoclastic and hugely
influential volume of short stories from Wales, Caradoc Evans's *My People*
(1915).[4] A comparative reading of the two "Celtic cousins," George Moore
in Ireland and Caradoc Evans in Wales, reveals that although they had
marked differences in style, tone, and authorial intention—Moore was a
revivalist, Evans wrote apparently to satirize "his people"—there are some
striking convergences in their two collections that beg further examination.
This chapter argues that a comparative reading of these collections draws
attention to dimensions often overlooked in criticism which focuses on
Moore or Evans alone. I contend that Moore still mobilizes negative stereotypes of the peasantry even as he promotes the Celtic Revival and that Evans
must be read in an international context to avoid the existing overemphasis
on his fracture with past literary traditions. Thus, the comparative approach
subtly alters the place and meaning of each writer in his respective national

canon while encouraging the construction of extranational critical frameworks.

The comparative approach adopted here is informed by recent "archipelagic" understandings of cultural and literary history that have begun to trace
some of the influences on and continuities and differences between experiences in the modern nations that make up the British Isles.[5] The "margins" in
particular—those nations which have been dominated or assimilated by
"Britain"—have been the focus of productive comparative studies. One
strength of archipelagic comparative studies lies in the effort "to move away
from rather than replicate [the] core/periphery model" even while the "margins" are sometimes nevertheless recognized as sharing a degree of common
experience with each other due to the dominance of the perceived center. In
order to move beyond the core/periphery model and "to question the term
'marginal' itself," Glenda Norquay and Gerry Smyth argue that we need "to
hear voices talking 'across' borders and not only to or through an English
centre."[6] In a Welsh-Irish context, Paul O'Leary similarly observes that "the
act of comparison de-centres the seductive—but simplistic—Ireland/England
and Wales/England oppositions that continue to dominate large parts of the
historiography about cultural nationalism."[7] This is very pertinent in the case
of Caradoc Evans. Cultural readings of *My People* have often been overshadowed by Welsh sensitivities borne of English dominance: Evans was and
sometimes still is regarded as a traitor to the Welsh, having delivered an anti-
Welsh satire for the entertainment of English audiences.[8] A comparison with
Moore's revivalist short stories complicates the analysis of Evans's works,
moving readings away from the England/Wales axis without sacrificing the
historical and cultural contexts from which both authors' collections of short
stories emerge.

Rather than seeking to find parallels and similarities in Irish and Welsh
comparisons, O'Leary, following Marc Bloch, emphasizes an attention to
difference as the best way to generate new or significant meanings in a
comparative historical analysis.[9] The differences between Moore and Evans
as authors and between the styles and approaches of their stories are profound. Moore was a well-established figure from a wealthy, English-speak-
ing background who wrote *The Untilled Field* as a contribution and restorative to Irish culture. *My People* was a harsh satire on the Welsh peasantry; it
was Evans's first book, which he wrote in highly innovative "English," even
though his first language was Welsh. His background was marked by poverty
and he had educated himself through evening classes in London. In historical
terms, Ireland and Wales were very different: in Ireland, the national language was in precipitous decline, but independence movements were relatively advanced, while in Wales, the national language had only just fallen
out of majority use while the Home Rule movement had stalled as a political
force. Ireland was Catholic with a disestablished Anglican Church, Wales

was Nonconformist Protestant but the Church of England remained estab-lished.[10] Wales had experienced enormous immigration during its industrial heyday, whereas Ireland had experienced catastrophic emigration and fa-mine.

Despite the differences, certain commonalities have long been acknowl-edged, and there was a rich and complex relationship between Irish and Welsh writers, intellectuals and politicians in the late nineteenth and early twentieth centuries. It could, as Moore himself acknowledged, be character-ized as a love-hate relationship. Delivering a speech in 1914 to the National Eisteddfod in Cardiff (the pre-eminent Welsh cultural event of the year), Moore averred that "the Irish and the Welsh are cousins—first cousins—and like all cousins we have loved and hated each other."[11] Points of tension included "progressive" Nonconformist Wales's hostility toward an Ireland mired deep in reactionary Catholicism and its alarm at violent expressions of Irish nationalism. Yet, the same Nonconformist Wales supported the parlia-mentary movement to secure Irish Home Rule, since it reinforced Wales's arguments for the disestablishment of the Church of England and also pro-vided nationalist movements like *Cymru Fydd* (Young Wales) with a model of limited devolution that could be adapted to the Welsh situation. Of equal, or even greater, significance to the Irish-Welsh relationship was the sense of common purpose, resulting in the Pan-Celtic networks between Welsh and Irish artists of the 1890s and early twentieth century, and in Irish admiration for Welsh cultural institutions such as the Eisteddfod.[12]

Emerging from two different yet comparable national contexts, then, Moore and Evans produced two roughly contemporaneous collections of short stories that, for all their stylistic differences, resemble each other in some extraordinary ways. Moore described *The Untilled Field* as a collection of short stories "dealing with peasant life."[13] The stories are connected by the use of recurring characters and locations and, in the 1914 and later editions, by the use of framing devices. *My People* is subtitled "Stories of the Peasant-ry of West Wales," and is structured as a series of interconnected short stories based in one fictionalized but representative village, Manteg, in the heart of Welsh-speaking West Wales. Moore and Evans's aims, however, were very different. Moore "sought . . . to redeem the presentation of Irish characters from British modes of perception"[14] with the intention of "the regeneration of the Irish race."[15] Far from challenging stereotypes of the Welsh, Evans's *My People* presented Wales as peopled by the worst kind of ignorant, spiritually impoverished, and vicious peasantry. Yet even when the trajectories of the two writers were so different—Moore viewing himself as a messianic savior returning to his native country, and Evans being character-ized as a demonic betrayer of Wales to English censure—a transnational comparative study reveals a series of important similarities of form and style that suggest comparable cultural influences. The form of each of their collections is influenced by the keen interest of both writers in folktales, oral storytelling, and indigenous languages, an interest shared by ethnographers and revivalists in both Ireland and Wales. Moore and Evans draw on these traditional forms of storytelling (in Gaelic and Welsh) in the style, syntax, and idiom of their own writing, and their stories can be seen as constituting or contributing to the development of varieties of non-standard "englishes." Both of their collections respond in different ways to national narratives emerging from their respective countries in the nineteenth century. This context and the manner in which these authors attempt to represent indigenous culture leads us to consider how their work might be read in some ways as "postcolonial," despite the fact that neither collection fits unproblematically into an anti-colonial mold.

This chapter considers the evidence for direct influence between Moore and Evans, before examining shared themes and features of their two collections, including their representations of peasants and abused women in particular, of the stranglehold of the clergy, of the artist as an exiled individual, and the creation of a new indigenous form of English suited to the aims of the writer.

My People was published in November 1915, twelve years after *The Untilled Field*, and so compelling is the resemblance between certain stories in the two collections that it prompts the question of possible direct influence.[16] Did Evans read Moore, recognize and respond to his stories of the peasantry, reworking his motifs of rural Ireland into a darker portrayal of rural Wales?[17] One may identify a series of tantalizing connections between Evans and Moore besides the suggestivity of the texts themselves that might indicate that Evans was familiar with *The Untilled Field* prior to the publication of *My People*. From 1910 onward, Moore published in the *English Review*, and this periodical included a review of the 1914 edition of *The Untilled Field*.[18] Evans also published in the *English Review*, and we know that Austin Harrison and Norman Douglas, the editor and sub-editor, were influential forces in his career.[19] Intriguingly, the publisher Stanley Unwin recalled three manuscripts submitted to his publishing company shortly after its establishment in the second half of 1914 that Unwin believed Austin Harrison had sent his way: Moore's *The Brook Kerith*, Evans's *My People*, and Thomas Burke's *Limehouse Nights*. He (reluctantly) rejected all three.[20] Evans's friend and countryman, writer and journalist Arthur Machen, is another connection: Machen had known Moore since the beginning of the century, and renewed his acquaintance with the author around 1912–1914 in a series of interviews for the *Evening News*.[21] Finally, Evans's avowed interest in naturalism would likely have made him aware of Moore, the champion of French naturalism in England. However, while it seems unlikely that as a journalist, editor, and aspiring writer Evans would have been unaware of Moore, we have no firm evidence that he read *The Untilled Field*.[22] In any case, concentration on the issue of direct influence might be unwise, since it obscures the deeper, more interesting question of why two writers from different, if closely adjacent, countries should have shared a common, or comparable, vision at this time.

Possible explanations for this coincidence or convergence of vision include the residual orality[23] of two semi-literate societies; the co-existence of Gaelic and Welsh alongside English in these societies; the shift of "ruling class" power in both Ireland and Wales as the "colonial class" was replaced by a new class emerging out of the previously subordinated mass of the native population; and the rise to dominance of the clergy in this new order. In literary terms, we can see these writers' works as examples of "fringe Modernism" or perhaps proto-Modernism in Moore's case. We can also read their convergences in the context of Ireland and Wales as countries or cultures exhibiting at least some significant features of colonial/postcolonial societies. Katie Gramich has argued that the figure of the peasant "embodies an essential national identity" in the "anti-colonial self fashioning that [took] place" in Welsh and Irish writing.[24] There is, therefore, a historical national and cultural context in which the synergies in the visions of Evans and Moore may be understood.

The biographical context from which their two collections emerge is of interest, too, since both writers became controversial national figures because of their portrayals of the Irish and Welsh. In *Confessions of a Young Man* (1888), the first of many autobiographical works, Moore claimed "[t]wo dominant notes in my character—an original hatred of my native country, and a brutal loathing of the religion I was brought up in."[25] This is a deliberately simplistic and characteristically provocative statement and one that might equally describe Caradoc Evans, who was regarded as a renegade and national pariah in Wales. The furor that greeted the publication of Evans's inflammatory *My People* included police intimidation of booksellers in Cardiff in an attempt to deter them from stocking the volume, apoplectic letters to the press denouncing the book, and, later, the slashing of a portrait of the author in a London theatre.[26] In Ireland, Moore also provoked outrage and hostility, prior to his reinvention as a supporter of the Gaelic League, with the publication of *Parnell and His Island* (1887), which denigrated the Irish as a "degenerate race."[27]

Evans and Moore came from rather different backgrounds (the former was raised in relative poverty in West Wales, while the latter had a privileged upbringing as the son of a Member of Parliament and major Irish landlord in County Mayo), but there are a surprising number of coincidental similarities in their biographies. For significant parts of their careers they lived and wrote away from their native countries as voluntary exiles. Both were outspoken critics of the dominant religions of their respective countries. Moore renounced Catholicism in a letter to the *Irish Times* in 1903 shortly after the publication of *The Untilled Field*, and, despite his continuing membership and attendance at various chapels in London, Evans's publication of *My People* was regarded as a similarly public break with Nonconformity. Religion and exile are thus of considerable importance in both collections.

Both writers regarded the clergy as a parasitical and prohibitive power. Nonconformity was once a radical force in Wales, on the side of the peasantry in the tithe wars for instance, but by the end of the nineteenth century, Evans perceived the Chapel and its doctrine of "respectability" as exercising a pernicious stranglehold on the nation. If Irish Catholicism was once allied with the peasantry in a subversive anti-colonial battle against landlordism and the Protestant Ascendancy, the balance of power had changed, giving the Catholic Church a stifling monopoly. Moore and Evans both wrote against a new order of clerical power that had ceased to be the champion of the peasantry and become a dominant and dominating force within the emerging nation, replacing rather than overthrowing the previous imperialist order.

Moore's attack on the clergy in Ireland closely echoes earlier criticism leveled at landlordism and, significantly, Moore all but ignores the landlord class in his stories, a class that was in reality still an important presence in Ireland, albeit one in decline. Evans quietly excludes the landed gentry who lived in the parish on which Manteg is modeled from his stories; their absence in the village allows him to focus all his criticism on the totalitarian rule of the Chapel. *My People* deliberately eliminates class and cultural differences represented by the presence of larger landlords whilst eliding the traditionally pronounced Welsh denominational rivalry to decry a single, all-powerful Capel Sion.[28] To the exclusion of all other factors, then, both Moore and Evans were concerned with exposing the imprisoning, claustrophobic, dictatorial role of organized religion in the lives of the Irish and Welsh peasantry.

The Untilled Field, as Adrian Frazier remarks, depicts "Ireland as a prison run by jailers who are priests."[29] Evans too represents Wales as oppressed by the institutionalized religion that ought to have led the nation to salvation:

> I write down our condition to the tyranny of the preachers and the Liberal politicians. They have not only robbed us and given us a god of their own likeness—a god who imparts neither charity nor love—but they have dominated us for so many generations that they have fashioned our mind. They have built a wall about us. Within that wall—within the Nonconformist compound—we are born and spend our days in captivity. There are men who can break from any prison and our captors—our leaders–are the prison breakers.[30]

Similarly, the Chapel is depicted as a force that suppresses art and creativity and the higher aspirations of the human spirit: "Nonconformity . . . has substituted God for the black-coated figures that oppress the people and drain them of their substance, [and] has succeeded in fashioning a large majority of Welsh peasants into creatures without stamina and without soul."[31] In *The Untilled Field*, the Church stamps all vitality out of the peasantry and stifles all art except the formulaic iconography sustained by relentless church-building. Oppressive and philistine influences, Church and Chapel are also presented by both writers as overtly materialistic, with religious respectability ascribed to affluence, as in Moore's "Some Parishioners," where Annie Connex's wealth is perceived as a sign of her closeness to the Church, while Evans's grotesque peasants imitate the Chapel's "immorality and hatred and avarice."[32]

In Moore's work, the priests are portrayed as a root cause of the exodus from Ireland as people flee their repressive regime. Diaspora and exile are major themes in *The Untilled Field* and America is a constant presence in the imaginations and finances of those still at home. For Evans's peasants, in contrast, there is no escape. Indeed, the very idea of a world existing outside the immediate ambit of their village and its market towns is largely absent. Apart from the odd letter from a son or daughter who is away, the importation of a wife from a distant town, or the expulsion of a troublesome daughter to the nearest county asylum, there *is* no outside world. The claustrophobia of the village of Manteg adds to the sense of tension and madness in the world of these Welsh peasants.

Yet, despite the very carefully closed world created by the author, there is an implicit idea of exile in *My People*, a subtextual and paratextual concern with distance and detachment that is bound up with the figure of the artist, storyteller, or writer. Artists, intellectuals, and authors often see themselves as outsiders, exiles, or renegades whose very detachment facilitates their originality and creativity. The figure of the artist, an individual detached from his community and occupying the privileged vantage point of both insider and outsider, is invoked by both writers in their fiction and autobiographies. Evans left his home village in South Cardiganshire at the age of fourteen, first to be apprenticed to a draper in Carmarthen, and thence traveling to London via South Wales, becoming a Fleet Street journalist in his twenties.[33] When he composed *My People*, he was writing from London about a people from whom he was removed, and about a village in which he had not lived for over half his life, although he maintained close links with it. The extraordinary original dust jacket on early editions of *My People* invoked Evans's status as exile while simultaneously foregrounding his claims to authenticity. The dust jacket gave neither the title nor author of the volume on the front cover. Instead, the bare text stated: "These stories of the Welsh peasantry, by one of themselves, are not meat for babes. The justification for the author's realistic pictures of peasant life, as he knows it, is the obvious sincerity of his aim, which is to portray that he may make ashamed."[34] The statement implicitly addresses an English audience with no experience of Evans's "people," asserting the authenticity of the "realistic pictures" as "he knows it." The emphasis on veracity also operated as a defense against anticipated outrage in Wales. Importantly, the author's voluntary exile from Wales is implicitly inscribed on this cover at the very moment he owns his "people" in print. In his judgmental condemnation and desire to "make [the Welsh peasantry] ashamed," Evans is by implication distanced and detached from the condemned group.

Like Evans, Moore had long been an exile from Ireland, searching for artistic inspiration and the avant-garde in Paris and London before returning to Dublin to find new inspiration in the Dublin Theatre and Gaelic League.[35] In the first edition of *The Untilled Field*, two framing stories depict a quasi-autobiographical portrait of the artist fleeing the tyranny of the Catholic Church, which suggests creativity within Ireland is impossible. The return to Ireland in the final story, "The Way Back," is highly ambivalent and both stories were dropped from later editions. Although *The Untilled Field* began as an act of cultural nationalism, Moore ultimately found that writing its stories became a process of writing himself into exile once again.[36]

Moore's fictional artists and, in later editions, his storyteller characters, are absent in Evans's stories. Ironically the ultimate storytellers in *My People* are the satirized ministers themselves, and it is the figure of a gifted preacher, Eben, in "The Talent Thou Gavest," who comes closest to a quasi-autobiographical portrait of the author. Indeed, the voice of the omniscient narrator in *My People*, with his biblical cadences and rhetorical flourishes, finds a direct parallel in Manteg's ministers. Robert Welch once commented that "There was in Moore (as in Joyce) a good deal of the priest,"[37] and this statement can be extended to Evans, an inveterate "sermon-taster" who as a boy apparently addressed his fellows from a purpose-built pulpit.[38] Eben is a powerful orator and speaker of unpleasant truths, a preacher who must ultimately be silenced or ostracized and who is thus analogous to the author as artist and moral critic.[39] Thus, in both Moore's and Evans's works, in different but comparable ways, the true artist is figured as an exile, while the artist who remains at home is stifled, in various ways, by the demands of religion.

Central to both writers' representations of organized religion as carceral and corruptive is their focus on the peasantry—the main victims and accomplices of the Church and Chapel. The peasantry in Welsh and Irish writing, as Gramich argues, symbolizes the national character and as such has been demonized or idealized depending on the competing ideologies espoused:

> The residual and the emergent may be seen to coalesce in the figure of the Celtic peasant. In so far as he represents a static, primitive past, the peasant must be quasi-ritualistically destroyed, and yet, to the extent that he embodies

the energetic *difference* of Celtic cultures [from English hegemony], he must continually be resurrected and re-created. [40]

The portraits of Irish and Welsh peasantry in *The Untilled Field* and *My People* are remarkably similar, despite the different aims—revivalism and satire—of the authors. *My People* is infamous for its scheming, bestial, self-ish peasants, and for its darkly comic and grotesque caricatures, which unsettle in their claims to naturalistic veracity. Moore's peasant figures in *The Untilled Field* are deliberately more sympathetic and sometimes romanticized, like the storytelling coach-driver in "A Play-house in the Waste," who is twice described as a "legitimate descendant of the ancient bards." [41] Yet Moore's ambivalence toward peasants surfaces repeatedly and, particularly in his representations of western Ireland, there are striking parallels with Evans's harsher depictions of these versatile national symbols.

A shared concern of both writers is the oppression and exploitation of women. Evans and Moore show women being demonized and punished by religious patriarchs who view them as the agents of a dangerous sexuality. In both of their collections, women are repeatedly reduced to the level of animals. In *My People*, women are imprisoned, tethered, and driven out of their homes in the service of male sexuality. For instance, a father who sexually abuses his daughter eventually ties her up and drives her to the madhouse "in the manner a colt is driven to market." [42] In his signature story "A Father in Sion," a woman is shut in the harness-loft and only let out for exercise wearing a cow halter when her husband, a prosperous farmer and Chapel elder, wants a new wife:

> Once a week when the household was asleep he placed a ladder from the floor to the loft, and cried: "Achsah, come you down now."
>
> Meekly the woman obeyed, and as her feet touched the last rung Sadrach threw a cow's halter over her shoulders, and drove her out into the fields for an airing.
>
> Once when the moon was full, the pair were met by Lloyd Schoolin', and the sight caused Mishtir Lloyd to run like a frightened dog, telling one of the women of his household that Achsah, the madwoman, had eyes like a cow's. [43]

In Moore's "A Play-house in the Waste," when a woman becomes pregnant outside of marriage, her mother "took a halter off the cow and tied Margaret to the wall, and she was in the stable until the child was born." [44] The images of animalized and victimized women in cow halters are reminiscent of other gendered punishments such as the imposition of the "brank" or "scold's bridle"—an adapted halter with a bit used to silence "unruly" women. [45]

Women are often aligned with livestock in stories about weddings. In Moore's "A Letter to Rome," a pig is to be part of a marriage settlement and will move in to the newly constructed house in the bog, along with the new wife, suggesting an equivalence between the animal and the woman. In Evans's "A Heifer Without Blemish," the heifer of the title refers both to the bride and to the cow that will belong to the couple upon marriage.[46] The use of such parallel images might suggest the low status of women in Irish and Welsh peasant culture, or perhaps it is an extension of the common allegorical function of women in literature and art, where tethered, objectified peasant women bear the burden of meaning in the respective critiques of religious oppression.[47]

The allegorical function of female peasants is particularly pronounced in Moore's work. In *The Untilled Field*, there is barely an important female figure who does not in some way constitute an allegory of nation, perhaps reflecting the author's close connection to nineteenth-century literary traditions. There are the vibrant, dancing young peasant women who are connected to an older, pre-Christian Ireland and who are broken or chased from Ireland by the priests.[48] There are the rather two-dimensional women who represent the nation in stories about questions of exile and home.[49] Finally, there are the old peasant women, starving or disabled, in thrall to the church. Bridget Coyne in "Julia Cahill's Curse" is a blind old woman living in poverty who becomes the central figure of an allegorical image of Ireland where the Church itself becomes a play-house in the waste: "'This blind woman . . . will be the priest's last parishioner,' and I saw the priest saying Mass in a waste church for a blind woman, everyone else dead or gone."[50]

The most important of these characters, as allegory and something more, is Biddy M'Hale, who appears in the 1903 edition in section V of "Some Parishioners," a story which became "The Window" (and Biddy's name eventually changed to "McHale") in later editions. She is physically crippled but, denied romantic or sexual fulfillment in her youth, she becomes a prosperous and therefore relatively powerful woman as a poultry farmer: "Her faith in her money was abundant; she knew that as long as she had her money the priest would come to her for it on one pretext or another, sooner or later."[51] But in the grip of a monomania revolving around her desire to erect a stained glass window in her church, Biddy is reduced to a maddened, soiled, semi-naked creature, living (like an animal) in an outhouse on scraps of food given to her by villagers, her poultry dead or lost. Enraptured as she is by her religious visions, she is indifferent to her material condition, and so it is possible to see her as a positive symbol of genuine faith in contrast to the empty rhetoric of the Church. Yet, as Mark Llewellyn points out, Biddy's "delusion is but an extreme form of the income-generating faith that the priest needs to stimulate in order to ensure that his parish, and his position within it, can survive."[52]

Evans's magnificently titled "Be This Her Memorial" is, typically, a more horrifying and uncompromising tale than anything found in *The Untilled Field*, but it nevertheless bears a remarkable resemblance to the tale of Biddy

M'Hale.[53] It is the story of the ancient Nanni (even her name corresponds to Biddy's, as a generic designation for elderly women), who starves herself in order to buy an illustrated bible for the minister she worships. Her "gaudy" bible is directly analogous, as Gramich observes, to Biddy's stained glass window.[54] The religious mania of Biddy and Nanni can, of course, be read as symptomatic of a national malaise where both Irish and Welsh cultures are reduced to ruin by their prostration before religious institutions: "Nanni [is] suffering Wales, duped by a Bible salesman, sacrificing herself in her rat-infested cottage,"[55] while Biddy is obsessed with the mass-produced iconography of the relentless church-building program.

Biddy starts out as a wealthy woman; Nanni is maintained, begrudgingly, on poor relief, one tenth of which she still "religiously" donates to the chapel (this "tithe" suggests that the Chapel has merely usurped the oppressive role of the established Anglican Church). Biddy resists the priest's direct appeals for funds, yet she rapidly comes to resemble Nanni in her impoverished state, and the disreputable appearance of the two women provokes censure. In Moore's story, Biddy's scruffy presence in church becomes an embarrassment and annoyance to the priest: "she wore a bright blue cloak, she seemed to wear hardly anything else, and tresses of dirty hair hung over her shoulders."[56] Nanni's physical decline attracts local disapproval when she appears in Chapel with running sores and a visitor recoils in horror from the stench of her mud-walled hovel: "'Old Nanni,' folk remarked while discussing her over their dinner tables, 'is getting as dirty as an old sow.'"[57] This gossipy censure of Nanni is, significantly, uttered across the dinner table, raising the specter of starvation that haunts the story as a subtext until the final revelatory scene when it becomes apparent that Nanni has been subsisting on rat only to be devoured by rats in turn. Of course the comment also reduces her home to a pigsty, which echoes Biddy's sheltering in an outhouse.

If some critics have maintained that Moore deliberately allows room for a variety of interpretations of "truth" in his story, including the one that insists that Biddy is indeed witness to religious visions that the priest cannot begin to understand,[58] Evans leaves no such room to maneuver in his story. As Biddy unravels physically, materially, and (arguably) mentally during the course of the story, we are told that she seems "a little astray, a little exalted."[59] If this is a sign of genuine spiritual insight. Nanni's equally exalted distraction and "gleaming eye[s]"[60] in Evans's story are most certainly caused by starvation rather than by spiritual elevation. The workmen building the church in Moore's story offer a diagnosis of Biddy's condition that comes closest to the bleakness of Evans's depiction of Nanni: they "laugh . . . at [Biddy] for [being] a crazy old woman" and in response to her claim that "'one can live on very little when one is doing the work of God' . . . [t]he man called her a vain old woman, who was starving herself so she could put up a window."[61] Evans unequivocally pronounces Nanni to be deluded: "in her search for God, she fell down and worshipped at the feet of a god"[62]—the local minister, "Respected Josiah Bryn-Bevan":

> She helped bring Josiah into the world; she swaddled him in her own flannel petticoat; . . . she knitted him four pairs of strong stockings to mark his going out into the world as a farm servant; and when the boy, having obeyed the command of the Big Man [God], was called to minister to the congregation of Capel Sion, even Josiah's mother was not more vain that Nanni. Hence Nanni struggled on less than three shillings and ninepence, for did she not give a tenth of her income to the treasury of the Capel?[63]

As we have seen, Evans rebuked Nonconformist leaders for failing Wales and his story is a damning attack on the clergy's disloyal, quasi-filial betrayal of the nation that nurtured and reared Nonconformity to its current position of strength.

If depictions of the peasantry and religion in *The Untilled Field* and *My People* are similar in content, an equally significant parallel is to be found in the way both writers are concerned to harness the power of oral or residually oral cultures in Wales and Ireland.[64] In their stories, both writers try to evoke the mood and structure of folktales. In Moore's work this is done through direct speech and framed narratives, while in Evans's, oral storytelling inflects the structure, language and style of the whole collection. The following is a passage from Moore's "A Play-house in the Waste"—an anecdote describing what happens when a girl becomes pregnant outside of marriage—related as a framed story told by a local driver:

> The girl had been led astray one evening returning from rehearsal—in the words of my coach-driver, "she had been 'wake' going home one evening, and when the signs of her 'wakeness' began to show upon her, her mother took the halter off the cow and tied the girl to the wall and kept her there until the child was born. And Mrs Sheridan put a bit of string around its throat and buried it one night near the playhouse. And it was three nights after that the storm rose and the child was seen pulling the thatch out of the roof."[65]

The anecdote stands out because it is markedly different in style from the larger story in which it is embedded. It displays characteristics of an oral folktale: there is little sense of causality or logical progression in the events described, just as there is no subordination of clauses that are linked by a series of "ands."[66] The rendition is unembellished, the terrible events being related without elaboration, without reference to emotion of any kind, recalling the directness of folktale. The mediating narrator, the agent of the "Irish Industrial Society" who is our guide into this dark western wasteland, appears unable to render the story as part of his own causal, rational narrative and must recreate the voice of the peasant in order to allow the power of the folk narrative to be conveyed intact.[67] The otherness, and indeed the authenticity, of this passage and the quoted storyteller are reinforced by the use of the word "wakeness,"[68] although the rest of the speech is given in standard English. The foreignness of the word and its euphemistic meaning are highlighted yet contained by the quotation marks.

In a statement about Yeats that could be applied to Moore, Jacqueline Genet writes that, for him, "the way of speaking of the peasants, like their imagination, is concrete, free from the abstractions and generalizations which have exhausted the sap of Victorian writing."[69] Moore's succinct narrative thus mimics the written form of oral folktales and other literary representations of peasant speech, anticipating Evans's development of a more pronounced but comparable style. In Moore's work, as in Evans's, the focus is on actions, on concrete events, rather than abstractions. Evans's stories are magnificently understated in their spare renditions of events and sayings, recalling Old Testament stories, and they are all the more shocking for the unemotional presentation of momentous happenings alongside minor details, as can be seen in the following example. A daughter whose father has "sinned against" her

> cast from her body her clothes, and went down the Roman road and into the village. The people closed their doors on her and for four days she wandered thereabouts nakedly. The men of the neighbourhood laid rabbit traps on the floor of the fields, and one trap caught the foot of Matilda, and she was delivered into Evan's [her father's] hands. Having clothed her, he took a long rope, the length and thickness that is used to keep a loac of hay intact, and one end of the rope he fastened round her right wrist and one end round the left wrist. In this wise he drove her before him, in the manner in which a colt is driven, to the madhouse of the three shires, which is in the town of Carmarthen, and the distance from Manteg to Carmarthen is twenty-four miles.[70]

While Moore frames short examples of peasant folk-culture within larger stories, Evans makes these examples the basis of his entire collection. Nevertheless, the attempt to convey the characteristics of orality and folktale, and traces of the original language of these traditions (Gaelic, or Hiberno-English, and Welsh), produces intriguingly similar results.

The endeavor to represent in written English an oral culture that is conducted in a language other than English can be read in the light of postcolonial paradigms as an example of the construction of new, hybrid "english." Both Moore and Evans were self-consciously concerned with disrupting and reinvigorating standard English with the syntaxes and idioms of Gaelic and Welsh. Moore dreamed of purifying and beautifying tired imperial English prose through "a bath in Irish,"[71] which, since he spoke no Gaelic, he sought to achieve by a complicated and rather bizarre process of translation from English to Gaelic and back again. There is limited evidence, however, of his retaining "translations" in his work and it should be noted that many stories in *The Untilled Field* were not translated at all. [72] Evans was a native speaker of Welsh who claimed not to have become fluent in English until adulthood; Fleet Street friends recalled his labored composition of copy in Welsh, which would then be translated into English. [73] The unique register he created for his short stories, which suggests Welsh syntax and vocabulary, also makes use of "aggressive mistranslation," [74] including "Big Man" as a mistranslation of "*Arglwydd Mawr*," or "great Lord," and the literal translation of the endearment "*bach*" as "little": "'Dear little Big Man,' she prayed, 'let not your son bach religious depart.'" [75] Thus, within the limits of their different resources, both writers used the defamiliarizing influences of Gaelic or Welsh and their awareness of oral culture and storytelling to disrupt, invigorate, and shape their "english" in comparable ways.

How far Evans's and Moore's hybrid "englishes" can be described as "postcolonial" is an interesting question. They certainly bear comparison with new languages developed in colonial contact zones and in postcolonial literatures, but while Evans's "english" is by far the more radical and artistically original creation, his is more difficult than Moore's to describe as unproblematically "postcolonial." Despite Moore's ambivalence, he wrote self-consciously to further the aims of the nationalist Gaelic League. Evans is a more difficult and paradoxical case. I have discussed the hybrid nature of Evans's non-standard "english" elsewhere, pointing out the similarities it bears to other postcolonial englishes in the disruptive, invigorating, and creative way it uses Welsh (and some of the English spoken in Wales) to construct a unique and immensely powerful literary language. Yet postcolonial models do not adequately accommodate Evans: while his extraordinary writing could be described as postcolonial in form, it is not obviously anti-colonial in content. [76] Retrospectively, Evans's literary contribution has been canonized as part of a nationalist assertion of Welsh difference and artistic vitality (and thus appropriated into a postcolonial critical discourse in Wales), yet it would be difficult to argue that his writing is really a "postcolonial" (read anti-colonial) text of subversion. Instead, Evans appears to use his stylized language to condemn the Welsh peasantry in terms that deliberately reference and mobilize the received colonial imagery of the Welsh, just as Moore tends to reinforce stereotypes of a backward, superstitious peasantry.

A transnational comparative approach refocuses our attention, drawing out different themes in part by extracting them from their respective national canons and literary histories without abandoning the specific national contexts from which they emerge. By studying *The Untilled Field* and *My People* together, it is evident that these controversial Irish and Welsh authors were drawing on similar cultural and literary traditions to forge innovative new writing. Oral folktale, with a naturalist inflection, and the influence of indigenous language both influenced form, while both writers mounted an attack on the established powers in their respective countries—religious institutions rather than the more distant political powers in Westminster.

Evans was writing against the more romanticized image of the peasantry as a cultural wellspring that Moore and his fellow Celtic revivalists had in some degree helped to construct. He was also engaging with specifically Welsh debates, rejecting in inflammatory terms the idea of a *Cymru Lân Cymru Lonyddd* (Pure and Peaceable Wales) that had been so painstakingly constructed in Wales to counter the (mis)representations of the Welsh Nonconformist peasantry as immoral and backward as published in an infamous 1847 government report.[77] But what a comparison with Moore reveals about Evans is that his iconoclastic modernist stories draw strength from similar techniques to those used in the Irish Renaissance. Moreover, Evans was not simply inverting the images and motifs of an earlier romanticized discourse to undermine that discourse. Rather, his authority and claims to authenticity paralleled those of Moore as indeed his diagnosis of the ills of Wales reflected Moore's analysis of Ireland's malady. To perform a comparison with the Celtic Renaissance writers, then, is to read Evans against the grain, to step outside the Welsh framework of canonical and critical formations, and thus to see connections with a wider, even "Pan-Celtic" tradition.

In reading Moore in light of Evans's overt attack on the Welsh, it is obvious that Ireland, and particularly the peasantry, are faulted as backward and blinkered. Indeed, his portrayal of the subjugated peasantry suggests that Moore has not moved all that far from the assumptions of *Parnell and His Island.* Old and culturally valuable traditions may indeed be available to be captured by ethnological and literary acts of preservation, but the Ireland Moore portrays is hardly poised on the brink of national revival.

Transnational comparative readings offer a different lens through which to view often familiar writers. Reading Evans and Moore in conjunction challenges both the stated intentions of each writer and the received critical viewpoint of their two seminal collections of Irish and Welsh short stories.

NOTES

1. I am grateful to M. Wynn Thomas and John Harris for some illuminating contributions and comments on earlier drafts of this chapter.

2. In *Ave,* Moore describes this call to move back to Ireland as a revelation akin to Paul's on the road to Damascus. See Adrian Frazier, *George Moore 1852–1933* (New Haven: Yale University Press, 2000), 273.

3. See also subsequent editions in 1926 and 1931. I have used the first edition (London: T. Fisher Unwin, 1903) as my primary text, but have included page references to the standard edition (based on the 1931 publisher edition) edited by Mark Llewellyn, *The Untilled Field (1931),* vol. 3 of *The Collected Stories of George Moore: Gender and Genre,* ed. Ann Heilmann and Mark Llewellyn (London: Pickering and Chatto, 2007). This edition will be referred to as 2007.

4. Similarly, *The Untilled Field* has been seen to have anticipated elements of James Joyce's *Dubliners* (1914): David Wheatley discussed Moore's influence on Joyce in "An Untilled Field: Moore's Influence on Joyce and Beckett" at the "George Moore and His Contemporaries" conference at the University of Hull in 2008. For a contemporary comparison of Joyce and Evans, see "A Study in Garbage," *Everyman*, February 23, 1917, 398, in *The Critical Heritage: James Joyce,* vol. 1, *1907–27*, ed. Robert H. Deming, (New York: Routledge, 1997), 85. For Evans's influence on Joyce, see Wim Van Mierlo, "James Joyce and Caradoc Evans," *Genetic Joyce Studies* 7 (Spring 2007): n.p., accessed June 21, 2014, www.geneticjoycestudies. org/.

5. See Glenda Norquay and Gerry Smyth, eds., *Across the Margins: Cultural Identity and Change in the Atlantic Archipelago* (Manchester: Manchester University Press, 2002); John Kerrigan, *Archipelagic English: Literature, History, and Politics 1603–1707* (Oxford: Oxford University Press, 2008); and Stefanie Lehner, *Subaltern Ethics in Contemporary Scottish and Irish Literature: Tracing Counter-Histories* (Basingstoke: Palgrave Macmillan, 2011). There are few detailed comparative studies of Anglophone literature in Wales and Ireland. The establishment of the Arts and Humanities Research Council funded Ireland-Wales Network based at Cardiff and Aberystwyth Universities was a major development in this field, hosting seminars and conferences (at one of which an early version of my chapter was delivered) and publishing a special issue of *Irish Studies Review* 17, no.1 (February 2009) on "Irish and Welsh Writing" guest-edited by Claire Connolly and Katie Gramich.

6. Norquay and Smyth, introduction to *Across the Margins*, 2.

7. Paul O'Leary, "Public Intellectuals, Language Revival and Cultural Nationalism in Ireland and Wales: A Comparison of Douglas Hyde and Saunders Lewis," *Irish Studies Review* 17, no.1 (February 2009): 15.

8. On the ways in which criticism of Evans's *My People* has negotiated the collection's problematic status as a canonical (anti-national) text, see Kieron Smith, "Constructing the Map: Welsh Criticism of Caradoc Evans," *Almanac: A Yearbook of Welsh Writing in English: Critical Essays* 16 (2012): 89–120.

9. O'Leary, "Public Intellectuals," 6.

10. The Welsh Church Act of 1914, which disestablished the Anglican Church, came into effect in 1920.

11. George Moore, "Epistle to the Cymry," included in the new and revised 1926 edition of *Confessions of a Young Man* (London: William Heinemann Ltd, 1933), 287.

12. Moore's speech at the National Eisteddfod in Cardiff in 1914, "Epistle to the Cymry," is an example, albeit a rather patronizing one, of the contemporary assertion of the common causes of cultural nationalism in Ireland and Wales. The title asserts Moore's claimed affinity to Wales, by his use of *"Cymry,"* which roughly translates as "comrade" or fellow countryman. Moore's friendship with playwright and patron of the arts Lord Howard de Walden (T. E. Ellis) and de Walden's attempt to establish a Welsh National Theatre are also interesting in this context. On Moore and de Walden's friendship, see Stoddard Martin's discussion in the next chapter.

13. From Moore's letter to Virginia Crawford, August 19, 1902, quoted in Mark Llewellyn's introduction to *The Untilled Field*, vii.

14. Richard Allen Cave, introduction to *The Untilled Field*, by George Moore (Gerrards Cross: Colin Smythe Ltd, 2000), xxiv.

15. From his memoirs, *Salve* (1912), quoted in Mark Llewellyn's introduction to *The Untilled Field*, vii.

16. For *The Untilled Field*'s potential influence on other writers, see also Bertha Thomas's collection of interlinked short stories focusing on the farmers, innkeepers, peasantry, and gentry of a parish in Carmarthenshire, *Picture Tales from Welsh Hills* (London: T. Fisher Unwin, 1912).

17. Evans's early short stories, published in *Reynolds Newspaper* and *London Chat* between 1904–1908, show no influence of *The Untilled Field*, although they do show early traces of concerns that would bloom in *My People*, so it is unlikely that Evans read *The Untilled Field* on its first publication. On the early stories, see Tomos Owen, "From Slum to Capel Sion: The

Early Fiction of Caradoc Evans and the Prehistory of 'Anglo-Welsh Literature'," in *Almanac: A Yearbook of Welsh Writing in English* 16 (2012): 121–150.

18. *The English Review* XIX (December 1914): 124. I am grateful to Martha S. Vogeler for drawing my attention to this.

19. David Caradoc Evans, "Two Welsh Studies," *The English Review* XX (April 1915): 25–36. Evans subsequently dropped the "David" from his name. This piece consisted of "The Man Who Walked With God" (revised and published in *My People* as "A Father in Sion") and "Be This Her Memorial." These two stories most closely resemble elements of Moore's "A Play-house in the Waste" and "The Window." In July 1915, another article entitled "Two Welsh Studies" by Caradoc Evans appeared in *The English Review*, 426–37. The two stories "The Devil in Eden" and "A Just Man in Sodom" appeared in *My People* with the same titles.

20. Stanley Unwin, *The Truth About a Publisher: An Autobiographical Record* (London: George Allen & Unwin Ltd, 1960), 133.

21. Mark Valentine, *Arthur Machen* (Bridgend: Seren, 1995), 107–108; Frazier, *George Moore*, 286, 380, 540 n75, 561 n31.

22. We do know that later in Evans's career, when he was acting editor of *T P's Weekly* (1923–1929), he published a front-page interview with Moore, written by John Austin (November 12, 1927). From Evans's own pen we know that as a developing writer he read *The Clarion*, *T P's Weekly*, and *Reynold's Newspaper*, none of which published Moore during the relevant period. Evans helped to compile *The World's Great Books* edited by Arthur Mee et al. (London: Amalgamated Press, 1909–10), but Moore does not appear in the five volumes of digested writings. Evans named a number of writers as influences, for instance, "Tolstoy, Gorki, Turgenief, Maupassant, Flaubert, Hardy, W. W. Jacobs, and . . . the bible . . . " and kept a picture of Dickens above his desk. We know that he had a complete set of Synge, but he never mentions Moore. See Evans, "The Road with One Fingerpost" and "W. H. Davies," in *Fury Never Leaves Us: A Miscellany of Caradoc Evans*, ed. John Harris (Bridgend: Poetry Wales Press, 1985), 121, 127. (The quotation is taken from "The Road with One Fingerpost," 121.)

23. Walter J. Ong uses this classification in *Orality and Literacy: The Technologizing of the World* (London: Methuen, 1982), 69.

24. Katie Gramich, "Creating and Destroying 'The Man Who Does Not Exist': The Peasantry and Modernity in Welsh and Irish Writing," *Irish Studies Review* 17, no. 1 (February 2009): 19–30.

25. George Moore, *Confessions of a Young Man* (1888), quoted in Patrick Ward, *Exile, Emigration and Irish Writing* (Portland, OR: Irish Academic Press, 2002), 201.

26. See John Harris, introduction to *My People*, by Caradoc Evans (Bridgend: Seren, 1987), 38–44.

27. George Moore, *Parnell and His Island* (London: Swan Sonnenshein, Lowrey & Co., 1887), 234. In fact, Moore is here describing the "aboriginal" Irish, "the Fins," whom he distinguishes from the Celts (ibid., 96), but the distinction is blurred.

28. The development of one all-encompassing Chapel can be seen when Evans rewrites an earlier satire on Nonconformist denominational rivalry, where the Methodists fear they may lose a burial (and thus material evidence of the size of their congregation) to the Dissenters, in "The Man Who Wouldn't Die" (*London Chat*, January 11, 1908, repr. in Evans, *Fury Never Leaves Us*, 58–62). The much revised and darker version, which appeared as "The Glory That Was Sion's" in *My People*, eliminates Nonconformist conflict/competition, using a shadowy off-stage Anglican Church to replace the second Chapel.

29. Frazier, *George Moore*, 309–310.

30. Evans, quoted in Harris, introduction to *My People*, 16.

31. Ibid., 44.

32. Ibid.

33. Trevor Lloyd Williams, *Caradoc Evans* (Cardiff: University of Wales Press on behalf of the Welsh Arts Council, 1970), 17–19.

34. Dust jacket of first edition of *My People*, published by Andrew Melrose, reprinted in Harris, introduction to *My People*, 34. It is not known whether the publisher or the author composed these lines, but the emphasis on veracity was already present in a letter Evans published in *The Carmarthen Journal* (a local Welsh paper) in defense of two short stories

from the collection that had been published earlier (April 1915) in *The English Review* (see note 17). Attacking "such a people" as those depicted, he wrote: "You know all this to be true, and you know incidents more remorselessly true than anything I have written about in my stories." Quoted in John Harris, introduction to *My People*, 44.

35. See Frazier, *George Moore*, 273, 284–286.

36. George Moore, *Hail and Farewell: Ave, Salve, Vale*, ed. Richard Cave (Gerrards Cross: Colin Smyth, 1976), 347. I am grateful to Adrian Frazier for drawing this point to my attention.

37. Robert Welch, "Moore's Way Back: *The Untilled Field* and *the Lake*," in *The Way Back: George Moore's* The Untilled Field *and* The Lake, ed. Robert Welch (Dublin: Wolfhound Press, 1982), 33.

38. Williams, *Caradoc Evans*, 16. M. Wynn Thomas considers the analogous roles of religious minister and (oral) storyteller in relation to some of Evans's later stories in his book *In the Shadow of the Pulpit: Literature and Nonconformist Wales* (Cardiff: University of Wales Press, 2010), 128–135, 179–180, 205–209.

39. Harri Roberts, "The Body and the Book: Caradoc Evans's *My People*," *Welsh Writing in English: A Yearbook of Critical Essays* 11 (2006–2007): 32–50. Eben chooses to compromise his gift and tone down his excoriations in return for a living.

40. Gramich, "Creating and Destroying," 19.

41. George Moore, *The Untilled Field* (London: T. Fisher Unwin, 1903), 225, 239. These words do not appear in the 1914 and later editions.

42. Evans, "Lamentations," *My People*, 144.

43. Evans, "A Father in Sion," *My People*, 51–52.

44. See the 1931 edition of Moore's "A Play-house in the Waste," *Untilled Field* (2007), 85. For the original rendering of the scene discussed later in my chapter, see Moore, "A Play-house in the Waste," *Untilled Field* (1903), 237.

45. I am grateful to Diana Wallace for drawing my attention to the connection between the haltered women in Evans's and Moore's stories and the scold's bridle.

46. See Harris, introduction to *My People*, 28.

47. For a feminist reading of Evans's peasant women, see Katie Gramich, "The Madwoman in the Harness Loft: Women and Madness in the Literature of Wales," in *Dangerous Diversity: Changing Faces of Wales*, ed. Katie Gramich and Andrew Hiscock (Cardiff: University of Wales Press, 1998), 20–33.

48. Julia Cahill (whose earlier model seems to be Mary Moran in "The Tenant Farmer," *Parnell and His Island*) is expelled from the church and village to live in exile with the fairies or in America. Kate Kavanagh rebels against the arranged marriage foisted upon her by the priest, refusing to allow her drunken husband into her bed and fleeing to America the next morning.

49. Examples include Margaret Dirken in "Homesickness," or Catherine who rejects the fit and able brother, choosing instead the dreamer in "The Exile"; Lucy the life model who flees Dublin in "The Way Back"; the unkind mother in "And So On He Fares," and Ellen Cronin in "The Wild Goose."

50. Moore, "Julia Cahill's Curse," *Untilled Field* (1903), 206. This passage doesn't appear in the 1931 edition, but the 1903 version is reprinted in the appendix to Llewellyn's 1931 edition of *The Untilled Field*, 230.

51. Moore, "Some Parishioners," *Untilled Field* (1903), 93; "The Window," *Untilled Field* (2007), 58.

52. Llewellyn, introduction to *The Untilled Field*, xviii.

53. "The Window" is itself very close to Flaubert's "*Un Coeur Simple*," as Gramich points out in "Creating and Destroying," 26.

54. Ibid.

55. Harris, introduction to *My People* , 31.

56. Moore, "Some Parishoners," *Untilled Field* (1903), 110; "The Window," *Untilled Field* (2007), 65.

57. Evans, "Be This Her Memorial," *My People*, 111.

58. See Cave, introduction to *The Untilled Field*, xv–xvi.

59. Moore, "Some Parishioners," *Untilled Field* (1903), 106; "The Window," *Untilled Field* (2007), 63.

60. Evans, "Be This Her Memorial," *My People*, 111.

61. Moore, "Some Parishioners," *Untilled Field* (1903), 94, 96; "The Window," *Untilled Field* (2007), 59.

62. Evans, "Be This Her Memorial," 108.

63. Ibid., 109.

64. On Moore and the oral tradition, see Vivien Mercier, "The Irish Short Story and Oral Tradition," in *The Celtic Cross: Studies in Irish Culture and Literature*, ed. Ray B. Browne, William John Roscelli and Richard Loftus (West Lafayette, IN: Purdue University Studies, 1964), 98–116.

65. Moore, "A Play-house in the Waste," *Untilled Field* (1903), 237. The 1931 version is slightly different, see note 41.

66. See Ong, *Orality and Literacy*, 37–39.

67. Moore, "A Play-house in the Waste," *Untilled Field* (1903), 185. In later versions of this and other western stories, Moore enhanced the role of the oral storyteller by providing layered frames, multiple storytellers, and including interjections from listeners. The tale of the coach-driver is retained with only minor modifications, but is now told by "Pat Comer, one of the organizers of the I.O.A.S," that is the Irish Agricultural Organization Society. See the 1931 version in Llewellyn's (2007) edition of *The Untilled Field*, 79.

68. "Wake" and "wakeness" suggest the "archaic" pronunciation of "ea" as "ay," so that the reported speech of the coach-driver links him to the past. See Terence Patrick Dolan's Hiberno-English Archive, accessed June 21, 2014, www.hiberno-english.com/index.html.

69. See "Yeats and the Myth of Rural Ireland," in *Rural Ireland, Real Ireland?*, ed. Jacqueline Genet (Gerards Cross: Colin Smythe, 1996), 154.

70. Evans, "Lamentations," *My People*, 144.

71. Moore, quoted in Declan Kiberd, *The Irish Writer and the World* (Cambridge: Cambridge University Press, 2005), 97.

72. There seems to be some disagreement between various critics' lists on what was translated into Gaelic and *An t-Úr-Ghort* (the six Gaelic-language stories published in 1902 that would a year later appear in their English-language versions in *The Untilled Field*). See Pádraigín Riggs, *"An t-Úr-Ghort and The Untilled Field,"* in *George Moore: Artistic Visions and Literary Worlds*, ed. Mary Pierse (Newcastle: Cambridge Scholars Press, 2006), 130–141; Ward, *Exile, Emigration and Irish Writing*, 213; Cave, introduction to *The Untilled Field*, xvii. Intriguingly, Cave (but not Riggs or Ward) suggests that "The Play-house in the Waste" appeared in *An t-Úr-Ghort*, but I have found no commentary on how direct speech is represented in this Gaelic version, or whether there is a clear shift in register corresponding to the English version. Nor can I ascertain whether the English version in *The Untilled Field* is supposed to be the result of a "bath in Gaelic."

73. Williams, *Caradoc Evans*, 19–20.

74. Harris, introduction to *My People*, 16.

75. Evans, "Be This Her Memorial," *My People*, 109.

76. See Kirsti Bohata, *Postcolonialism Revisited: Writing Wales in English* (Cardiff: University of Wales Press, 2004), 106–107.

77. On the 1847 government report into the state of education in Wales (known as the "Treachery of the Blue Books") and its moral, cultural and religious condemnation of the Welsh, see Gwyneth Tyson Roberts, *The Language of the Blue Books: Wales and Colonial Prejudice* (Cardiff: University of Wales Press, 2011) and Prys Morgan, "From Long Knives to Blue Books," in *Welsh Society and Nationhood: Historical Essays Presented to Glanmor Williams*, ed. R. R. Davies, Ralph A. Griffiths, Ieuan Gwynedd Jones and Kenneth O. Morgan (Cardiff: University of Wales Press, 1984), 199–215. On Evans's attack on *Cymru Lan Cymru Lonydd* (the pacific image of Wales nurtured in response to the Blue Books report) see Hywel Teifi Edwards, "Y Pentre Gwyn and Manteg: From Blessed Plot to Hotspot," in *Beyond the Difference: Welsh Literature in Comparative Contexts*, ed. Daniel Williams and Alice von Rothkirch (Cardiff: University of Wales Press, 2004), 8–20.

Chapter Eleven

Moore, Wagnerism, and the Shape of the Later Career

Stoddard Martin

George Moore's interest in Wagner lasted for fifty years and had both social and aesthetic aspects, as has been noted and explored by Moore scholars.[1] The present chapter extends investigation into Moore's Wagnerism as it pertains to cultural attitudes and associations, especially with Anglo-Welsh man of letters Lord Howard de Walden, Italian novelist Gabriele D'Annunzio, and French critic and novelist Edouard Dujardin. It also engages with the writing of "Wagnerian" prose, notably *The Brook Kerith*, as it links to Wagner's *Parsifal* and his unrealized "Jesus of Nazareth" scenario.

Moore's Wagnerism began with the French during his early days in Paris, especially in his friendship with Dujardin, then editor of *La Revue wagnérienne*. French poets had been fascinated by Wagner at least since Baudelaire had written *Richard Wagner et Tannhäuser à Paris* during the celebrated battle over Wagner's revision of that work for the Opéra in 1861—largely a matter of heightened sensuality in the Venusberg music.[2] Moore's interest was quickened in the 1890s by association with the poet/critic in English most devoted to Baudelaire and *les Décadents*, Arthur Symons; it was solidified in the Edwardian decade by trips to Bayreuth with his Wagner-mad fellow Irish grandee Edward Martyn and his great lady friend and beloved Maud Cunard.[3] Others who stimulated this interest included Howard de Walden, Moore's "protégé" as he was seen at the time, as affirmed by Max Beerbohm in his 1907 cartoon "Mr George Moore, Preacher to Lord Howard de Walden."[4] Moore's recent biographer Adrian Frazier has suggested that Howard de Walden replaced Sir William Eden, the Maecenas who took Moore on his earliest trips to Bayreuth.[5] In 1908, Howard had indeed taken Moore to the festival, in company with Josef Holbrooke, the so-called

"Cockney Wagner,"[6] and Margherita Van Raalte, who later became Lady Howard de Walden. They saw *The Ring* and *Parsifal*, prompting Moore to write to Lady Cunard some of his most salient reflections on Wagner, Bayreuth, and travel in South Germany, of which he would remain fond.[7] Margherita for her part would relate in a memoir sixty years later how she suffered an attack of claustrophobia in the first act of Wagner's last work and fled to her room, whereupon her landlady, disgusted, knowing how rare seats for performances were, snatched the ticket from her hand and rushed off to enjoy the final two acts herself.[8]

Howard de Walden was twenty-eight years Moore's junior. On accession to his title in 1899 and marriage to his opera-singing heiress in 1912, he was reputedly the richest man in Britain.[9] He wrote verse drama under the name T. E. Ellis and backed theaters and theater ventures, including a production of Maeterlinck's *Blue Bird* at the Haymarket in 1909.[10] From his residence in Wales, Chirk Castle, he would seek to do for native theatre what he saw Lady Gregory, Moore, and Yeats as having done for Ireland, an ambition Moore would extol almost obsequiously in "Epistle to the Cymry."[11] Howard eventually became a patron of Dylan Thomas, whose first name was inspired by the title character of the middle play in Howard's trilogy *Children of Annwn* (1912), *Dylan Son of the Wave*, which was produced at Drury Lane as an opera, with music by Holbrooke, under the direction of Thomas Beecham in the year of the Welsh poet's birth.[12] This being the year too of the outbreak of World War One, the opera was lambasted for its "German method" and dropped from view,[13] inflicting on Howard one of many wounds he would suffer from a cultural world that seemed to favor his money over his output, partly as a result of the sturdy middle-class prejudice that work of value could hardly come from persons of such privilege. In later years he would withdraw, teased by his wife for faulty knowledge of "real" music[14] and satirized by a scribbling son-in-law as sipping his morning coffee while reading *The Times* clad in a full suit of armor.[15] The lampooning was not quite as cruel as that which Munich had lavished on "mad" King Ludwig for his patronage of Wagner and erection of fantasy castles, nor would Howard de Walden end in death by drowning, though whisky became his most reliable companion in middle age and probably hastened his end.

Before family and status had done their worst—that is, during the Edwardian decade—this grand poetaster more or less let Moore make Seaford House in Belgravia his London address, which had the advantage of providing Moore with geographical and social proximity to his beloved Maud. Moore encouraged and was encouraged by the younger man's passion for Wagner, symbolism and Arthurian legend. They fell out when Moore claimed co-authorship of Howard's play *Lanval* on the basis of having offered discussion and advice rather than having put pen to paper. The putative co-author took umbrage, causing Moore to complain to Lady Cunard: "Howard's a lunatic and there's an end of it." Eventually, however, he "sent G. M. a cheque for the entire proceeds of the production (which came to exactly 17/6) and the dispute was resolved in laughter."[16] A few years on, newly married, Howard would invite Moore for Christmas at Chirk with him, his wife, and his incipient brood. To Lady Cunard, Moore would now write, "He is a great dear . . . like Jesus Christ—I mean very much in the same way—an affectionate nature like myself."[17] Coming as it did on the eve of Moore's journey to the Holy Land to collect material for his "Christ" book, *The Brook Kerith*, the remark seems to have been portentous. The book may indeed owe motifs to the presence in Moore's life of this aristocratic, serene, or just increasingly resigned individual, who seems to have borne—at least in Moore's flattering reflection of him—comparison to a *parfait esprit* or "guileless fool," a pre-Parsifalian persona.

Moore's most thoroughgoing attempts to write Wagnerian or musical prose in experimental and/or Symbolist mode come, as I have argued elsewhere,[18] from this period between the end of the nineteenth century and the Great War, which saw a kind of *Götterdämmerung* of an English phase of Wagnerism, as of most things Victorian. His friendships with Howard de Walden and with Maud Cunard, who half-broke Moore's heart by taking up with Beecham instead of with him once she had left her husband, were mixed into it. As readers of the original edition of *The Lake* will know, the writer who takes the heroine to Europe is named Ellis, not Poole, as in the 1921 edition; the novel was to be dedicated to Maud, who refused the honor; and a long central chapter is devoted to an aesthetic journey leading to Bayreuth and performance of *The Ring*, styled "the greatest musical work the world has ever known."[19] The cutting or altering of these features for the later edition indicates how Moore attuned himself to a *Zeitgeist* in which *fin-de-siècle* enthusiasms were no longer in vogue, Wagner and things German were to be downplayed and abstraction and obliquity were preferred. He also would grow less eager or needy to invoke the link to Howard de Walden. A distancing from the *passé* may also be seen in a change of the heroine's name from the Symonsian "Rose Leicester" to the Joycean "Nora Glynn." But while these revisions may shed light on the trajectory of Moore's presentation of himself in later years, toward a figure designed to impress Maud Cunard's daughter perhaps as much as "Emerald"[20] herself, they do not alter what is well-known of the Wagnerian inspiration for *The Lake* overall: the style of the prelude to *Lohengrin* and the content of the letters of Wagner and Mathilde Wesendonck,[21] which had been translated into English and published in the 1890s by Moore's friend William Ashton Ellis (another Ellis, though no relation), head of the London Wagner Society.[22]

Both Wagner and his most extreme disciple among novelists, Gabriele D'Annunzio, were influential over Moore in this era. We know this from

numerous letters Moore wrote to Maud as well as an "interview" he gave to
The Musician while composing *Evelyn Innes*, his most explicit statement on
Wagnerian aesthetics as they apply to the novel. [23] In this interview, he described the Italian—also a favorite of Symons's and linked at the time to
Eleanora Duse, for whom Symons would go to Italy to offer his ill-fated
poetic drama *Tristan and Iseult* [24]—as a systematic adaptor of *leitmotif* in
verbal detail. Moore said that he did not want to go to D'Annunzian lengths
in building up descriptive details as if into chromatic chords; his main concern in "a music novel" was to pursue Wagner's devotion to certain grand
"motives"—the Parsifal motif of redemption notably, a recurring favorite—also to the characters' psychological/emotional lives, [25] which were not
easy to dissociate from the music that broods beneath Wagnerian avatars'
words. One may detect a hint of Moore's well-known flippancy here, perhaps
even his covering of sources, for in D'Annunzio he surely spotted a wealth of
the very elements he extolled.

He had in fact been reading the Italian avidly, spurred on by the enthusiasm of Maud, to whom he wrote:

> You speak about *The Triumph of Death* by d'Annunzio; I have just finished
> *L'Intrus*, another book by him. I think it quite wonderful. You know that I
> seldom praise a novel—well, I could write twenty pages about *L'Intrus*. He
> writes as that fellow whose name begins with P and whose hair is red plays the
> piano [Paderewski]. In him we get the psychological novel . . . He is a little
> wanting in outline—but what wonderful writing! [26]

Later, reporting on an evening of music by Wagner, he asked Maud to send
him a copy of *Le Triomphe de la Mort* (Moore read D'Annunzio in French,
presumably because he did not know enough Italian, though he said that the
translation of *L'Intrus* was "at least equal to the original"). [27] Later still,
having half-digested another D'Annunzio novel, he wrote:

> *Les Vierges aux Rochers* I did not finish. It did not seem to me nearly so good
> as the others. He is a wonderful writer and he has interesting things to say, but
> he has no power for the massing and the ordination of events, I add for the
> symbolisation of events. I don't know if you will understand this last phrase; it
> requires explanation but it would take too long . . . *une lettre n'est pas un
> cours de littérature.* [A letter is not a literature tutorial.] [28]

To sum up: while immersing himself in the works of a composer who, he
told Maud, held "the deepest secrets . . . the secrets of life . . . in our
hearts . . . beyond words," [29] and composing his own first "music novel,"
Moore paid his chief contemporary *literary* attention to the most ardent Wagnerian novelist of the day. His dismissal of *Le Vergine delle Rocce* (*Les
Vierges aux Rochers*) may in this light mix his reasonable fatigue in the

cours de littérature with an urge to distance himself from what appeared a formidable rival—part of an effort, signaled in *The Musician*, to depict his work as an advance on, or at least different from, D'Annunzio's. There may also be an element of Anglo-Saxon disdain in Moore's taste such as that which Henry James would sum up in the phrase "queer high flavoured fruit from overseas."[30] Years later at a party in Paris, Moore would quip to another American, "[D'Annunzio] is a 'hair-dresser' who knows just what brushes and scents to use,"[31] even though Moore would have known that for the Parisian *haute monde*, D'Annunzio, having recently fled Italy to escape a Wagnerian mountain of debt, was the most sought-after of society lions, beloved by Comte de Montesquiou and Princess de Polignac alike[32] and envied by Proust, whose vast *oeuvre* was just then beginning to be (self) published.

Of this figure so widely seen as a foremost genius of his epoch, we might also note that the young Joyce, who *did* read Italian, had stated in "The Day of the Rabblement" (1901): "Mr. Moore is really struggling in the backwash of that tide which has advanced from Flaubert . . . to D'Annunzio: for two entire eras lie between *Madame Bovary* and *Il Fuoco*."[33] *Il Fuoco* is an apt reference point. Set in Venice in the year of Wagner's death there, it constituted the Italian's most extreme effort in literary Wagnerism, focusing on a hero devoted to chromatic aesthetics, a vast interior life, Tristan-like romanticism, and a national theater to rival Bayreuth. Projected to be the first volume in a *Ring*-like sequence (further volumes were never written), it is a prime example of what native critics would call *dannunzianismo*:[34] a characteristic pre-Proustian blend of autobiography with fiction, feeding from and into authorial celebrity. It ends with the hero escorting Wagner's casket to the funeral train that will take it to "*la collina bàvara*"[35] and with its heroine, based on the actress Eleonora Duse, preparing to leave the stage for retreat into a convent. This detail, given that it was published in 1900, could not have affected Moore as he wrote *Evelyn Innes* (1898), but it is portentous for its sequel *Sister Teresa* (1901). Even if, unlike early D'Annunzio novels, Moore did not read it or, like *Les Vierges aux Rochers*, he set it down unfinished, he would surely have heard of it; for not only did his callow young Irish critic, Joyce, absorb it, but so did his beloved Maud and his artistic conscience of the *Evelyn Innes* period, Arthur Symons.

Richard Cave has suggested that Moore created a *monologue intérieur* in *The Lake* that was not merely sequential,[36] revealing workings of mind such as Dujardin had deployed in *Les Lauriers sont coupés* (1888) or as Joyce would develop in Leopold Bloom, but also cumulative in its power like the monologues in Wagner, thus potentially transformational for its characters. This was a feat Henry James and Virginia Woolf would achieve in their ways, yet neither with such self-conscious inspiration from Wagner as Moore, like

D'Annunzio, was pleased to invoke. Evocation of psycho-erotic underlife is of course where Wagner had advanced standard operatic procedure the most, achieving effects that appealed to artists and moralists of a "new age" as well as to decadent dreamers on color, imagery, and what D'Annunzio calls the "orgasmo" of feeling.[37] Such literary techniques are where Moore's later works may claim their most permanent attention in my view, also an attribute shared with and largely inspired by Wagner and imitated by D'Annunzio—extravagantly in *Il Fuoco*, but also in earlier works Moore had read. This was the all-absorptive, rhythmical narration: what Nietzsche disparaged, in part disingenuously, as "unending melody,"[38] and what Moore's literary "son" Joyce would spend his last two decades attempting to achieve in an experimental novel whose river runs back to "riverrun" and out to the vastest of all efforts by a mere writer to compose a modernist, post-Wagnerian work, using words as notes and building up waves of harmony and dissonance out of verbal *leitmotifs*—that "book to go beyond all books":[39] *Finnegans Wake*.

The Brook Kerith may be such a book in its way, or aspire to be. While not a world-historic epic, it takes on what, in popular thought, would be seen as "the greatest story ever told" and deals with it in a manner that would cause Shaw to quip, "I read about thirty pages of *The Brook Kerith*. It began to dawn on me that there was no mortal reason why Moore should not keep going on like that for fifty thousand pages, or fifty million for that matter."[40] Shaw of all people! In content, the novel links back to Wagner's unrealized scenario "Jesus of Nazareth," about which Moore had written in the same journal in which he espoused ideas for a "music novel" on Wagnerian lines: "Neither Shakespeare nor Sophocles could have contrived a nobler or more dramatic telling of the story . . . In [one] incident Wagner has divined a lost fragment of the history of the time. But how exquisitely it fits with the known facts, how it completes and explains! . . . The beauty of Wagner's music has shadowed his genius as a writer."[41]

The longest of any scenario Wagner did not turn into an opera, "Jesus" was conceived shortly after *Siegfried's Tod*, the *ur*-version of the last part in *The Ring*, though it was sketched earlier. It comes from the pivotal phase of Wagner's career surrounding the Dresden rising of 1849, participation in which caused him to be condemned to death, a sentence commuted to exile from Germany, leading to years of compositional drought yet vast literary activity organizing his thoughts for the future, along with self-justification. The scenario is set as a five-act play, the French operatic or Shakespearean grid that Wagner had abandoned after *Rienzi* in favor of the three-act or Greek model of all his mature work, a fact that may underline how turbulent a period of reassessment this was for him, in terms of form as well as content, aesthetics and ideas. The sketch that Moore praises takes up only a third of Wagner's essay, which runs to nearly sixty pages of the last volume of his

Prose Works. Another third consists of free-form exegesis—Ashton Ellis dubs it "Feuerbachian hermeneutics"[42]—and ardent speculation on the nature of sex, man, woman, family, child, egoism, and death. A final third lists passages to be used in the text, all taken from Luther's German edition of the Bible and displaying close reading of the Gospels.

Ellis argues that Wagner relies mostly on the Gospel of St. John. He also seeks to combat a charge that the composer was taking off from the *Leben Jesu* of David Strauss, published in 1835 and in several popular editions by the time Wagner sat down to write.[43] The point here was surely to promote "Jesus of Nazareth" as the vanguard work of a later nineteenth-century, pan-European fascination with the historical Jesus, which gave rise not only to Ernest Renan's famous *Vie de Jésus* in 1863 but also to Dujardin's *La source du fleuve chrétien* four decades on. Because of its extent and the way it appeared in the last volume of *Prose Works* labeled "Posthumous," Wagner's sketch could strike disciples as indicating a further path for the "artwork of the future"[44] now that *Parsifal* had been fixed as a last word. The scenario could thus be a last beyond last word, a grail beyond grail, for the happy few. Such an impression no doubt helped impel the quest of the most avid of old Wagnerians at the turn of the century into the historical facts leading to the coming of Christ.

I have noted the influence of Lady Cunard and Howard de Walden on Moore in this phase, the first with an erotic tinge, the second with an existential and social tinge; but Dujardin was equally important, not least as correspondent. He remained a beacon and sounding-board for Moore decades beyond his heyday as editor of *La Revue wagnérienne* and its successor *La Revue independante*. Moore's letters to him, which John Eglinton translated and published shortly before Moore's death,[45] are as heavy with revelation about the author's turn of mind in this phase as were the letters to Maud that Rupert Hart-Davis published following *her* death two decades later.

Eglinton introduces his small volume by observing that Moore, in contrast to many contemporaries, was less an "ideas man" than an observer: "nearer to the true Buddhistic vision."[46] This image evokes *Parsifal*, also perhaps Wagner's other great unrealized scenario "The Victors" (which involves aspects of Indian religion) and signals an overall drift in his Schopenhauer-affected later years. In the same way as one might envisage Howard de Walden playing paraclete from this mix, Moore appears as Gurnemanz—the old tale-teller, hermit, and fond if somewhat displaced member of a "grail order." This is indeed how the author came to relate to the two worlds he dwelt in most as he aged: the literary and the social. A watershed, Eglinton states, arrived in Moore's career during or just after composition of *The Lake* and led on to a new style—"direct, unemphatic, following the line of narrative with patient adequacy."[47] The description might be of the mode, so boring to the giddy, of the post-Dresden Wagner who had the chutzpah to

deploy the monologues of Wotan in *The Ring* and the narrative of Gurnemanz in that first act of *Parsifal* that sent young Margherita Van Raalte
fleeing the theatre. A style of an old sage—confident, consummate, apparently no longer burdened by motives of riches or fame—was apt for the creator
of a "stage consecration play," so too for one of limited editions on fine
paper. Of Moore's style, Eglinton concludes: "His style is his wisdom, his
vision of life, his whole experience. There is no more distinguished achievement in present day literature, nor—in spite of some monotony of manner-
isms— . . . so limpid a flow between mind and subject matter."[48]

Moore's letters to Dujardin trace the realization of this later style: its
origins, the critical moment leading to it, and its relation to Moore's earlier
"musical" aesthetics during and after his phase of greatest interest in Wagner.
In 1887, the era of the *Revues*, Moore writes to congratulate Dujardin on *Les
Lauriers*, which he calls "a kind of symphony in full stops and commas."[49] A
decade on, when discussing Wagner and "Jesus of Nazareth" for *The Musician*, as well as conceiving *Evelyn Innes*, he returned to Dujardin some notes
on *Parsifal* that he had borrowed, along with a recommendation of
D'Annunzio as "a writer of the first rank," and went on to solicit notes on
Tannhäuser and *Tristan*, though confessing, "What I like best of Wagner is
Lohengrin."[50] After 1903, the era of *The Lake*, which Eglinton calls pivotal,
he followed Dujardin's interest from Wagner into biblical study. This carried
on into the era of Moore's closest association with Howard de Walden (letters to Dujardin are often sent from Seaford House), with Moore referring to
his next work as "my *messianic* book 'Hail and Farewell.'"[51] By 1908, he
was asking Dujardin to take on a scenario about the Irish heroine Deirdre,
suggestive not only of Wagner and Howard de Walden's Celtic projects but
also of Yeats. He asked Dujardin to persuade a composer, probably Paul
Dukas, to render it into opera. Dujardin apparently would have preferred
Moore to drop this fantasy and travel with him to Palestine, causing Moore to
retort, "You see, my good friend, in life one must choose: it is either the
opera or exegesis."[52] There is further exchange on topics for opera, no doubt
iterating ideas discussed at Seaford House, with Holbrooke, or on the way to
Bayreuth. Then, by the summer of 1909, Moore wished to meet Dujardin
himself at the Wagner festival and go with him after to "the glaciers."[53]

Dramatic sensation, whether artistic or natural, was exercising a simpler
fascination over Moore by this stage: "What I want to write now is pure
aesthetics."[54] Wagnerian operatic yearnings having reached a summit previously largely unachieved, he began to descend into the valley of exegesis. He
talked of writing *The Apostle*; of Paul versus Luke regarding *The Acts*.[55] By
1913, he was referring to "our interminable conversations on Jesus, Wagner
and Dukas," in that order.[56] By 1914, "After a pretty close study of the
Gospels I have come over to your belief that Jesus never existed on this earth.
I am by no means sure that I shall get anywhere with him. Stripped of his

miracles, the Lord is a sorry wight."[57] A gap of six years followed, explained largely by the intervention of war. Following this, Dujardin was impoverished and Moore much taken up with wiring money to him. The friendship never quite regained its old footing, though *Letters* came out in 1928. By this time, Dujardin, having been lionized by Joyce, as Moore was not, had moved on to devote himself to the clarifications of *Le Monologue intérieur, son apparition, ses origines, sa place dans l'oeuvre de James Joyce* (1931), a work one imagines not entirely designed to thrill his *ancien ami.*

The writing of *The Brook Kerith* occupied the first years of the wartime hiatus, when trips to Bayreuth and Germany were forcibly ended and relations with Howard de Walden diminished as that friend drifted more toward family and Wales, having failed in *his* high designs for theatrical art on a more cosmopolitan stage. In this era, the Gurnemanz persona became fixed, that of old Moore as *parfait*, hermit of Ebury Street, storyteller, and refiner of a "style [which] is his wisdom."[58] *The Brook Kerith* reflects as much, the book being not so much a version of Wagner's Jesus scenario or a dramatization of the history Dujardin explores in *La Fleuve* as an excursus on related subject and theme. A spirit of the music of *Parsifal* seems to hover over it, as well as ghosts of the content of that "last word." The achievement is Wagnerian in *feel* in a way that explicitly Wagner-related works such as *Evelyn Innes* are not. This is apparent in the long, sensual evocations of landscape (waste, forest, lake, rock) or animal (ram, eagle, bear, lamb) as in a glorification of simple, individual existence in nature and brotherhood divorced from the degradation of urban power struggle and decadence. This is in tune with the ethos of Wagner's last work as well as parts of *The Ring.*

The book seems to sum up years of semi-conscious dreaming in the opera house or the armchair on how to accomplish in writing what Moore had long accepted as the highest achievement in art. An unobtrusive tripartite structure, from the narrative of Joseph of Arimathea to the career of Jesus to the arrival and flight of Paul, mirrors Wagnerian form at its most typical, while the normative milieu of the Essenes, resonant of Cathars and their love-feast, recalls Wagner's representation of a Grail order. That young Jesus should have no rival among slingers of shot in the hills,[59] that his voice should be tender and conversation with him induce "sweet reverie,"[60] that he should become a *pure* who cannot be "inflamed by the sight of every woman"[61] and worshipper of God in spirit rather than in conformity to Law, that he should prove a *mensch* yet remain a mere man who errs and ends by wondering if love of God itself is not "the last uncleanliness of mind,"[62] is all in harmony with ideals a "happy few" would have seen Wagner driving at in his last work. The final clench of the novel—Paul's decision to go on preaching of Christ after being confronted by a Jesus who "did *not* rise from the dead" and who regards his youthful messianism as "folly"[63]—is pure Moore: a gloss on the development of a religion that, not least as an Irishman, had troubled him

all of his life. But from a dramatic point of view, the conception is Wagnerian too, or perhaps post-Wagnerian in its quieter, more rarefied guise, analogous, say, to the post-*Parsifal*ian yet still Wagner-derived new direction
Debussy was seen to be taking in music with *Pélléas et Mélisande*.

Beyond *The Brook Kerith*, output of the aging Moore flows with a calm-
er, more gently resigned self-assurance than that which characterized earlier
work—certainly work prior to the moment of aesthetic crisis Eglinton notes
regarding *The Lake*. In *Perronik the Fool* (1924), a version of the *Parsifal*
tale, and *Héloïse and Abélard* (1921), perhaps a version of *Tristan*, as in
other late books, all carefully executed and in numbered edition, we may, if
inclined, see a shade of the aging Wagner at his desk, wondering where to
return to or to go on to now that his swan-song of *Bühnenweihfestspiel*
(*Parsifal*) existed—to that old Jesus sketch? to the Buddhist scenario? to
some dramatization of the element of the Feminine in Man he was essaying
at his desk at Palazzo Vendramin when his heart stopped?[64] In a *Zeitgeist*
captivated by this *Übermensch* among artists, a *finis* like Moore's seems apt.
Had Moore died like *Der Meister* at age sixty-nine, the great work he had
achieved in a previous decade, *The Brook Kerith*, might have stood as a
magisterial last word: a *Parsifal*, as it were. Had Wagner lived, he would
have wished to craft smaller, more essentially modernist pieces, in verse as
well as music drama: mere *jeux d'esprit* compared to his earlier works, yet no
less transcendental or reaching after the sublime. Thus, in his sphere, Moore
arguably realized what the great forerunner had projected, yet had been unable to achieve.

NOTES

1. See William F. Blissett, "George Moore and Literary Wagnerism," *Comparative Litera-
ture* 12, no.1 (Winter 1961): 52–71, reprinted in *The Man of Wax: Critical Essays on George
Moore*, ed. Douglas Hughes (New York: New York University Press, 1971). My work on
Moore began with chapter 6 of *Wagner to "The Waste Land": A Study of the Relationship of
Wagner to English Literature* (London: Macmillan, 1982) and continued in "George Moore and
Literary Wagnerism: A Revisitation," in *George Moore: Across Borders*, ed. Christine Huguet
and Fabienne Dabrigeon-Garcier (Amsterdam: Rodopi, 2013), 33–41.

2. For Wagner's appeal to French writers, see *Wagner to "The Waste Land,"* chapter 1.

3. Though Wagner's influence on writers in English traveled mainly via francophone figures of the post-Baudelaire era, it is worth noting that Wagner's career began with English
inspirations, including a historical novel by a Victorian with occult interests, Edward Bulwer-
Lytton. Wagner read *Rienzi* in 1837 and, during a crucial period in Paris three years later,
adapted it into what would become his breakthrough opera, which premiered in Dresden shortly before he became *Kapellmeister* (musical director) there in 1842. (See "Autobiographical
Sketch," first published in *Zeitung für die elegante Welt*, no. 8, February 1 [1843], reprinted in
Wagner: A Documentary Study, ed. Herbert Barth, Deitrich Mack and Egon Voss, trans. P. R. J.
Ford and Mary Whittall [London: Thames and Hudson, 1975], 14). This was followed by a
work conceived during a sea voyage to London preceding the year in Paris that also drew on
English sources including Coleridge, De Quincey, Marrayat, and a tale published in 1821 in
Blackwood 's magazine: *The Flying Dutchman* (see Ernest Newman's *Wagner Nights* [London:

Putnam, 1949], 9–28). Wagner claimed inspiration from English sources, both early and late, notably Shakespeare, whose plays he adored (Barth, Mack and Voss, *Documentary Study*, 11). As a boy, he studied English in order to translate *Romeo and Juliet*; a few years before his death, when sketching *Parsifal*, he considered writing a funeral march for that play but instead merged ideas for it, along with an unfinished *Trauersymphonie*, into the funeral music of Titurel in the final act of his last work (Newman, *Wagner Nights*, 761–764). *Parsifal*, like *Tristan* before it, was based in legend dear to English contemporaries, origins mixed from British and troubadour sources. Add to this that in his first serious job, in Königsberg in 1835, the sole work Wagner wrote was an overture entitled "Rule Britannia" (Barth, Mack and Voss, *Documentary Study*, 13–14) and that his first opera performed, in Riga the next year, was a version of *Measure for Measure* (*Das Liebesverbot*), and you have the portrait of an artist whose impulsion, far from being violently, nationalistically German as later mutation would have it, was as Anglo-inspired as that of the great French Romantics Berlioz and Hugo or his exact contemporary, the young Verdi.

4. The cartoon is printed in Rupert Hart-Davis, ed., *George Moore: Letters to Lady Cunard 1897 – 1933* (London: Hart-Davis, 1957), page opposite 54. The friendship is memorialized in thirty-eight letters from Moore to Howard de Walden, and four to his wife, among unpublished papers in possession of the Howard de Walden estate, and also including letters from Kipling (five), Shaw (one), Belloc (forty-two), Chesterton (twenty-one), Rodin (twenty) and Felix Weingartner (three), among other cultural notables of the period, c. 1900–1930.

5. Adrian Frazier suggested this in conversation at the "George Moore: Crossing Borders" conference at the University of Lille (2007). He added that Moore had been friendly with Eden's wife, as he would be with Howard de Walden's. Not only did Moore know how to conduct himself in these circles, and enjoy it, he also "genuinely liked women."

6. David Hamilton, "The Neglect of English Classical Music," *New English Review* (August 2009), accessed June 25, 2014, www.newenglishreview.org/David_Hamilton/The_ Neglect_of_English_Classical_Music/.

7. Moore to Cunard, August 16 and 18, 1908, in Hart-Davis, *Letters to Cunard*, 62–66; also 96, where, in a letter undated from 1918, Moore asks Maud to ask Lord Curzon to spare Cologne Cathedral from bombardment.

8. Margherita Howard de Walden, *Pages from My Life* (London: Sidgwick & Jackson, 1965), 70–71.

9. Prior to marriage to this heiress of Dutch/Sephardic descent, reputed to be the richest in Britain, Howard de Walden was estimated to share in a fortune of £16,000,000. See Hart-Davis, *Letters to Cunard*, 50 n1.

10. Moore's own feeling for this play, and for Maeterlinck's trope, is indicated in September 1909 letters he wrote to Maud addressing her as "My dear Blue Bird"; Hart-Davis, *Letters to Cunard*, 73–74.

11. George Moore, "Epistle to the Cymry," included in the new and revised 1926 edition of *Confessions of a Young Man* (Harmondsworth: Penguin, 1939), 265–77. Moore was not above seeking flattery of his protégé/patron. Several letters mentioned in n4 above suggest this, as does Moore's depiction of the character Ellis in the first edition of *The Lake* mentioned later in this essay (London: Heinemann, 1905), though that portrait is ambiguous, even barbed. Ambiguity also arises in the Cymry epistle, where Moore notes: "when I used to come over from Ireland and stay at Seaford House I used to confide to Lord Howard all my plans for the revival of the Irish language" (272). Here, he appears to lay claim to a kind of co-authorship in the man's Welsh endeavors, as he would to composition of plays (see n16 below). Regarding Moore and Wales, see also Kirsti Bohata's discussion in the previous chapter.

12. I am grateful for information provided by Thomas Seymour, a grandson of Howard de Walden who has edited three of his plays and is accumulating materials for a biography (in conversations, October 2007 and after).

13. "If English opera is to be sung and performed in English, it must not be founded on German methods," *The Era* (June 1914). *Children of Annwn* was translated into German in 1922.

14. Another of Howard de Walden's grandchildren, Tatiana Mallinson, has recalled to me in conversation (October 2007) that her grandmother, being a "serious" musician, was less im-

pressed with Wagner than was her husband, whom she felt to be partly ignorant of that art, though in an amateurish way he played clarinet and organ. Moore appears to confirm this when he relates to Maud how he described her to Howard as "like music, like Wagner's music," to which Howard replied, "Not a bit like Wagner's music," which Moore amended, "You are quite right . . . she is more like Mozart. The Symphony in G Major. She is as joyous." The letter goes on: "Howard didn't know the G Major Symphony or he thought my remark foolish" (July 13, 1905, Hart-Davis, *Letters to Cunard*, 42).

15. Spanish journalist José Luis de Villalonga, married to Howard de Walden's daughter Priscilla. I rely here again on the recollections of Tatiana Mallinson in conversations (see previous note).

16. December 4, 1909, Hart-Davis, *Letters to Cunard*, 74–75; also 75 n1.

17. December 28, 1913, ibid., 85.

18. See "George Moore and Literary Wagnerism: A Revisitation." This is also the view of Richard Allen Cave in his *Study of the Novels of George Moore* (Gerrards Cross, Bucks: Colin Smythe, 1976).

19. See George Moore, *The Lake* (London: Heinemann, 1921); and Richard Allen Cave's "Afterword" to his edition of *The Lake* (Gerrards Cross, Bucks: Colin Smythe, 1980).

20. Maud had adopted this new first name by then, regarding her own as plain or *passé*. Moore adapted to it, though he was shocked when he first heard it, fearing that she might have run off with an unknown rival. Moore's friendship with Maud's daughter Nancy is well known; see also my essay "Moore and Hemingway" in *George Moore: Dublin, Paris, Hollywood*, ed. Conor Montagu and Adrian Frazier (Dublin: Irish Academic Press, 2012), 137–146.

21. See *Wagner to "The Waste Land,"* chapter 6. Elements in *The Lake* relating to Wagner's work include *Lohengrin* and its prelude, mirroring the lake in the sky and the sense of mystical oneness at the end of chapter 11 (of the 1921 edition). Other examples are, in relation to *Parsifal*, the condition of the priest as hermit in a wood by a (sacred) lake and the importance of the augury of a bird (cormorant/swan) shot down by irresponsible huntsmen (1980 edition, 141), and, in relation to *Götterdämmerung* and the Norns scene, an image of weaving a thread out from one spool and onto another (ibid., 146). These are in addition to obvious *Tristan* overtones and themes: the Celtic locale, the "wistful [depressive?] Irish note," the character of the beloved ("mysterious, evanescent as breath, with the same irresponsible seduction," ibid., 134), and her role in "revealing the soul" of the man and luring him to escape into a larger, more sublime existence; and also the extraordinary aesthetical/Wagnerian milieu that the hero-ine travels to in Europe (chapter IX of the 1905 version, cut in the 1921 revision).

22. Ellis was known to Symons, Shaw, Howard de Walden, and all figures of the day in England for whom Wagner was a beacon. His translations of the *Prose Works* appeared throughout the 1890s, attracting major interest. Though I know of no blood connection between W. A. and T. E. Ellis, it is not impossible that this link to the name of the most prominent of English Wagnerians was a subliminal element encouraging the youthful Howard de Walden to use his family name rather than title when operating as author.

23. "Mr George Moore on Music and Literature," *The Musician* (1897): 392–394, quoted and discussed in my *Wagner to "The Waste Land,"* 103.

24. Symons regarded D'Annunzio as "the greatest figure in Italian letters" and championed him in England. He wrote an introduction for Georgina Harding's translation of *The Child of Pleasure* (London: Heinemann, 1898) and translated himself three plays, *La Gioconda* (1901), *Francesca da Rimini* (1902) and *The Dead City*, performed in 1918. See Karl Beckson and John M. Munro, eds., *Arthur Symons: Selected Letters, 1880–1935* (London: Macmillan, 1989), esp. 117 and 174. For his *Tristan* disappointment, see also *Wagner to "The Waste Land,"* chapter 4, esp. 67–68.

25. Moore coined the term in "Since the Elizabethans" (*Cosmopolis* [October 1896]: 57). Cave quotes it in his *Study of the Novels* (135 and elsewhere) and in his "Afterword" to *The Lake* (182).

26. September 10, 1897, Hart-Davis, *Letters to Cunard*, 23–24.

27. October 1897, ibid., 24–25.

28. February 10, 1898, ibid., 26–27.

29. October 1897, ibid., 25.

30. Henry James, "Gabriele D'Annunzio, 1902," *Quarterly Review* (April 1904), quoted in Roger Gard, ed., *Henry James: The Critical Muse* (London: Penguin, 1987), 10. This now neglected essay is a key critical statement from James's "major phase." Two of his three last novels bear D'Annunzian elements: *The Wings of the Dove*, set partly like *Il Fuoco* in Venice, and *The Golden Bowl*, scrutinizing like *L'Innocente* a sympathetic heroine's marriage to an adulterous Italian aristocrat. Symbolic damaging of the eponymous gift in *The Golden Bowl* may echo a climactic scene between the hero and heroine in *Il Fuoco*.

31. Reported in a letter to Fania Marinoff, June 2, 1913. See Bruce Kellner, ed., *Letters of Carl Van Vechten* (London: Yale University Press, 1987), 5–6, quoted by Adrian Frazier in *George Moore: 1852–1933* (New Haven: Yale University Press, 2000), 387.

32. See, for example, Philippe Jullian, *Robert de Montesquiou: A Prince of the Nineties*, trans. John Haylock and Francis King (London: Secker & Warburg, 1965), esp. 217–28.

33. Ellsworth Mason and Richard Ellmann, eds., *The Critical Writings of James Joyce* (Ithaca: Cornell University Press, 1989), 71, quoted and discussed by Frazier, *George Moore*, 317–318.

34. See *Il Fuoco*, ed. Giansiro Ferrara (Milano: Mondadori, 1967), introduction by Ferrara, esp. 27.

35. *Il Fuoco*, concluding sentence. The reference ("the Bavarian hill") is to Bayreuth.

36. Cave made this suggestion in his extensive discussion in *Study of the Novels of Moore*, especially in the chapter entitled "The Wagnerian Novel."

37. A word used frequently by the author, particularly in *L'Innocente*, at moments when the interior monologue of the hero reports feelings so strong as to induce involuntary shivers and/or welling of tears.

38. In Friedrich Nietzsche, "Wagner as a Danger, 1," *Nietzsche Contra Wagner: The Brief of a Psychologist* in *The Complete Works of Friedrich Nietzsche*, ed. Oscar Levy (Edinburgh: T. N. Foulis, 1911), vol. 8, *The Case of Wagner*, trans. Antony M. Ludovici, 61. See also *Wagner to "The Waste Land,"* 7.

39. A concept embodying obvious Wagnerian ambitions and enunciated influentially in not dissimilar terms by both Nietzsche and Mallarmé. See *Wagner to "The Waste Land,"* 153 and elsewhere.

40. Quoted in Joseph Hone, *The Life of George Moore* (London: Victor Gollancz, 1936), 333; see *Wagner to "The Waste Land,"* 114.

41. "Wagner's 'Jesus of Nazareth,'" *The Musician* (1897): 8, quoted by W. A. Ellis in his Preface to "Posthumous," vol. 8 of *Richard Wagner's Prose Works* (London: Kegan Paul), 1899, xvii.

42. The phrase refers to the German philosopher and anthropologist Ludwig Feuerbach's method of exegesis. See Ellis, "Posthumous," xvi.

43. Strauss was a figure of such note that the young Nietzsche, after writing *The Birth of Tragedy out of the Spirit of Music* to glorify Wagner, divided the first volume of his next work, *Thoughts out of Season,* into complementary essays, "David Strauss, the Confessor and the Writer" and "Richard Wagner at Bayreuth." Ellis would have been keen to combat views of the later Nietzsche and his apostasy from "the Wagner cult."

44. Richard Wagner, *Das Kunstwerk der Zukunft* (Leipzig: Otto Wigand, 1850).

45. John Eglinton, ed., *Letters from George Moore to Ed. Dujardin, 1886–1922* (New York: Crosby Gaige, 1929).

46. Eglinton, introduction to *Letters to Dujardin*, 11–12.

47. Ibid., 14.

48. Ibid., 15.

49. Moore to Dujardin, May 17, 1887, in *Letters to Dujardin*, 20.

50. Undated and April 22, 1897; see also November 3, 1897; ibid., 37–38.

51. April 4, 1908, ibid., 66 (emphasis added).

52. November 18 and 19, 1908, ibid., 68–69.

53. June 15, 1909, ibid., 78.

54. July 22, 1909, ibid., 79.

55. April 13, 1911, ibid., 88.

56. May 2, 1913, ibid., 98.

57. April 30, 1914, ibid., 104.

58. Eglinton, introduction, ibid., 15.

59. George Moore, *The Brook Kerith: A Syrian Tale* (London: T. Werner Laurie, 1916), 103.

60. Ibid., 122 and 153.

61. Ibid., 194.

62. Ibid., 357.

63. Ibid., 458.

64. An event crucial to the plot that galvanizes the ambitions of the artist-hero in D'Annunzio's *Il Fuoco*.

II

Collaboration

Co-Authorship, Desire, and Conflict

An Introduction to the Moore/ Craigie Collaboration

Ann Heilmann

The Fool's Hour was the first of several ventures in collaborative playwriting undertaken by George Moore and Pearl Craigie. The comedy revolves around a young lord's infatuation with an actress and two women's resourcefulness in achieving their ends (to marry the men of their desire). Its three acts were drafted in the first four months of 1894, but only the first act saw publication, in the inaugural April 1894 issue of *The Yellow Book*. This outlet, so suitable for a decadent co-production, was probably chosen at Craigie's suggestion. Ironically, she later expressed her dismay at the magazine's "vulgar" contents.[1] Published here in its entirety for the first time, the play is collated from manuscript sources held in the Pearl Craigie/George Moore Papers in the Mark Samuels Lasner Collection, on loan to the University of Delaware Library.[2]

The history of Moore and Craigie's co-authorship has a distinctly dramatic quality in itself. Tragicomic in its collision of two incompatible personalities who kept attracting and repulsing each other, the story of their relationship does not altogether lack some of the more farcical aspects of *The Fool's Hour*. As outlined in this book's Introduction, collaboration was always a game with high stakes for Moore: a stimulus to creative thought, yet ever at risk of turning into a source of irritation and antagonism, sometimes lifelong enmity when friendships soured in the clash of temperaments, or when Moore's co-author proved unreliable or worse, ran off with what he considered his intellectual property. Even more hung in the balance when it came to collaboration with women: an arrangement in which, for Moore at least, the textual inevitably merged with the sexual. In Craigie, Moore was to meet his match.

Initially, it appeared as if two brilliant conversationalists had found each other. To John Butler Yeats (the father of the poet), Moore was without doubt "the most stimulating mind" he had ever encountered; and for all the caricatures that Moore's appearance inspired, his words, as Max Beerbohm attested, were so eagerly awaited that the room would fall silent when he started to speak.[3] Classically educated[4] and highly cultured, Craigie, for her part, enjoyed the reputation of being "the only rival to Wilde in the making of epigrams."[5] Not only was she witty, she also delighted in the verbal flirtation that Moore relished. But he almost missed his opportunity of becoming acquainted with her. His side of the story is related in the "Lui et Elle" section of the second American (1920), third English (1921), and (as chapter II) in the Carra (1923) editions of *Memoirs of My Dead Life*. After responding casually in late 1893 to an unfamiliar author, "John Oliver Hobbes," wishing to know whether his recent novel—according to Moore himself, *Some Emotions and a Moral* (1891), though more likely *A Bundle of Life* (1893), which Craigie started to adapt in January 1894[6]—might make suitable material for a comedy, Moore was mortified to discover from Arthur Symons that Hobbes "was a woman, and a pretty one" at that.[7] His hastily dispatched apology led her to invite him, probably in December 1893,[8] to Lancaster Gate, the location of the elegant London residence of her American parents to which she had returned with her newly born son after separating from her husband some years earlier.[9] Shortly after their first encounter, work on *The Fool's Hour* took off, with Craigie providing drafts and Moore offering suggestions from early January 1894.[10] That the initial script was Craigie's is indicated in her choice of names and a few passages that appear partially drawn from an incomplete earlier draft of a story entitled "The Love Monger."[11]

As *The Fool's Hour* gained in pace, so did the frequency of Moore and Craigie's correspondence alongside regular outings to galleries, parks, concerts, and dinners. Moore's head was soon turned. In *Memoirs* he recounts asking himself "doubtfully if I were falling in love; I could not believe that such a disaster could happen to me."[12] That it did happen he later blamed on Craigie's deliberate deployment of sex appeal, for while "suspicions often crossed my mind that she was fooling me," what man, especially of Moore's cast of mind, could have resisted witty banter about sex: "No one's talk turned oftener on the subject of sex . . . she admitted sex to be her subject; her brain was certainly possessed of it."[13] Interwoven with art, sex was of course Moore's very own domain. Craigie excelled in the art of sensual allusion and teased Moore mercilessly, such as when she spiced praise of *Esther Waters* with a pretend-disclaimer of her awareness that "you are a man and I am a woman and I like you" and, from the safe distance of the Continent, sighed for sensual abandon: "Why must duty invariably come before pleasure? Oh, to be an unconscious sinner for at least five-and-twenty minutes!"[14]

The problem, from Moore's point of view, was that every expression of desire was accompanied by a simultaneous retraction. If "this eternal restraint . . . tire[d her] to death," Craigie also sounded a warning note: "Life has made me fearful of my best impulses"; she was "a lover of souls, but people scare me out of my wits"; the "trouble" was that "my thoughts are too mature for my body."[15] Her rhetoric of refutation is easily recognizable in Moore's 1895 *Celibates* portrait of "Mildred Lawson."[16] In fairness, Craigie alerted Moore early on that "sex relations did not appeal to her," but he chose to ignore the hint: "one attaches no real significance to the confession."[17] This was a grave error, particularly in light of her marital history, one so reminiscent of the social purity scripts of New Woman novels like Sarah Grand's *The Heavenly Twins* of 1893 or Emma Frances Brooke's *A Superfluous Woman* of 1894 (Craigie's husband was violent and afflicted with syphilis, which she was terrified of contracting and passing on to her child).[18] An equally weighty consideration must have been the divorce suit in which she was then engaged (a wife petitioning for custody of her child at a time when the law privileged the rights of men had to conduct herself with the strictest propriety; any imputation of adultery would have proved fatal to her lawsuit).[19] As a convert to Roman Catholicism who had made a vow of chastity,[20] she had an additional bulwark of defenses that only further aggravated Moore, that fiercest of iconoclasts (though here, too, he would turn his experience to good account in his writing: in the eponymous Evelyn Innes's abject submission to Monsignor Mostyn, Craigie was, in 1898, appalled to recognize a parody of her relationship to her own confessor, Monsignor Brown).[21]

Given the complex personal circumstances within which the Moore/Craigie collaboration advanced, it is not surprising if work on *The Fool's Hour* stalled after the publication of the first act. Initially, though, matters progressed well. On January 4, 1894, Craigie sent Moore "a short sketch of Acts I and II, for, following your excellent advice, I have not even thought of any dialogue. Do you like the name of 'Sarah Sparrow'? I am thinking of an actress of the Mrs. Bancroft and Ada Rehan type—I mean a blend of the two."[22] This earliest manuscript version of the play (handwritten manuscript sheet C; see "Note on the Text") indicates that she had a larger cast of characters in mind. A note at the end of the outline of the first act seeks reassurance: "I want you to see this before I write anything further . . . I think the above little scene is, on the whole, good." In this version the Doldrummonds are called Skeppertons and Sarah's fellow actor and love interest, Mandeville, appears as Bob Norton. There is some confusion about Sarah's role in the draft of Act II because another actress, Kitty Carew (who receives

only fleeting mention in the published version), is presented as Cyril's seduc-
tress. Intriguingly, this is the name given in *Vale* (the final volume of *Hail
and Farewell*) to one of the Mayfair cocottes with whom Moore and his
friends Colville and Belfort Bridger spent their time and money in 1869. Did
Moore suggest the name or co-opt it later for his autobiography?[23]

The opening scenes of the first act are well-developed, introducing a
context for Cyril's bid for independence and rebellion against his mother's
regime through a satirical juxtaposition of his hen-pecked father with a bachelor friend. Plot and character constellation, however, were still in process. In
reply to a subsequent query, Moore offered an overview of how he envisaged
the remainder of Act I:

> You asked me if I thought that news of the Sparrow should come from the
> mother of the young girl. I couldn't answer the question offhand, I cannot
> answer it now but I think I can throw some light on the question.
>
> When Cyrils mother has defended her system of education and sufficiently
> reproved the friend who has suggested that Cyril should be allowed more
> liberty she announces ᵖᵉᵃᵏˢ of her projects of marriage for him. This leads up to
> description of the girls mother—she has two admirers, Cyrils mother defends
> her—ᵗʰᵉ ᵍⁱʳˡ ʷⁱˡˡ ᵇᵉ an excellent marriage for Cyril. This brings on the lady with her
> two admirers and her daughter. You then paint the scene of the second family.
> The girls mother is going to marry one of her admirers—she is full of her
> marriage and explains ᵉˣᵖˡᵃⁱⁿˢ it at length—the admirers comment on the ar-
> rangement, she is going to marry A but B is always going to remain their
> friend, how otherwise would they pass their evenings. This ought to come out
> very comic. The lady says that her daughter will have two stepfathers—the
> [illegible] question of the step father brings the daughter into the conversation
> or rather makes her the subject of it. She will need no stepfather ˢᵃʸˢ Cʸʳⁱˡˢ ᵐᵒᵗʰᵉʳ she
> is going to marry Cyril. Cyril becomes the subject of the conversation. Where
> is he?
>
> Here his relations [illegible] with Miss Sparrow might be mentioned by the
> lady with the two admirers—she has just remembered having heard that—or
> perhaps it might come ᶠʳᵒᵐ ᵗʰᵉ ᵃᶜᵗᵒʳ at the end of the act, just before Cyril comes in.
> Then it would come as an equal surprise on both parties. But you will see
> which way works out best. Do just as you please. I send this letter [illegible]
> hoping that it may suggest a new turn of thought and start you off afresh if you
> should happen to stick at a scene.[24]

Mrs. de Trappe's unconventional domestic arrangements (a comic scenario
that Moore redeployed in his 1915 Preface to *Muslin*),[25] her role as the
catalyst of Cyril's defection, and Mandeville's conversation with Julia in
preparation for Cyril's first entry were all laid out.

The drafting of Act II proved to be more challenging a process, as signaled by the diversity of the manuscript variants. On January 28, 1894,
Craigie wrote, "Yesterday afternoon I began Act III, and this morning I have
been working at the Sarah and Mandeville scene [in Act II]. It has left me all

but lifeless: how difficult it is. . . . The Sarah and Mandeville scene is horribly clever, but too realistic for the stage."[26] In a follow-up letter, she expressed her relief that Moore "rather like[d]" the scene, even if "it need[ed] elaboration."[27] When Moore proposed how to rework Sarah, she remained firm: "You must let me write Sarah my own way."[28] It was not only Sarah's character but also Mandeville's that underwent several revisions. Initially, while Sarah appears more self-assertive about her emotional needs, she is subjected to greater sexual exploitation when a resentful and cynical Mandeville exerts pressure on her to show herself "sympathetic" to Cyril's suit and allow him to "kiss" her (surely a euphemism) in order to extract money from him for the theatre Mandeville wants to set up (see manuscript H, *The Fool's Hour*). Although it transpires that Mandeville and Sarah have been lovers for five years (in the typescript version, the precise nature of their relationship is more uncertain), there is no indication of the later Mandeville's sentimental interest in Sarah. In the final manuscript version, the typescript (A, *The Fool's Hour*), Mandeville is depicted more in the light of a dandy than of a pimp, and Sarah gains in independence when she forces Cyril's hand by publicly announcing their engagement, while at the same time teaching Mandeville a lesson about her desirability as a wife. There is also some variation in the act's opening scene between Soame and Cyril and in the exchange between Cyril and Sarah after Mandeville's intervention. For all its troublesome reconceptualizations, this turned out to be the act Moore liked best; he later told Craigie's father that he preferred it to Act I.[29]

Act III, by contrast, as Craigie wrote apologetically, is "only a sketch"; its "untidy[ness]," she added, left her "quite miserable."[30] The shortest act, it lacks the satirical edge and witty dialogue of Act I and the probing inquiry into class and gender relations of Act II. The writing partnership with Moore had run out of steam. Perhaps Moore was too preoccupied with shifting the parameters of their relationship, or Craigie felt that his increasing pressure was wearing her down. The absence of manuscript variants of this act may suggest that it was typed up without much feedback or discussion. Moore later acknowledged that "the fault was [his]," and that, unhappy "that the third act did not work out satisfactorily," Craigie "decided . . . not to go on with the play."[31]

Another reason for suspending work on *The Fool's Hour* was that a new project had intervened: Craigie now wanted to produce a one-acter for Ellen Terry. (Terry was later to acknowledge in her autobiography just how important the play was in bringing "about a friendship . . . which lasted until [Craigie's] death.")[32] Glad to oblige, Moore quickly drafted a seventeen-page sketch[33] based on a French source, Clément Caraguel's *Le Bougeoir* (1852).[34] As Moore later explained to John Morgan Richards, Craigie's father and biographer, "The French play and JOURNEYS END IN LOVERS MEETING were both founded on a folk story, at least a thousand years old, and both plays follow the folk tale. When I told Mrs. Craigie the tale she asked me to write it out for her, and I wrote the play from end to end. She retouched the dialogue that I supplied her with."[35] Craigie chose the Shakespearean title[36] for this comedy about the reconciliation of an estranged aristocratic couple in which the philandering husband begins to appreciate his wife just as she is on the brink of contemplating adultery. On her return from a ball, she discovers an admirer hiding in her rooms, and hastily shuffles him into her bedroom when she hears her husband entering the house and making his way to her boudoir. The entertainment derives from the imaginative maneuvers required of the wife to prevent her husband from discovering the would-be lover and enable him to depart undetected.

With this one-act play, the roles were reversed: Moore provided the first draft, and Craigie offered suggestions and emendations. Ironically, what turned out to be the singularly most popular product of their collaboration spelled the end of their relationship, just as "Moore's one successful play"[37] happened to be one for which he was not credited after the first round of performances. Craigie's summary dismissal of him in May 1894 hit like a bombshell.[38] Moore was heartbroken.[39] He was also furious: he had been dropped, he told friends, for "a handsome lordling," priggish Lord Curzon (the "other" George, whom Craigie was repeatedly rumored to be planning to marry between 1894 and 1906). His resentment never quite left him.[40]

Although a reconciliation of sorts was effected, not least when in the immediate aftermath of the affair Moore discovered Maud Burke,[41] he did not attend the premiere of *Journeys End with Lovers Meeting* on June 5, 1894 (with Ellen Terry, Johnston Forbes-Robertson and William Terriss as the cast)[42] but heard from Craigie that it was "an extraordinary success . . . I enjoyed it extremely—no actors could have wished for warmer, more spontaneous applause."[43] The play continued to draw enthusiastic audiences, in the Lyceum and elsewhere, in July 1894, October and December 1895, November 1896, and May 1898.[44] At the end of 1895, Terry took the comedy to the States, where it was performed to great acclaim in New York's Abbey Theatre (December 1895, with Craigie in attendance) and the Chestnut Street Opera House in Philadelphia (January 1896). In 1902 the play was published, under Craigie's sole authorship, in her short story collection *Tales about Temperaments*, and in January 1905, Terry sold the performance rights to an American buyer.[45] By then, Moore was smarting with a renewed sense of injury. When in 1905, in the middle of another authorship dispute, Craigie set about preparing a new edition of *Journeys End*, with their joint publisher Fisher Unwin, Moore's patience was at an end. Unwin, at a loss as to how to address the situation, proved reluctant to offend Craigie, causing an incandescent Moore to sever his relations with the firm. Craigie, meanwhile, claimed that Moore, never a gentleman, had finally gone mad: "Seriously, I believe his brain is touched . . . it is now a case of mental illness."[46] After her death in 1906, his irritation again rose to fever pitch when, following his explanation of the circumstances of composition, the first edition of John Morgan Richards's *The Life of John Oliver Hobbes* (March 1911) only credited him for the initial idea and attributed authorship to Craigie alone. After a volley of letters Richards smoothed the waters by publishing Moore's account in the second edition of his biography in June 2011.[47]

The fresh grievance Moore nursed in 1905 revolved around yet another quarrel with Craigie. After a chance re-encounter in Bayreuth in 1899, their paths had crossed again in 1904, when Moore—never able to learn a lesson where a woman was concerned—suggested that, in exchange for waiving his rights to *Journeys End*, Craigie help him with a play he had in mind based on his correspondence with "Gabrielle" (Cecile Gabrielle, Baronne Franzi Ripp).[48] Set in 1860, the plot of what was to become *Elizabeth Cooper* (1913) and *The Coming of Gabrielle* (1920)[49] is organized around an aristocratic Austrian admirer of an established older British author. After agreeing to meet his epistolary devotee and attend the German-language premiere of his play in Vienna, he sends his secretary (a nephew) to impersonate him; the nephew promptly falls in love, and the couple gets married under the author's name. Inevitable complications arise on their honeymoon visit to Britain.

This time, Moore was not going to risk his work falling hostage to fortune and immediately drew up an agreement of joint authorship rights with Craigie, which both authors signed on May 26, 1904.[50] Ironically, in his eagerness to establish joint copyright, the thought that "Gabrielle" might object to the free use made of her letters does not appear to have crossed Moore's mind.[51] The frisson of sharing a playfully suggestive correspondence he was entertaining with one woman with another to whom he was renewing his attentions was clearly irresistible, prompting a considerable bout of creative energy:

> So here I am dictating all day. I dictated the whole of the first act yesterday. This morning I attacked the second and dictated till the man had to beg me to stop on account of wrist-cramp. If he comes back this evening I shall finish the second act and I have no doubt I shall be able to dictate the third tomorrow. That will be a comedy dictated in three days. Mrs. Craigie will go over the dialogue but I am surprised at the ease with which I am doing it. . . . I shall return to London on Monday leaving Mrs. Craigie to finish the play.[52]

His collaborator's role, he wrote to Edouard Dujardin, merely consisted in undertaking "a little clearing up" and, being "very strong on the business side," to take "charge of all the arrangements"; although the play would "be signed by both of us . . . almost all of it is mine."[53] Predictably, of course, the idyll did not last. All too soon the old problems returned with a vengeance; temperaments clashed and tempers flared.

In Craigie's unpublished sketch of Moore, "Scene between Diggs and Julia," written most likely at this time, Diggs (in anticipation of what Moore would say about the kick in the park in *Memoirs*) accuses Julia of having "the power of calling out all that is worst and meanest in my character."[54] Julia, for her part, is exasperated by the man's stubborn inability to take no for an answer:

> *Julia.* This is a scene which grows more tedious every time we rehearse it . . . I am tired of you now! Tired of you!! Do you understand[.] Tired of you! Hate you!

> *Diggs.* Very pretty, but as women cannot hate until they have learned how to love, perhaps you will tell me, as you seem in a comparatively truthful mood, who is the other man.

> *Julia.* There can be no other for me.

> *Diggs.* Beware of false sentiment[,] my dear Julia. You are still young. You may yet die respectable.[55]

> *Julia.* If I may live so, it would please me better.

> *Diggs.* Virtue is a dull companion! A damn dull companion!!

> *Julia.* It is a pity that you have so little in common with innocence.

> *Diggs.* Not when I have so much with wisdom, and such wisdom, with such a superior instinct for the comforts of life.[56]

When Julia asks him to leave, and a friend enters the room, Diggs announces his imminent departure to the Continent. Shocked about his appearance, the friend cautions Julia: "He would make a dangerous enemy!" Julia is unconcerned: "It seems to me that in our effort to avoid making enemies, we have surrounded ourselves with treacherous friends."[57] Craigie evidently no longer cared. She reworked *The Peacock's Feathers* (also titled *Elizabeth Cowper* and *Elizabeth Cooper*)[58] into a play of her own, *The [Three] Lovers*,[59] prompting strong objections from Moore, who now suddenly cast the quality of her work in doubt, declaring that he wanted nothing to do with it: "I dont [sic] think that your writing mixes with mine naturally and I am of [the] opinion that two people cannot *write* a play; the writing must be done by one. I offered you the scenario and invited you to write the play but you insisted that I should write it. I am quite willing to give you another subject and let you write it or to accept your subject and write it but I will not consent to my writing being hashed up with yours."[60] (This professed disdain for Craigie's writing did not prevent Moore from paraphrasing an epigram from *The Sinner's Comedy* in *The Coming of Gabrielle* and *Memoirs*.)[61] The conflict intensified when Craigie took her script to Arthur Bourchier and started rehearsals in December 1904.[62] By now, Moore had revised his own version and pushed for "leave to publish my dialogue[;] I shall not deny that you helped me with the construction"; his addition that "I do not tell lies" signals the heated temperature of the exchange.[63] The dispute, further aggravated by Craigie's plans to bring out a new edition of *Journeys End*, continued throughout 1905, while the variants of the play sat untouched.[64]

After her death in August 1906, Moore suggested to her father that either he "should use such portions of [Craigie's version] as I think right, the profits arising from the play to be equally divided between us," or that he be given "complete liberty to make use of my own text, and agree that all profits arising from the play shall belong to me."[65] From 1909 onward he was in correspondence with Dujardin about a French adaptation but, apparently not overly happy with parts of Dujardin's play, proposed in 1914 that he translate into French the German version he had commissioned from his English text.[66] The play that in Craigie's lifetime already existed in several differently authored and disputed variants had become a hopeless tangle of collaborative-adaptive transactions. None of the eventual productions of *Elizabeth Cooper*—London 1913, Paris 1914 (as *Clara Florise*), and London 1923 (as *The Coming of Gabrielle*)—proved a box office hit, and William Archer was particularly scornful.[67] Surely Adrian Frazier is right in concluding that if Moore spent such inexhaustible energies on minor literary projects it was because the "imbroglios caused by collaboration and play production were the equivalent of 'light literature' in his life."[68] Ultimately, then, for all its emotional fallout, the drama of collaboration assured Moore of a "fool's hour" of entertainment—galvanizing at the moment of experience, diverting in writerly recollection—to counterbalance the demands of a life dedicated to art.

NOTES

1. In a letter of January 11, 1894, Craigie asked Moore whether he "kn[e]w anything about a new illustrated Quarterly to be called *The Yellow Book*? Harland and Aubrey Beardsley are the Editors"; John Morgan Richards, *The Life of John Oliver Hobbes Told in Her Correspondence with Numerous Friends* (London: John Murray, 1911), 79. Later in 1894 (date unspecified) she wrote that the *Yellow Book* had rightly received bad reviews: "I have never seen such a vulgar production." (Ibid., 85).

2. The editors are grateful to Mark Samuels Lasner for giving us permission to reproduce material from this collection.

3. Adrian Frazier, *George Moore 1852–1933* (New Haven: Yale University Press, 2000), 327. For Beerbohm, see his description of the impact Moore had on others: "*Voilà Moore qui parle! Silence, la compagnie, Moore parle*" [Listen, Moore is speaking! Be quiet, everybody, Moore is speaking], quoted in David Cecil, *Max: A Biography* (Boston: Houghton Mifflin, 1965), 202 (emphasis in original).

4. Shortly after her marriage, Craigie enrolled in Classics at University College, London; see Mildred Davis Harding, *Air-Bird in the Water: The Life and Works of Pearl Craigie (John Oliver Hobbes)* (Madison: Fairleigh Dickinson University Press, 1996), 55.

5. Frazier, *George Moore*, 231.

6. Writing to Craigie's father, John Morgan Richards, on December 4, 1909 (letter reprinted in the latter's *Life of John Oliver Hobbes*, 86), Moore refers to the 1891 novel. Craigie's more recent biographer mentions *A Bundle of Life*: Harding, *Air-Bird*, 101. With its fast-moving multiple love triangles and happy ending, this text might indeed lend itself more easily to comedic treatment than the earlier novel, whose entanglements end on a much more serious note, involving separation and suicide. In her first extant letter to Moore of January 4, 1894, Craigie writes that she "had a sudden impulse to call on Daly and suggest to him a dramatized version of 'A Bundle of Life.' Oddly enough, he had read the book, and was about to write to me on the subject!" (Richards, *Life of John Oliver Hobbes*, 78.) Was that a second attempt at persuading Moore that the project was viable? At least one page of the first act was drafted, probably around this time, and was later filed with the manuscript of *The Fool's Hour* (see manuscript B, *The Fool's Hour*). Fifteen years later, Moore perhaps misremembered the title; "some emotions and a moral" certainly provides an aptly ironic caption for the relations, literary and otherwise, between Moore and Craigie.

7. George Moore, *Memoirs of My Dead Life*, Carra edition (New York: Boni and Liveright, 1923), 16.

8. Frazier, *George Moore*, 523 n15.

9. Harding, *Air-Bird*, 56. Craigie left her husband in 1891, after the birth of her son in the preceding year. The marriage, contracted in 1887, had been overshadowed by incompatibility, marital violence, the spectre of syphilis and her (possibly psychosomatic) illness from the start (ibid., 53–56).

10. Craigie's earliest published letter to Moore dates from January 4, 1894; see her father John Morgan Richard's biography, *Life of John Oliver Hobbes*, 78. The typescript of *The Fool's Hour* contains two pasted half-pages in Moore's hand, but otherwise the manuscript is in Craigie's hand.

11. Pearl Craigie's "The Love-Monger" [ca. 1890s?] is held in the Pearl Craigie/George Moore Papers in the Mark Samuels Lasner Collection, on loan to the University of Delaware Library [hereafter Craigie/Moore Papers, MSL Collection]. A number of characters from *The Fool's Hour* already feature, albeit in different constellation, in this story fragment: Sarah Sparrow is here the daughter of a hotel proprietor who runs away with a married Sir Digby Soame and after his death becomes engaged to the widowed banker Mr. Banish, scandalizing his son and female relatives. Among the latter figures is a Mrs. Maramour; the name Maramour also appears in the first draft of Act I of *The Fool's Hour* (manuscript C) and was later selected by Craigie for Lady Soupire's admirer in *Journeys End with Lovers Meeting*. Some passages from the story resurface in the play: a father's complaint that "No man has had a kinder father. . . . Did I not say to you 'You are a fool, but please yourself': No man has had a kinder father!" (unnumbered page) is given to Lord Doldrummond in conversation with Sir Digby Soame at the start of Act I, and a son's declaration of independence ("So I am going away. If I am to live at all, I must discover see life," unnumbered page, sentence struck through) resembles Cyril's (considerably tamer) statement at the end of Act I that if he continues at home, "I can do everything, in fact, but live."

12. Moore, *Memoirs*, 17.

13. Moore, *Memoirs*, 18.

14. Craigie to Moore, January 11 and February 14, 1894, in Richards, *Life of John Oliver Hobbes*, 79, 82.

15. March 8, 1894, in Richards, *Life of John Oliver Hobbes*, 83–84.

16. See Nathalie Saudo-Welby's discussion in chapter 7. Moore's first *Lady's Pictorial* version of the story in 1888 predated his relationship with Craigie and depicts a character who is more authentically concerned with the New Woman's quest for independence, a purpose and an occupation.

17. Moore, *Memoirs*, 18.

18. Harding, *Air-Bird*, 54.

19. Craigie sued for, and in 1895 was granted, a divorce on the grounds of adultery combined with cruelty. Male adultery was not admissible by law as sufficient cause in itself, even though husbands could file for divorce on the grounds of adultery alone. See Mary Lyndon Shanley, *Feminism, Marriage, and the Law in Victorian England* (Princeton: Princeton University Press, 1989), 39–44. Fathers usually retained the right to determine the education of their children. While Craigie refused to permit Reginald contact with his son, she was bound by law to have him educated in the Church of England, his father's faith. See Harding, *Air-Bird*, 148–149.

20. Harding, *Air-Bird*, 77.

21. Hone, *Life*, 203; Harding, *Air-Bird*, 239.

22. Richards, *Life of John Oliver Hobbes*, 78.

23. George Moore, *Vale* (London: William Heinemann, 1914), 35; also Frazier, *George Moore*, 21.

24. Moore to Craigie, "King's Bench Walk, Temple, Thursday night," [Undated] Craigie/Moore Papers, MSL Collection. Errors have been retained.

25. Mrs. de Trappe's eccentric *mariage à trois* resembles the marital arrangements of the Kilcarneys as explored in Moore's "Preface"; when Violet's lover dies, the couple is inconsolable until they decide on a suitable replacement. The two polyandric women bear the same Christian name. The name of Mrs. de Trappe's lover (Arthur) additionally recalls the triangular relationship between Mr. Barton (Arthur), his wife and Lord Dungory, her established lover. See George Moore, 1915 "Preface" to *Muslin* (the revised and retitled version of *A Drama in Muslin*], Uniform edition (London: William Heinemann, 1936), xiii–xvii.

26. Richards, *Life of John Oliver Hobbes*, 81.

27. "London, Thursday night," in Richards, *Life of John Oliver Hobbes*, 82.

28. Craigie to Moore, January 28, 1894, in Richards, *Life of John Oliver Hobbes*, 81.

29. Moore to John Morgan Richards, December 4, 1909, Letters to John Morgan Richards 1, Craigie/Moore Papers, MSL Collection; the letter is reproduced in Richards's *Life of John Oliver Hobbes*, 86.

30. Both quotations are taken from the undated letter headed "London, Thursday night" (composed after February 14 and before March 8, 1894), in Richards, *Life of John Oliver Hobbes*, 82.

31. Moore to John Morgan Richards, December 4, 1909, also in Richards, *Life of John Oliver Hobbes*, 86.

32. Ellen Terry, "'Beefsteak' Guests at the Lyceum," *The Story of My Life: Recollections and Reflections* (New York: Doubleday, Page and Co, 1909), gutenberg.org/ebooks/12326 (accessed March 23, 2014).

33. The draft is in Moore's hand. Craigie/Moore Papers, MSL Collection, Section 1, Manuscripts.

34. I am grateful to Michel Brunet for identifying the mysterious French author. The name is misspelled—as "Caraquel" or "Caraquell"—in contemporary and critical literature. "Caraquel" appears in the summary of a letter of Craigie's dated June 23, 1895 (addressee unknown), in which she requests that the program of the play should acknowledge "Caraquel and George Moore"; ET ZI, 116 letter (BL), Ellen Terry and Edith Craig Database: A Guide to the Papers from Smallhythe Place, University of Hull, www.ellenterryarchive.hull.ac.uk/ (accessed March 23, 2014). This version of the name is also referenced by her biographers; see Richards, *Life of John Oliver Hobbes*, 78, and Harding, *Air-Bird*, 129. "Caracuell" is the spelling given in Edmund Gilcher's *A Bibliography of George Moore* (DeKalb: Northern Illinois University Press, 1970), B11, 157, and in Colin Smythe's "Selected Checklist of the Writings of George Moore and Edward Martyn," in *Selected Plays of George Moore and Edward Martyn*, ed. David B. Eakin and Michael Case (Gerrards Cross and Washington: Colin Smythe and Catholic University of America Press, 1995), 367. The French title, *Bougeoir* (not to be mistaken for "bourgeois"), refers to the candlestick the wife passes on to the young man to light his way out of her boudoir and house, while her blindfolded husband is demonstrating his skills in picking up a perfume bottle from her toiletry table in the endeavor to prove that he spent a previous night at his club watching a friend performing a similar trick, rather than having entertained himself with a mistress elsewhere. In Moore's version (which Craigie adapted), the husband

has long been unfaithful and his wife calls his bluff when he declares that he would find the book they loved reading together as young lovers even in complete darkness. When, blindfolded, he enters her bedroom in quest of the right bookcase and shelf, Captain Armatage is able to make his exit.

35. Moore to John Morgan Richards, October 22, 1909, Letters to John Morgan Richards 1, Craigie/Moore Papers, MSL Collection. A more detailed version of the story is given in his letter of December 4, 1909, which is reproduced in Richards, *Life of John Oliver Hobbes*, 86.

36. Letter to Richards, December 4, 1909, reproduced in Richards, *Life of John Oliver Hobbes*, 86. The title is derived from *Twelfth Night* (Act II, scene 3).

37. Hone, *Life*, 203.

38. While taking a stroll round Hyde Park, Craigie announced that she no longer wished to see Moore. This was the context which led to the notorious kick referenced in this volume's introduction. Horrified and distraught, Moore describes in his *Memoirs* that he suddenly became aware of the staged nature of the scene: "we walked up and down the long walk many times, she listening to my pleading. . . . At last my stunned brain awoke, and I saw she was enjoying my grief as she might a little comedy of her own invention, conscious of her prettiness in black crêpe de Chine with the hat to match. . . . [T]he ill-repressed smile that I caught sight of under her hat cast me out of myself" (Moore, *Memoirs*, 22).

39. Even a trip to Paris did not help. Relief only came when, back in London, Moore (re-)encountered Maud Burke. See Moore, *Memoirs*, 22–24; Frazier, *George Moore*, 239–240.

40. William Geary to Hone, quoted in Frazier, *George Moore*, 238. A handsome and widely traveled aristocrat as well as a successful politician and shortly to become Viceroy of India, Curzon was indeed a force to be reckoned with. Craigie had known him since 1890, but was probably not aware of the secret engagement he entered into with Mary Leiter in 1893. Her biographer suggests that Curzon may have considered terminating his engagement for Craigie, but as a married woman seeking a divorce, and a Roman Catholic who would have to abandon her faith to remarry, she was not a likely marriage prospect for an ambitious man. Curzon reaffirmed his vows to Leiter in March 1894 and this, Harding speculates, may have been the cause of Craigie's depression at the time, hinted at in letters through references to bodily pain and an overwhelming sense of isolation ("The silence of my life overwhelms me," January 28, 1894, in Richards, *Life of John Oliver Hobbes*, 80). By the time she broke with Moore, she knew that Curzon was a lost cause. His marriage took place in April 1895, a few months before her divorce came through. (See Harding, *Air-Bird*, 112–21). If Craigie was genuinely in love with Curzon and mourning his loss, Moore's expectation that he would consummate his relationship with her would have added further pressure. It is not surprising that she backed out shortly before being presented to his brother at Moore Hall, presumably as his mistress(-to-be). (See Moore to Maurice Moore, May 1, 1894, in Robert Stephen Becker, ed., "The Letters of George Moore, 1863–1901," 5 vols [PhD diss., University of Reading, January 1980], 3: 922.) Whether, as she claimed, she had actually refused Curzon (see Harding, *Air-Bird*, 120) is uncertain; but her deep attachment evidently continued, extending to his wife. This led Moore to suspect that her close friendship with the Curzons was a long-term strategy meant to secure George in the event of his ailing wife's death. When Craigie suddenly suffered cardiac arrest in August 1906, a mere month after Mary Curzon's own death, he was convinced that she had taken her life after being snubbed by Curzon (Frazier, *George Moore*, 338). At the time of her death Moore professed to have forgiven Craigie: "She gave me a great deal of annoyance, but all that is forgotten and I dream of the affection I once felt for her" (September 23, 1906, in *Letters from George Moore to Ed Dujardin, 1886–1922*, ed. John Eglinton [New York: Crosby Gage, 1929], 59). Yet the revised version of "Mildred Lawson," "Henrietta Marr" (*In Single Strictness*, 1922), features a cold-blooded schemer who inveigles herself into the confidence of an invalid in order better to seduce her husband in front of her nose. Moore was not alone in conjecturing Craigie's suicide (if by misadventure); her own family appears to have believed that, overcome by depression aggravated by serious debt and her father's refusal of a loan, she may have overdosed on sleeping pills (Harding, *Air-Bird*, 470–472).

41. Harding, *Air-Bird*, 121. For Moore's encounter with the young woman "in fine health, high spirits, blonde hair and tiny hands" whose invitation to join her company brought about

his "cure" in late May 1894, see *Memoirs*, 24, where Cunard is figured as "Elizabeth" and Craigie as "Agate"; see also Frazier, *George Moore*, 239–240.

42. Harding dates the premiere to a matinee in July 1895 (*Air-Bird*, 125), but the summary of the program notes refers to the "First Night 1894" as June 5, 1894, ET-D159 program (BL), Ellen Terry and Edith Craig Database (accessed March 22, 2014). See also Eakin and Case, "Introduction" to their *Selected Plays of George Moore and Edward Martyn*, x.

43. Letter headed "Thursday," in Richards, *Life of John Oliver Hobbes*, 85.

44. See summaries of ET-D163 program (BL) [July 18, 1894]; ET-D711 program (BL) [October 26, 1895] Lyceum Theatre Company; ET-D718 program (BL) [December 11, 1895] Lyceum Theatre Company; ET-D720 program (BL) [December 16, 1895] Lyceum Theatre Company; ET-D183 program (BL) [November 25, 1896] ET-D203 play program (BL) [May 26, 1898] Ellen Terry and Edith Craig Database (accessed March 22, 2014).

45. Harding, *Air-Bird*, 171–172; John Oliver Hobbes, *Tales about Temperaments* (London: T. Fisher Unwin, 1902); summary of ET-5,050 postcard (BL) [January 3, 1905] "From N [Ellen Terry] to [Unknown] [Elizabeth Rumball]." The database notes on the latter item read that "She has just sold her little play Journey's End in Lovers' Meeting to an American," Ellen Terry and Edith Craig Database (accessed March 22, 2014). This presumably refers to the performance rights as Craigie retained the rights to the text.

46. Craigie to Unwin, February 1, 1905, quoted in Vineta Colby, *The Singular Anomaly* (New York: New York University Press, 1970), 218. See also Frazier, *George Moore*, 357.

47. See Richards to Moore, April 25, 1911; Moore to Richards, May 22, 1911; and Richards to Moore, June 1, 2011; the account published in the second edition is Moore's letter to Richards of December 9, 1909 (*Life of John Oliver Hobbes*, 86); Craigie/Moore Papers, MSL Collection.

48. See *George Moore's Correspondence with the Mysterious Countess*, ed. David B. Eakin and Robert Langenfeld (Victoria, BC: English Literary Studies, University of Victoria, 1984). The correspondence covers the period 1903–1906 and was thus still in process when Moore conceived of the idea of the play.

49. George Moore, *Elizabeth Cooper* (Dublin: Maunsel & Co, 1913); *The Coming of Gabrielle* (1920), in *Selected Plays of George Moore and Edward Martyn*, ed. David B. Eakin and Michael Case (Gerrard's Cross: Colin Smythe, 1995), 117–174.

50. "We the undersigned agree to write a comedy to be called correspondence or some more appropriate title the proceeds of which are to be equally divided between ourselves as joint authors." Signed by both authors on May 26, 1904; Craigie/Moore Papers, MSL Collection.

51. He also drew on her letters in chapter XIII of *Memoirs*, 228–229. In one of the early co-authored versions of the play, *Elizabeth Cowper* (written in 1904), Moore's alter ego Lewis Davenant, when challenged by a female friend about his use of the correspondence, justifies himself by arguing, "what breach of confidence is there in reading the unsolicited letters of a stranger; of a woman one has never seen and does not want to see?" He is pulled up by his nephew/secretary Sebastian Dayne: "you engaged in this correspondence willingly, you led her on, you tempted her to confide in you, she would have written no more of these letters except perhaps the first if you hadn't angled for them." Act I of "'ELIZABETH COWPER'[:] A PLAY IN THREE ACTS," signed by Arthur Bourchier and inscribed "Version received by me from George Moore on [November/December] 19–1904," 35, 40, Craigie/Moore Papers, MSL Collection.

52. Moore to Virginia Crawford, September 7, 1904, from Steephill Castle, Ventnor, Isle of Wight, in *George Moore on Parnassus: Letters (1900–1933) to Secretaries, Publishers, Printers, Agents, Literati, Friends, and Acquaintances*, ed. Helmut E. Gerber with the assistance of O. M. Brack, Jr. (Newark: University of Delaware Press, 1988), 117.

53. September 13, 1904, in Eglinton, *Letters from George Moore to Ed Dujardin*, 54.

54. Pearl Craigie, "Scene between Diggs and Julia" [ca. 1895–1905], Craigie/Moore Papers, MSL Collection, (unnumbered) typescript page 1. In *Memoirs*, Moore wrote that "Agate" "took pride in the fact (I know she did later) that her power over me should have caused me to put off all conventions and to have become, as it were, another George Moore" (22).

55. This latter phrase also appears in a variant of Act II of *The Fool's Hour* (manuscript H), when Mandeville tells Sarah to wheedle money out of Cyril if she wants him (Mandeville) to make her respectable by agreeing to marry her.

56. Craigie, "Scene between Diggs and Julia," typescript pages 2–3.

57. Ibid., typescript page 10.

58. The Craigie/Moore Papers at the MSL Collection hold two partial manuscript versions: Acts I and III of "Elizabeth Cowper" (1904) and Act I of "'ELIZABETH COOPER': A Comedy in Three Acts by George Moore and John Oliver Hobbes," undated, inscribed "This manuscript is the property of George Moore 4 Up. Ely Place Dublin." This version of *Elizabeth Cooper* is also likely to date from 1904.

59. The play is referenced as "*The Three Lovers*, written in collaboration with Mr. George Moore" in Richards, *Life of John Oliver Hobbes*, 35. A partial manuscript (typescript with handwritten notes) of Act III, entitled *The Lovers*, is held in the Craigie/Moore Papers, MSL Collection.

60. Moore to Craigie, November 20, [1904], 4 Upper Ely Place, Craigie/Moore Papers, MSL Collection. Years later Moore would restate his point towards Craigie's father, writing on October 7, 1909, to Richards that *The Three Lovers* was "quite worthless . . . and if it were produced would only disgrace everybody concerned in its production. It . . . would fail, as much from a commercial as from a literary point of view. . . . [T]o see her name attached to such wretched stuff would do your book a great deal of harm." (Ibid.)

61. See John Oliver Hobbes, *The Sinner's Comedy* (London: T. Fisher Unwin, 1905): "love comes to a man through his senses—to woman through her imagination" (148). The relevant passages in *The Coming of Gabrielle* and chapter II of *Memoirs* read: "a man's love is attracted in the beginning by the eye . . . but a woman's love . . . arises out of her imagination" (Sebastian in *Gabrielle*, 134); "a man loves in the first instance through the eye . . . whereas a woman loves through her imagination" (*Memoirs*, 24–25). In an interesting twist, the statement is here applied to the developing relationship with "Elizabeth" after Moore's recovery from "Agate."

62. Frazier, *George Moore*, 338. The (exercise book) cover of the manuscript of Act III of *The Lovers* is inscribed by Arthur Bouchier (Craigie/Moore Papers, MSL Collection).

63. Telegram, Moore to Craigie, December 7, 1904, Craigie/Moore Papers, MSL Collection.

64. The cast of characters in both co-authored versions (*Elizabeth Cowper*, *Elizabeth Cooper*) and Craigie's *The Lovers* is longer than in Moore's published plays (*Elizabeth Cooper* and *The Coming of Gabrielle*); Craigie/Moore Papers, MSL Collection. Two of the characters who are later omitted appear in Act III of *The Lovers* (Birchill and Rose) and also feature in *Elizabeth Cowper* (Burchell and Rose) and the early version of *Elizabeth Cooper* (Burchell). *Elizabeth Cowper* begins with a long discussion of Davenant by two groups of altogether five female characters, of whom only Lady Thurlow reappears in Moore's published version of *Elizabeth Cooper*. In *Elizabeth Cowper*, Rose is a love interest for Davenant, thus acting as a counterweight to the Austrian countess. Lady Thurlow's and Rose's roles are combined in the flirtatious—and safely married—admirer Lady Letham in *The Coming of Gabrielle*. The published plays add a comic interlude with the sailor husband of another, working-class devotee of Davenant's work, who unwittingly corresponded not with the author but with his secretary. In both variants, the Countess is aware of Sebastian's imposture early on and revenges herself on the men (in *Gabrielle* on Davenant only) by pretending to be ignorant of the deception. The final act of *The Coming of Gabrielle* is closer to the original versions in featuring a (temporary) rupture between the lovers, with Gabrielle considering divorce and flirting with Davenant, before a reconciliation is effected.

65. Moore to Richards, August 29, 1906, Craigie/Moore Papers, MSL Collection.

66. Richards agreed to a French adaptation for half the share of the profits and in exchange for Craigie's letters (Frazier, *George Moore*, 357–538). For Moore's correspondence with Dujardin, see March 8, March 16, April 10, May 12, June 15, and July 22, 1909, in Eglinton's *Letters from George Moore to Ed. Dujardin*. Moore enquired about progress but proved unwilling to respond to Dujardin's request to "help [him] out with the scene in the third act," which he had presumably found lacking; for Moore, "the whole play is a dish from which I have eaten too often" (March 16, 1909, ibid., 76). Unsurprisingly, Dujardin was irritated; on July 22, 1909,

Moore conceded that, "As you say, collaboration by correspondence is an impossibility" (ibid., 79) and on November 15, 1909, he admitted that, "With regard to the comedy, I think the game is up" (ibid., 81). However, after *Elizabeth Cooper* was published and performed in 1913, his interest in a French version revived, prompting him to exert renewed pressure on Dujardin: "A German has just done a lovely adaptation of the play. . . . It is ten times better than anything you have succeeded in doing, or I, or both of us together. You will have nothing to do but to translate." (February 11, 1914, ibid., 101). He still disliked Dujardin's third act (February 14, 1914, ibid., 102).

67. Frazier, *George Moore*, 358.
68. Ibid.

The Fool's Hour: A Play

By John Oliver Hobbes [Pearl Craigie]
and George Moore

Edited by Ann Heilmann

NOTE ON THE TEXT

Act I, the only known act of the play, was published in the *Yellow Book* 1, no. 1 (April 1894), 253–272. As the "final" version, this act is reproduced from the printed text. Substantial variants of passages (in the typescript or handwritten manuscript pages) are discussed in the notes.

The text of Acts II and III has been edited from the undated typescript (paginated 1–35 and 1–12, with corrections in both Moore's and Craigie's hands) and handwritten sources (Act II, all in Craigie's hand) held in the Pearl Craigie/George Moore Papers in the Mark Samuels Lasner Collection on loan to the University of Delaware Library. The typescript of Act II misses two pages (4, 33): to provide a continuous text, the editor here draws on the handwritten manuscript sources of Act II (details are given in the notes). For reasons of consistency formatting has been aligned. Cyril's surname is spelt Aprile throughout (the handwritten text of Act II refers to "April"). Manuscript abbreviations such as the ampersand are rendered in full. With the exception of letters or notes by the co-authors, typographical and punctuation errors have been silently corrected. Minor manual corrections on the typescript are not indicated; significant corrections are given or discussed in the notes.

MANUSCRIPT VERSIONS, PEARL CRAIGIE/GEORGE MOORE PAPERS, MARK SAMUELS LASNER COLLECTION

Typescript of manuscript (A)

Act I: individual sheets, but no continuous typescript, manually corrected (in both co-authors' hands); pages 2, unpaginated, 12, unpaginated, 19, 20, 21, 22

Act II, pages 1, 2, unpaginated (3), 5–32, 34
Act III, pages 1–12

Handwritten manuscript sheets (all in Pearl Craigie's hand): B-K

Act I

B. "Act I," single sheet. This is the start of a play based on Craigie's novel *A Bundle of Life* (1893). The sheet most probably dates from early January 1894. The fragment includes a reference to a Lady Bonnejoy, who does not feature in the novel but also appears in manuscript C.[1]

C. "Act I, At Lord Skepperton's house in Brighton," 6 pp. This is probably the earliest version of what was to become *The Fool's Hour*. The Doldrummonds are called Skepperton, and there is a wider cast of characters. The manuscript also contains a sketch of the start of Act II.[2]

D. "Act I, Library at Lord Doldrummond's," unnumbered, 1p

E. "Act I, The Library in Lord Doldrummond's house at Brighton," 2 pp

Act II

F. Untitled, 1 sheet (exchange between Cyril and Soame; from Rubens to Julia de Trappe)

G. Untitled, 1 long sheet (Cyril and Soame on painters)

H. Untitled, 11 unnumbered pages, roughly equivalent to pages 16 to end of typescript

I. Untitled, 1 sheet variant of part of Cyril and Sarah's scene

K. "Cyril and Sarah," 3 unnumbered pages, roughly equivalent to pages 22–27 of typescript

Act III

Continuous typescript, numbered 1–12.

THE TEXT

Characters of the Comedy

Lord Doldrummond
Cyril, *his Son* (Viscount Aprile)
Sir Digby Soame
Charles Mandeville, *a tenor*
Mr. Banish, *a banker*
The Hon. Arthur Featherleigh
Mr. Samuel Benjamin, *a money-lender*
Lady Doldrummond
Julia, *an heiress*
The Hon. Mrs. Howard de Trappe, *her mother, a widow*
Sarah Sparrow, *an American prima donna*

Act I

SCENE—*The Library in Lord Doldrummond's house at Brighton. The scene represents a richly-furnished but somewhat oppressive room. The chairs and tables are all narrow, the lamp-shades stiff, the windows have double glasses. Lord Doldrummond, a man of middle-age, handsome, but with a dejected, browbeaten air, sits with a rug over his knees, reading "The Church Times." The Butler announces "Sir Digby Soame." Sir Digby is thin and elderly; has an easy smile and a sharp eye; dresses well; has two man-ners—the abrupt with men, the suave with women; smiles into his beard over his own witticisms.*

Lord Dol. Ah, Soame, so you are here at last?[3]

Soame. [Looking at his watch.] I am pretty punctual, only a few minutes late.

Lord Dol. I am worried, anxious, irritable, and that has made the time seem long.

Soame. Worried, anxious? And what about? Are you not well? Have you found that regularity of life ruins the constitution?

Lord Dol. No, my dear Soame, no. But I am willing to own that the existence which my wife enjoys, and which I have learnt to endure, would not suit every one.

Soame. I am glad to find you more tolerant. You used to hold the very harshest and most crude opinions. I remember when we were boys, I could never persuade you to accept the admirable doctrine that a reformed rake makes the best husband![4]

Lord Dol. [Timidly.] Repentance does not require so large an income as folly! This may explain that paradox. You know, in my way, I, too, am something of a philosopher! I married very young, whereas you entered the Diplomatic Service and resolved to remain single: you wished to study women. I have lived with one for five-and-twenty years. *[Sighs.]*

Soame. Oh, I admit at once that yours is the greater achievement and was the more daring ambition.

Lord Dol. I know all I wish to know about women, but men puzzle me extremely. So I have sent for you. I want your advice. It is Cyril who is the cause of my uneasiness. I am afraid that he is not happy.

Soame. Cyril not happy? What is he unhappy about? You have never refused him anything?[5]

Lord Dol. Never! No man has had a kinder father! When he is unreasonable I merely say "You are a fool, but please yourself!" No man has had a kinder father!

Soame. Does he complain?

Lord Dol. He has hinted that his home is uncongenial—yet we have an excellent cook! Ah, thank heaven every night and morning, my dear Digby, that you are a bachelor. Praying for sinners and breeding them would seem the whole duty of man. I was no sooner born than my parents were filled with uneasiness lest I should not live to marry and beget an heir of my own. Now I have an heir, his mother will never know peace until she has found him a wife!

Soame. And will you permit Lady Doldrummond to use the same method with Cyril which your mother adopted with such appalling results in your own case?

Lord Dol. It does not seem my place to interfere, and love-affairs are not a fit subject of conversation between father and son!

Soame. But what does Cyril say to the matrimonial prospect?

Lord Dol. He seems melancholy and eats nothing but oranges. Yes, Cyril is a source of great uneasiness.

Soame. Does Lady Doldrummond share this uneasiness?

Lord Dol. My wife would regard a second thought on any subject as a most dangerous form of temptation. She insists that Cyril has everything which a young man could desire, and when he complains that the house is dull, she takes him for a drive!

Soame. But *you* understand him?

Lord Dol. I think I do. If I were young again—

Soame. Ah, you regret! I always said you would regret it if you did not take your fling! The pleasures we imagine are so much more alluring, so much more dangerous, than those we experience. I suppose you recognise in Cyril the rascal you might have been, and feel that you have missed your vocation?

Lord Dol. [*Meekly.*] I was never unruly, my dear Soame. We all have our moments, I own, yet—well, perhaps Cyril has inherited the tastes which I possessed at his age, but lacked the courage to obey.

Soame. And so you wish me to advise you how to deal with him! Is he in love? I have constantly observed that when young men find their homes unsympathetic, it is because some particular lady does not form a member of the household. It is usually a lady, too, who would not be considered a convenient addition to any mother's visiting-list!

Lord Dol. Lady Doldrummond has taught him that women are the scourges of creation. You, perhaps, do not share that view!

Soame. Certainly not. I would teach him to regard them as the reward, the compensation, the sole delight of this dreariest of all possible worlds.

Lord Dol. [*Uneasily.*] Reward! Compensation! Delight! I beg you will not go so far as that. What notion would be more upsetting? Pray do not use such extreme terms!

Soame. Ha! ha! But tell me, Doldrummond, is it true that your wife insists on his retiring at eleven and rising at eight? I hear that she allows him nothing stronger than ginger ale and lemon; that she selects his friends, makes his engagements, and superintends his amusements? Should he marry, I am told she will even undertake the office of best man!

Lord Dol. Poor soul! she means well; and if devotion could make the boy a saint he would have been in heaven before he was out of his long clothes. As it is, I fear that nothing can save him.

Soame. Save him? You speak as though you suspected that he was not such a saint as his mother thinks him.

Lord Dol. I suspect nothing. I only know that my boy is unhappy. You might speak to him, and draw him out if occasion should offer—but do not say a word about this to Lady Doldrummond.

[Enter Lady Doldrummond.—She is a tall, slight, but not angular woman. Her hair is brown, and brushed back from her temples in the simplest possible fashion. Self-satisfaction (of a gentle and ladylike sort) and eminent contentment with her lot are the only writings on her smooth, almost girlish countenance. She has a prim tenderness and charm of manner which soften her rather cutting voice.]

Lady Dol. What! Cyril not here? How do you do, Sir Digby? I am looking for my tiresome boy. I promised to take him to pay some calls this afternoon, and as he may have to talk I must tell him what to say. He has no idea of making himself pleasant to women, and is the shyest creature in the world!

Soame. You have always been so careful to shield him from all responsibility, Lady Doldrummond. Who knows what eloquence, what decision, what energy he might display, if you did not possess these gifts in so preeminent a degree as to make any exertion on his part unnecessary, and perhaps disrespectful.

Lady Dol. Ah! mothers are going out of fashion. Even Cyril occasionally shows a certain impatience when I venture to correct him. As if I would hurt any one's feelings unless from a sense of duty! And pray, where is the pleasure of having a son if you may not direct his life?

Lord Dol. Cyril might ask, where is the pleasure of having parents if you may not disobey them.

Lady Dol. [To Soame.] When Herbert is alone with me he never makes flippant remarks of this kind. *[To Lord Doldrummond.]* I wonder that you like to give your friends such a wrong impression of your character.

[Turning to Sir Digby.] But I think I see your drift, Sir Digby. You wish to remind me that Cyril is now at an age when I must naturally desire to see him established in a home of his own.

Soame. You have caught my meaning. As he is now two-and-twenty, I think he should be allowed more freedom than may have been expedient when he was—say, six months old.

Lady Dol. I quite agree with you, and I trust you will convince Herbert that women understand young men far better than their fathers ever could. I have found the very wife for Cyril, and I hope I may soon have the pleasure of welcoming her as a daughter.

Soame. A wife! Good heavens! I was suggesting that the boy had more liberty. Marriage is the prison of all emotions, and I should be very sorry to ask any young girl to be a man's goalkeeper.

Lord Dol. Sir Digby is right.

Lady Dol. The presence of a third person has the strangest effect on Herbert's moral vision. As I have trained my son with a care and tenderness rarely bestowed nowadays even on a girl, I think I may show some resentment when I am asked to believe him a being with the instincts of a ruffian and the philosophy of a middle-aged bachelor. No, Sir Digby, Cyril is not *my* child if he does not make his home and his family the happiest in the world!

Soame. Yes?

Lady Dol. He has not taste for cards, horses, brandy, or actresses. We read together, walk together, and drive together. In the evening, if he is too tired to engage in conversation, I play the piano while he dozes. Lately he has taken a particular interest in Mozart's classic light opera. Any interest of that kind is so elevating, and I know of nothing more agreeable than a musical husband.

Lord Dol. You see she is resolved on his marriage, and she has had Julia de Trappe on a visit with us for the last five weeks in the hope of bringing matters to a crisis.

Lady Dol. And why not? Our marriage was arranged for us, and what idle fancies of our own could have led to such perfect contentment?

[Lord Doldrummond avoids her eyes.]

Soame. Julia de Trappe? She must be the daughter of that Mrs. Howard the Trappe who gives large At Homes in a small house, and who spends her time hunting for old lovers and new servants.

Lady Dol. I own that dear Julia has been allowed to meet men and women who are not fit companions for a young girl, no matter how interesting they may be to the general public. Only yesterday she told me she was well acquainted with Mr. Mandeville, the tenor. Mrs. de Trappe, it seems, frequently invites him to dinner. Still, Julia herself is very sensible, and the family is of extraordinary antiquity.

Soame. But the mother? If she has not been in the divorce court, it is through no fault of her own.

Lady Dol. [Biting her lip.] Mrs. de Trappe is vain and silly, I admit; but as she has at last decided to marry Mr. Banish, the banker, I am hoping she will live in his house at Hampstead, and think a little more about her immortal soul.

Soame. Does Cyril seem at all interested in Miss Julia?

Lady Dol. Cyril has great elegance of mind, and is not very strong in the expression of his feelings one way or the other. But I may say that a deep attachment exists between them.

Soame. A man must have sound wisdom before he can appreciate innocence. But I have no desire to be discouraging, and I hope I may soon have the pleasure of congratulating you all on the wedding. Good-bye.

Lord Dol. What! Must you go?

Soame. Yes. But *[aside to Lord Doldrummond.]* I shall bear in mind what you say. I will do my best. I have an engagement in town to-night. *[Chuckles.]* An amusing one.

Lord Dol. [With envy.] Where?

Soame. At the Parnassus.

Lady Dol. [With a supercilious smile.] And what is the Parnassus?

Soame. A theatre much favoured by young men who wish to be thought wicked, and by young ladies who *are*. Good-bye, good-bye. *[Shakes hands with Lord and Lady Doldrummond and goes out.]*

Lady Dol. Thank goodness, he is gone! What a terrible example for Cyril. I was on thorns every second lest he should come in. Soame has just those meretricious attractions which appeal to youth and inexperience. That you should encourage such an acquaintance, and even discuss before him such an intimate matter as my hope with regard to Julia, is, perhaps, more painful than astonishing.

Lord Dol. They are both too young to marry. Let them enjoy life while they may.

Lady Dol. Enjoy life? What a degrading suggestion! I have often observed that there is a lurking taste for the vicious in every Doldrummond. *[Picking up Cyril's miniature from the table.]* Cyril is pure Bedingfield: my second self!

[The Butler announces Mrs. De Trappe, Mr. Arthur Featherleigh, Mr. Banish. Mrs. de Trappe is a pretty woman with big eyes and a small waist; she has a trick of biting her under-lip, and looking shocked, as it were, at her own audacity. Her manner is a little effusive, but always well-bred. She does not seem affected, and has something artless, confiding, and pathetic. Mr. Featherleigh has a nervous laugh and a gentlemanly appearance; otherwise inscrutable. Mr. Banish is old, well-preserved, rather pompous, and evidently mistakes deportment for dignity.]

Mrs. de Trappe. [Kissing Lady Doldrummond on each cheek.] Dear Edith, I knew we should surprise you. But Mr. Banish and I are house-hunting, and I thought I must run in and see you and Julia, if only for a second. I felt sure you would not mind my bringing Arthur *[indicating Featherleigh.]* He is so lonely at the prospect of my marriage that Mr. Banish and I have promised to keep him always with us. We have known each other so long. How should we spend our evenings without him? James admits they would be tedious, don't you, James? *[Indicating Banish.]*

Banish. Certainly, my dear.

Lady Dol. [Stiffly.] I can well understand that you have learned to regard Mr. Featherleigh as your own son. And as we advance in years, it is so pleasant to have young people about us.

Mrs. de Trappe. [After a slight pause.] How odd that it should never have struck me in that light before! I have always thought of Arthur as the trustee, as it were, of my poor fatherless Julia. *[To Banish.]* Have I not often said so, James?

Banish. [Drily.] Often. In fact I have always thought that Julia would never lack a father whilst Arthur was alive. But I admit that he is a little young for the responsibility.

Feather. [Unmoved.] Do not forget, Violet, that our train leaves in fifty-five minutes.

Lord Dol. [Catching a desperate glance from Lady Doldrummond.] Then I shall have time to show you the Russian poodles which the Duke of Camden brought me from Japan.

Mrs. de Trappe. [Peevishly.] Yes, please take them away. *[Waving her hand in the direction of Banish and Featherleigh.]* Edith and I have many secrets to discuss. Of course she will tell you *[to Lord Doldrummond]* everything I have said when we are gone, and I shall tell Arthur and James all she has said as we go home. But it is so amusing to think ourselves mysterious for twenty minutes. *[As the men go out laughing, she turns to Lady Doldrummond with a sigh.]* Ah, Edith, when I pause in all these gaieties and say to myself, Violet, you are about to marry a second husband, I cannot feel sufficiently thankful that it is not the third.

Lady Dol. The third?

Mrs. de Trappe. To face the possibility of a third honeymoon, a third disappointment, and a third funeral would tax my courage to the utmost! And I am not strong.

Lady Dol. I am shocked to see you so despondent. Surely you anticipate every happiness with Mr. Banish?

Mrs. de Trappe. Oh, yes. He has money, and Arthur thinks him a very worthy sort of person. He is a little dull, but then middle-class people are always so gross in their air when they attempt to be lively or amusing; so long as they are grave I can bear them well enough, but I know of nothing so unpleasant as the sight of a banker laughing. As Arthur says, City men and butlers should always be serious.

Lady Dol. Do you think that the world will quite understand—Arthur?

Mrs. de Trappe. What do you mean, Edith? A woman must have an adviser. Arthur was my late husband's friend, and he is my future husband's friend. Surely that should be enough to satisfy the most exacting.

Lady Dol. But why marry at all? why not remain as you are?

Mrs. de Trappe. How unreasonable you are, Edith! How often have you urged me to marry Mr. Banish, and now that it is all arranged and Arthur is satisfied, you begin to object.

Lady Dol. I thought that you liked Mr. Banish better.

Mrs. de Trappe. Better than Arthur? No, I am not so unkind as that, nor would James wish it. I am marrying because I am poor. My husband, as you know, left nearly all his money to Julia, and I feel the injustice so acutely that the absurd settlement he made on me is spent upon doctor's bills alone. If it were not for Arthur and one or two other kind friends who send me game and other little things from time to time, I could not exist at all. *[Draws off her gloves, displays a diamond ring on each finger, and wipes her eyes with a point-lace handkerchief.]* And when I think of all that I endured with De Trappe! How often have I been roused from a sound sleep to see the room illuminated and De Trappe, rolled up in flannel, sitting by the fire reading "Lead, kindly Light." What an existence! But now tell me about Julia. I hope she does not give you much trouble.

Lady Dol. I only hope that I may keep her always with me.

Mrs. de Trappe. How she must have improved! When she is at home I find her so depressing. And she does not appeal to men in the least.

Lady Dol. I could wish that all young girls were as modest.

Mrs. de Trappe. Oh, I daresay Julia has all the qualities we like to see in some other woman's daughter. But if you were her mother and had to find her a husband, you would regard her virtues in another light. Fortunately she has eight thousand a year, so she may be able to find somebody. Still, even money does not tempt men as it once did. A girl must have an extraordinary charm. She is so jealous of me. I cannot keep her out of the drawing-room when I have got callers, especially when Mr. Mandeville is there.

Lady Dol. I have heard of Mr. Mandeville. He is an actor, a singer.

Mrs. de Trappe. A lovely tenor voice. All the women are in love with him, except me. I would not listen to him. And now they say he is going to marry Sarah Sparrow—a great mistake. I should like to know who would care about him or his singing, once he is married.

Lady Dol. And who is Sarah Sparrow?

Mrs. de Trappe. Don't you know? She is the last great success. She has two notes: B flat and the lower G—the orchestra plays the rest. You must go to the Parnassus and hear her. To-night is the dress rehearsal of the new piece.

Lady Dol. And do you receive Miss Sparrow?

Mrs. de Trappe. No, women take up too much time. They say, too, that she is frantically jealous because Mandeville used to come and practise in my boudoir. He says no one can accompany him as I do!

Lady Dol. I hope Cyril does not meet Mr. Mandeville when he goes to your home.

Mrs. de Trappe. Let me see. I believe I introduced them. At any rate, I know I saw them at luncheon together last week.

Lady Dol. At luncheon together! Cyril and this person who sings? What could my boy and Mr. Mandeville have in common?

Mrs. de Trappe. They both appear to admire Sarah Sparrow very much. And I cannot find what men see in her. She is not tall and her figure is most innocent; you would say she was still in pinafores. As for her pretti-ness, I admit she has fine eyes, but of course she blackens them.[6] I think the great attraction is her atrocious temper. One never knows whom she will stab next.[7]

Lady Dol. [Half to herself.] Last week Cyril came in after midnight. He refused to answer my questions.

Mrs. de Trappe. You seem absent-minded, my dear Edith. *[Pause.]* I must be going now. Where are Arthur and James? We have not a moment to lose. We are going to choose wedding presents. James is going to choose Arthur's and Arthur is going to choose James's, so there can be no jealousy. It was I who thought of that way out of the difficulty. One does one's best to be nice to them, and then something happens and upsets all one's plans. Where is Cyril?

Lady Dol. I am afraid Cyril is not at home.

Mrs. de Trappe. Then I shall not see him. Tell him I am angry, and give my love to Julia. I hope she does not disturb you when you are in the drawing-room and have visitors. So difficult to keep a grown-up girl out of the drawing-room. Where can those men be? *[Enter Lord Doldrum-*

mond, *Mr. Featherleigh, and Mr. Banish.]* Ah! here they are. Now, come along; we haven't a moment to lose. Good-bye, Edith.

[Exeunt (after wishing their adieux) Mrs. de Trappe, Mr. Featherleigh, and Mr. Banish, Lord Doldrummond following them.]

Lady Dol. [Stands alone in the middle of the room, repeating.] Cyril and—Sarah Sparrow! My son and Sarah Sparrow! And he has met her through the one woman for whom I have been wrong enough to forget my prejudices. What a punishment!

[Julia enters cautiously. She is so unusually beautiful that she barely escapes the terrible charge of sublimity. But there is a certain peevishness in her expression which adds a comfortable smack of human nature to her classic features.]

Julia. I thought mamma would never go. I have been hiding in your boudoir ever since I heard she was here.

Lady Dol. Was Cyril with you?

Julia. Oh, no; he has gone out for a walk.

Lady Dol. Tell me, dearest, have you and Cyril had any disagreement lately? Is there any misunderstanding?

Julia. Oh, no. *[Sighs.]*

Lady Dol. I remember quite well that before I married Herbert he often suffered from the oddest moods of depression. Several times he entreated me to break off the engagement. His affection was so reverential that he feared he was not worthy of me. I assure you I had the greatest difficulty in overcoming his scruples, and persuading him that whatever his faults were I could help him to subdue them.

Julia. But Cyril and I are not engaged. It is all so uncertain, so humiliating.

Lady Dol. Men take these things for granted. If the truth were known, I daresay he already regards you as his wife.

Julia. [With an injured air.] Perhaps that is why he treats me so unkindly. I have often thought that if he were my husband he could not be more disagreeable! He has not a word for me when I speak to him. He does not hear. Oh, Lady Doldrummond, I know what is the matter. He is in love, but I am not the one. You are all wrong.

Lady Dol. No, no, no. He loves you; I am sure of it. Only be patient with him and it will come all right. Hush! is that his step? Stay here, darling, and I will go into my room and write letters. *[Exit, brushing the tears from her eyes.]*

[Butler ushers in Mr. Mandeville. Neither of them perceive Julia, who has gone to the window.]

Butler. His Lordship will be down in half an hour, sir. He is now having his hair brushed.

Julia. [In surprise as she looks round.] Mr. Mandeville! *[Pause.]* I hardly expected to meet you here.

Mandeville. And why, may I ask?

Julia. You know what Lady Doldrummond is. How did you overcome her scruples?

Mandeville. Is my reputation then so very bad?

Julia. You—you are supposed to be rather dangerous. You sing on the stage, and have a tenor voice.

Mandeville. Is that enough to make a man dangerous?

Julia. How can *I* tell? But mamma said you were invincible. You admire mamma, of course. *[Sighs.]*

Mandeville. A charming woman, Mrs. de Trappe. A very interesting woman; so sympathetic.

Julia. But she said she would not listen to you.

Mandeville. Did she say that? *[A slight pause.]* I hope you will not be angry when I own that I do not especially *admire* your mother. A quarter of a century ago she may have had considerable attractions, but—are you offended?

Julia. Offended? Oh, no. Only it seems strange. I thought that all men admired mamma. *[Pause.]* You have not told me yet how you made Lady Doldrummond's acquaintance.

Mandeville. I am here at Lord Aprile's invitation. He has decided that he feels no further need of Lady Doldrummond's apron-strings.

Julia. Oh, Mr. Mandeville, are you teaching him to be wicked?

Mandeville. But you will agree with me that a young man cannot make his mother a kind of scribbling diary?

Julia. Still, if he spends his time well, there does not seem to be any reason why he should refuse to say where he dines when he is not at home.

Mandeville. Lady Doldrummond holds such peculiar ideas; she would find immorality in a sofa-cushion. If she were to know that Cyril is coming with me to the dress rehearsal of our new piece!

Julia. It would break her heart. And Lord Doldrummond would be indignant. Mamma says his own morals are so excellent!

Mandeville. Is he an invalid?

Julia. Certainly not. Why do you ask?

Mandeville. Whenever I hear of a charming husband I always think that he *must* be an invalid. But as for morals, there can be no harm in taking Cyril to a dress rehearsal. If you do not wish him to go, however, I can easily say that the manager does not care to have strangers present. *[Pause.]* Afterwards there is to be a ball at Miss Sparrow's.

Julia. Is Cyril going there, too?

Mandeville. I believe that he has an invitation, but I will persuade him to refuse it, if you would prefer him to remain at home.

Julia. You are very kind, Mr. Mandeville, but it is a matter of indifference to me where Lord Aprile goes.

Mandeville. Perhaps I ought not to have mentioned this to you?[8]

Julia. *[Annoyed.]* It does not make the least difference. In fact, I am delighted to think that you are taking Cyril out into the world. He is wretched in this house. *[With heroism.]* I am glad to think that he knows any one so interesting and clever and beautiful as Sarah Sparrow. I suppose she would be considered beautiful?

Mandeville. [With a profound glance.] One can forget her—sometimes.

Julia. [Looking down.] Perhaps—when I am as old as she is—I shall be prettier than I am at present.

Mandeville. You always said you liked my voice. We never see anything of each other now. I once thought that—well—that you might like me better. Are you sure you are not angry with me because I am taking Cyril to this rehearsal?

Julia. Quite sure. Why should I care where Cyril goes? I only wish that I, too, might go to the theatre to-night. What part do you play? And what do you sing? A serenade?

Mandeville. [Astounded.] Yes. How on earth did you guess that? The costume is, of course, picturesque, and that is the great thing in opera. A few men can sing—after a fashion—but to find the right clothes to sing *in*—that shows the true artist.

Julia. And Sarah; does she look *her* part?

Mandeville. Well, I do not like to say anything against her, but she is not quite the person I should cast for la Marquise de la Perdrigonde. Ah! if you were on the stage, Miss de Trappe! You have just the exquisite charm, the grace, the majesty of bearing which, in the opinion of those who have never been to Court, is the peculiar distinction of women accustomed to the highest society.

Julia. Oh, I should like to be an actress!

Mandeville. No! no! I spoke selfishly—if you only acted with *me*, it would be different; but—but I could not bear to see another man making love to you—another man holding your hand and singing into your eyes—and—and—Oh, this is madness. You must not listen to me.

Julia. I am not—angry, but—you must never again say things which you do not mean. If I thought you were untruthful it would make me so—so miserable. Always tell me the truth. *[Holds out her hand.]*

Mandeville. You are very beautiful!

[She drops her eyes, smiles, and wanders unconsciously to the mirror.]
[Lady Doldrummond suddenly enters from the boudoir, and Cyril from the middle door. Cyril is handsome, but his features have that delicacy and his

expression that pensiveness which promise artistic longings and domestic disappointment.]

Cyril. [Cordially and in a state of suppressed excitement.] Oh, mother, this is my friend Mandeville. You have heard me mention him?

Lady Dol. I do not remember, but—

Cyril. When I promised to go out with you this afternoon, I forgot that I had another engagement. Mandeville has been kind enough to call for me.

Lady Dol. Another engagement, Cyril?

[Lord Doldrummond enters and comes down, anxiously looking from one to the other.]

Cyril. Father, this is my friend Mandeville. We have arranged to go up to town this afternoon.

Lady Dol. [Calmly.] What time shall I send the carriage to the station for you? The last train usually arrives about—

Cyril. I shall not return to-night. I intend to stay in town. Mandeville will put me up.

Lord Dol. And where are you going?

Mandeville. He is coming to our dress rehearsal of the "Dandy and the Dancer."

Cyril. At the Parnassus. *[Lord and Lady Doldrummond exchange horrified glances.]* I daresay you have never heard of the place, but it amuses me to go there, and I must learn life for myself. I am two-and-twenty, and it is not extraordinary that I should wish to be my own master. I intend to have chambers of my own in town.

Lady Dol. Surely you have every liberty in this house?

Lord Dol. If you leave us, you will leave the rooms in which your mother has spent every hour of her life, since the day you were born, planning and improving. Must all her care and thought go to nothing? The silk hangings in your bedroom she worked with her own hands. There is not so much as a pen-wiper in your quarter of the house which she did not choose with the idea of giving you one more token of her affection.

Cyril. I am not ungrateful, but I cannot see much of the world through my mother's embroidery. As you say, I have every comfort here. I may gorge at your expense and snore on your pillows and bully your servants. I can do everything, in fact, but live. Dear mother, be reasonable. *[Tries to kiss her. She remains quite frigid.]*

[Footman enters.]

Footman. The dog-cart is at the door, my lord.

Cyril. You think it well over and you will see that I am perfectly right. Come on, Mandeville, we shall miss the train. Make haste: there is not time to be polite. *[He goes out, dragging Mandeville after him, and ignoring Julia.]*

Lord Dol. Was that my son? I am ashamed of him! To desert us in this rude, insolent, heartless matter. If I had whipped him more and loved him less, he would not have been leaving me to lodge with a God knows who. I disown him. The fool!

Lady Dol. If you have anything to say, blame *me*! Cyril has the noblest heart in the world; I am the fool.

Curtain.

Act II

SCENE—*Sarah Sparrow's boudoir. Furnished with a piano, a divan and a quantity of Mandeville's photographs. Some of them hang on the walls but the greater number (in gaudy and eccentric frames) are on the tables and mantelpieces. The boudoir door is open and shows ballroom where guests are dancing. During the dancing the door is usually closed. At left another door leads to the supper room.*

[Enter Soame and Cyril]

Cyril. Ah! this is life, this is the world, this is the real thing. Wasn't the opera charming. Didn't Sarah sing divinely? Isn't she pretty? Did you ever see anyone so beautiful?

Soame. She is a pretty woman.

Cyril. You have never met anyone so lovely, have you?

Soame. I will not go so far as that. You know I have seen a great many pretty women. . . Have you ever been to Rome, Cyril?

Cyril. No; but tell me, what fault do you find? I defy you to find any fault.

Soame. She is rather small. She is a small woman.

Cyril. I like small women.

Soame. In Rome—

Cyril. Are they all fine women in Rome? I don't want to go to Rome.

Soame. [Throwing himself on the divan and speaking dreamily as he watches the smoke of his cigarette.] I was thinking of the sublime types of female beauty. All the great artists painted and carved fine women. Michael Angelo's women are immense Titanic creatures, long and lithe of limb, sinewy . . . beautiful in their way but not helpless enough for me. I think a woman should be helpless. It rouses a man's heroic instincts. Always be heroic, Cyril.

Cyril. [Yawning.] I will.

Soame. Raphael's women? Fair creatures with those fair eye-lashes that give a summer softness to the eyes—those downward-gazing eyes which he painted so often . . . You should go to the National Gallery.

Cyril. I do not admire blond women.

Soame. Correggio's women, somewhat colourless, but dainty, winsome . . . A classical anticipation of those delicious little creatures of Fragonard, all slim waist, high heels and silk stockings, lost in a mist of frills.

Cyril. I think I should like those better.

Soame. Women of Veronese! Opulent women trailing yards of brocade, heavy hair and heavy white arms and cruel red mouths like venomous flowers.

Cyril. There's nothing venomous about Sarah, is there?

Soame. [Dreamily.] Women of Tintoretto! Enigmatic women who lean out of the clouds which decorate the ceiling of a Doge's palace. You have never been to Venice, have you, Cyril?

Cyril. [With impatience.] I have never been anywhere.[9]

Soame. Rubens's women . . . *[Waking up to a sense of responsibility.]* But the best of all, my dear Cyril, is to avoid women altogether. The strong man thinks of other things.

Cyril. Are you a strong man?

Soame. Yes, indeed. I bury myself in diplomacy: I dig in my garden every morning.

Cyril. Did digging help Adam? How about Samson and Hercules, and Lord Nelson and Dante? I am not a fool and I am proud to confess that I have a great and honourable . . . admiration . . . for Miss Sparrow.

Soame. For God's sake, speak lower. Honour is the one word you must never mention before a woman: if she is virtuous it will remind her of the very scruples you wish her to forget, and if she is not virtuous, it will only give her one more claim to your pocket-book. Remember, too, that the world finds it much easier to forgive an expensive mistress than a poor wife.

Cyril. I admit I am rather young to think of marriage.

Soame. I will not say that. Julia de Trappe is a charming girl.

Cyril. Julia! . . . She is a mere child; very pretty, of course, but she has no experience. My wife must be a woman of the world!

Soame. I try to advise you for the best, my dear Cyril, and if you will not listen . . . well, youth is headstrong . . .][10] [If I had] known that you were likely to take Miss Sparrow seriously—I shouldn't have come. Besides, it's so unnecessary. She doesn't want you to take her seriously [illegible annotation].

Cyril. Do you think so? Well, I [am] sure I don't want to marry anyone. I am too young.

Soame. Cyril, your mother is most desirous that you should marry Julia. Be guided by your mother, Cyril. She is a wise woman and only desires your good. All this *[pointing towards the ball-room]* is as nothing.

Cyril. Surely it helps to cultivate our tastes for beauty.

Soame. [Dreamily] I doubt if it even does that. I don't see a really pretty woman in the room. Marriage, Cyril, is the one thing: the rest is nothing.

Cyril. Then why did you never marry?

Soame. Ah! that is a long story. Miss de Trappe is a charming girl. She will make you an admirable wife.

Cyril. Yet she is not a Rubens woman. Which is she? A Raphael woman? What's the name of the other fellow you spoke about? Tin—Tin—

Soame. Tintoretto. One of these days we must go abroad and study the old Masters. But by the bye, who was that tall fair girl you were dancing with when I came in? You might introduce me. [11]

Cyril. With pleasure.

[At that moment the music ceases and some of the guests pass across the stage on their way to the supper room. Cyril introduces Sir Digby to Miss Gwendoline Bellamy, and they go off together. Mandeville comes forward.]

Mandeville. Are you enjoying yourself?

Cyril. Enormously. What a relief to get away from home. If it had not been for you . . . Ah! you have been a real friend. *[Shyly.]* But . . . women are so unreasonable . . . Do you think my mother was crying when I left this afternoon.

Mandeville. [Impatiently.] If you allow yourself to be moved from any purpose by the fear that some women may cry, you can make up your mind at once that all enjoyment in life is at an end . . . But tell me, is Sir Digby Soame a friend of your father's?

Cyril. An old friend.

Mandeville. Is he safe?

Cyril. Oh yes. He admires Rubens! I have just introduced him to Gwendoline.

Mandeville. Well, he ought to be satisfied . . . And what did you think of the piece?

Cyril. Splendid. When Sarah tucked up her skirts and danced the jib and when she sang that song about the brandy and the brigadier—

Mandeville. [Pensively]. Yes, so long as Sarah herself has a good part she does not care what becomes of me, but I am glad you liked the piece. I only hope that the public will agree with you. One never knows.

Cyril. How can it fail. Besides you will have a great success in any case.

Mandeville. [With greater cheerfulness.] Yes. I think I may do something with it. They seem to like the serenade.

Cyril. And the duet went magnificently.

Mandeville. Ye-es. Sarah was a little too loud. She spoiled three of my best effects.

Cyril. [In a consoling tone.] No one observed it! And how pretty she looked. Didn't you think so?

Mandeville. To tell the truth I forgot to notice. I was so wrapped up in my part . . .

Cyril. I have promised her to remain in town for the first night. Are you sure you don't mind my stopping at your place?

Mandeville. Not in the least, my dear fellow.

Cyril. I will send my people word. My only difficulty is . . . you will not tell anyone, will you?

Mandeville. Of course not.

Cyril. I should like to send Sarah a present. It is so nice to be able to leave something at the stage door, but I am short of money . . . I suppose there will be no difficulty about finding someone who will make me an advance?

Mandeville. Not the least. I will see to that.

Cyril. There is not much time. I want it tomorrow morning before twelve.

Mandeville. I saw Benjamin in the rooms just now. He does business as cheaply as anyone. He won't charge you more than 40 per cent.

Cyril. Thank you so much. I wonder whether Sarah would come out with me tomorrow and choose something.

Mandeville. Ah! you must settle that matter yourself. I cannot interfere one way or the other . . . I hope Benjamin has not gone.

Cyril. I hope not.

[More guests cross the stage. Among them Mr. Benjamin with his partner.]

Mandeville. There he is now.

Cyril. But he is with a lady.

Mandeville. That does not matter. *[Calls to Benjamin.]* Benjamin, I want you a moment. *[Going up stage.]* Excuse me, Florence, but I must have a word with Mr. Benjamin . . . A matter of business.

Florence. Very well, but don't keep me waiting long. You'll find me at the buffet. *[Exit Florence.]*

Mandeville. [Aside.] Look here, Benjamin, I am bringing you a nice bit of business, as safe as houses. *[As he comes down the stage.]* Lord Aprile, son of Lord Doldrummond. Only son, good for any amount. *[To Cyril.]* Allow me to introduce a friend of mine. Mr. Benjamin, Lord Aprile.

Mr. Ben. Very pleased, I'm sure, to make your acquaintance. Were you at the rehearsal?

Cyril. *[Nervously.]* Yes.

Mr. Ben. Pretty piece, isn't it? Pretty women, pretty dresses, and with our friend here to sing the serenade, I thought it ought to succeed.

Cyril. [Gaining courage.] The best piece I ever saw in my life. The music is so good: you find yourself humming it as you go out of the theatre.

Mandeville. You are not very complimentary, old chap. You forgot those who sing the music.

Mr. Ben. Aren't these tenors touchy? Well, I will say I never heard a serenade better sung. Wasn't it first rate, my Lord?

Cyril. Rather. Wasn't Miss Sparrow charming. She is the prettiest girl I ever saw in my life. He is a lucky fellow to sing a duet with her. I wish I were a tenor and stood in your place.

Mandeville. I should not mind if you were. Her B flat loosens every tooth in my head.

Mr. Ben. Are you coming to the first night?

Cyril. Yes. It is so jolly to get away from home. I could stop here a month if I were not so short of money . . . That reminds me. Mr. Mandeville told me that he thought you would not mind . . . that you would be kind enough to advance me a little.

Mr. Ben. Only too pleased, my Lord. I am happy to do business with any friend of Mr. Mandeville's.

Mandeville. I should think that Lord Aprile could dispense with my intro-duction! It was only because he told me that he wanted the money imme-diately. Tomorrow morning in fact.

Mr. Ben. Of course! I quite understand. If Lord Aprile will do me the honour to call at my office tomorrow morning I will write him a cheque for whatever sum he requires.

Cyril. Thank you. I'm sure it's extremely good of you. It will not be for long, you know.

Mr. Ben. When it suits your convenience, Lord Aprile.

Cyril. Tomorrow morning then, about half past eleven. Excuse me, I hear the music. I think I am engaged to Miss Sparrow for this waltz. *[Exit.]*

Mandeville. This is really good business. You can pluck him at your leisure.

Mr. Ben. [Annoyed.] I don't go in for plucking. Hard cash paid down, without cigars, wine or jewellery. 15 per cent commission.

Mandeville. 15 per cent; really! Then for the future I will not trouble you with my friends. I will take them over the way.

Mr. Ben. How much commission do you expect?

Mandeville. Twenty.

Mr. Ben. Twenty per cent out of forty!

Mandeville. My charge is twenty. You can charge what you like.

Mr. Ben. You say it is quite safe?

Mandeville. You know as much about it as I do. Come, Sam, don't put it on too thick. The eldest son of Lord Doldrummond.

Mr. Ben. Very well: 20 per cent, but if I were you I'd give up singing and turn bill discounter. Now I've another matter to talk about.

[Peals of laughter are heard. Sarah Sparrow enters followed by Cyril and several other young men. Sarah is of the adorable type, pretty, weak, and insolent. She sees Mandeville and at once loses all interest in her flirtations.]

Cyril. I assure you that you promised me the next waltz.

Sarah. But how can I remember when I have lost my card?

A Guest. You promised me the next, Miss Sparrow.

Sarah. Then I cannot dance with either of you. That's fair. I am the fairest woman in the world . . .. Besides I am too tired. Lord Aprile, you must let me find you a partner.

Cyril. If I do not dance with you, I do not care to dance with anybody.

Sarah. Oh yes, you must dance, to please me.

[Some guests come from the supper-room. Sarah beckons to a girl, who leaves her partner and comes down stage.]

Alice, let me introduce you to Lord Aprile. Miss Alice Grove—Lord Aprile. *[Turning to another girl who has followed.]* Miss Guinevere Montague—Lord Aprile. *[Cyril looks in despair] [Aside.]* To please me. I am so tired.

Cyril. May I have the pleasure of the next waltz with you, Miss Grove?

Miss G. I shall be most happy, Lord Aprile, and so will my cousin, Miss Guinevere, dear Lord Aprile. *[Cyril books two dances and with one last look at Sarah goes up to the ball-room with Miss Grove on his arm. They are followed by other dancers, and the stage is left to Sarah, Mandeville and Benjamin.] [Sarah closes the door.]*

Mandeville. [Angrily.] Why on earth did you refuse to dance with him?

Sarah. Because I do not feel like dancing.

Mandeville. But why did you send him away?

Sarah. Because I do not want him.

Mandeville. If you can afford to throw over a young Lord with heaps of money on the eve of a failure, I've nothing more to say. That is sense, isn't it, Sam?

Mr. Ben. It sounds like it.

Sarah. *[Looking hard at both.]* I wonder what you are planning. Nothing good, I can be very sure. *[Pause.]* And what were you saying about a failure? Who says the Opera will fail? Our duet went splendidly.[12]

Mandeville. I am glad you were satisfied.

Sarah. What do you think, Mr. Benjamin?

Mr. Ben. I thought you charming, my dear. But—

Sarah. But what?

Mandeville. *[Angrily.]* Now do not lose your temper, Sarah. You never can keep your temper.

Mr. Ben. Look here. I've got money in this theatre, but I'm not going to throw good money after bad. If the piece takes the public I'll go on: if it doesn't, I'll close the theatre.

[A girl enters from the supper-room.]

Girl. Well, Sam, have you done talking business?

Mr. Ben. Yes, dear, in a moment. *[To Sarah and Mandeville.]* Think over what I have said. I'll give the piece a week, and if it does not succeed I close the theatre. *[Goes out with the girl on his arm.]*[13]

Sarah. Do you think he means that?[14]

Mandeville. I do indeed. He only puts money in the theatre to please Kitty Carew. She has thrown him over and he will close the theatre if we aren't paying expenses at the end of the week.

Sarah. You think there is no chance of the piece catching on?

Mandeville. Not much.

Sarah. Why? Wasn't I all right? I got an encore for my dance.

Mandeville. But your dance isn't everything. You spoiled my best scene by coming out of the balcony before I was half through the second verse, and then fidgeting there dangling your legs about, making faces. I never saw such damn selfishness in my life. So long as you keep the house in a roar you don't mind what becomes of me.

Sarah. Indeed I do. You can cut my dance out if you think it interferes with you. I only came on the balcony because I thought it more artistic that you should sing to someone.

Mandeville. What! are you crying? I declare women are never happy unless they are miserable. Do you want to spoil my evening?

Sarah. You have spoilt mine.

Mandeville. *[Putting his arm round her waist.]* You know I am fond of you.

Sarah. But you ought to remind me of it sometimes. One forgets.

Mandeville. *[Kissing her.]* Come, cheer up. Perhaps the piece will go better the first night. The public may take to it. If we could only keep the theatre open,—if we could just give the piece a chance.

Sarah. I can't think how Benjamin can be so short-sighted.

Mandeville. Short-sighted? I like that. And you suppose it was not short-sighted of you to refuse a dance with that young ass, Lord Aprile? You actually sent him off to dance with Alice Grove.

Sarah. Do you think he would have put money in the theatre?

Mandeville. Do I think? A thousand pounds. A wretched two thousand pounds, say a miserable three thousand pounds.

Sarah. I can easily get him back.

Mandeville. I wish you would. Benjamin and I could work it together.

Sarah. He is so young, so confiding. It seems a shame.

Mandeville. As you like. If you want to see the piece go to the wall and the theatre closed, you know the way to go about it.

Sarah. Charles!

Mandeville. Three thousand pounds is nothing to him, even if he should lose it. He'll get it all back if the piece catches on.

Sarah. Is he very rich, then?

Mandeville. I wish I had a quarter of what he has. Lord Doldrummond is a rich man, and Aprile is engaged to a girl with eight thousand a year, Julia de Trappe.

Sarah. Is she pretty?

Mandeville. Yes, I should call her a pretty girl.

Sarah. Then he won't think of me.

Mandeville. Rubbish! He doesn't care a brass farthing about her. Aprile is stage struck. He talks of nothing but operas, rehearsals, and soprano voices.

Sarah. The girl is I suppose in love with him?

Mandeville. Well, she does sometimes seem to care for him, but I don't think it's very deep. It will wear off.

Sarah. Do you know her?

Mandeville. Yes, I've met her.

Sarah. And do you care for her?

Mandeville. Care for her? Not I. She's merely a pretty girl with eight thousand a year. She was in the drawing-room when I went to fetch Cyril yesterday.

Sarah. And you talked to her?

Mandeville. How curious you are.

Sarah. Is she coming to see the piece?

Mandeville. Yes. She said she'd be here on the first night.

Sarah. She is coming to see you.

Mandeville. Now Sarah, don't be nonsensical. You know I don't like it.

Sarah. Tell me. Do you like her as much as you like me?

Mandeville. I never gave her a thought. But come, don't let's start a quarrel.

Sarah. We shouldn't have any quarrels if we were married.

Mandeville. Do you think not? You're a dear sweet girl. I'd marry you tomorrow if we could afford it. *[Kisses her.]*

Sarah. Will you, if this piece should catch on?

Mandeville. I don't see why we shouldn't marry. We are very fond of each other. If the piece catches on we shall be able to afford it. And the way to make it catch on is to get Aprile to put a couple of thousand pounds into the theatre.

Sarah. How should I do that?

Mandeville. By being a little nice to him. You can twist him round your little finger if you like. He only wants to tell you that you are the prettiest woman in the world and the greatest singer in London. Let him.

Sarah. But if he should ask me to be his wife?

Mandeville. Ask you to marry him? Oh, he wouldn't do that.

Sarah. *[Changing her voice.]* You think that an impossibility?

Mandeville. I mean that you can always keep him from coming to the point.

Sarah. *[Pointedly.]* But he is so young, so impulsive.

Mandeville. Now what is it, Sarah?

Sarah. *[Pause.]* Nothing.

Mandeville. Come, what is the matter?

Sarah. I understand! Because I've been a fool about you, because in all that concerns you I have no spirit, no will of my own, nothing but the most miserable heart in the world.

[The door of ball-room opens.]

Mandeville. Hush! I know all that. They are coming in. *[She looks at him contemptuously.] [He attempts to speak again, but guests come in from the ball-room. Mandeville slips off in the crowd and Cyril, who is very excited, rushes forward when he sees Sarah.]*

Cyril. Ah! how can I thank you for letting me come here this evening?[15]

Sarah. I'm glad you're amused . . . I introduced you to a pretty girl, Miss Alice Grove, didn't I?

Cyril. Oh! I don't care a bit for her . . . But she dances very well.

Sarah. You are fond of dancing?

Cyril. I should think I was, of dancing and music and your singing—of you. Oh the dullness of my father's house cannot be imagined. We only ask each other how we slept, and whether anything we had for dinner disagreed with us. Sometimes we give a dinner party and the only excitement then is to watch the effect of my father's bad champagne on a few bilious peers.

Sarah. [Smiling.] I hope you didn't find my champagne bad?

Cyril. Excellent! You're a judge of wine. But why do you look at me in that way. Do you think I have drunk too much? I am not talking nonsense, am I?

Sarah. No, you're very nice. Go on. I like to hear you.

Cyril. Is that really true? I must tell you, I think of you all day. When I am with you I am mad with happiness and when I leave you I only live by the memory of what you said and wondering what you'll say when I next see you. I am sure there is no one that loves you half as desperately.

Sarah. Now you are talking nonsense. You'll regret that you've said these things to me when—

Cyril. When what? *[Sarah looks at him significantly.]*Ah, I see Mandeville has told you about Julia. That is all a mistake. Julia and I are the best friends in the world. We have known each other all our lives . . . but we are not in love with each other, indeed we are not. I admit that my mother has some ideas of a match, but I'm not going to marry to please my mother. It isn't fair of her to ask me to do so, is it? I don't want to marry and settle down. I love you. You don't believe me. No one has ever loved you as I do.

Sarah. They have said so, at all events.

Cyril. Oh! they may say so, but do not believe them. *[Taking her hand.]* Have you travelled?

Sarah. Why?

Cyril. I thought you might like to go to Japan, or Tunbridge Wells, or Paris, or anywhere.

Sarah. People would talk if I travelled about alone.

Cyril. Oh, not alone. With me. Say yes. Dearest, dearest, my very dearest, look at me again. How lovely your eyes are. I could worship you for ever. Only say yes. Come tonight. Do not wait till tomorrow. I hate tomorrow. Do you mind when I kiss you? It is terrible to love anyone as much as I do you. But you will come. Say yes. Tonight—tonight, it must be tonight.

Sarah. Ah! you are like the rest. I am to spend a week with you in Paris, and you will worship me for ever. Your week would be more amusing than my Eternity.

Cyril. If I am like the rest, I do not love like the rest, but it is so difficult for a fellow to be honourable when his parents are religious! If I gave you my mother's pearl necklace it would not cause her half as much grief as if we married and had respectable lodgings at Ealing. They would never consent to our marriage, or if they did, it would be deferred till so late a day that out of perversity or impatience we should each by that time be in love with someone else.

Sarah. Why ask your father's consent? In these matters a man must decide for himself. I think it would be very wrong to place such a responsibility on Lord Doldrummond's shoulders. Whether he said yes or no he could only tremble for the consequence.

Cyril. But if the consequences were bad, it would be so much more agreeable to blame him than to find fault with you, dearest. Why not be philosophical. Have you not said a thousand times that love and marriage are the most ill-assorted couple in the world, and are at the root of every divorce. You have no silly whims about virtue, thank goodness. You have taught me the folly of mine.

Sarah. Oh Cyril, I never knew I had so apt a pupil. Ah! I wish I had no conscience. We must never see each other again. We must forget the happy life we might have spent together, if marriage had only been possible. *[Pretends to cry.]*

Cyril. But it is possible. I never suspected that you had these scruples, forgive me.[16] You are quite right. If I thought that any other man would dare speak to you as I have spoken, I would thrash him with a horse whip.

Sarah. Do you find it so easy to forgive yourself?

Cyril. I love you. That makes a difference. But promise that you will marry me.

Sarah. [Dreamily] I could give up singing and we could go and live in the country and have friends to stop with us from Saturday till Monday.

Cyril. *[Alarmed.]* O, if you're going to be quiet and live in the country I might as well marry Julia. Ah no, we must be married privately. No one must know of it, at least for a few months. For the present we must continue just as we are—a little more intimate of course, and I shall see you often . . . People may think what they like . . . it will be most amusing. No one will guess our secret.

Sarah. [Sullenly.] I hate secrets.

Cyril. Still, for my sake, dearest, for my sake. Surely if I sacrifice a whole career for you, you can keep a little secret for me!

Sarah. But what is the use of being married if no one knows of it? If I cannot tell all these horrid jealous women . . . I should like to see their faces when they hear . . . Cats.

Cyril. Ah! be patient. If one does a foolish thing one can at least do it with discretion. Darling! *[He kisses her just as the guests, headed by Mandeville and Benjamin, return from the supper-room.]*[17]

Sarah. [With a little scream, and affecting great confusion.] [Eyes downcast and speaking in gasps.] He has . . . the sight . . . Oh Cyril, I must explain. *[To Mandeville with ill-concealed triumph.]* Lord Aprile has asked me to marry him and I have accepted.

Cyril. [With desperate gaiety.] You must all drink our health. Come Mandeville, propose the toast. I suppose you never guessed . . . *[laughs hysterically]* what I meant when I told you that this was the happiest moment in my life.

Mandeville. Surely she has not accepted you? . . . How sly these lovers are. *[Signals to Footman.]*

Soame. [Aside to Cyril.] Cyril, for God's sake . . .

Cyril. I tell you it's too late . . . I am a man of my word . . . *[Aloud]* Make haste with the champagne.

[The Footman enters with champagne. Pours out wine.]

Mandeville. My friend Lord Aprile has called upon me to propose the health of the future Countess of Doldrummond. Her ladyship, if I may anticipate, the peerage has no firmer friend than myself. I have watched her career from the beginning with unfeigned admiration. There are those who are born as the popular superstition has it, under a lucky star. Miss Sparrow is one of those fortunate mortals. Her stage career has been one of uninterrupted success. Tonight we saw her create the part of La Marquise de Perdrigonde in "The Dandy and the Dancer." Her singing and dancing filled us with admiration. The true artist always obtains praise first from her fellow artists. Professional jealousy is, I am convinced, a myth. We applaud tonight what the public will applaud tomorrow. My friend Lord Aprile has made a wise choice, and our friend Miss Sparrow will prove as brilliant an ornament to the aristocracy as she has done to the stage. To their health. *[They drink.]*

Mr. Ben. I beg to be allowed to propose Lord Aprile's health. Lord Aprile is a young man of distinguished family. He has got wealth and youth in his favour. Tonight he has proved that he is a man of taste. I have not had the pleasure of knowing him for long: my friend Mr. Mandeville introduced him to me tonight, but I may say he has long been known to me by name. The interest he takes in the drama has reached me and I am sure that you will all here agree with me that the stage needs the support of the aristocracy as much as the aristocracy needs the culture and amusement that the stage affords. I do not wish to detain you. I can see that Miss Sparrow is looking tired, but there is a subject on which I must say a word. The union of the stage, particularly the lighter stage, has long been a noticeable feature in modern society. Tonight this union has been legitimised, but as there can be no divorce without marriage I venture to hope that this marriage, the health of which we have drunk tonight, will not lead to any divorce, at least to no immediate divorce of Miss Sparrow and the stage. May we hope that Miss Sparrow's secession from the stage will not be immediate. She will remember, although her old fortunes have been elevated to another sphere, that the fortunes of her friends and comrades are still centred in the success of "The Dandy and the Dancer!" We hope that we may count on her loyal support at all events until the success of the piece is firmly established.

Cyril. I think I may venture to say that my future wife does not intend at least for the present to sever her connection with the stage.

Mr. Ben. To their health. *[They drink.]*

Miss B. Good-night dear, I am so pleased. There will be paragraphs in all the papers tomorrow. The piece is sure to be a success now. *[She retires up the stage.]*

Miss G. I'm so pleased, darling. I assure you I mean it, although I say it.

Mr. Ben. I hope you won't forget your old friends in your future brilliant surroundings.

Sarah. Thank you, thank you. *[Hysterically]* But I'm so tired.

Mandeville. [With an air of authority.] The fact is she has had a very hard day, and is not able to shake hands with you all.

Mr. Ben. We quite understand.

[Sympathetic murmurs among the guests, who gradually file out; Mandeville and Benjamin follow them.]

Soame. [Aside.] Cyril, this is madness . . . this is . . .

Cyril. I know my own mind. Good night.

Soame. You must come with me.

Cyril. Why? *[He shows signs of extreme drowsiness and accepts Soame's arm.]*

Soame. Good night, Miss Sparrow.

Sarah. Good night.

Cyril. Why should I go with you, Soame? It will give you so much trouble. Good night, Sarah.

Sarah. Shall I see you tomorrow?

Cyril. Tomorrow? When is tomorrow?

Sarah. Good night.

[Soame and Cyril go off. Sarah marches up and down the room in a fury, rests for a moment on the divan, and then flies to the piano and thumps the key-board with both fists.]

Mandeville. [Entering cautiously.] Sarah! what's the meaning of all this?

Sarah. I never want to see you again. You have driven me to this. Do not reproach me because I will not listen. *[Pause] [He says nothing.]* Do you hear, I will not listen. I have made up my mind to forget you, and if you say another word . . . *[Snatches his photograph from the table and flings it down on the floor.]* There, this is the end! *[Snatches several from the wall.]* And now, go. Do you hear? Go, go, go!

Mandeville. This is absurd. [18]

[*Sarah.* Go!

Mandeville. You will make yourself ill.

Sarah. Go! *[Falls sobbing on the divan.]*

Mandeville. Let me take out those beastly hair-pins.

Sarah. Do not touch me!

Mandeville. Those cheap things will ruin your magnificent hair.

Sarah. I do not care; it does not matter: nothing matters now. O, I am so tired of you. Go!

Mandeville. You do not care for Cyril.

Sarah. He loves me! I have not the strength to argue. Leave me.

Mandeville. You want me to go? Then say you hate me and I will go at once. You are not the only woman on this earth.

Sarah. [Roused.] What? You can think of other women when I am so ill that I am not responsible for what I have said[?] What did I say? I forgot. *[Throwing herself into his arms.]* Do not let me marry Cyril. Take me away. Save me from myself. Do not let me marry Cyril.][19]

Mandeville. That will be all right. Lord Doldrummond will never give his consent.

Sarah. He said he would marry me without his father's consent.

Mandeville. That's easier said than done. They'll send him abroad, for a trip round the world. You surely never took this marriage seriously, did you?

Sarah. What do you mean? I can get him to marry me if I wish.

Mandeville. But don't you see there's something much better than marriage in this?

Sarah. What's that?

Mandeville. A breach of promise. Twenty thousand pounds damages.

Sarah. And then?

Mandeville. Why, then we can have our own theatre. [20]

Sarah. Oh Charles!

Mandeville. Now we are beginning to understand each other. This is sense.

Sarah. [Embracing him.] Oh, it's wonderful how everything works out for the best after all.

Mandeville. A little common sense—that's what does it. You're very tired, dear. *[He lifts her from the divan, and as they go up the stage, the curtain falls.]*[21]

Act III

SCENE—*Library at Lord Doldrummond's. Lord Doldrummond is discovered looking through a pile of bills. Lady Doldrummond stands facing him on the opposite side of the table.*

Lady Dol. Fifteen hundred pounds! So Cyril has squandered fifteen hundred pounds on flowers, suppers, wine and jewels for the creature. I cannot believe it. I will not think that he could be infatuated even for one evening with a painted adventuress. I will not believe it: I cannot. O, there is no such thing as purity! If ever a boy looked honest, noble and high-minded it was Cyril. And this woman—a woman who sings to the mob! If it had been some young inexperienced girl, I could bear it better. I could even try to understand it a little . . . one reads in books that with some natures youth is a sort of madness; but it is the disappointment . . . the disappointment, Herbert. When I once lose faith in man, I shall lose faith in God, for they are His witnesses. That is the fear! The terrible fear!

Lord Dol. I would not care if it were fifty times the sum so long as Cyril has learnt his lesson.

Lady Dol. He has learnt how to enjoy life. Do you think that is a knowledge he will readily forget? You wished him to have more liberty—more pleasure. He has taken both and I have lost him. There is a man who calls me Mother but my son is gone. I can only remember how I loved him, how I trusted him, how kind, how true he was and remembering this I miss him. That is all! I must be patient: it is wrong to complain. God knows best: perhaps I loved him too much . . . But the pain of it!

Lord Dol. Does Julia know?

Lady Dol. Cyril walked out to meet her yesterday as she returned from Church. She looked pale when they came in and soon went to her room. When I saw her next she had been crying.

Lord Dol. Then he told her?

Lady Dol. I, too, had been crying. No, we did not speak. There was nothing to say.

Lord Dol. Does she forgive him?

Lady Dol. [*After a pause.*] She is a woman, Herbert.

[Butler announces Sir Digby Soame. Lady Doldrummond merely bows and ignores his hand. Lord Doldrummond tries to atone for her coldness by a forced cordiality.]

Lord Dol. My dear Soame, this is indeed kind.

Soame. [To Lady Doldrummond.] You make me feel that my visit is an intrusion, Lady Doldrummond.

Lady Dol. [Firmly.] My husband, I am sure, is more than glad to see you and I would leave you both together if I did not fear that your sympathy would lead to even greater disaster than your advice.

Lord Dol. Edith! A guest!

Lady Dol. A traitor!

Soame. Lady Doldrummond!

Lady Dol. Sir Digby, we have known each other many years. I never liked you: you never cared for me: people told me you were agreeable and I owned that you were clever, but I felt you were evil and I knew that you would bring trouble to this home.

Soame. My dear Lady Doldrummond, I know that I am not popular with good women. I am not a sufficiently bad man. I cannot play the hypocrite. But when you blame me for your son's extravagant indiscretion, I must protest.

Lady Dol. Indiscretion! You only call it indiscretion? For the first time in my life I wish I could agree with you.

Lord Dol. [Testily.] This is no time to quarrel about a definition. Tell us your news, Soame.

Soame. Have I Lady Doldrummond's permission to speak plainly? *[She inclines her head.]* Sarah Sparrow will certainly sue Cyril for a Breach of Promise.

Lady Dol. God!

Lord Dol. The scandal!

Soame. [Lifting his hands.] And the expense.

Lord Dol. How much does the woman want?

Soame. She will ask for twenty thousand pounds.

Lady Dol. Can the matter be settled privately?

Soame. I fear not. Miss Sparrow would no doubt regard a public trial as the chiefest of her compensations.

Lord Dol. Thank Heaven, we have sent Cyril out of the country.

Soame. What! Has he gone away?

Lady Dol. He left England last night.

Soame. Alone?

Lady Dol. No: he has his conscience for companion.

[Soame shrugs his shoulders. Butler announces Mrs. de Trappe. She enters, appropriately attired in half mourning]

Mrs. de Trappe. Dear Edith! What trouble! *[Shakes hands mechanically with the two men, who go up stage.]* What trouble, Edith! They talk of nothing else in London. No one blames poor Cyril—some blame Sarah. The world is so cruel—they say you have always been too strict with the unfortunate boy. But I have fought your battle and you may be quite sure that no matter how severely you are judged, I shall always maintain—and Arthur is of my opinion—that you at least intended to be a kind mother! But where is Julia? *[Lady Doldrummond touches bell.]* May I see her? In the circumstances, I think it is most improper that she should remain here. James and Arthur quite agree with me.

[Footman enters.]

Lady Dol. Tell Miss de Trappe that Mrs. de Trappe has called.

[Footman goes out.]

Mrs. de Trappe. I cannot express my grief, Edith. If I had less heart, I would be a happier woman, but, as it is, I feel for others far more than they feel for themselves. Although Cyril is not my son, I am certain that my suffering at the present moment is far greater than your own.

[Julia enters. She looks graver—paler, no longer the young girl of the first Act.]

Julia. Did you wish to see me, Mama?

[Lady Doldrummond goes up stage to Soame and Lord Doldrummond.]

Mrs. de Trappe. How ill you look! This is shocking. Have you heard this disgraceful story about Cyril? There will be a Breach of Promise case.

Julia. I have heard the story.

Mrs. de Trappe. Have you quarrelled with Cyril?

Julia. No.

Mrs. de Trappe. What does he say?

Julia. If he said anything, it was in confidence.

Mrs. de Trappe. Nonsense! He is well aware that no nice girl has secrets from her mother and he cannot have much respect for you if he tells you things which you dare not repeat to me! Were you engaged to him? Are you engaged to him? This mystery is not respectable and if you do not choose to explain yourself, I shall appeal to Cyril.

Julia. He has gone abroad.

Mrs. de Trappe. What! Then he will never have the courage to return.

[Footman enters and hands a card to Julia. She shows some agitation.]

Footman. I have shown the . . . young person into the morning room. *[Exit.]*

Lady Dol. [Reading.] Miss Sarah Sparrow!

Julia. Dear Lady Doldrummond, I hope you will not be angry but she has called at my invitation. Ah, before you say anything let me tell you why I wrote to her. I thought if we could only meet each other face to face . . .

Lady Dol. My poor child—what could you have to say to such a creature?

Mrs. de Trappe. I forbid you to see her. A woman of that kind could make a hundred pounds out of every word you utter.

Julia. I am not afraid: she may know the world. I only know that I love Cyril and she does not. Do you think she would be any match for me?

Lady Dol. Ah, then you do love him, Julia?

Julia. Yes.

Mrs. de Trappe. O, this is very pretty and romantic, no doubt, but when girls have sentiment, mothers at least must have sense. What is to be done with Sarah Sparrow?

Julia [To Lady Doldrummond.] Let me see her. Only believe in me—only trust me, and all will go well. I know it will.

Lady Dol. [Kissing her.] A loyal heart never yet worked mischief. I will believe in you—I do trust you. Your mother and I will go into the boudoir and you can see Miss Sparrow here. Come, Violet.

Mrs. de Trappe. [Following.] Whatever trouble comes of this will not be my work.

[Lady Doldrummond and Mrs. de Trappe go out. Julia rings bell. Footman enters.]

Julia. I will see Miss Sparrow here. *[Exit Footman.] [Alone.]* I have but one fear. Will Cyril ever forgive me for helping him? A man always forgets that if his pleasures are only for himself, his trouble belongs to the woman who loves him.

[Footman announces Miss Sparrow.]

Sarah. Miss de Trappe?

Julia. I am very glad you were able to come, Miss Sparrow.

Sarah. Yes, I have come. But I daresay it was not wise.

Julia. Why?

Sarah. [Seating herself.] What can I say to you? what can you say to me? I have been infamously treated and all the talk in the world would not make me forget Lord Aprile's dishonourable conduct. I come of an ancient Puritan family, Miss de Trappe, and I am not the sort of person one makes love to merely for amusement!

Julia. I am sure that Lord Aprile could never have thought so.

Sarah. O, I know that Cyril is deeply attached to me: he has sworn over and over again that I am the only woman he loves and could love, but if he can forget his vows and protestations simply because Lord Doldrummond disapproves of our marriage, his is a flimsy devotion I am the happier for lacking! At least, I try to think so. I am too proud to break my heart without a struggle. I have struggled. *[She wipes her eyes.]* You see how vainly!

Julia. Life is full of disillusions, Miss Sparrow.

Sarah. [Who has evidently studied her part well.] It is not only the disillusion, Miss de Trappe. To every woman the prospect of a home, means, carriages, horses and a distinguished position is dangerously alluring, but to one who has had to fight with poverty, who has worked from five in the morning till twelve o'clock at night, who has had to dance for her lodging and sing for her supper, such an offer of Lord Aprile's would mean more than a lover and an engagement bring! To have dreamt of peace and then to go back again to the old trials, the old temptations, the old privations, and old humiliations,—ah, what money could atone for the anguish of the awakening?

Julia. [Timidly.] I believe your solicitor has suggested that ten thousand pounds would relieve the difficulty—to a certain extent.

Sarah. Ah, these lawyers can sell our bitterest sorrow for a song! How little they know women!

Julia. It is not as though you were old and plain, Miss Sparrow, and that Cyril was your last and only chance of a husband. You must receive offers of marriage every week: no jury in the world could see you and think otherwise! In fact, with no desire to flatter you, you are far too fascinating to excite sympathy as a woman with no future! Your story is only effective so long as you are not seen: if you appear in Court, you will not only make the women envious, but for every pound you receive, you will create a hundred enemies. How much better and more dignified to settle the matter privately?

Sarah. I was extremely indiscreet to come here. This is a conspiracy and no doubt you have witnesses and a solicitor's clerk concealed behind every curtain.

Julia. [Indignant.] Miss Sparrow!

Sarah. Oh, I should not blame you, for if I were in love with a man, I would stick at nothing to get him out of trouble! Good Lord! I am as great a fool as yourself and wish I had never been born. *[Bursts into tears.]* Why do you want to help Cyril? He will not give you a Thank you for your pains.

Julia. He will never know anything about them.

Sarah. [Drily.] I see you understand men!

Julia. Let me tell Lord Doldrummond that you will accept the money without a trial?

Sarah. Why should I? I do not pretend to be an angel and revenge is something.

Julia. Be kind! be generous! Why do you wish to make such trouble and unhappiness for all of us? It does not matter to me what Cyril has done, what disgrace he may be in, and what ruin you may bring upon him. Do your worst and he will still remain my best and dearest! But a man is for the world—not for one woman only. Lord Aprile was not born to dream away his life on my devotion. He is very young and he has been very foolish, but he has a soul, he has ability, he may do much. I know he has the courage to live down any shame, yet the world is cruel,—I was not brought up in a nursery, and I have never yet seen any man or woman get the better of a public scandal.

Sarah. It is unfair to appeal to my feelings in this way. My solicitor would be indignant. These things are not done, Miss de Trappe.

Julia. Mr. Mandeville has been in love with you for some years: he was the first to believe in your genius and he knew you were beautiful before the world told him so. Few women have such devotion offered them.

Sarah. I am not bad-hearted but business is business and I owe something to my profession.

Julia. You can have the money at once.

Sarah. [After a pause.] The whole amount?

Julia. Of course.

Sarah. Who will give it to me?

Julia. Lord Doldrummond.

Sarah. Why should I do all this merely to oblige you?

Julia. One cannot always say what motive prompts a noble act!

Sarah. Oh Lord, I am not working the nobility trick! This is business and nothing else. If you make it worth my while to accept your terms, the trial is off! Right off! If not, it is *on*. Right on! What's the use of beating about the bush? I haven't the strength. I like to be natural and straightforward: all this splandee-and-splandum wears me out!

Julia. Then will you see Lord Doldrummond

Sarah. Oh, I don't mind seeing him! I have done nothing to be ashamed of!

[Julia goes to door of boudoir and calls "Lord Doldrummond." He enters followed by Sir Digby.]

Julia. Allow me to introduce Miss Sparrow.

Sarah. [Holding out her hand.] I am very happy to meet you, Lord Doldrummond, although I cannot suppose that you are especially glad to see me. *[He bows coldly.]* How are you, Sir Digby? I daresay you knew it would come to this when you drank my health at the ball! And now, Miss de Trappe, what am I to do next?

Julia. Miss Sparrow has consented to abandon the action and she will accept ten thousand pounds in settlement of all claims.

Sarah. I know I shall be sorry for this!

Lord Dol. [To Sir Digby.] She must sign a paper to that effect at once. *[Sir Digby sits down and writes hurriedly.] [To Sarah.]* A wise decision, Miss Sparrow.

Sarah. Not at all. My solicitor will take my head off! Your son has treated me very badly and no money can compensate for the mortification, disappointment, distress of mind, and . . .

Soame. May I ask you to sign this, Miss Sparrow?

Sarah. [Reading it through.] That seems fair enough. I am not unreasonable and there is not a grain of malice in my nature. Here goes! *[Signs
with a flourish.]* And now, where's my cheque?

NOTES

1. The full text of this manuscript (B), entitled "Act I," is given below:

Scene. Dining-room at Sir Sidby Warcop's.
The table is set up for dinner. The diners are Sir Sidney and Lady Warcop, Mrs.
Portcullis, Lady Twacorbie, the Hon. Felicia Gorm, ~~Lady Bonnejoy~~, Captain Sa-
ville Rookes, Sidney Wiche, Sir Ventry Coxe, Mr. Waddilove and others. The seat
at the left of Sir Sidney and the right of Rookes is vacant. ~~Desert is~~ being ~~handed~~
^{Desert is being handed}. A footman enters and says something to Lady Warcop.

Warcop.

[The next exchanges are crossed out diagonally, and are therefore enclosed in square
brackets.]

[Lady Warcop. Ah, Lady Mallinger has at last arrived. She must come in at once and not
think of dressing after dinner.

Footman. She has been shown to her room, my lady.

Sir Sidney. Nonsense! Go to her, Blanche ~~crossed out half-sentence~~ [,] if you do not, she
will keep us ~~longing for~~ ^{in suspense} ~~waiting~~ ^{for} at least another hour.

~~Lady Warcop rises from the table.~~]

Sir Sidney. How disappointing that Lady Mallinger has not yet arrived. I hope we shall
not have to wait much longer.

Van Huyster. I would rather wait than do anything else in the world. Indeed, I have even
maintained that suspense is the one truly indispensable emotion,—for without it every
other would be extremely tedious. Certainty robs grief of its tears, love of its nonsense,
and life of its delicious mystery.

Wiche. ~~Lady Twacorbie~~. ^{Lady Warcop} You speak of affection and melancholy, ^{Mr. Van Huyster}, with the
confidence of one who has never loved and would never mourn. [Sighs]

Van Huyster. Good Heavens! You were never more mistaken. I have constantly observed
in myself a capacity for adoration which narrowly verges on the abandoned. If I were
once to love with the whole power of my soul . . . but I dare not think of it! ~~Crossed-out
sentence?~~

2. Manuscript C starts with a list of seven scenes: "I. Lord Skepperton and Sir Digby
Soame," "II. Lord Skepperton. Sir Digby Soame, and Mrs. Gaye-West," "III. Mrs. Gaye-West
and Lady Bonnejoy," "IV. Mrs. Gaye-West, Lady Bonnejoy, and Lady Skepperton," "V. Mrs.
Gaye-West, Lady Bonnejoy, Lady Skepperton, and Cyril," "VI. Mrs. Gaye-West, Lady Bonnejoy, Lady Skepperton, Cyril, and Norton," "VII. Lord Skepperton and Cyril." On the second
page Lady Skepperton's name is crossed out and replaced with Doldrummond. (Two later

manuscript sources, D and E, locate Act I in Lord Doldrummond's library; D closely resembles the printed version.) Lady Bonnejoy also appears in the draft version of the first act of the adaptation Craigie was planning for *A Bundle of Life* (see manuscript B). Unnumbered page 4 of manuscript C ends with a note to Moore: "I want you to see this before I write anything further. I shall have a fearful fight with the critics before I convince them! I must not, however, ask others to join in the struggle. (By the by, did you see the Pall Mall review? I have had the pleasure of pointing out to the Editor that the phrase "We had some words," which he objected to as a vulgarism, has been used by Shakespeare, Swift and Tennyson.) I think the above little scene is, on the whole, good. [Short illegible sentence crossed out] ^{May I have it back please as soon as possible.} J. O. H." To provide a context for the way in which the co-authors' ideas developed, the text is given in full. It reads:

> Act opens with a scene between Lord Skepperton (who is recovering from bronchitis), and his friend, Sir Digby Soame. He confides to him his anxieties with regard to his son, Cyril and how he has a young, rich and handsome widow visiting them in the hope of marrying him off and getting him settled. He tells how he is in constant association with an actor called Norton: describes the character of Norton. Mrs. Gaye-West enters. The two men talk of Cyril with the idea of getting her opinion of him: she seems a little too enthusiastic on the subject of Norton. This to hood-wink her questioners. Lady Bonnejoy is announced. The two men soon withdraw and the two women are left. Lady Bonnejoy at once asks whether Mrs. G-W. has heard the rumours with regard to Cyril and Kitty Carew. She goes on to say that she herself has met Miss Carew.
> Act I. *Library at Lord Skepperton's.*
> Scene I. Lord Skepperton and Sir Digby Soame.

Lord S. Thank heaven every night and morning of your life, my dear Digby, that you are a bachelor. Praying for sinners and breeding them would seem the whole duty of man. I was no sooner born than my parents were filled with uneasiness lest I should not live to marry, and beget an heir of my own! Now I have an heir, his mother will never know peace until she has found him a wife. And he is the worst fellow in the world for matrimony for, on my soul, I believe he has inherited all the unruly tastes which I possess but lack the courage to obey. If I did not understand him so well I would be more severe,—as it is, whenever I assert my authority I am hoping he will have the audacity to defy me. I recognise in Cyril the rascal I might have been, and I feel I have missed my vocation!

Soame. You have always been so respectable that I fear you have not so much as the remembrance of a repented sin to stir the intolerable calm of domesticity. But in all seriousness, I am greatly surprised to hear this report of Cyril. I thought that Lady ~~Skepperton~~ ^{Doldrummond} held views on the subject of a young man's education and had brought him up on a system of her own.

Lord S. Ah, that is the trouble! My poor wife has taught him that women are the scourges of creation and if he had met no other example than herself, no doubt he would have accepted the doctrine. But I fear his only prejudices are directed against the virtuous and discreet, and I am convinced that there is not a young man in London who could give you so many admirable reasons for going straight to the devil!

Soame. I have heard that Lady Skepperton insists on his retiring at eleven and rising at eight: that she allows him nothing stronger than ginger ale and lemon-juice: that she selects his friends, makes his engagements and superintends his amusements, and when he marries, I am told, she will even undertake the office of best man!

Lord S. Poor soul! She means well and if devotion could have made the lad a saint, he could have been in Heaven before he was out of his long-clothes! Her one idea, now, however is to get him a wife. She is constantly inviting Julia de Trappe to the house, in the hope of bringing matters to a crisis.

Soame. Julia de Trappe! She must be the daughter of that Mrs. Howard de Trappe who gives large At Homes in a small house and spends her time hunting for old lovers and new servants.

Lord S. Yes, I am afraid Julia has had a very bad bringing-up and has been allowed to meet men and women who are certainly not fit companions for a young girl. But I find her singularly modest and sensible, and if anything can save my unhappy son it will be her worldly wisdom—not his mother's unsettling prudence.

Soame. Save Cyril? You speak as though—

Lord S. Ah, Digby, I know the whole story. You like all the rest of my friends have conspired to keep me in ignorance of the one matter which most concerns me. What would become of us if it were not for our enemies: they alone will tell one the truth. I knew of Cyril's infatuation for this actress called Sarah Sparrow before he had been three times to see her act. I can tell you the number of letters he has written, the presents he has given her, and the debts he has incurred. I dare not break the news to my wife, for her interference would only make matters worse. My only hope now lies in Julia.

Soame. What is a young girl against such a woman as Sarah Sparrow? A man must have a sound knowledge of evil before he can appreciate innocence. I have no wish to be discouraging, but do not pin much faith to Julia and the power of pure affection!

[JULIA is heard singing.] And the best and the worst of this is / That neither is most to blame, / If you've forgotten my kisses, / And I've forgotten your name!"
[JULIA enters.]

[This page ends with Craigie's note to Moore. Page 5 begins with the final paragraph to Act I and the start of Act II]—see the following text:

[. . .] there is really no time to be lost: the gong sounds: they must not stay for luncheon: Cyril tells Norton to get into the dog-cart which the footman announces is waiting at the door: Norton says good-bye and goes: the others go into the dining-room at Lady Skepperton's suggestion to watch them drive off. Cyril is just about to leave when he encounters Lord Skepperton and Sir Digby who have returned from their walk: there is a stormy scene and the father and son part in anger.
Act II: Supper party at Kitty Carew's after "The Dandy and the Dancer." She has two chaperons:—Lady Mankin and Miss Maramour. Norton, Cyril, a dramatic author, several critics, another actress (with her husband), and some artists are present. The party is breaking up. Cyril wishes Kitty good-night but gives her to understand that he intends to return. Bob is on the point of leaving when Kitty begs him to stay. She proposes to him: draws pathetic picture of Art struggling with poverty but eventually succeeding. Bob does not see it: she reproaches him for sneering at her "whenever she tries to soar above her mud-heap." He drily remarks—glancing about the room—"that he would say that she had the strongest mud-heap in London!" Goes on to define his idea of a fireside—"one at one theatre, and the other at another" etc. etc. She taunts him with Cyril as a rival: Bob seems to doubt her power in that direction: [illegible] with his account of a deuced pretty and rich widow "with an easily encountered eye" whom he has met several

times at the Skeppertons: Kitty unholy jealous. They part company. Cyril returns: makes desperate love: she accepts him: questions him about Mrs. Gaye-West. He dwells rather too long on her beauty and attractiveness adding "that even Bob was impressed and talked about her from morning till night." Kitty becomes absent-minded: Cyril fears she is over-tired: the two chaperons return and insist that she will not be able to act on Monday if she does not get her proper rest. Cyril departs. Lady Bonnejoy is announced: obliged to call and congratulate her on her splendid performance and invite her to dinner the following night. Several charming people are coming: the lovely Mrs. Gaye-West, Cyril: Lord and Lady So-and-So (rattles off a lot of titles). Norton (if she can get hold of him: By-the-bye, how splendid it would be if Kitty and Norton were to marry and manage a theatre: such a handsome couple and they act so magnificently together. Surely he must be hopelessly in love with her to play the lover with such touching effect: everyone can see that he worships the ground under her feet. Poor fellow! So distinguished-looking, too. And so many women running after him: the Countess of S. and the Duchess of B. are out of the Divorce Court through no fault of their own. K. admits that she would marry Bob if she only had capital: he is certainly most fascinating. [This is where the manuscript ends.]

3.   Manuscript page D introduces Soame as "a relic of the Diplomatic service: has an easy smile and a sharp eye: dresses well: speaks abruptly and smiles into his beard over his own witticisms." He immediately launches into satirical mode, noting, "with a disappointed air," that "You look far better than I hoped to find you. You are rather yellow and you have certainly lost flesh: your eyes, too, are dull, and your hair is much greyer than when I saw you last, but otherwise I should say that there was nothing on earth the matter with you!" The page ends with Lord Doldrummond's response to Soame's enquiry about his wife's health.

4.   A dig at New Woman fiction, especially of the social purist kind, which cautioned women readers to steer clear of the "Old Man" with a sexual past if they wished to safeguard their health as well as that of their future children.

5.   This is where the typed manuscript pages (A) start (part of Lord Doldrummond and Soame's prior exchange, heavily edited in Moore's handwriting, is glued onto the first half of the page).

6.   A variant of the last two sentences is inserted in Craigie's hand to Moore's handwritten additions to the typescript (A, Act I, unnumbered page).

7.   Intertextual reference to the provincial French actress Laure whom Lydgate finds so beguiling in George Eliot's *Middlemarch* (1871–1872) until she tells him that the fatal accident that befell her husband during a performance was intentional and that she meant to stab him. See chapter XV of *Middlemarch*, ed. Gregory Maertz (Peterboro, Ontario: Broadview, 2004), 145–146.

8.   Julia's response in the typescript (A, Act I, pages 21–22, with Craigie's handwritten annotations) is underpinned by dry wit; she is more spirited here, and Mandeville is figured as a dandy: "It does not make the least difference. Perhaps you are right in taking Lord Aprile into society. He wearies in this house. He complains of sleepless nights, eats nothing but oranges, discourses enchantingly on suicide, wonders at the stars, gazes at the moon, weeps at the sound of music, sighs at the mention of a dance and smiles to hear of lovers in one grave! Sarah and her supper party may change his thoughts!" This is followed by the exchange below:

Mandeville. I am afraid you attach an importance to a dress-rehearsal and a supper party that neither deserve. A party at Sarah Sparrow's is not such a wild affair as you think. Just a slice of cold chicken and—

Julia. A glass of ginger ale. Cyril will think that he is in his father's house. And now, tell me, Mr. Mandeville, what part you take in this new piece. Are you satisfied with it?

Mandeville. I play the part of a dandy.

Julia. Oh, you will be splendid as a dandy.

[Mandeville looks at her curiously.]

Mandeville. The costume is of course picturesque, and that is the great thing in an opera. A few men can sing but to find the right clothes to sing *in*—that shows the true artist!

9. (Unnumbered) page 3 of the typescript (A) of Act II ends with a crossed-out reply by Soame: "Not to the low countries. Rubens's women, golden-haired, fair as roses. Those great roses, Marchal Neil [Maréchal Niel], I think they are called." The next page is missing, and the text is here partially reconstructed from a page of the handwritten manuscript (F) which also begins with Rubens and then moves to Sarah Sparrow. However, the end of this page does not lead into the fragmented sentence on page 5 of the typescript; this sentence has been completed by the editor, the insertion being indicated by square brackets. There is a second, longer, handwritten manuscript page (G, numbered 3) relevant to the passage. This sheet breaks off in mid-sentence and does not connect thematically with page 5 of the typescript. Following Cyril's exclamation that "I have never been anywhere," the variant reads:

Soame. No wonder then that you are attracted by little women . . . one of these days we may go abroad . . . your father has asked me to talk to you and give you the benefit of my experience.

Cyril. And this is, that fine women are prettier than little women.

Soame. Ha! ha! . . . I am a critic not a lover . . . As in Italy, so in the low countries Rubens's women are immense . . . golden hair and fair skin clear as roses, sumptuous as sun-flowers . . . You have not been to the low countries, Cyril?

Cyril. No and there would be no use in my going there. I do not admire fat women . . . I like Sarah.

Soame. [Working up to a sense of responsibility.] But the best of all, my dear fellow, is to avoid women altogether.

Cyril. But if one cannot.

Soame. The strong man has nothing to say to them.

Cyril. And are you a strong man?

Soame. Yes indeed . . . I bury myself in diplomacy; I spend ten hours a day writing on Egyptian affairs; in the summer I dig in my garden every morning; I . . .

Cyril. Did digging help Adam? . . . How about Samson and Hercules and Lord Nelson and Dante? I am not a fool.

Soame. When one reaches a certain age one can discriminate between love as a fine art and love as a spring fever!

Cyril. I am not at all ashamed of being young . . . But you are mistaken if you think I have left home merely because I admire Sarah. The tedium of my father's house is not to be imagined. We only ask each other how we slept last night or whether anything we eat [page breaks off; the latter sentences appear later in the typescript of Act II].

10.   The handwritten manuscript page of the dialogue between Cyril and Soame (F) ends with a passage that features later in the typescript and has been omitted here: "By the bye, who was that tall, fair girl you were dancing with when I came in? You might introduce me." To fit the different manuscript versions together, I continue with page 5 of the typescript (A, Act II) and have inserted a few words to complete the sentence.

11.   Soame's speech is crossed out, but no replacement text is added. It is included here to provide a lead into the dialogue between Cyril and Mandeville.

12.   Sarah's final sentence is crossed out.

13.   The following two exchanges between Sarah and Mandeville and Sarah's reply are crossed out. They are retained here to lead into Mandeville's statement "But your dance isn't everything."

14.   In the handwritten version (H) of this part, Mandeville is presented in a harsher and Sarah, initially, in a more self-assertive light. The play here shifts uneasily into a more existential mode concerned with class resentment and sexual exploitation. Mandeville's first speech follows Sarah's question "Do you think he means that?"

Mandeville. Mean it? Did you ever hear Benjamin make jokes about money? The theatre will be closed next week. And it is your fault.

Sarah. My fault? Good God! What more could I have done?

Mandeville. You have said it. You did altogether too much.

Sarah. Ah, that is the curse. I live too much, I love you too much, I work too much, sometimes I think too much: But speak out! You are not often afraid to speak out. What more could I have done? I danced till my heart stood still and sang myself sick. And what for?

Mandeville. Your own vanity. Nothing else. Your own vanity. Where was I? Nowhere. What opportunities did I have? Not one. Are you crying? Then you must cry. I suppose you want to spoil my whole evening.

Sarah. You have spoilt my whole life.

Mandeville. O, women are only happy when they are miserable. . . . To close the theatre. . . . Damn Benjamin. This comes of doing business with a man who is not a gentleman. A gentleman *[as though struck by a sudden idea.]* Cyril! Cyril, of course. Cyril . . . and you refused to dance with him. There is judgment! If anyone had told me that you had it in you to be such a fool . . .O, I cannot talk.

Sarah. You think Cyril would help us?

Mandeville. Do I *think*? If he gave us a thousand pounds . . . a wretched two thousand . . . say, a miserable three thousand.

Sarah. Is he so rich?

Mandeville. His father has money. His mother was an heiress and he is going to marry Julia de Trappe—a girl with eight thousand a year. What in the devil has he done to deserve such luck. While I have to make myself [nice?] to a scoundrel like Benjamin merely to sing—not to *live*—but to sing!

Sarah. If Cyril is engaged to be married . . .

Mandeville. My dear woman. He is not in love with Julia, he does not admire her . . . he . . .

Sarah. Is she plain?

Mandeville. She is a pretty, innocent, little fool. Any other man would think himself fortunate to get her. Even I would be faithful for eight thousand pounds a year.

Sarah. *[Suspiciously]* Do you know this Julia?

Mandeville. Naturally.

Sarah. Do you often meet her[?]

Mandeville. I saw her this afternoon.

Sarah. Have you ever made love to her? . . . Answer me. Have you ever made love to her?

Mandeville. What has that to do with you?

Sarah. This much. When I once know that you are flirting with other women, I shall not be the only one to suffer! So take care.

Mandeville. *[Uneasily.]* What is the matter? I hate these quarrels.

Sarah. If we were married, we should not quarrel.

Mandeville. O, is that all? Well, get money and you may yet die respectable. Ha! ha! Make money, Sarah. Here am I, Cyril is there: one of us has three thousand pounds and the other would spend it . . . Work that!

Sarah. How?

Mandeville. By being a little . . . sympathetic. That is all.

Sarah [*Half-voice*] Devil.

Mandeville. Eh? He only wanted to tell you that he loves you to distraction, that he would like—to kiss your hand. Let him!

Sarah. But if he should ask me to be his wife.

Mandeville. Ask you to be his wife? Oh, he will not do that. I see no cause for alarm.

Sarah. *[Changing her voice.]* You think he would not.

Mandeville. What is the matter now? Don't be a fool. Get the money.

Sarah. I understand! Because I adore you. Because where you are concerned I have no spirit, no will of my own, no conscience, no hope, no reason—nothing, nothing, nothing but the most miserable heart in the world. You think I would be the same with any other, with all the others! We have been . . . friends . . . for five years, and you know less about me than the boy who cleans my boots!

[The door is opened.]

Mandeville. Hush! They are coming in. Don't be a fool. *[She looks at him contemptuously, he attempts to speak but guests come in from the ball-room and cross stage. Mandeville glides away in the crowd and Cyril, who is violently excited, lurches forward when he sees Sarah.]*

15. Manuscript source H here again assumes a more serious, class-inflected tone:

Cyril. Ah! How can I thank you for allowing me to come here this evening! What a charming life you lead! All music and flowers and light and beautiful colours! Nothing dull, nothing ugly, nothing to make you wretched!

Sarah. So you think I ought to be happy? Are you?

Cyril. O! the dullness of my father's house is not to be imagined. We only ask each other how we slept or whether anything we [ate] disagreed with us.

Sarah. Your evenings must indeed be dull if one can only be distinguished from another by a fit of indigestion or no fit!

Cyril. Sometimes we give a party and then the chief excitement is to watch the effect of my father's bad champagne on a few bilious peers. And the conversation! Dull stuff about match-making, medicine and morality. Pugh! I am sick of it all.

Sarah. What? *[With a glance.]* The match-making?

Here the text merges with the typescript (A, Act II), with Cyril denying any interest in Julia, declaring his love for Sarah, asking her to go away with him, and finding his match in Sarah, who responds to his proposal of a secret tryst by making their engagement public.
    Manuscript source K starts in the same way but continues in a more light-hearted vein by omitting details of Cyril's domestic circumstances, moving directly from Sarah's question "So you think I ought to be happy" to Cyril's reply "Not so happy but I could wish to make you even happier. O, Sarah, no one could ever love you so well as I do. I think of you all day! When I am with you I am mad with happiness and when I leave you I can only live by remembering what you have said and wondering what you will say when I next see you. I am sure that no one has ever loved you so desperately." This is followed by Sarah's "They have said so, at all events." The remainder is close to the typescript (A, Act II), with a variant that also appears in manuscript I and is discussed below.
    16. Handwritten variant K: Cyril's speech ends here, and Sarah replies: "Why should I forgive you when you have really paid me the compliment of assuming that I have no silly whims about virtue! Ah, why do men ask us for favours which they can only despise us for granting. And most of us learn this too late." This is followed by Cyril's rest of the speech in the typescript, "Forgive me. If I thought any other man would dare speak to you as I have spoken, I would thrash him with a horse-whip."
    17. A separate variant (I) outlines a very different outcome of the dialogue between Cyril and Sarah in Act II. Here, their relationship seems to have gone much further than in the other versions and ends with a break-up—which appears to be overheard by Mandeville. The tone of their exchange is different from the rest of the play. It is tempting to read the passage biographically, as a coded warning to Moore on the part of Craigie to curb his increasing demands of a change to their relationship or risk losing her (this version has more deletions and corrections than the other manuscript pages):

Cyril. It is not for me to remind you how I have endured your caprices, your impatience, your never-changing moods, likes, dislikes, jealousies and what not. I should be the last to preach that we are under an obligation to those who love us, who would give their lives for us, whose every thought is for our happiness, our amusement. For your sake I myself have treated others as you are treating me. I am too ashamed of my own ingratitude to find fault with yours . . . But . . . how I would love you even now—if you would let me. If you would only tell me that under all this apparent indifference you still care for me . . . a little.

Sarah. My dear, I am very fond of you . . . no one has ever been so kind to me . . . I am not ungrateful . . . but you do not understand women . . . We never love a man because he deserves us: we like to throw ourselves away. It is so interesting to suffer, to sacrifice our peace of mind, our looks, our [illegible], our past, present and future to some one [who] would write on our tomb-stone "To-morrow to fresh woods and pastures new" . . . O, you are so young, dear, o you have so much to learn. I feel like your grandmother . . . Kiss me*! [Holds up her cheek.]*

Mandeville. No one knows how I worship that woman.

18.   Here a page (34) is missing from the typescript (A, Act II). The subsequent text enclosed in square brackets is taken from manuscript source I. The insertion ends with n19.
19.   I have replaced the first two exchanges on page 34 of the typescript (A, Act II), which read:
   sits down beside her.]

Mandeville: You are the only woman on this earth.

Sarah. What? you think of other women when I'm so ill, that I'm not responsible for what I said. *[Pause.]* Do not let me marry Cyril. Take me away. Do not let me marry Cyril.

20.   Handwritten variant (H): "Why then we can marry and each have our own Theatre!"
21.   In the handwritten version (H) the Act ends as follows:

Mandeville. This is sense. Now we are talking sense.

Sarah. You will come and see me tomorrow?

Mandeville. Of course. *[As he goes, she kisses her hand to him.]*

Sarah. [Alone and speaking mechanically.] This is Sense!

   [Curtains.]

Journeys End in Lovers Meeting

Untitled manuscript by George Moore

Edited by Mark Llewellyn

EDITOR'S NOTE

The collaboration that produced *Journeys End in Lovers Meeting* and the manuscript version by Moore presented here need some unpicking. The divide between Moore and Craigie on authorship rested on the role each played in the development of the idea from Ellen Terry's original request for a one-act text. In one version, Moore just "drafted a scenario and rough dialogue" that Craigie then "embellished."[1] Moore's scenario, as a July 1894 playbill from the Lyceum made clear, generated the "situations . . . from the French of Caraquel" [Caraguel].[2] Although the manuscript in Moore's hand indicates how sketchy the outline was in places, it does support his view that he did more than provide rough dialogue. Craigie's published version uses a fair number of Moore's own phrasings, admittedly subject to more extensive characterization and development of the text.

There are notable differences in Moore's text to the performed and published version. The characters' names are all different: Moore's manuscript has Mr. and Mrs. Austin and Captain Armatage, whereas Craigie changed these to Sir Philip Soupire, Lady Soupire and Captain Maramour. The scene of the drawing room remains the same, and it is Lady Seagrave's party from which the female protagonist has returned. Moore's manuscript is clearly a first sketch of the material. He confuses the name of the Captain—often within the same speech—which variously appears as Armatage, Athelstone (once), and Armstrong. In several places the names of off-stage female characters at the ball are given merely as "Mrs. —," presumably to be completed later, and at one point in a speech by Mr. Austin, his male card-playing

273

friends are given only as "so and so and so and so." There is relatively little by way of stage or character direction, compared to Craigie's published version.

NOTE ON THE TEXT

Held in the Pearl Craigie/George Moore Papers in the Mark Samuels Lasner Collection, on loan to the University of Delaware Library,[3] the manuscript comprises seventeen handwritten pages by Moore, with no title page or title header. Page 17 ends mid-scene with a signal that the next person to speak will be Mr Austin, but no words are provided. Given the manuscript's status as an outline piece, it is perhaps unsurprising that there is relatively little revision by Moore to the first drafting. The edited version presented here includes strikethrough text where this could be deciphered, and superscript is used to indicate write-over words and phrases. Moore's punctuation, especially the use of question marks and full stops/periods, is absent in several places. Where these features have been added, this is signaled through use of square brackets. Moore's stage directions are often—but not always —presented through underlining. To ensure consistency with the edited text of *A Fool's Hour*, these, and the characters' name markers in the script, have been italicized, and full stops have been added to characters' names preceding dialogue. Typographical and orthographic errors (such as Moore's absent apostrophes) have been silently corrected.

THE TEXT

Scene a lady's drawing room. Enter Mrs. Austin. She has returned from a ball and seems a little tired.

Mrs. Austin. Oh, how tired I am. But what a charming ball. I haven't enjoyed a dance as much for years. I thought that my dancing days were over. I really believe I must have danced seven or eight waltz[e]s . . . I am tired. But ~~what a charming ball~~ Lady Seagrave's parties always are amusing. They say ~~her set's very fast,~~ that all the women ~~there have admirers~~ ^{who go there have admirers}. There were certainly a number ~~about easily~~ of rakish looking military men about with ~~calm well-bred faces leaning about the doorways~~ ^{They stood} watching the women as they came in. ~~Mrs~~ The women were ~~half~~ ^{beautifully} dressed, ^{but} very de [illegible] ~~They carried carrying bouquets in their hands and looked around a circular glance as they came~~ ^{and they swept with their eyes as they came in seeking} their ~~partners~~ ^{admirers}. Captain Armatage was one of the group of men around the door leading to the ballroom. When I entered he saw me at once. He expected me, he knew I was coming. We met at a dinner party a fortnight ago. He spoke to me the whole time of dinner and when the men came up from dinner he came and sat down by me. I could see that he was smitten. He asked if he might call, but I told him I was going out of town. I thought it better so; I didn't want to begin a flirtation with him. Then we met at Lady Athelstone's at home . . . He paid me a great deal of attention and I told him I thought I was going to Lady Seagrave's ball. There was no reason why I shouldn't have told him. There was no reason why I should have refused to dance with him. He dances divinely. We sat out three or four dances together. It was so cool and quiet in the conservatory. In that distant nook behind the palms ~~were~~ we were quite alone. No one could say that Captain Athelstone *[sic.]* is not excellent company. We talked of a great many things. He said things that—I don't think I encouraged him. I hope he did not think I did. When he caught my hands and kissed them I'm sure I showed him how surprised I was that he should dare. Then he apologised and there was nothing more to be said. But we did ~~[illegbile]~~ remain talking some time longer. I suppose I did wrong, but ~~I dare say that~~ in that set ~~of nothing would be thought of it~~ very little time is wasted [when] a man admires a woman and he tells her so. But I am not like ~~the~~ other women ~~there~~ I have scruples, I have never let myself go and never will. I did not want to go to that ball; I do not like that fast set, but my husband insisted. What was I to do? It so happened that I surprised myself. . . . I was admired. I do not think I ever looked better. This dress suits me. . . . Captain Armstrong admired it. And what if he did pay a few compliments. I don't think he meant any harm and I'm sure my husband ~~wouldn't have cared if he~~ would approve. He did say however that the dress suited me [,] that he had never seen me looking better. I ~~have not heard him say so~~ didn't think he ever noticed what I had on. It is the first time for ~~the last four~~ many years at least that [he] ever seemed to notice whether I looked well or ill. ~~He didn't seem~~ I suppose he must compliment someone and Mrs Fairfax really did look so bad tonight that it would have been impossible to compliment her. Edward seemed hardly to notice her and ~~five years he was~~ three months ago he was so attentive. I wonder if there was ever anything really between them. He said he was going to his club[;] perhaps that was an excuse to see her home. If I only knew, if only true I would leave him. But one cannot know for certain. Ah how I once loved that man, and how he once loved me. ~~What is marriage~~ Two, three years of love and affection and then ~~neglect~~ polite indifference. That's marriage. I suppose people think one a lucky woman. A ~~residence~~ large house ~~illegible~~, fashionable society, jewels, carriages, horses; ~~and I could~~ and I am envied ~~illegible~~ when I sit at ~~illegible~~ the head of my husband's table and my dresses and ~~I have my~~ diamonds are taken as proofs of ~~illegible~~ the excellence of his behaviour towards me.

But it is not for himself, it is not because he wishes me to look well that he gives me these things but because he thinks I should do him credit. It was for that that he told me to wear my diamonds tonight. He wanted the world to see that he refuses me nothing, that I had everything his wife should have. So my life passes and when I go with him into society it is only to meet women who are, well, I don't wish to wrong him. ~~So~~ I will say women whom he admires more than me. I suppose every love story ends as mine has ended and yet ~~these women~~ and yet one always thinks that it ~~might~~ would not be so if one could only find the right person. These illegitimate loves [I] wonder if they endure; ~~if these~~ the women for instance I saw tonight I wonder if they are happy with their lovers. If I had ~~not~~ no scruples, ~~illegible~~ if I were sure that nothing remained of any love for my husband, if I were to ~~believe~~ listen to Captain Armatage I wonder. Would he dispose of his love too.

The door opens and Captain Armatage enters. Mrs. Austin starts to her feet.

Good heavens! ~~What does this mean. He comes~~ here.

Captain A. Hush, don't be alarmed. I must speak to you only a minute.

Mrs. Austin. Must speak to me! only a minute! I don't understand. How did you come here?

Captain A. Forgive me, ~~but I felt that I~~ I could not help myself. I felt I must pass through your street only to look up at your windows.

Mrs. Austin. But how are you here?

Captain A. Some other people—people who live here . . . I saw them come up the street and when they opened the door[.]

Mrs. A. You followed them in.

Captain A. Yes, I could not help myself. I felt I that I must speak to you.

Mrs. A. Speak to me!

Captain A. I felt I must tell you—

Mrs. A. This is madness! How did you get in [.] Who let you in?

Captain [A]. I knew your number. I knew that you would be alone[.]

Mrs. A. Knew that I would be alone!

Captain A. Yes, I heard your husband say that [he] was going to his club[.]

Mrs. A. Heard my husband say he was going to his club[.]

Captain A. Yes, I saw him go off with two other men[,] otherwise I shouldn't have risked it.

Mrs. Austin. But how did you get in here? . . . Oh this is dreadful. You must go away at once.

Captain A. One moment to tell you. I had to speak with you. ~~I knew~~ You see[,] I knew you would be alone[,] that no one would be up except your maid. I had thought to rap gently [~~illegible~~] and when your maid came to ask if I could say a few words to you.

Mrs. Austin. But my maid is ill . . . she is in bed. There is no one up[;] you must go at once.

Captain [A]. You let the door open. I saw a light. No one heard me[,] no one knows I am here. A few words, only a few words.

Mrs. Austin. Oh this is shameful. Have you thought how you are compromising me.

Captain A. I had to speak to you. Will you listen?

Mrs. Austin. No[,] I will not listen to you. This is unworthy of you, of a gentleman. If my husband were to return it would be impossible to explain your presence here. He never would believe that you were not here at my invitation—at least that I had not gravely encouraged you.

Captain A. But he has gone to play cards at his club, he will not return for at least two hours.

Mrs. Austin. For two hours! But you must go at once. There is not a moment to lose . . . If ~~you were to meet~~ he were to meet you on the stairs or when in the street he would suspect. If my servants were to find you here I should be impossibly compromised. You [illegible] in all this it was a shameful [illegible] a scene. Oh this was unworthy of you. I should not have believed you capable of such treachery.

Captain A. It was wrong of me perhaps but I could not help myself. ~~I had to ask~~ You do not know how I love you. Listen, try to forgive me. I was wrong to follow you here.

Mrs. Austin. What ~~have I done~~ did I say or do that you should speak to me in this way.

Captain A. You said and did nothing. Nor did I. It was fate ~~when~~ The first evening I met you I fell in love with you. You must have seen it. I [have] hardly spoken to any one else. I had eyes and ears only for you. I asked if I might come and see you ~~and~~

Mrs. A. And I told you that I was going out of town[.]

Captain A. Yes, and I despaired. But when met the second time you seemed to relent a little. You told me that you were going to Lady Seagrove's ball.

Mrs. Austin. I meant nothing by that. ~~It was~~ If you thought it was because I wished to see you you are mistaken; the subject came up in conversation[,] that was all.

Captain A. I dare say I was mistaken. But then one believes what one wants to believe and I hoped it was because you wished to see, see you again.

Mrs. A. Wished to see you again!

Captain [A]. At least that it would not be disagreeable to you to see me again. Ah how I counted the days and hours. I was watching for you and the moment you entered I saw you and asked you for a dance.

Mrs. Austin. When one goes to a ball it is to dance. There was no reason why I should have refused to dance with you.

Captain A. You danced many times with me. You seemed to like to dance with me. We sat out several dances and so far as I dared I tried to make you to understand that you were the one woman in the world for me.

Mrs. Austin. But Captain Armstrong you ~~should~~ must not say these things to me. You must go. I beseech you[,] go [!] Think of my position if my husband should return. I beg of you to go.

Captain [A]. Very well. I will go. But say that you forgive me this intrusion.

Mrs. Austin. Yes[,] if you will go.

[*Captain A.*] You will remember that the temptation is not resistible.

Mrs. Austin. Yes, I will remember[.]

Captain A. You are very good. ~~I could~~ It was not my fault. You will remember that. I felt that I must tell you how much I love you. I wanted to know that there is nothing I would not do. Yes, any thing. Your husband it is said is not kind to you. It is said you do not live happily.

Mrs. Austin. Who says this.

Captain A. The world.

Mrs. Austin. With what right and with what knowledge does the world speak of our private lives and presuming on ~~those~~ such idle evidence you come here ~~at this hour [illegible]~~ late at night to make love to me. You expect me to listen [.]

Captain A. I expect nothing. You know that I love you.

Mrs. Austin. Love me. I must beg of you to leave. If you don't leave this instant I shall ring for my servants.

Captain A. I am sorry you found it necessary for threats. I ought not to have delayed. I hope I may see you again.

Captain Armstrong is about to leave when Mrs. Austin hears a step on the stairs.

Mrs. Austin. That is my husband. You cannot pass on the stairs without his seeing you[;] what is to be done?

Captain A. This is most unfortunate.

Mrs. Austin. You see what your visit has cost me. Your presence cannot be explained. I am a compromised woman and without having done anything to deserve it.

Captain A. What is to be done.

Mrs. Austin. Nothing that I can see except to tell the truth.

Captain A. He will not believe it. I will jump from the window.

Mrs. A. You'll be killed.

Captain A. That does not matter if I succeed in saving you.

Mrs. A. Your dead body would be interpreted as conclusive proof.

Captain A. We must do something.

Mrs. Austin. There's nothing to be done but for me to hide you in my bedroom. Fortunately my husband—He will probably go to his room in a few moments. Then I will let you out. You see what your indiscretion has cost me.

Captain [A.] Which is your room?

Mrs. Austin. Here[,] this way. Quick[,] he is in the passage.

Captain Armstrong slips into Mrs. Austin's room. She closes the door. [Illegible] throws herself on the ottoman and assumes an air of confidence. Enter Mr. Austin.

Mr. Austin. Ah, still sitting up. It was a pleasant ball[,] was it not?

Mrs. Austin. Yes, very pleasant. I enjoyed myself[.]

Mr. Austin. I noticed that you danced a good deal. You see I was right to persuade you to come. I know no pleasanter house than Lady Seagrave's . . . I am glad you were amused. But you look tired. You ought to go to bed [.] Why are you sitting up?

Mrs. Austin. I have only just come in.

Mr. Austin. Only just come in.

Mrs. Austin. ~~I will~~ A few minutes at most. The coachman drove slowly. But you're back very early. Mrs.— was not looking very well this evening.

Mr. Austin. I did not see Mrs.— home. I went to the club.

Mrs. Austin. To play cards.

Mr. Austin. Yes ~~to play cards~~ I did think of cards but when I got there I did not feel in the humour and refused to play. It is foolish to play when you don't feel like it.

Mrs. Austin. And what made you feel out of humour. Mrs.—

Mr. Austin. No. I assure you. I did not think of her. I felt sorry—well, would you like me to tell you why I left the club.

Mrs. Austin (yawning). You can if you like.

Mr. Austin. That is not very encouraging. It was because I felt sorry that I had let you go home alone.

Mrs. Austin. But since you had let me go home alone ~~leaving your game of cards should~~ you could not relieve your error by leaving your game of cards.

Mr. Austin. No, but I wished to tell you that I was sorry.

Mrs. Austin. You could have done that tomorrow morning, if you thought it necessary.

Mr. Austin. If I had known that you would be so indifferent I should not have left the club. I should have enjoyed a game[;] there was so and so and so and so[,] all excellent players.

Mrs. Austin. It is not very late yet. If you went back at once you'd still be in time.

Mr. Austin (taking up his hat). Would you like me to go back?

Mrs. Austin (struggling to maintain her composure). I really cannot advise you. You must please yourself.

Mr. Austin goes to the door. He holds it open for a moment and then turns towards his wife.

Mr. Austin. Why cannot you advise me. Is it because you think I would not listen to you.

Mrs. Austin (yawning). Perhaps

Mr. Austin. If so you're mistaken. I know no more sensible woman. I should often be glad of your advise *[sic]*.

Mrs. Austin. About Mrs.— bonnets.

Mr. Austin. No, I do not care and have cared much what she wore. You were the best dress[ed] woman at the ball tonight.

Mrs. Austin. I'm glad you admired me.

Mr. Austin. Every one admired you and I most of all. That was why I came back from the club.

Mrs. Austin. ~~That~~ [illegible] you say that that is why you came back from the club. (*With sudden confidence.*) That was your motive.

Mr. Austin. Are you not satisfied with it. Do you not think it a worthy motive?

Mrs. Austin. I ~~like you~~ liked the first motive you pleaded better.

Mr. Austin. That I regretted having let you come home alone.

Mrs. Austin. There was another ~~reason~~ motive.

Mrs. Austin. Another motive (*pause*)

Mr. Austin. Yes; I remembered that you did not approve of gambling. You always advised me against it and although we are not unfortunately on such affectionate terms as we used to be[.]

Mrs. Austin. Unfortunately! You say unfortunately.

Mr. Austin. Yes; for I should well remember that we were very happy once.

Mrs. Austin. But we are very happy now. Far happier than we have ever been. We have not had a serious quarrel for at least two years. I ask you no questions and address [to] you no reproaches.

Mr. Austin. But do you never think that indifference is not happiness.

Mrs. Austin. It was not I who made the schism.

Mr. Austin. But if I admitted my mistake.

Mrs. Austin. Perhaps it was no mistake.

Mr. Austin. Do you really think so. It's true that we used to quarrel but quarrels are better than indifference. They are easier made up.

Mrs. Austin. You see I am very tired. It is too late to discuss such questions. You must let me ~~get to~~ go to bed. Goodnight.

She extends her hand[;] he takes her in his arms and kisses her.

Mr. Austin. How charming you look. You were ~~the~~ prettiest woman at the ball. I almost regretted that I was your husband for I wanted to ask you for a dance. I noticed that you danced many times with Captain Armstrong. ~~He was very attentive.~~

Mrs. Austin. ~~Yes he was very attentive.~~ You insisted on my going to the ball. I suppose you did not wish me to sit in a corner by self.

Mr. Austin. ~~He is liked by you~~ No. I was glad to see you amused.

Mrs. Austin. Yes I was amused. Captain Armstrong is excellent company. No one could say he was not.

Mr. Austin. You sat out several dances with him.

Mrs. Austin. Yes, I did. Surely you see nothing to object to in that. You're not jealous[,] are you. That would be absurd.

Mr. Austin. No. I'm not so foolish as to be jealous but I don't see why jealously on my part should be absurd.

Mrs. Austin. For all the toleration I extend to you may I not ask for some in return. You to[o] sat out many dances and were not remiss in your attentions to

Mr. Austin. To whom? Woman I never saw before. Tiresome woman whom I hope never to see again. You don't know how they all bored me.

~~Mrs Austin Not to Mrs ----you seemed one [illegible] and shamefully. It was not her fault if she is not looking her best. She [illegible]~~

Mrs. Austin. They seemed pleased enough notwithstanding. The conversation did not seem to lag. I suppose you left the love making to them.

Mr. Austin. Mrs.— of whom you were once so jealous. You cannot say that my attentions were very masked.

Mrs. Austin. ~~Neglect of~~ That you should have tired of her was no more than might be expected of you but it is too much to ask me to accept your [illegible] for a virtue.

Mr. Austin. There never was any love between us—we were merely friends. I swear to you[,] I dare say I could prove to you that I am speaking the truth. Do you wish for proof?

Mrs. Austin. She or another[,] what matter. I thought all such discussion was over between us. ~~[illegible]~~ We have agreed to live separate lives. That is your side of the house. This is mine. Goodnight. I am very tired.

Mrs. Austin holds out her hands[;] Mr. Austin takes her hands looks at her

Mr. Austin. Yes you look tired. You have sat up too late.

He moves towards her room. With a quick movement she gets between him and the door.

Mrs. Austin. No you shall not enter that room[.]

Mr. Austin. Why.

Mrs. Austin. You have lost the right.

Mr. Austin. Really—is it so bad as that then. Shall I never require the right again?

Mrs. Austin. That I cannot say. [~~illegible~~] Rights relinquished, abandoned for years, cannot be regained easily, certainly not in a few moments of facile pleading.

Mr. Austin. ~~I see I must be on I must become your~~ You're quite right. I must plead like a lover. I must try to win your love.

~~*Mrs. Austin* You must~~

Mrs. Austin. Yes, you must win back my love.

Mr. Austin. I wonder if I shall succeed.

Mrs. Austin. That I cannot say[.]

Mr. Austin. It will be [a] long courtship[.]

Mrs. Austin. That I cannot say. [~~Illegible~~] Good night.

Mr. Austin turns to go and an expression of relief comes over Mrs. Austin's face. He turns suddenly.

Mr. Austin. But you said years have passed. Not years. I dare say there have been faults. I will not pretend that I am faultless in the matter but I have never loved anyone but you. Years! Two years at most. It seems like yesterday. Have you forgotten ~~those~~ the days when we thought of nothing but one another? They were happy days.

Mrs. Austin. I thought you did not remember anything.

Mr. Austin. I remember all that concerns you. We used to be together for hours talking and reading in that room.

Mrs. Austin. ~~So you have not forgotten my room.~~ Do you remember what we used to read.

Mr. Austin. We used to read the poets—we read ~~Maud~~ Tennyson's Maud, and Shelley's sensitive plant and Swinburne's Triumph of Time. You like Tennyson best of all. I remember the little book case where the volumes stood. I could go there with closed eyes and put my hand on the ~~volumes~~ copy.

Mrs. Austin. You haven't forgotten my room then.

[*Mr. Austin.*] No. I could go there blindfolded and find—

Mrs. Austin. ~~I will~~ The Tennyson.

Mr. Austin. Yes. ~~I am sure I could.~~

Mrs. Austin stands looking at him. She moves herself towards the bedroom.

~~Mrs. Austin The books stand on the same shelf?~~

~~Mr. Austin In the same place. Third shelf from the bottom?~~

Mrs. Austin. ~~I will not say.~~ That's telling

Mr. Austin. *(With a pleading expression)* But if I find it all will be forgiven? [I may remain?]

Mrs. Austin. ~~You couldn't find it blindfolded~~ But could you fetch it blindfold.

She takes a handkerchief from her pocket.

Mr. Austin. ~~You promise not to~~ A handkerchief is unnecessary. I shall not open my eyes.

Mrs. Austin. ~~Yes, we must have a handkerchief~~ It is difficult to keep our eyes closed. You might open them involuntarily.

Mr. Austin (turning for her to tie the handkerchief). That is true. I should like to see if I can find the book. I believe I can lay my hand on it at once. You're tying that handkerchief very tight.

Mrs. Austin. Is it too tight? (*Loosening it)* Is that better.

Mr. Austin. Yes that is better[.]

Mrs. Austin. You are sure you can see nothing.

Mr. Austin. Nothing. All is ~~just~~ utterly darkness.

Mrs. Austin ~~Before I open the door for you you give me your word~~

Half opening the door of her room

Before I let you pass you give me your word of honour you will not ~~look un~~ lift the handkerchief.

Mr. Austin. My word of honour.

Mrs. Austin. You give me your word of honour that you will not look under the handkerchief.

Mr. Austin. My word of honour[.]

Mrs. Austin. You are quite sure you cannot see underneath it.

Mr. Austin. I can see nothing. . . You must give me my stick. Every blind man has a stick. I shall knock my self against [. . .] I may fall on the furniture[.]

Mrs. Austin. You shall have your stick.

She gives him his stick. He taps about and it is difficult for Captain Armstrong to pass him[;] at last he manages to do so[.] Mrs. Austin stands terrified. Captain [A.] gains the door of the apartment and disappears.

Mr. Austin (from the inner room). I have found the bookcase . . . (*pause*). [illegible] Third volume third row. (*Enter Mr. Austin, a book in his left hand*) I am sure I'm right. This is your Tennyson.

Mrs. Austin. Yes. You're quite right.

Mr. Austin

NOTES

1. Adrian Frazier, *George Moore 1852–1933* (New Haven: Yale University Press, 2000), 234.

2. As discussed in Ann Heilmann's introduction to Part II, Moore drew on Clément Caraguel's one-acter *Le Bougeoir* (1852). Playbill, *Journeys End in Lovers' Meeting*: A Proverb in One Act, by John Oliver Hobbes, Pearl Craigie/George Moore Papers, Mark Samuels Lasner Collection, on loan to the University of Delaware Library. (Apart from featuring on the playbill, the apostrophe does not appear in the title of Craigie's published version nor in Moore's references.)

3. The editor is grateful to Mark Samuels Lasner for granting permission to reproduce the text.

Index

About the Contributors

Dr. **Kirsti Bohata** is associate professor of English literature and director of CREW (Centre for Research into the English Literature and Language of Wales) at Swansea University, United Kingdom. Her most recent book is a collection of essays co-edited with Katie Gramich, *Rediscovering Margiad Evans: Marginality, Gender and Illness* (2013).

Michel Brunet is senior lecturer (associate professor) of English at the University of Valenciennes and Hainaut-Cambrésis, France. He wrote his doctoral thesis on William Trevor's short stories. His main areas of research lie in Irish literature, with a particular focus on Anglo-Irish writing and George Moore. He also has a strong interest in Irish minorities and issues related to identity.

Adrian Frazier is a graduate of Pomona College (BA 1971), Trinity College Dublin (Diploma in Anglo Irish Literature, 1973), and Washington University in St. Louis (MA 1976; PhD 1979). He has been on the faculty at Nanjing Teachers University (1979–1981), Union College in New York (1981–2000), and the National University of Ireland at Galway (2000–), where he holds a professorial chair and is the director of the MA in drama and theatre studies and the MA in writing. He has published on Irish poetry, drama, and fiction of the twentieth century, including *Yeats, Horniman, and the Struggle for the Abbey Theatre* (1990), a guest-edited issue of the *Irish Review* on *Irish Theatre* (2002), and *Playboys of the Western World: Production Histories* (2004). He is the author of *George Moore 1852–1933* (2000) and *Hollywood Irish: John Ford and the Irish Revival in Hollywood* (2011).

Elizabeth Grubgeld, professor of English at Oklahoma State University, has published many articles on Irish literature, autobiography, and disability studies and is the author of *George Moore and the Autogenous Self* (1994), awarded the American Conference for Irish Studies Prize for Best Book of Literary and Cultural Criticism. She is also the author of *Anglo-Irish Auto-biography: Class, Gender, and the Forms of Narrative* (2004), which won the Robert E. Rhodes Prize for Irish Literature. Her most recent work on George Moore includes "George Moore's Correspondence as Social Prac-tice" in *George Moore: Dublin, Paris, Hollywood*, ed. Adrian Frazier and Conor Montague (2012), "Framing the Body: George Moore's 'Albert Nobbs' and the Disappearing Realist Subject" in *George Moore: Across Borders,* ed. Christine Huguet and Fabienne Garcier (2013), and "George Moore's Autobiographies and the Vampiric Grasp of Home" in *George Moore and the Quirks of Human Nature*, ed. Maria Elena Jaime de Pablos and Mary Pierse (2014). She has served on the national board of the American Conference for Irish Studies and is a three-time past president of its board of its Southern division.

Anna Gruetzner Robins is professor in the history of art at the University of Reading, United Kingdom. Born in Toronto, she was educated at the Univer-sity of Toronto and the Courtauld Institute of Art, London. She was curator of the British section in the Royal Academy's *Post-Impressionism* exhibition (1979), curated *Modern Art in Britain 1910–1914* (1997), and co-curated *Degas, Sickert and Toulouse Lautrec* (2005). Among her books are *Walter Sickert: Drawings, Theory and Practice: Word and Image* (1996), *Walter Sickert: The Complete Writings on Art* (2000) and *A Fragile Modernism: Whistler and his Impressionist Followers* (2007). She is currently completing a book on the 1890s.

Ann Heilmann is professor of English literature at Cardiff University, Unit-ed Kingdom. She previously held professorial chairs at the Universities of Hull and Swansea and lectureships at Manchester Metropolitan, Bradford, and Leeds universities, United Kingdom. Her doctorate was awarded by the University of Tübingen, Germany. The author of *New Woman Fiction: Wom-en Writing First-Wave Feminism* (2000), *New Woman Strategies: Sarah Grand, Olive Schreiner, Mona Caird* (2004), and (with Mark Llewellyn) *Neo-Victorianism: The Victorians in the Twenty-First Century, 1999–2009* (2010), she is the co-editor (with Mark Llewellyn) of *The Collected Short Stories of George Moore* (5 vols, 2007). Other (co-)edited work includes three essay collections and four anthologies. She is the general editor of Routledge's "History of Feminism" and Pickering and Chatto's "Gender and Genre" series.

Dr. **María Elena Jaime de Pablos** is a senior lecturer of English literature at the University of Almería, Spain. The author of two Spanish-language studies on George Moore, she is the editor of *Análisis de género en los estudios irlandeses* (Gender Analysis in Irish Studies, 2007). She is also co-editor of the *Nuevas perspectivas críticas en los estudios de literatura irlandesa* (New Critical Perspectives on Irish Literature Studies, 2003), *Irish Landscapes* (2003), and *Joyceana: literaria hibernica* (2005). The general editor of *Revista AUDEM*, a Gender Studies journal published by Almería University, she was the organizer of the fourth International George Moore conference, at Almería University, in 2010, which resulted in the co-edited collection on *George Moore and the Quirks of Human Nature* (2014).

Dr. **Jane Jordan** is a senior lecturer (associate professor) in English Literature at Kingston University, United Kingdom, where she teaches Victorian Literature. Jane co-founded the Victorian Popular Fiction Association in 2009. She is the author of two biographies, the Victorian feminist and social reformer *Josephine Butler* (2001; 2007), and *Kitty O'Shea* (2005), mistress of Charles Stewart Parnell, whose scandalous divorce in 1890 wrecked the campaign for Irish Home Rule. She also co-edited the five-volume collection *Josephine Butler and the Prostitution Campaigns* (2003). She has published widely on Ouida and co-edited *Ouida and Victorian Popular Culture* (Ashgate, 2013).

Mark Llewellyn is John Anderson Research Professor in English at the University of Strathclyde, Glasgow, United Kingdom. He holds a doctorate from the University of Wales. Together with Ann Heilmann, he is the author of *Neo-Victorianism: The Victorians in the Twenty-first Century, 1999–2009* (2010). Co-edited work includes, with Dinah Birch, *Conflict and Difference in Nineteenth-Century Literature* (2010), and with Heilmann, *Metafiction and Metahistory in Contemporary Women's Writing* (2007) and *The Collected Short Stories of George Moore* (5 vols, 2007).

Dr. **Stoddard Martin** is a graduate of Stanford University and of University College London. He has taught writing and literature at Harvard University, Kellogg College Oxford, and the Universities of Łódź and Warsaw in Poland, where he was for a decade a visiting professor. He is the author of *Wagner to "The Waste Land"* (1982), *California Writers* (1984), *Art, Messianism and Crime* (1986), *Orthodox Heresy* (1989), and *The Great Expatriate Writers* (1992). His editions of Byron, Nietzsche, and D. H. Lawrence appeared in the Duckworth "sayings of" series, which he helped to conceive; his *Colin Haycraft: Maverick Publisher* was also published by Duckworth. He has been a critic and reviewer for many publications and has for some years been proprietor of a small press, Starhaven, devoted to belles-lettres.

He writes short novels under the name of Chip Martin. He has served on the management committee of English PEN and is an associate fellow of the Institute of English Studies, University of London.

Dr. **Katherine Mullin** is senior lecturer (associate professor) of modern literature, School of English, at the University of Leeds, United Kingdom. She is the author of *James Joyce, Sexuality and Social Purity* (2003) and various articles on sexuality, censorship, and working women in late-Victorian and Modernist literature and culture. Her current project, *Working Girls: Literature, Labour and Sexuality, 1880–1925*, explores representations of typists, shop-girls, and barmaids at the turn of the nineteenth century.

Dr. **Mary S. Pierse** currently teaches the literature of Irish feminisms for the women's studies MA at University College Cork, Ireland. She compiled the five-volume anthology *Irish Feminisms 1810–1930* (2010), and is editor of *George Moore: Artistic Visions and Literary Worlds* (2006) and the co-editor of *George Moore and the Quirks of Human Nature* (2014). She has published on Moore's works, Franco-Irish artistic connections, contemporary Irish women writers, Kate Chopin, Arthur Conan Doyle, and poets Dennis O'Driscoll and Cathal Ó Searcaigh. Organizer of the first trilingual International Moore Conference (2005), she is a board member at National Centre for Franco-Irish Studies and serves on editorial boards/scientific committees for publications in France and Spain.

Dr. **Nathalie Saudo-Welby** is a senior lecturer (associate professor) of English literature at the Université de Picardie in Amiens, France. She has published extensively on *Dracula*, degeneration, New Woman fiction, and the influence of scientific discourse on *fin-de-siècle* literature. She is currently working on late nineteenth-century feminism (Mona Caird, George Egerton, Sarah Grand, Olive Schreiner, H. G. Wells).